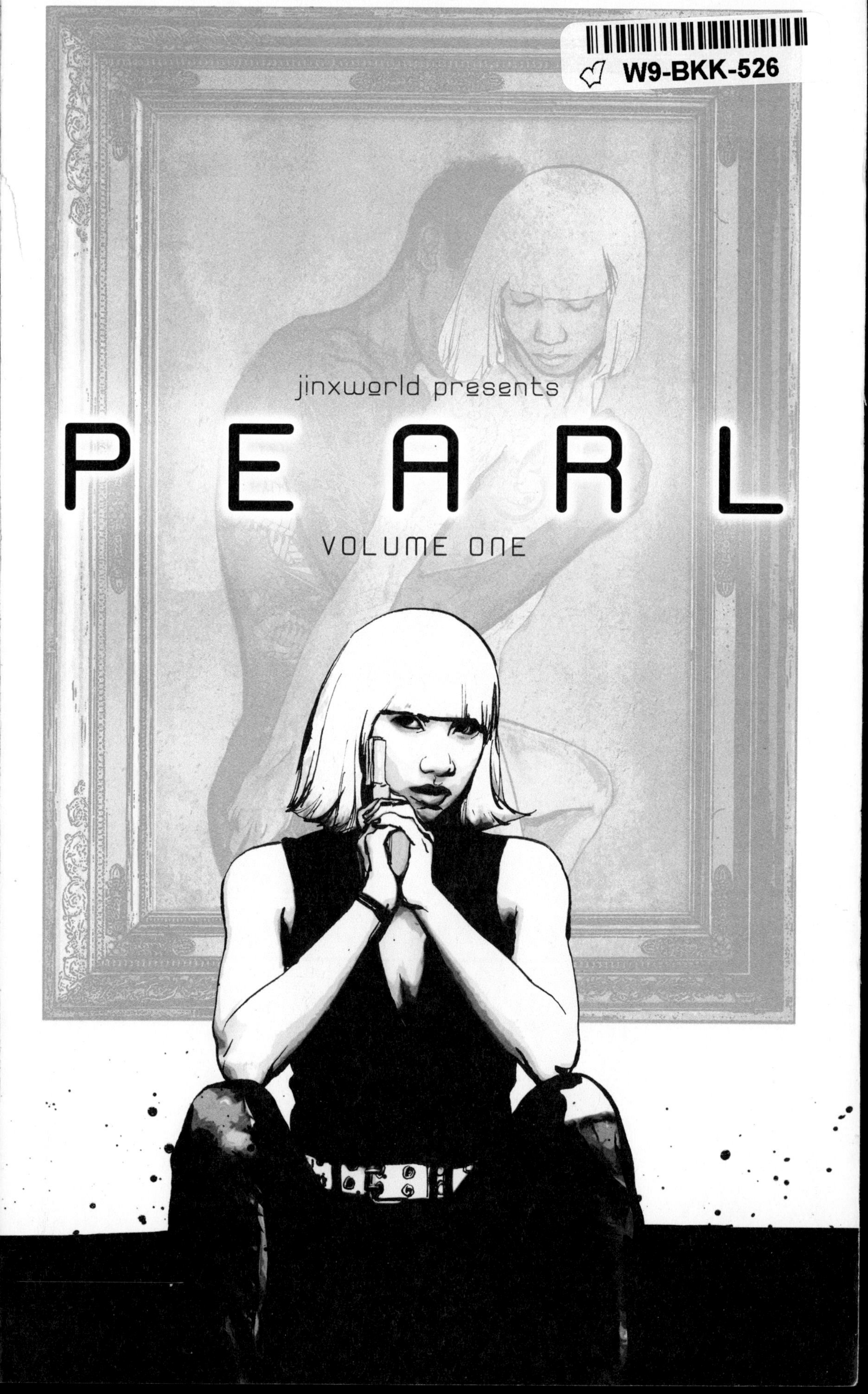
jinxworld presents
PEARL
VOLUME ONE

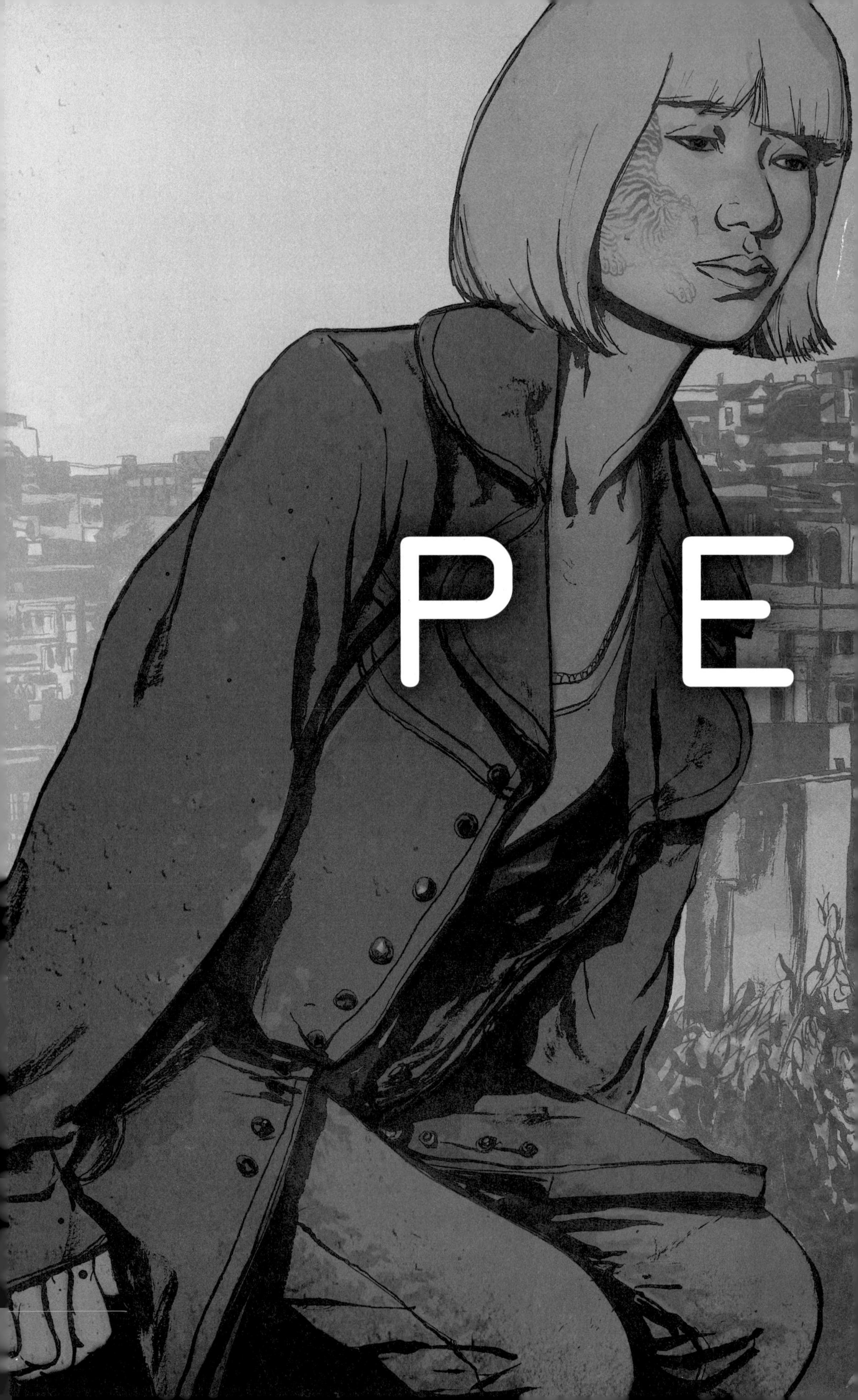
P E

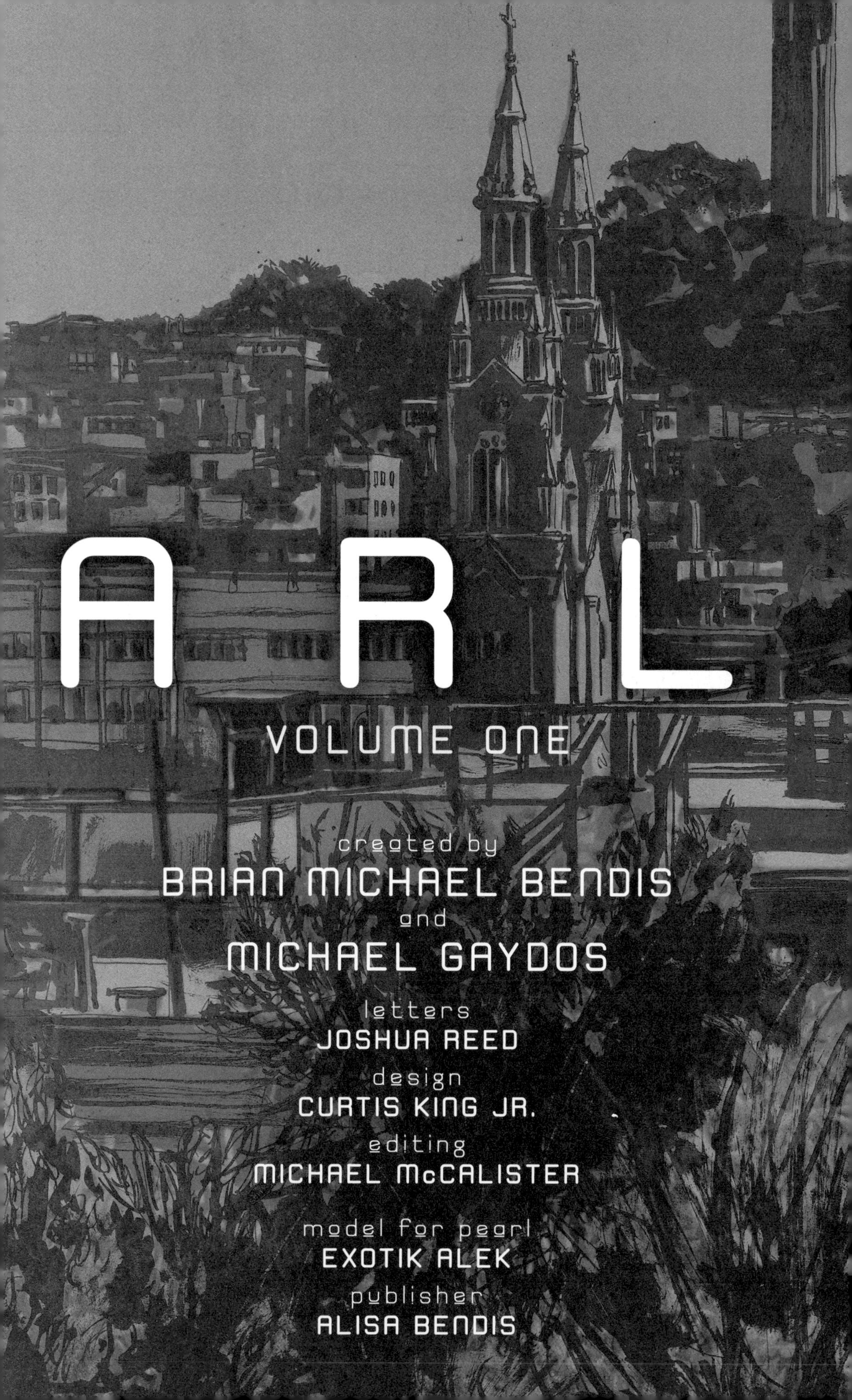

A R L

VOLUME ONE

created by

BRIAN MICHAEL BENDIS

and

MICHAEL GAYDOS

letters

JOSHUA REED

design

CURTIS KING JR.

editing

MICHAEL McCALISTER

model for pearl

EXOTIK ALEK

publisher

ALISA BENDIS

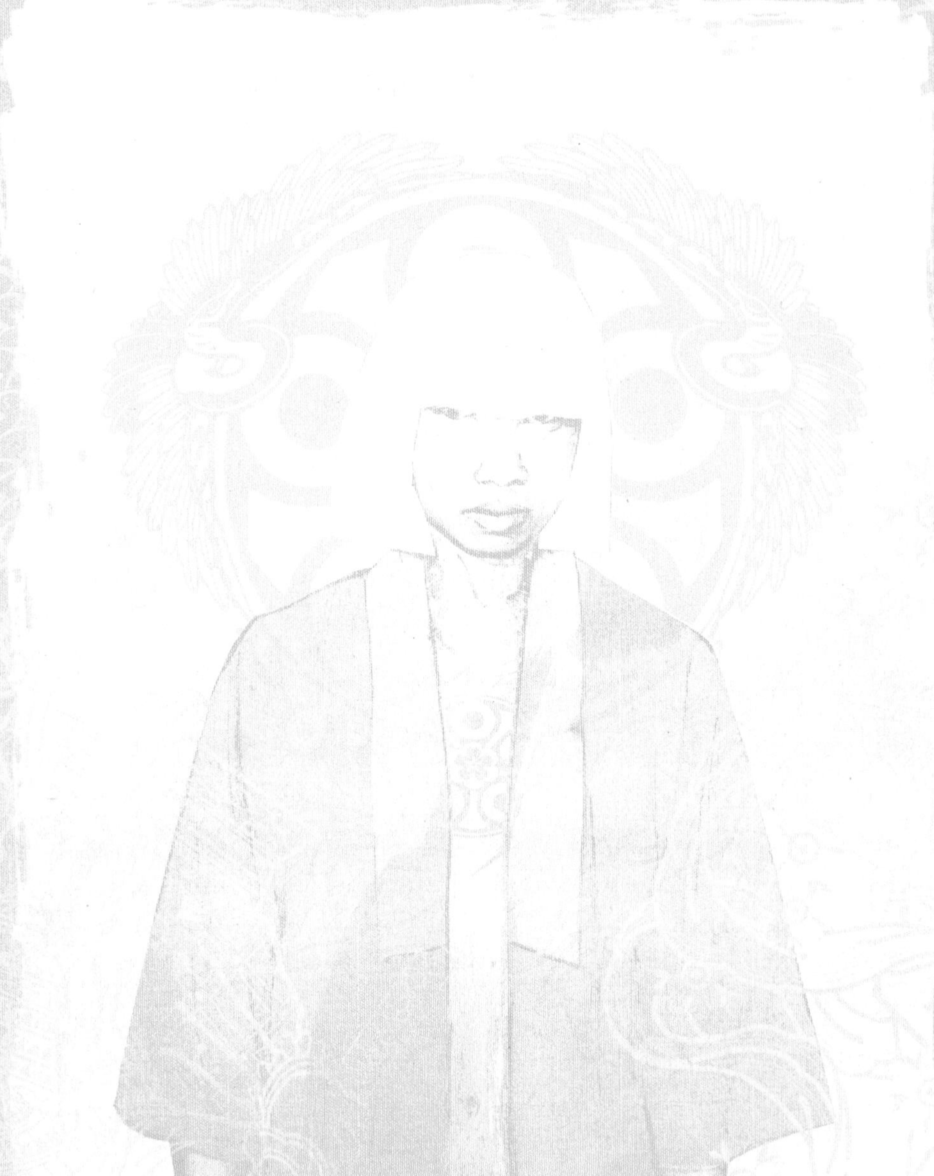

PEARL VOLUME ONE

Published by DC Comics. Compilation and all new material Copyright © 2019 Jinxworld, Inc. All Rights Reserved.

Originally published in single magazine form in PEARL 1-6. Copyright © 2018, 2019 Jinxworld, Inc. All Rights Reserved. Pearl, its logo design, the Jinxworld logo, all characters, their distinctive likenesses and related elements featured in this publication are trademarks of Jinxworld, Inc. The stories, characters and incidents featured in this publication are entirely fictional. DC Comics does not read or accept unsolicited submissions of ideas, stories or artwork.

PEFC Certified
This product is from sustainably managed forests and controlled sources
PEFC/29-31-337
www.pefc.org

DC Comics, 2900 West Alameda Ave., Burbank, CA 91505
Printed by LSC Communications, Owensville, MO, USA. 4/5/19.
First Printing. ISBN: 978-1-4012-9061-0
Library of Congress Cataloging-in-Publication Data is available.

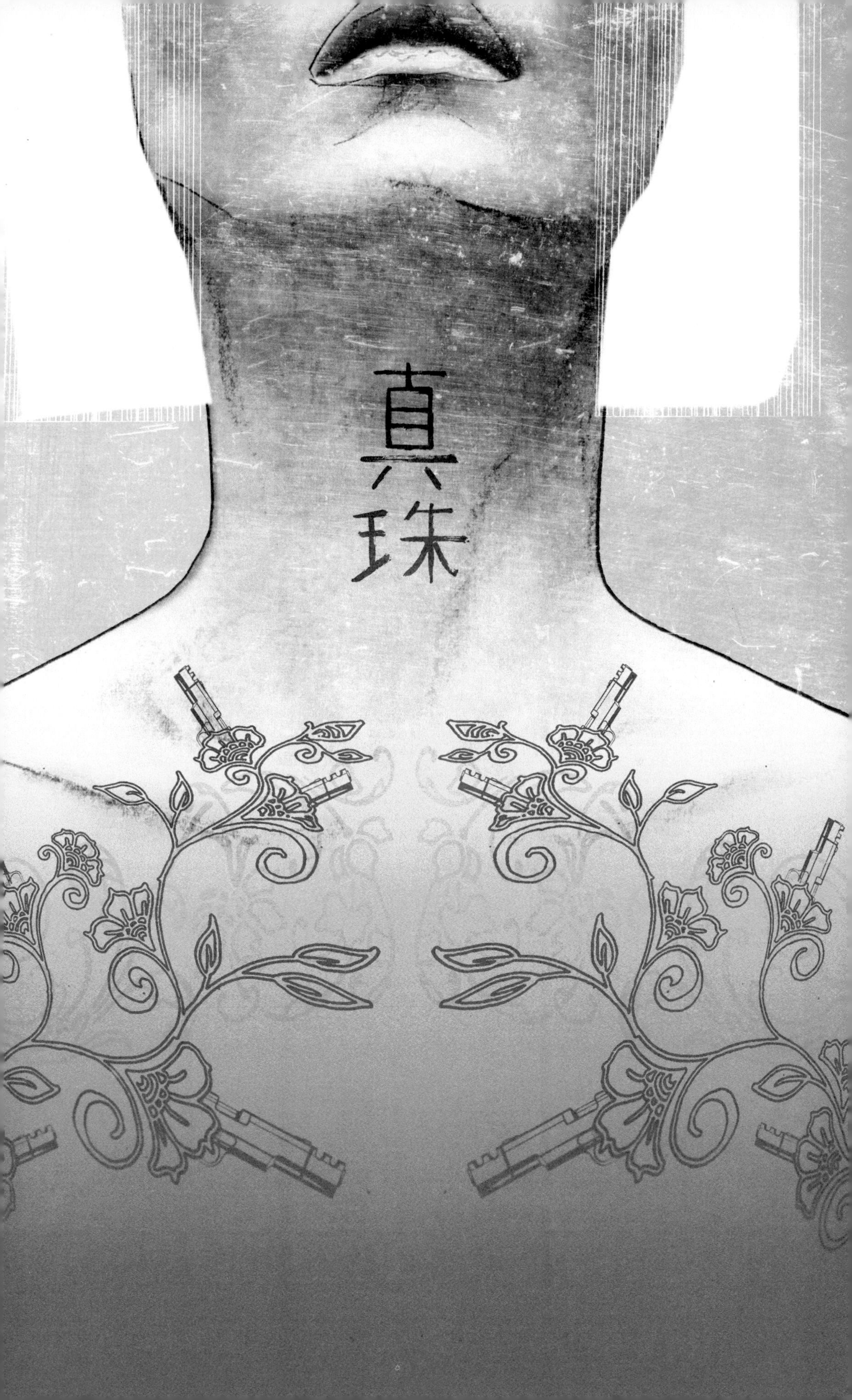
真珠

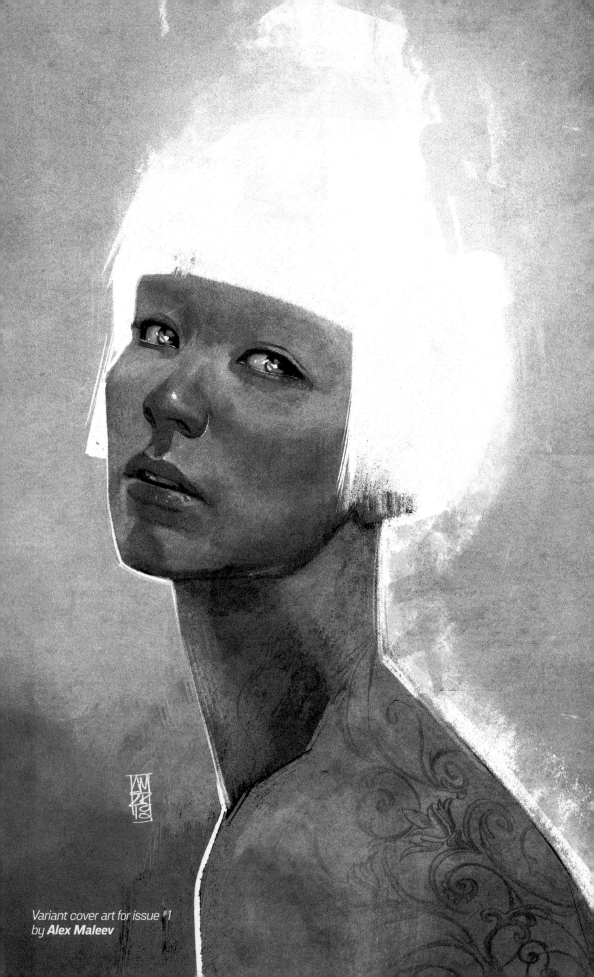

Variant cover art for issue #1
by **Alex Maleev**

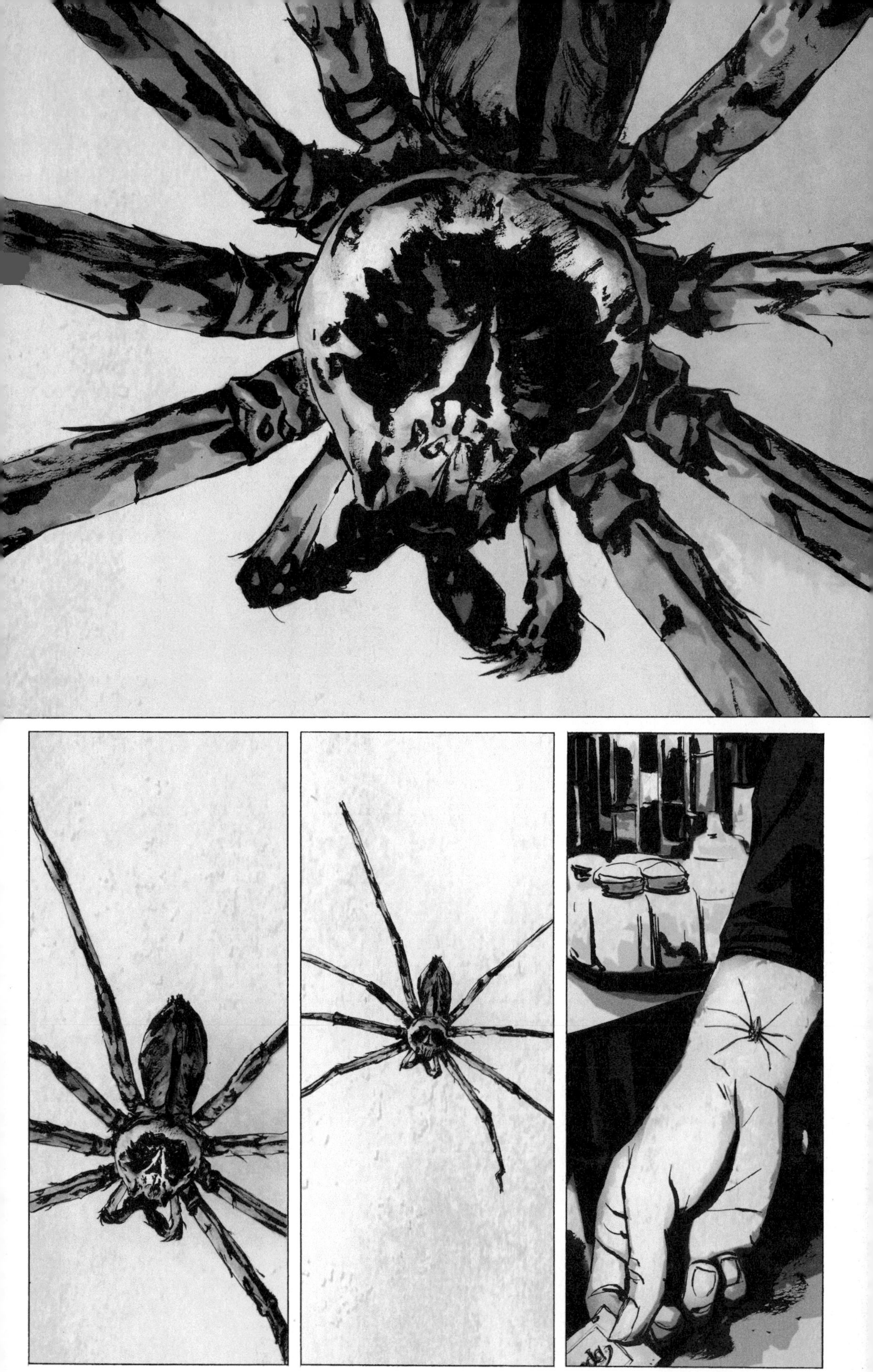

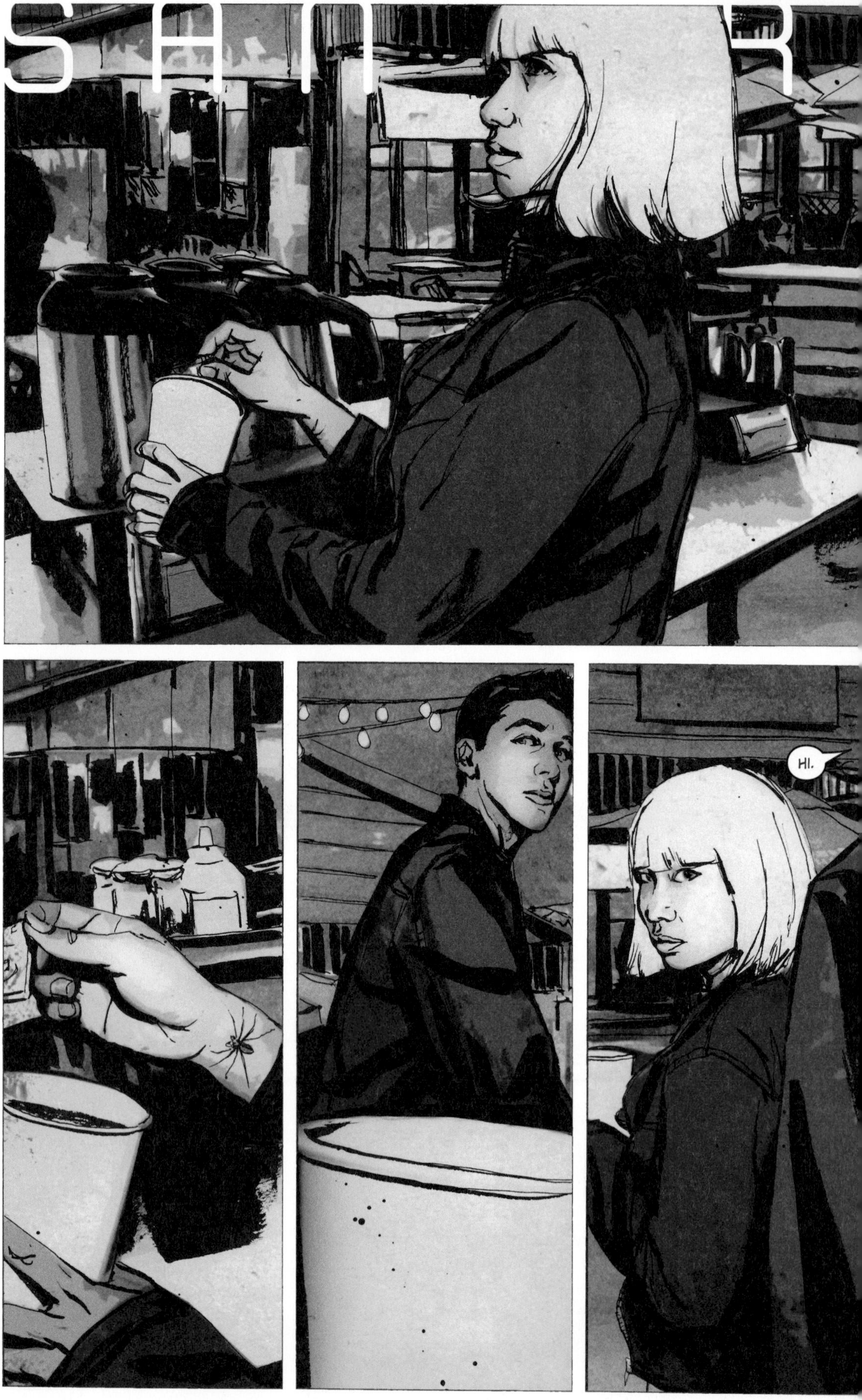
HI.

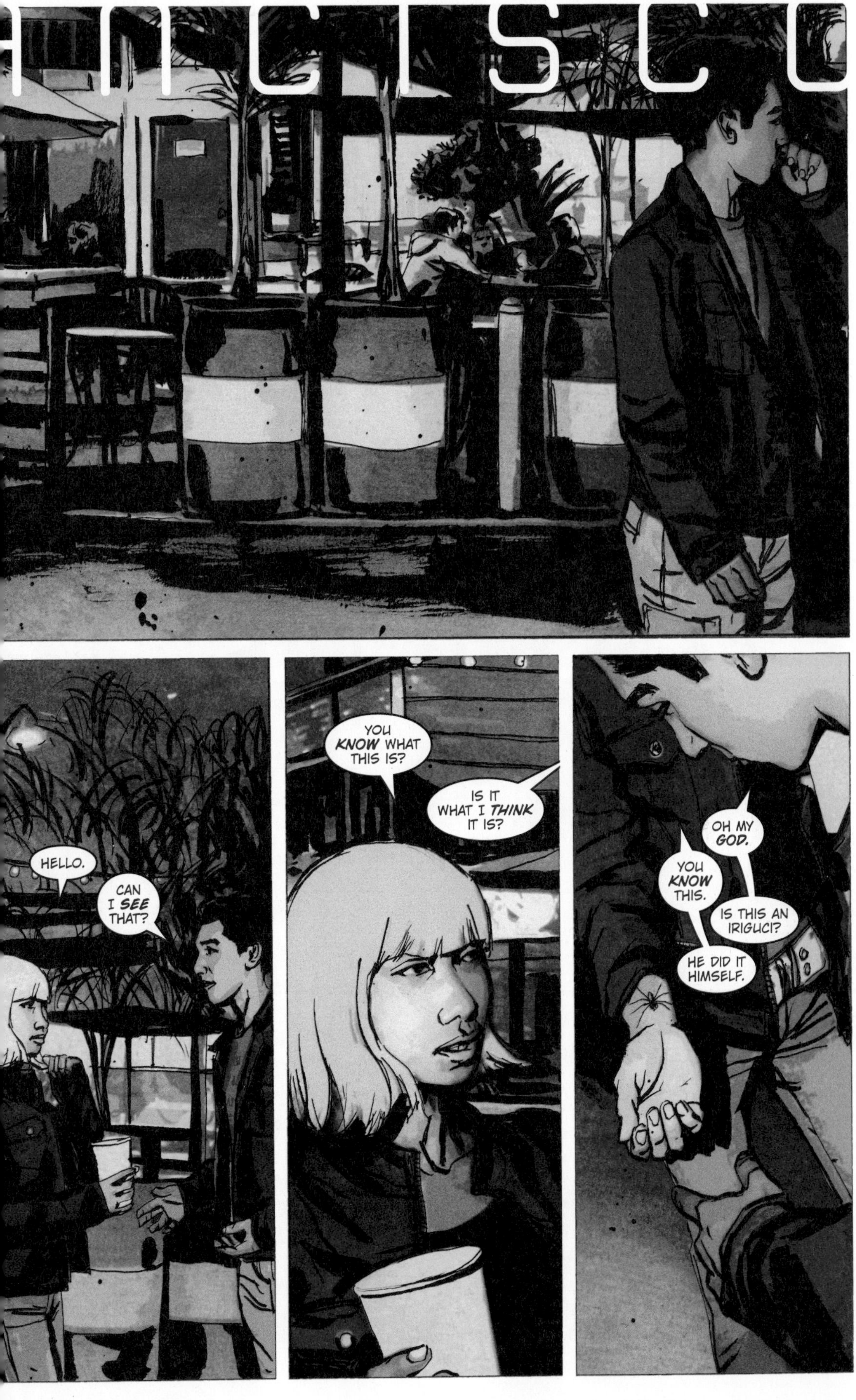
ANCISCO
HELLO.
CAN I SEE THAT?
YOU KNOW WHAT THIS IS?
IS IT WHAT I THINK IT IS?
OH MY GOD.
YOU KNOW THIS.
IS THIS AN IRIGUCI?
HE DID IT HIMSELF.

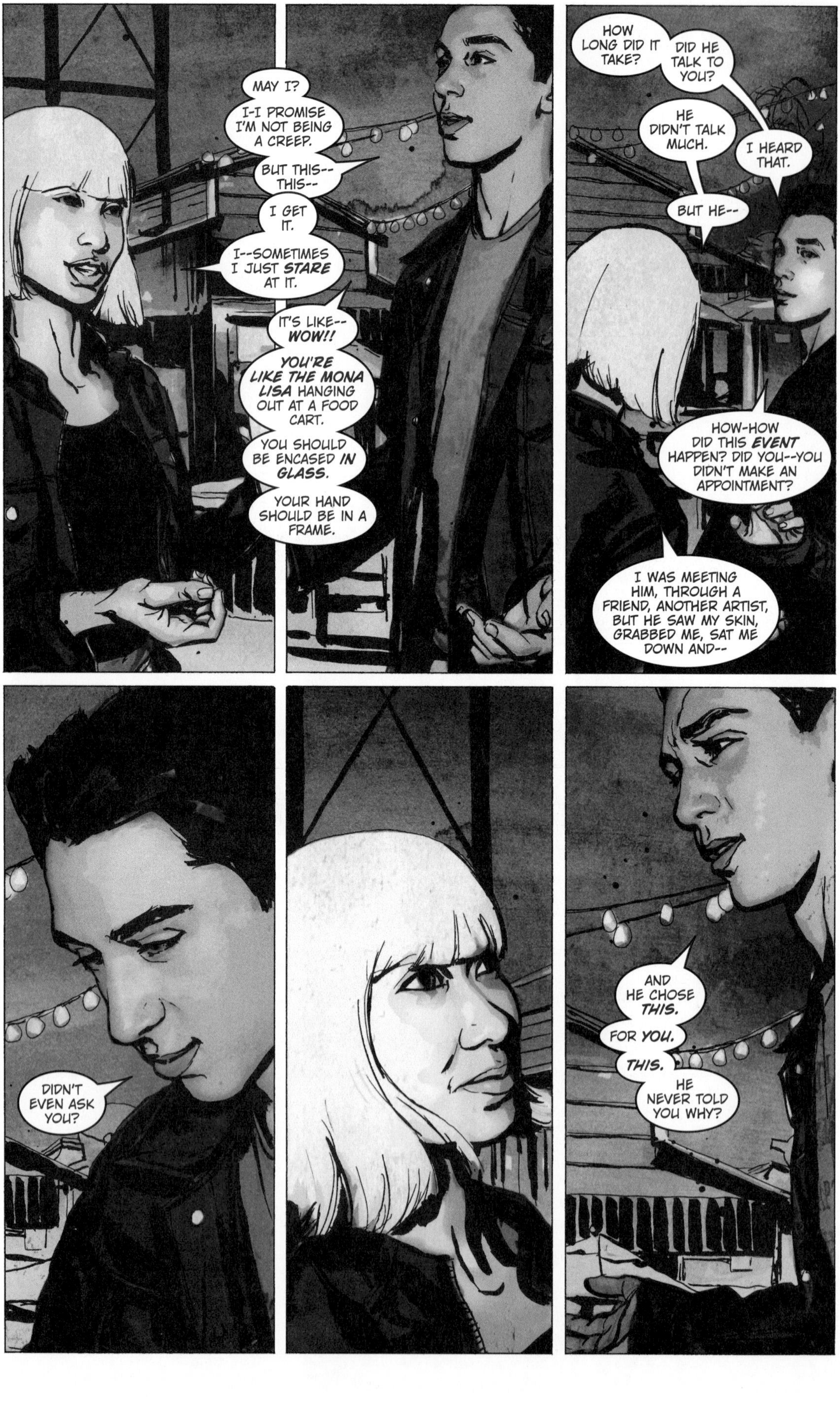
MAY I?
I-I PROMISE I'M NOT BEING A CREEP.
BUT THIS-- THIS--
I GET IT.
I--SOMETIMES I JUST STARE AT IT.
IT'S LIKE-- WOW!!
YOU'RE LIKE THE MONA LISA HANGING OUT AT A FOOD CART.
YOU SHOULD BE ENCASED IN GLASS.
YOUR HAND SHOULD BE IN A FRAME.
HOW LONG DID IT TAKE?
DID HE TALK TO YOU?
HE DIDN'T TALK MUCH.
I HEARD THAT.
BUT HE--
HOW-HOW DID THIS EVENT HAPPEN? DID YOU--YOU DIDN'T MAKE AN APPOINTMENT?
I WAS MEETING HIM, THROUGH A FRIEND, ANOTHER ARTIST, BUT HE SAW MY SKIN, GRABBED ME, SAT ME DOWN AND--
DIDN'T EVEN ASK YOU?
AND HE CHOSE THIS.
FOR YOU.
THIS.
HE NEVER TOLD YOU WHY?

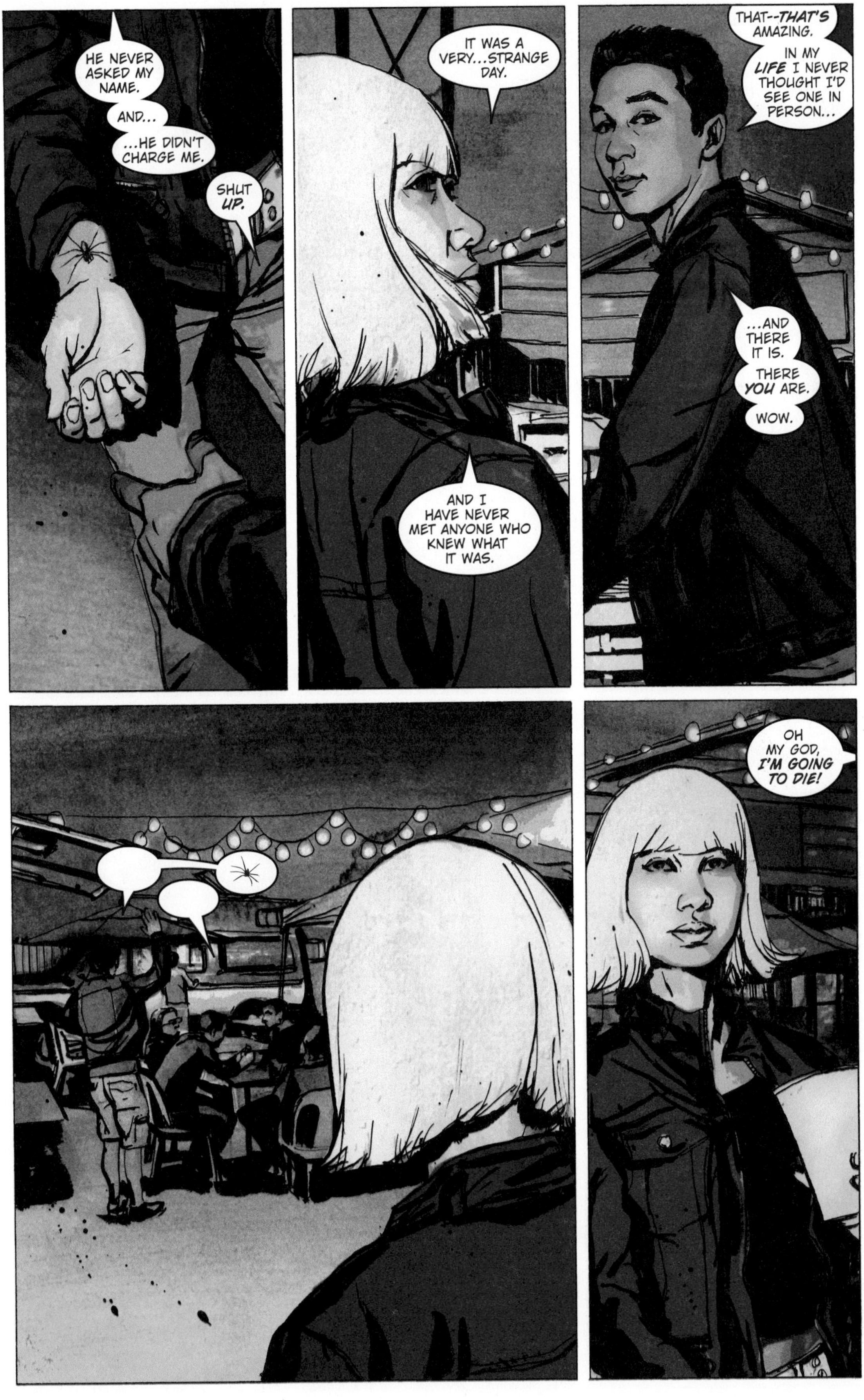
HE NEVER ASKED MY NAME.
AND...
...HE DIDN'T CHARGE ME.
SHUT *UP.*
IT WAS A VERY...STRANGE DAY.
AND I HAVE NEVER MET ANYONE WHO KNEW WHAT IT WAS.
THAT--*THAT'S* AMAZING.
IN MY *LIFE* I NEVER THOUGHT I'D SEE ONE IN PERSON...
...AND THERE IT IS.
THERE *YOU* ARE.
WOW.
OH MY GOD, *I'M GOING TO DIE!*

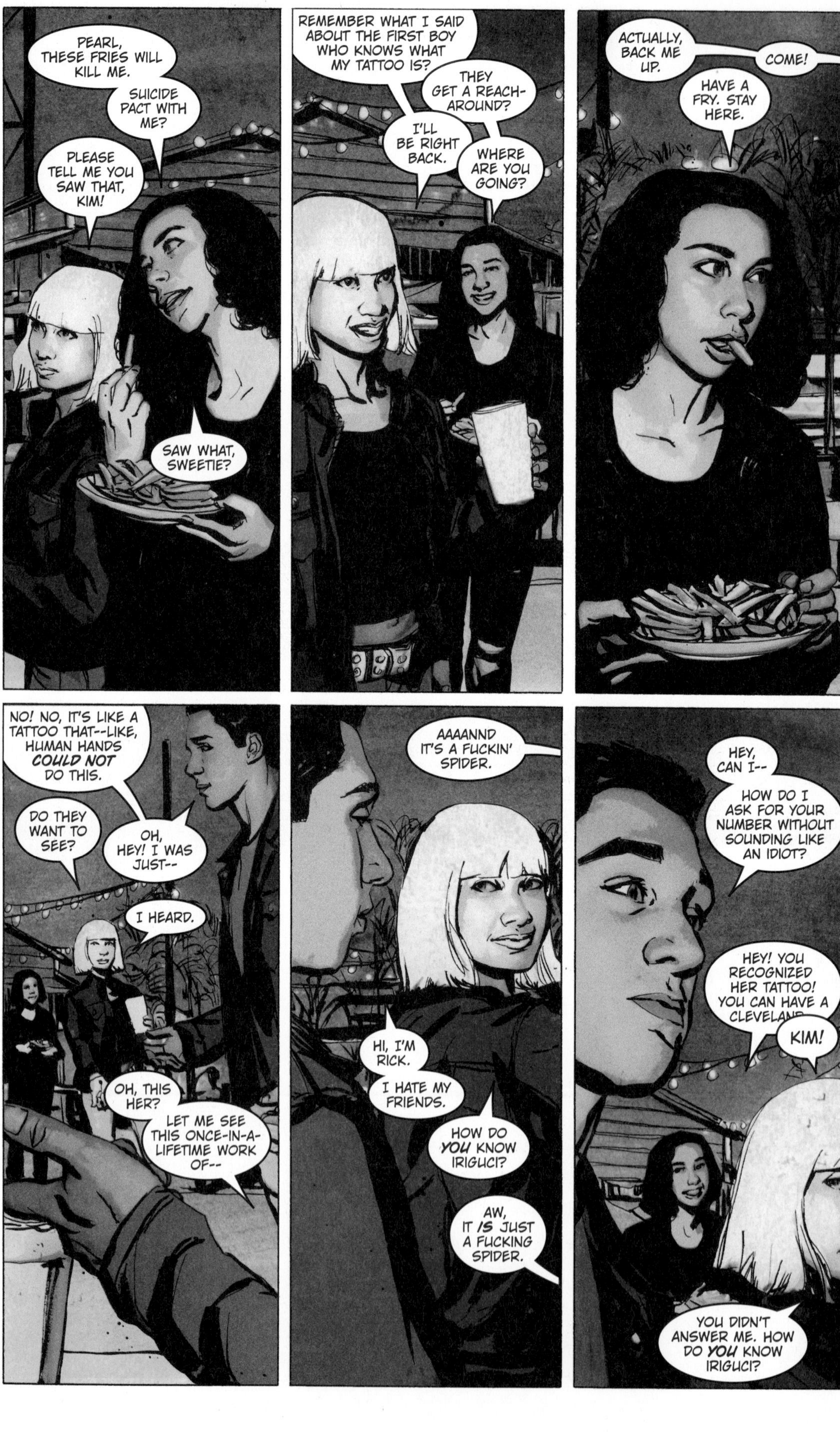
PEARL, THESE FRIES WILL KILL ME.
SUICIDE PACT WITH ME?
PLEASE TELL ME YOU SAW THAT, KIM!
SAW WHAT, SWEETIE?
REMEMBER WHAT I SAID ABOUT THE FIRST BOY WHO KNOWS WHAT MY TATTOO IS?
THEY GET A REACH-AROUND?
I'LL BE RIGHT BACK.
WHERE ARE YOU GOING?
ACTUALLY, BACK ME UP.
COME!
HAVE A FRY. STAY HERE.
NO! NO, IT'S LIKE A TATTOO THAT--LIKE, HUMAN HANDS **COULD NOT** DO THIS.
DO THEY WANT TO SEE?
OH, HEY! I WAS JUST--
I HEARD.
OH, THIS HER?
LET ME SEE THIS ONCE-IN-A-LIFETIME WORK OF--
AAAANND IT'S A FUCKIN' SPIDER.
HI, I'M RICK.
I HATE MY FRIENDS.
HOW DO ***YOU*** KNOW IRIGUCI?
AW, IT ***IS*** JUST A FUCKING SPIDER.
HEY, CAN I--
HOW DO I ASK FOR YOUR NUMBER WITHOUT SOUNDING LIKE AN IDIOT?
HEY! YOU RECOGNIZED HER TATTOO! YOU CAN HAVE A CLEVELAN
KIM!
YOU DIDN'T ANSWER ME. HOW DO ***YOU*** KNOW IRIGUCI?

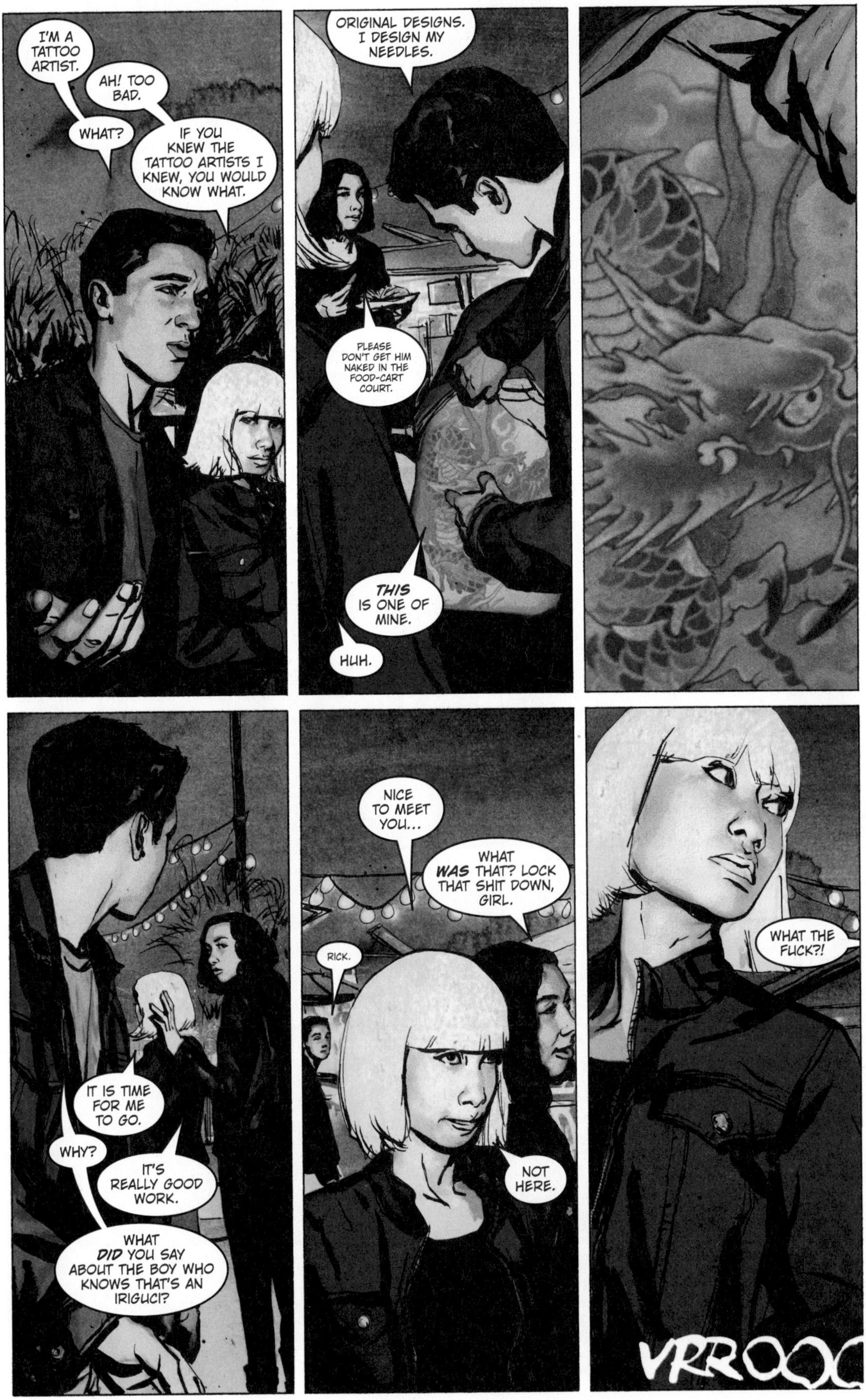
I'M A TATTOO ARTIST.
AH! TOO BAD.
WHAT?
IF YOU KNEW THE TATTOO ARTISTS I KNEW, YOU WOULD KNOW WHAT.
ORIGINAL DESIGNS. I DESIGN MY NEEDLES.
PLEASE DON'T GET HIM NAKED IN THE FOOD-CART COURT.
THIS IS ONE OF MINE.
HUH.
IT IS TIME FOR ME TO GO.
WHY?
IT'S REALLY GOOD WORK.
WHAT DID YOU SAY ABOUT THE BOY WHO KNOWS THAT'S AN IRIGUCI?
NICE TO MEET YOU...
WHAT WAS THAT? LOCK THAT SHIT DOWN, GIRL.
RICK.
NOT HERE.
WHAT THE FUCK?!
VRROOO

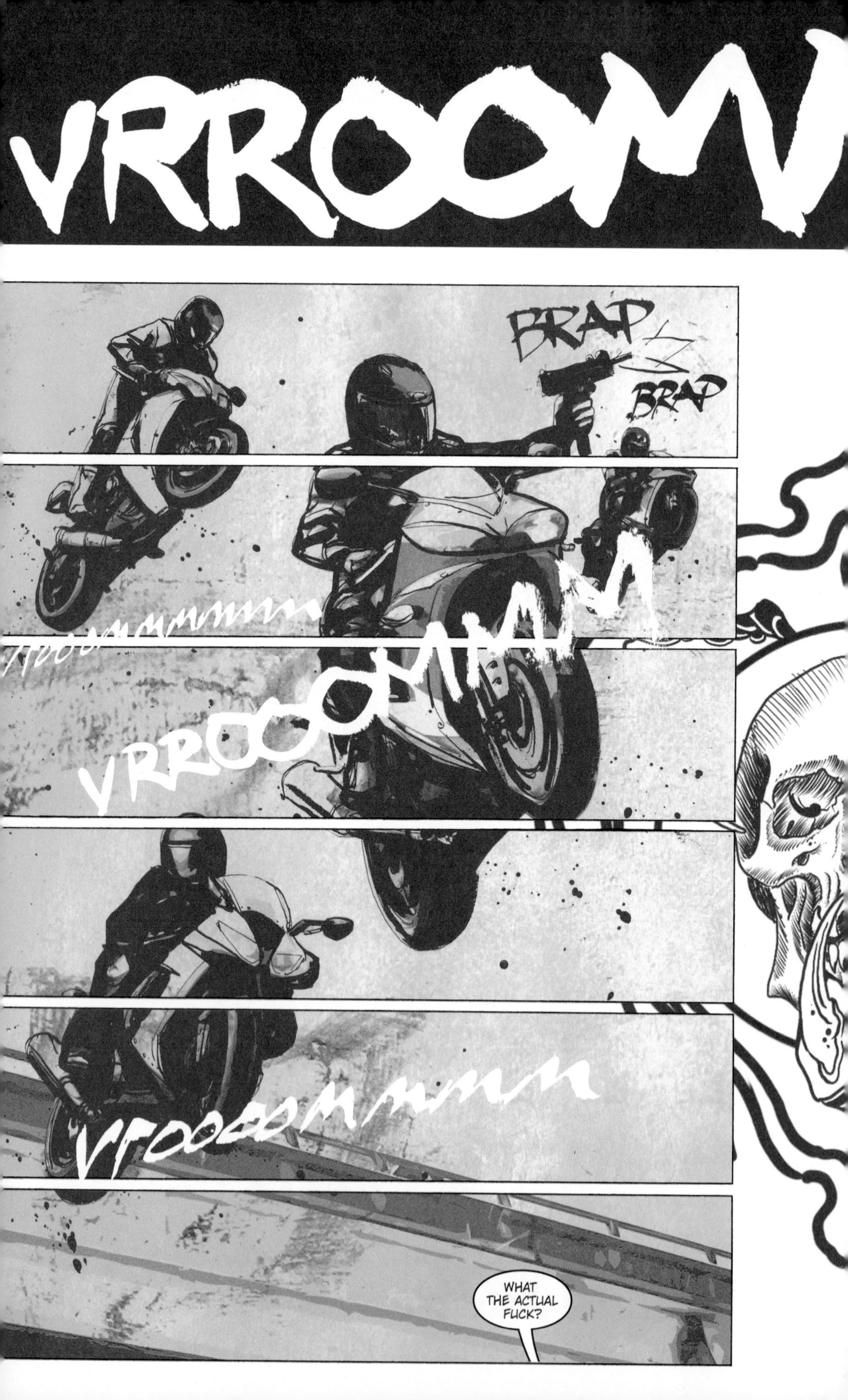
VRROOM
BRAP
BRAP
VROOOMMMMMM
VRROOOOMMMM
VROOOOMMMMM
WHAT THE ACTUAL FUCK?

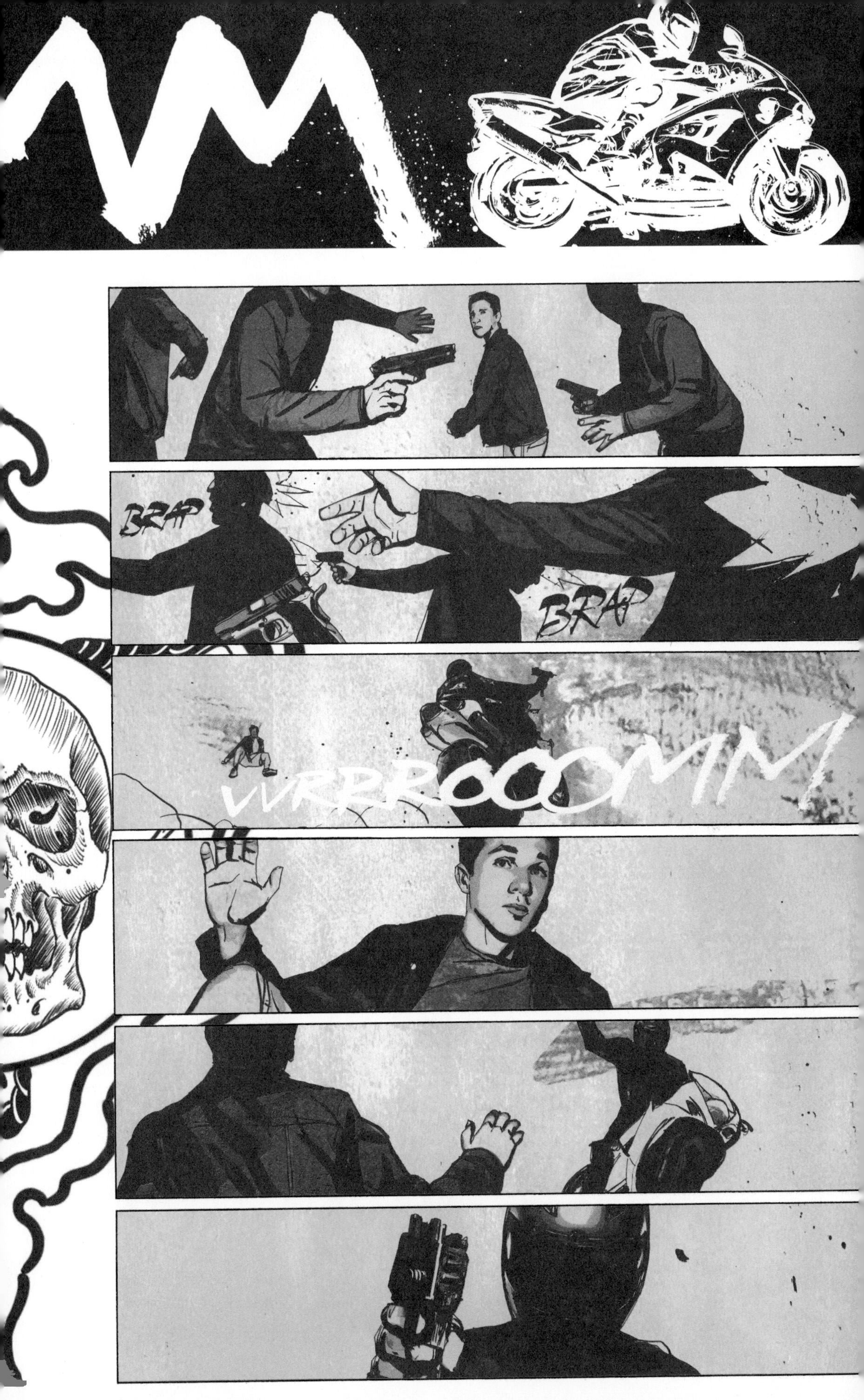
BRAP
BRAP
VVRRROOOMM

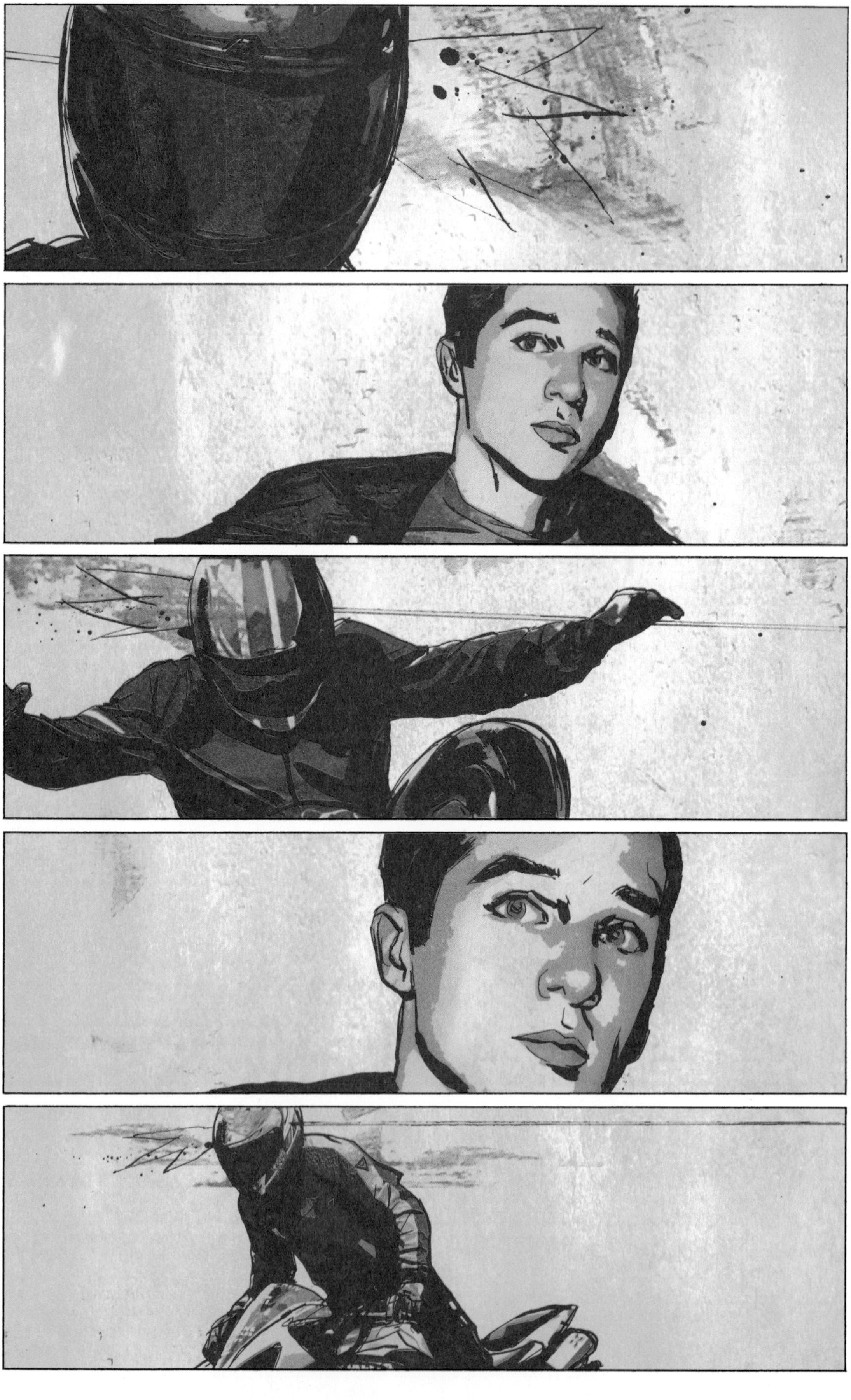

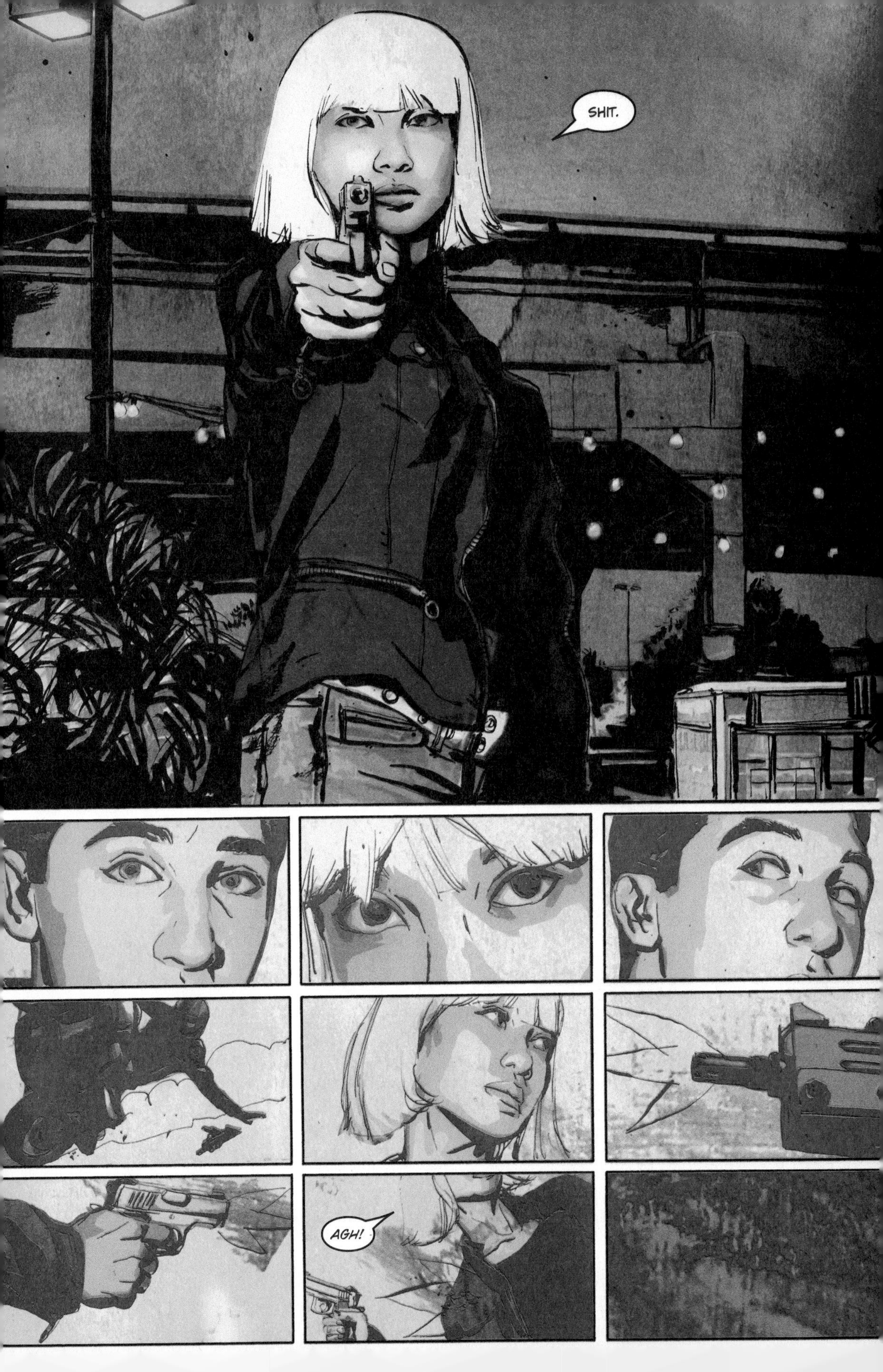
SHIT.
AGH!

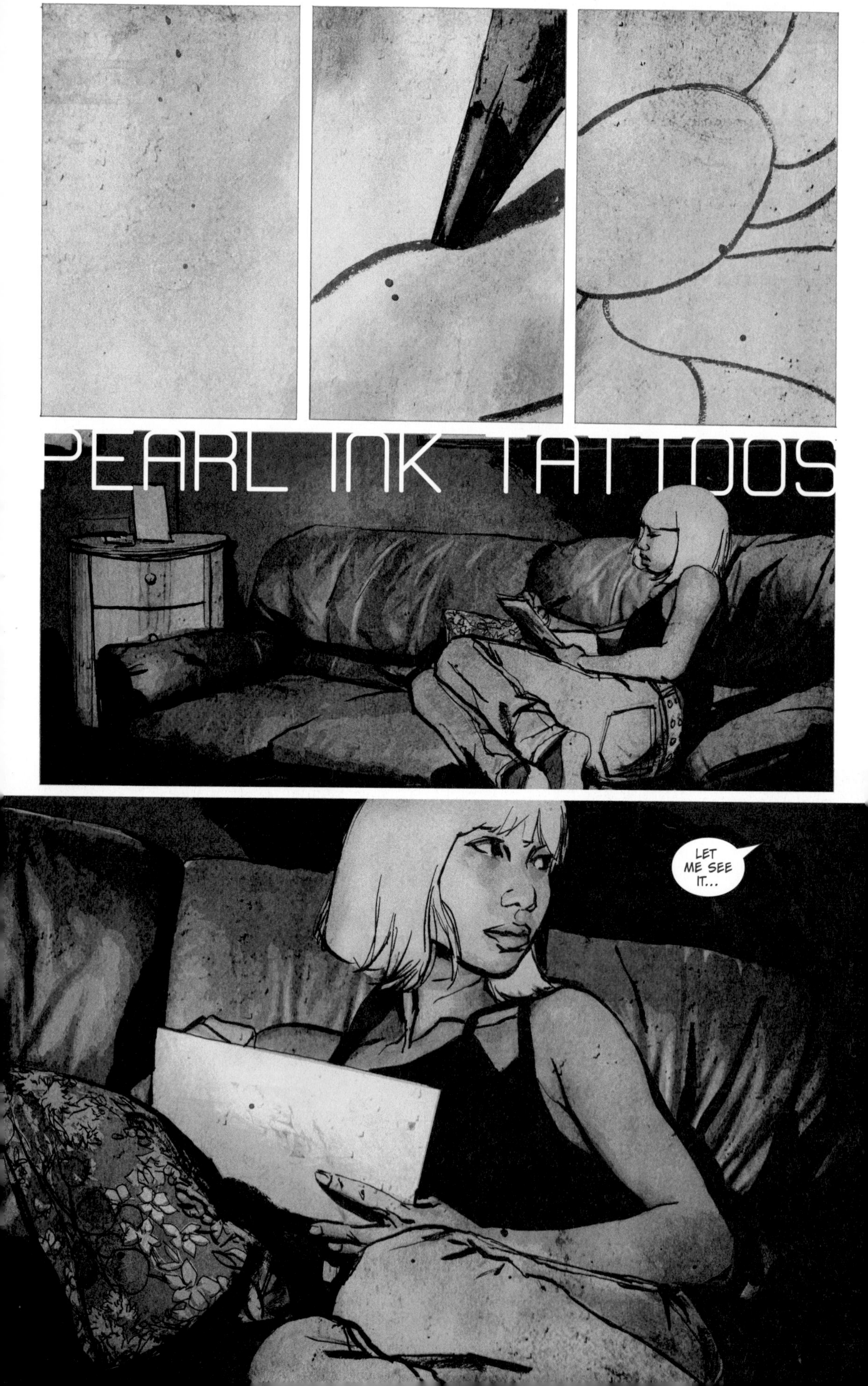
PEARL INK TATTOOS
LET ME SEE IT...

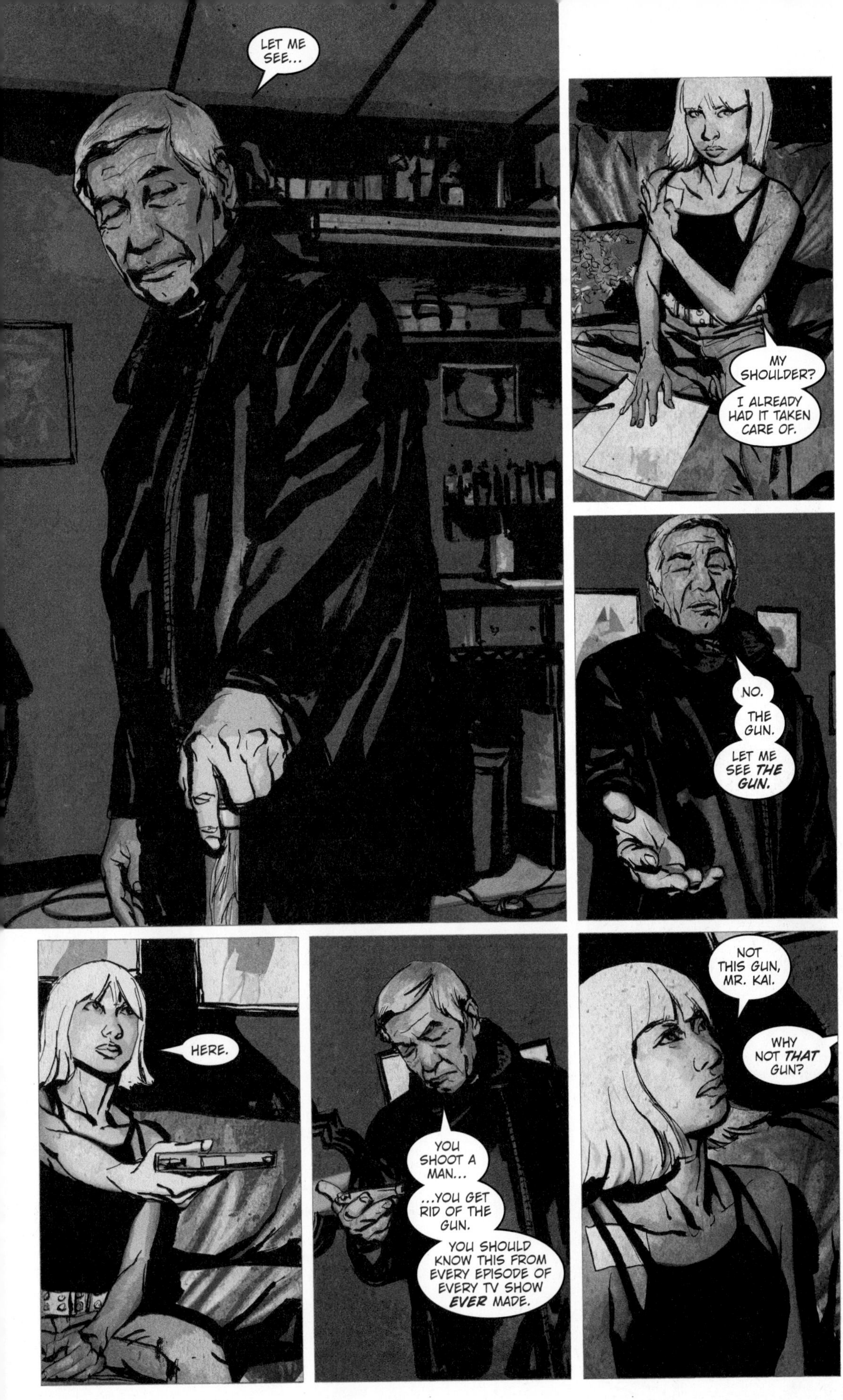
LET ME SEE...
MY SHOULDER?
I ALREADY HAD IT TAKEN CARE OF.
NO.
THE GUN.
LET ME SEE *THE GUN.*
HERE.
YOU SHOOT A MAN...
...YOU GET RID OF THE GUN.
YOU SHOULD KNOW THIS FROM EVERY EPISODE OF EVERY TV SHOW *EVER* MADE.
NOT THIS GUN, MR. KAI.
WHY NOT *THAT* GUN?

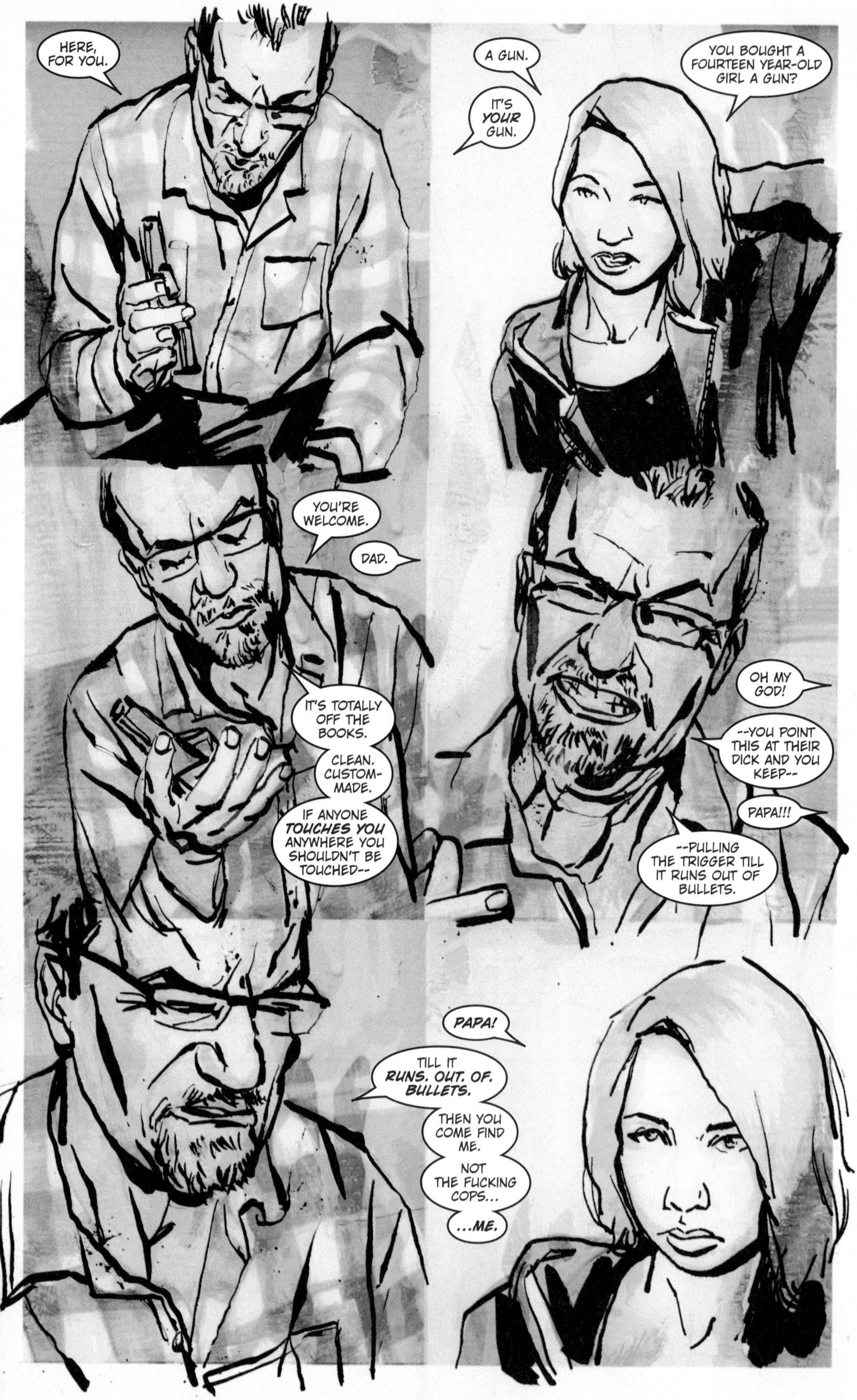
HERE, FOR YOU.
A GUN.
IT'S *YOUR* GUN.
YOU BOUGHT A FOURTEEN YEAR-OLD GIRL A GUN?
YOU'RE WELCOME.
DAD.
IT'S TOTALLY OFF THE BOOKS.
CLEAN. CUSTOM-MADE.
IF ANYONE *TOUCHES YOU* ANYWHERE YOU SHOULDN'T BE TOUCHED--
OH MY GOD!
--YOU POINT THIS AT THEIR DICK AND YOU KEEP--
PAPA!!!
--PULLING THE TRIGGER TILL IT RUNS OUT OF BULLETS.
PAPA!
TILL IT *RUNS. OUT. OF. BULLETS.*
THEN YOU COME FIND ME.
NOT THE FUCKING COPS...
...ME.

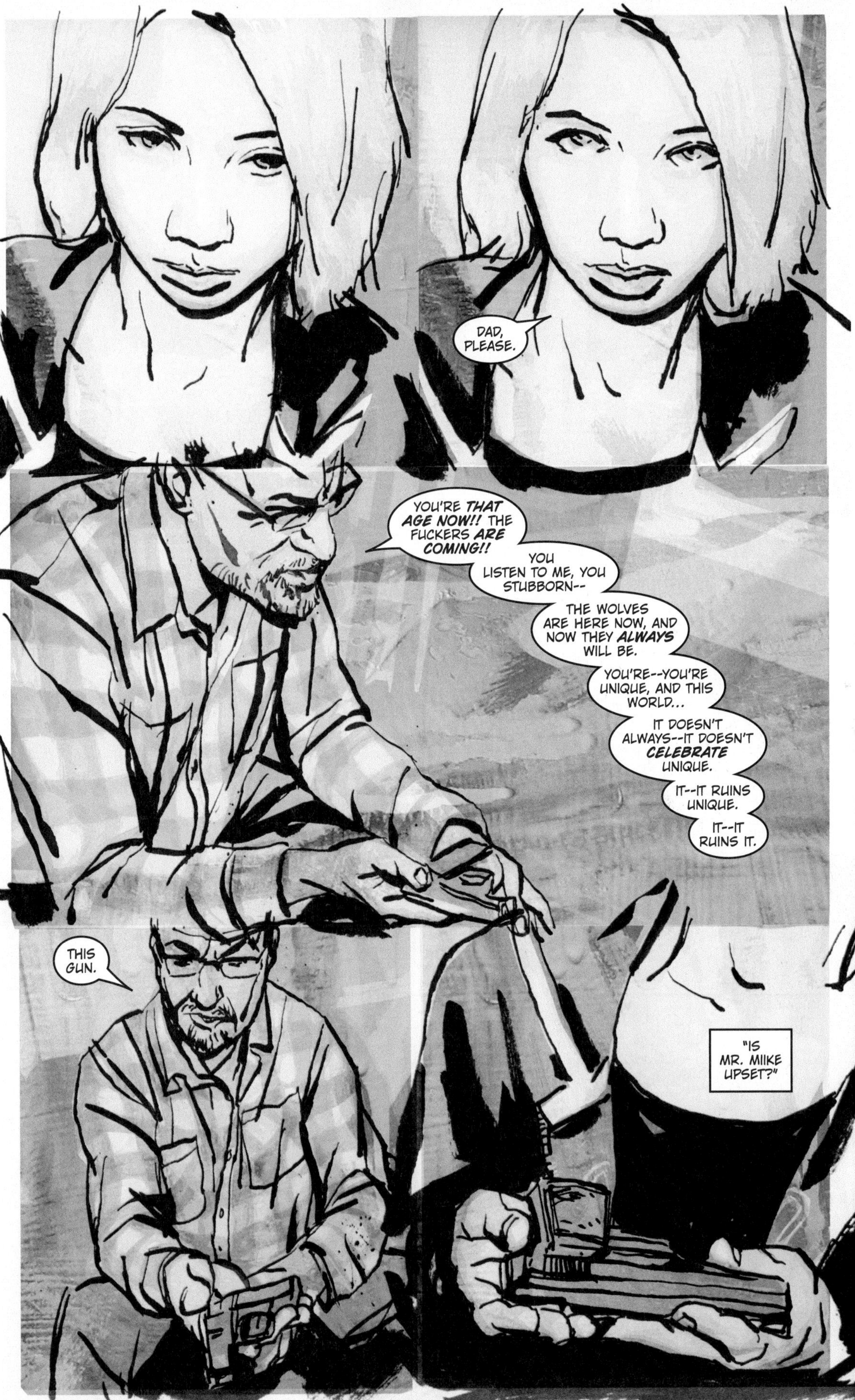
DAD, PLEASE.
YOU'RE *THAT AGE NOW!!* THE FUCKERS *ARE COMING!!*
YOU LISTEN TO ME, YOU STUBBORN--
THE WOLVES ARE HERE NOW, AND NOW THEY *ALWAYS* WILL BE.
YOU'RE--YOU'RE UNIQUE, AND THIS WORLD...
IT DOESN'T ALWAYS--IT DOESN'T *CELEBRATE* UNIQUE.
IT--IT RUINS UNIQUE.
IT--IT RUINS IT.
THIS GUN.
"IS MR. MIIKE UPSET?"

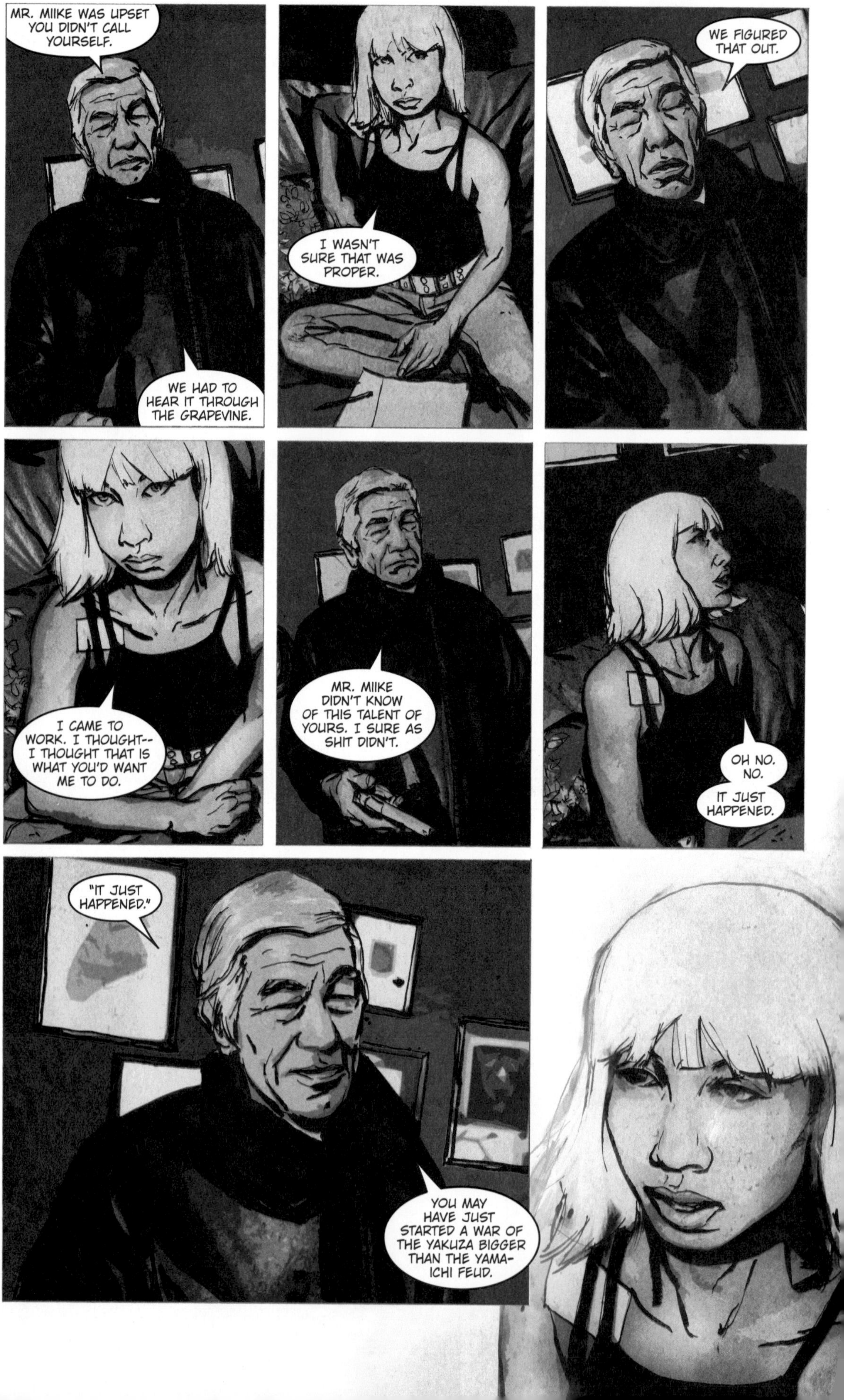
MR. MIIKE WAS UPSET YOU DIDN'T CALL YOURSELF.
WE HAD TO HEAR IT THROUGH THE GRAPEVINE.
I WASN'T SURE THAT WAS PROPER.
WE FIGURED THAT OUT.
I CAME TO WORK. I THOUGHT-- I THOUGHT THAT IS WHAT YOU'D WANT ME TO DO.
MR. MIIKE DIDN'T KNOW OF THIS TALENT OF YOURS. I SURE AS SHIT DIDN'T.
OH NO. NO.
IT JUST HAPPENED.
"IT JUST HAPPENED."
YOU MAY HAVE JUST STARTED A WAR OF THE YAKUZA BIGGER THAN THE YAMA-ICHI FEUD.

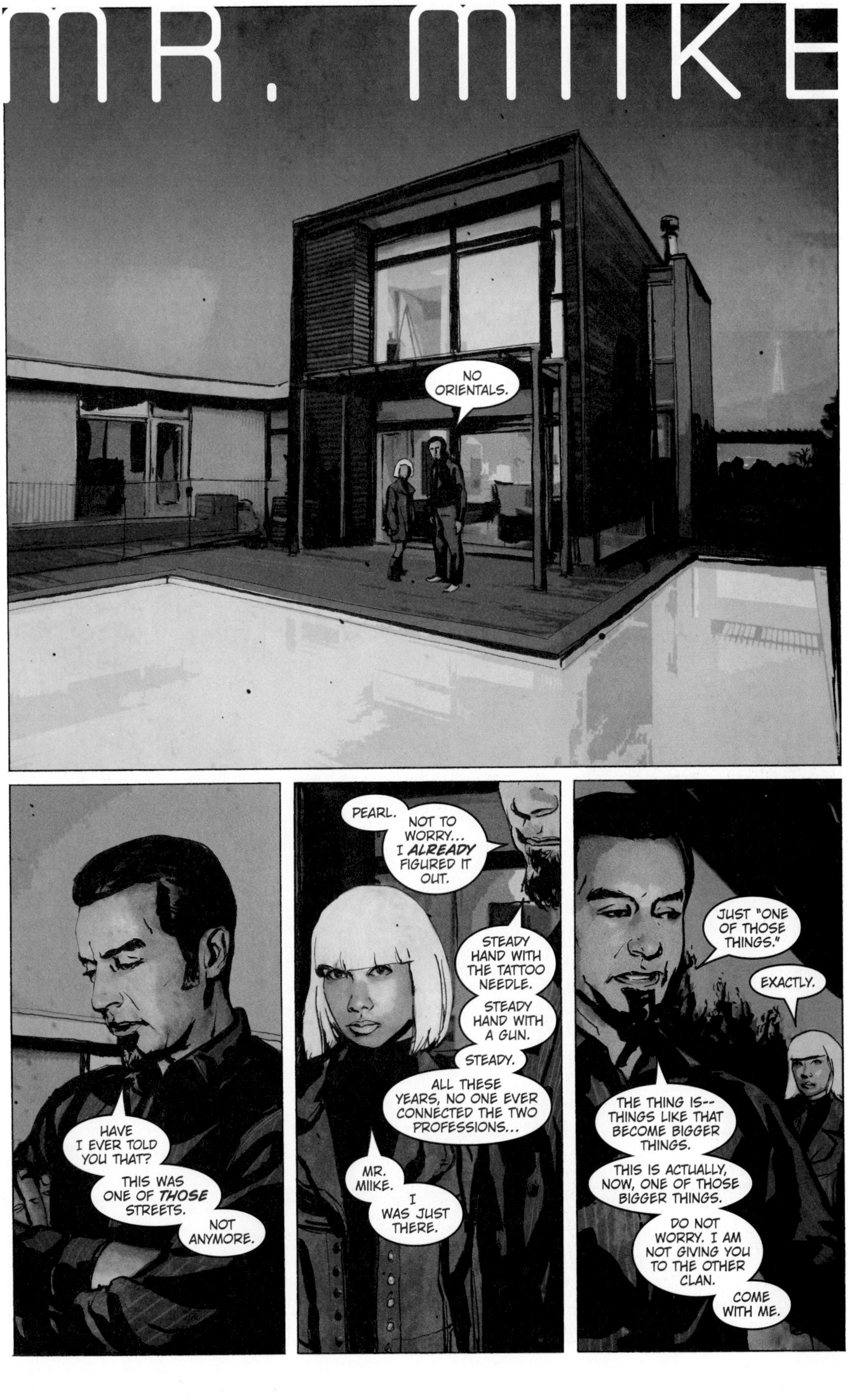
MR. MIIKE
NO ORIENTALS.
HAVE I EVER TOLD YOU THAT?
THIS WAS ONE OF *THOSE* STREETS.
NOT ANYMORE.
PEARL.
NOT TO WORRY... I *ALREADY* FIGURED IT OUT.
STEADY HAND WITH THE TATTOO NEEDLE.
STEADY HAND WITH A GUN.
STEADY.
ALL THESE YEARS, NO ONE EVER CONNECTED THE TWO PROFESSIONS...
MR. MIIKE.
I WAS JUST THERE.
JUST "ONE OF THOSE THINGS."
EXACTLY.
THE THING IS-- THINGS LIKE THAT BECOME BIGGER THINGS.
THIS IS ACTUALLY, NOW, ONE OF THOSE BIGGER THINGS.
DO NOT WORRY. I AM NOT GIVING YOU TO THE OTHER CLAN.
COME WITH ME.

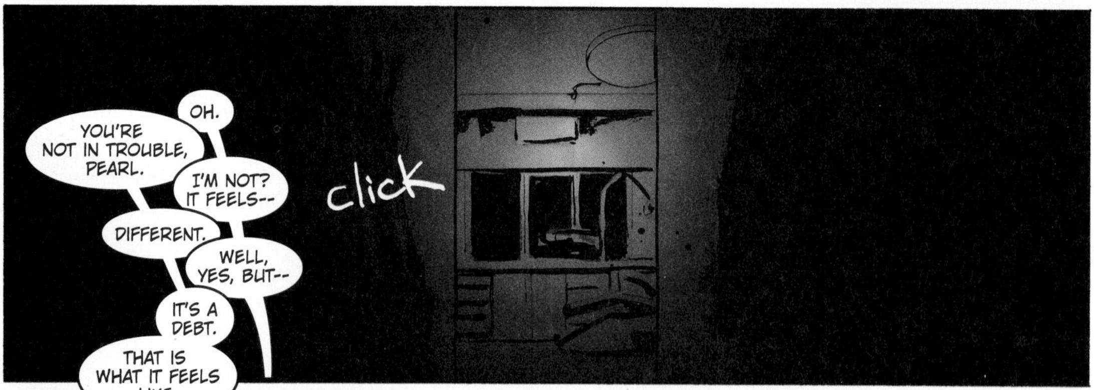
OH.
YOU'RE NOT IN TROUBLE, PEARL.
I'M NOT? IT FEELS--
DIFFERENT.
WELL, YES, BUT--
IT'S A DEBT.
THAT IS WHAT IT FEELS LIKE.
click

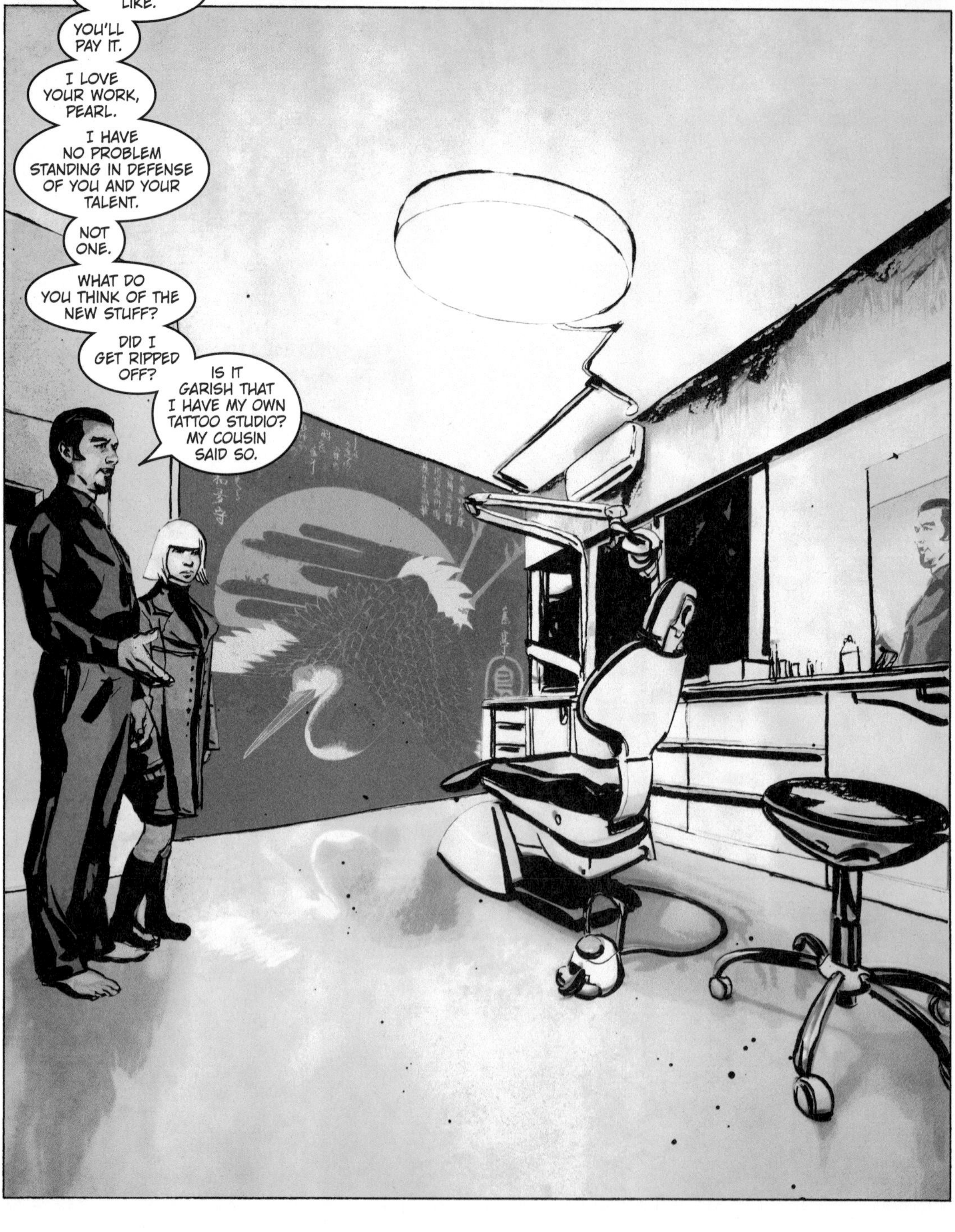
YOU'LL PAY IT.
I LOVE YOUR WORK, PEARL.
I HAVE NO PROBLEM STANDING IN DEFENSE OF YOU AND YOUR TALENT.
NOT ONE.
WHAT DO YOU THINK OF THE NEW STUFF?
DID I GET RIPPED OFF?
IS IT GARISH THAT I HAVE MY OWN TATTOO STUDIO? MY COUSIN SAID SO.

IT'S BEAUTIFUL.

GOOD. I COULD USE A TOUCH-UP.

THAT ONE PART OF MY SKIN *DID* HEAL SMOOTH IN THAT ONE PLACE.

YOU WERE *RIGHT* TO MAKE ME WAIT.

I TOLD YOU.

HOW MANY TATTOOS DO I HAVE TO DO TO REPAY YOU?

TATTOOS?

PEARL...

...NOW YOU'LL *WORK* FOR A LIVING.

THE YOUNG MEN FROM LAST NIGHT.

YOU'LL HAVE THEIR NAMES TOMORROW.

YOU'LL TAKE THEM OUT. QUICKLY AND--

I WAS GOING TO SAY "QUICKLY AND QUIETLY" BUT I HONESTLY *DON'T CARE* IF IT'S QUIETLY.

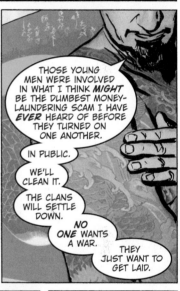

THOSE YOUNG MEN WERE INVOLVED IN WHAT I THINK *MIGHT* BE THE DUMBEST MONEY-LAUNDERING SCAM I HAVE *EVER* HEARD OF BEFORE THEY TURNED ON ONE ANOTHER.

IN PUBLIC.

WE'LL CLEAN IT.

THE CLANS WILL SETTLE DOWN.

NO ONE WANTS A WAR.

THEY JUST WANT TO GET LAID.

YOU WANT *ME* TO KILL THOSE MEN?

AND YOU WILL HAVE ARRIVED.

ME?

YOU STRIKE A POSE.

YOU'RE KIND OF UNFORGETTABLE.

I THINK YOU'LL BE *VERY* GOOD FOR CLAN RELATIONS.

I CAN'T DO THAT.

MR.
MIIKE...

THE PROBLEM
WITH TELLING
PEOPLE YOU THINK
THEM SPECIAL...

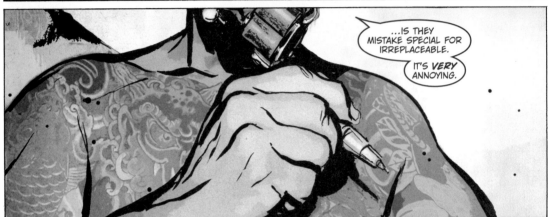

...IS THEY
MISTAKE SPECIAL FOR
IRREPLACEABLE.

IT'S *VERY*
ANNOYING.

AND
YET, THAT
FACE.

I WOULD
NEVER TOUCH
THAT FACE.

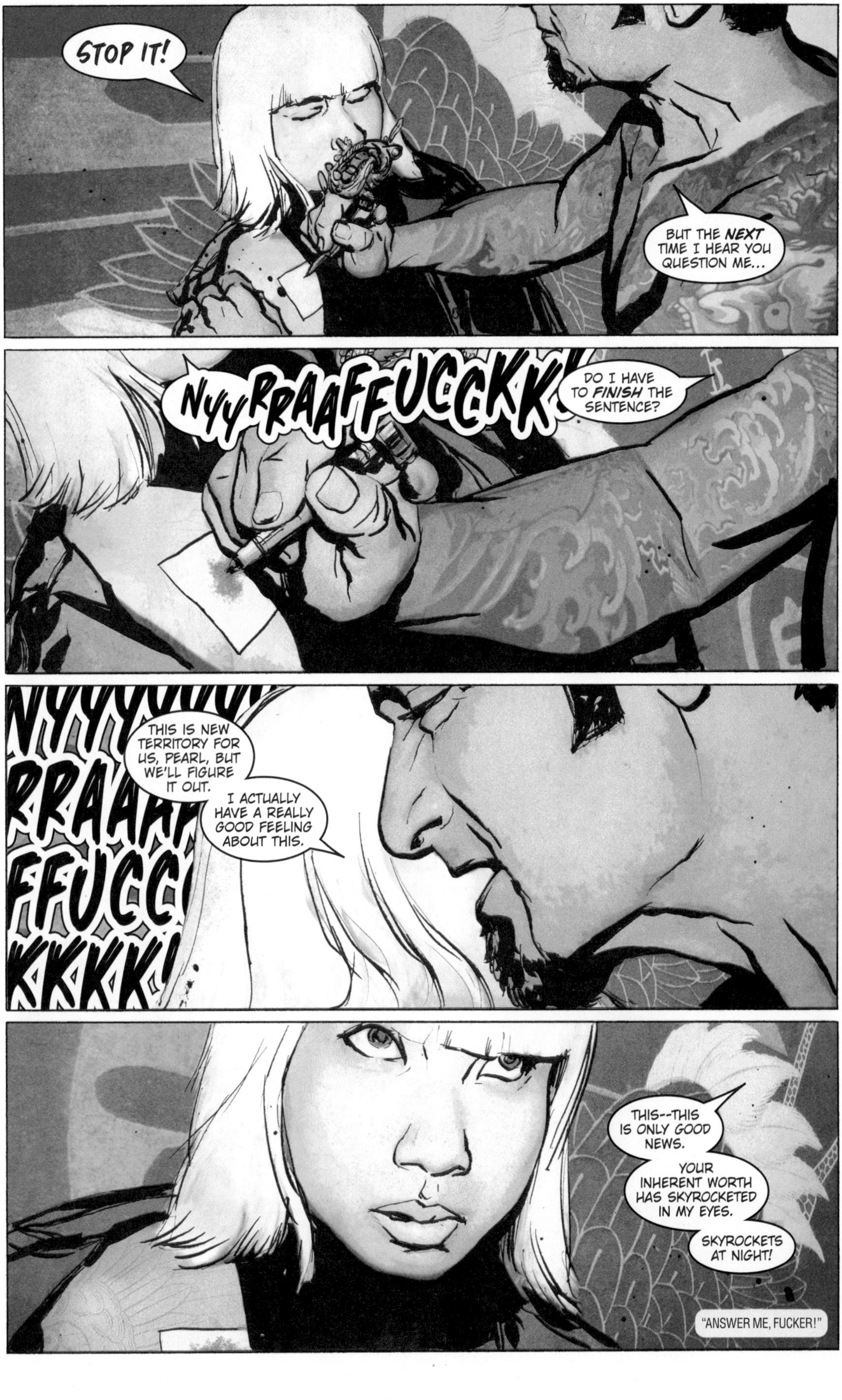
STOP IT!
BUT THE NEXT TIME I HEAR YOU QUESTION ME...
NYYRRAAFFUCCCKK
DO I HAVE TO FINISH THE SENTENCE?
NYYY
RRAA
FFUCC
KKKK
THIS IS NEW TERRITORY FOR US, PEARL, BUT WE'LL FIGURE IT OUT.
I ACTUALLY HAVE A REALLY GOOD FEELING ABOUT THIS.
THIS--THIS IS ONLY GOOD NEWS.
YOUR INHERENT WORTH HAS SKYROCKETED IN MY EYES.
SKYROCKETS AT NIGHT!
"ANSWER ME, FUCKER!"

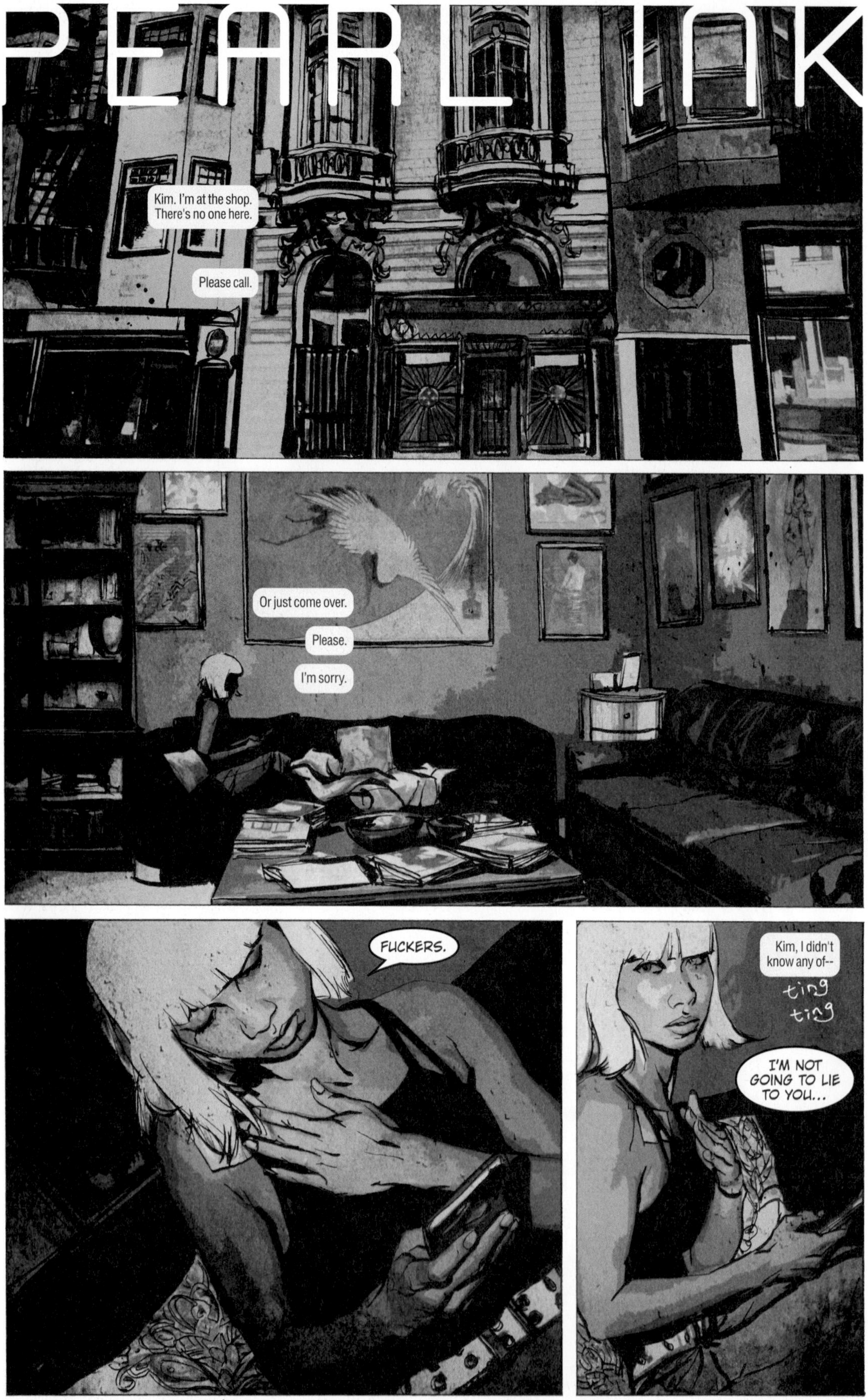
PEARL INK
Kim. I'm at the shop. There's no one here.
Please call.
Or just come over.
Please.
I'm sorry.
FUCKERS.
Kim, I didn't know any of--
ting ting
I'M NOT GOING TO LIE TO YOU...

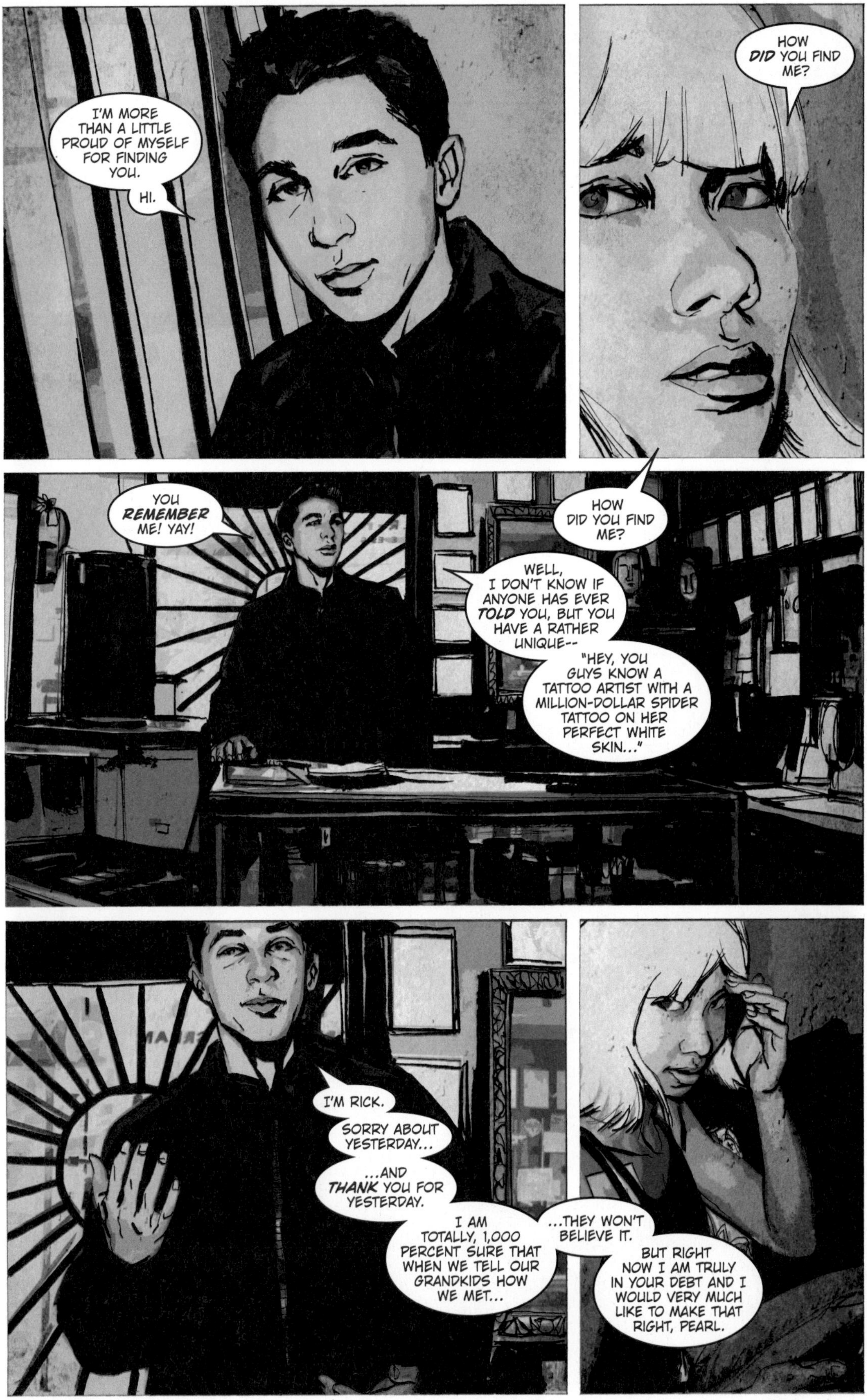
I'M MORE THAN A LITTLE PROUD OF MYSELF FOR FINDING YOU.
HI.
HOW *DID* YOU FIND ME?
YOU *REMEMBER* ME! YAY!
HOW DID YOU FIND ME?
WELL, I DON'T KNOW IF ANYONE HAS EVER *TOLD* YOU, BUT YOU HAVE A RATHER UNIQUE--
"HEY, YOU GUYS KNOW A TATTOO ARTIST WITH A MILLION-DOLLAR SPIDER TATTOO ON HER PERFECT WHITE SKIN..."
I'M RICK.
SORRY ABOUT YESTERDAY...
...AND *THANK* YOU FOR YESTERDAY.
I AM TOTALLY, 1,000 PERCENT SURE THAT WHEN WE TELL OUR GRANDKIDS HOW WE MET...
...THEY WON'T BELIEVE IT.
BUT RIGHT NOW I AM TRULY IN YOUR DEBT AND I WOULD VERY MUCH LIKE TO MAKE THAT RIGHT, PEARL.

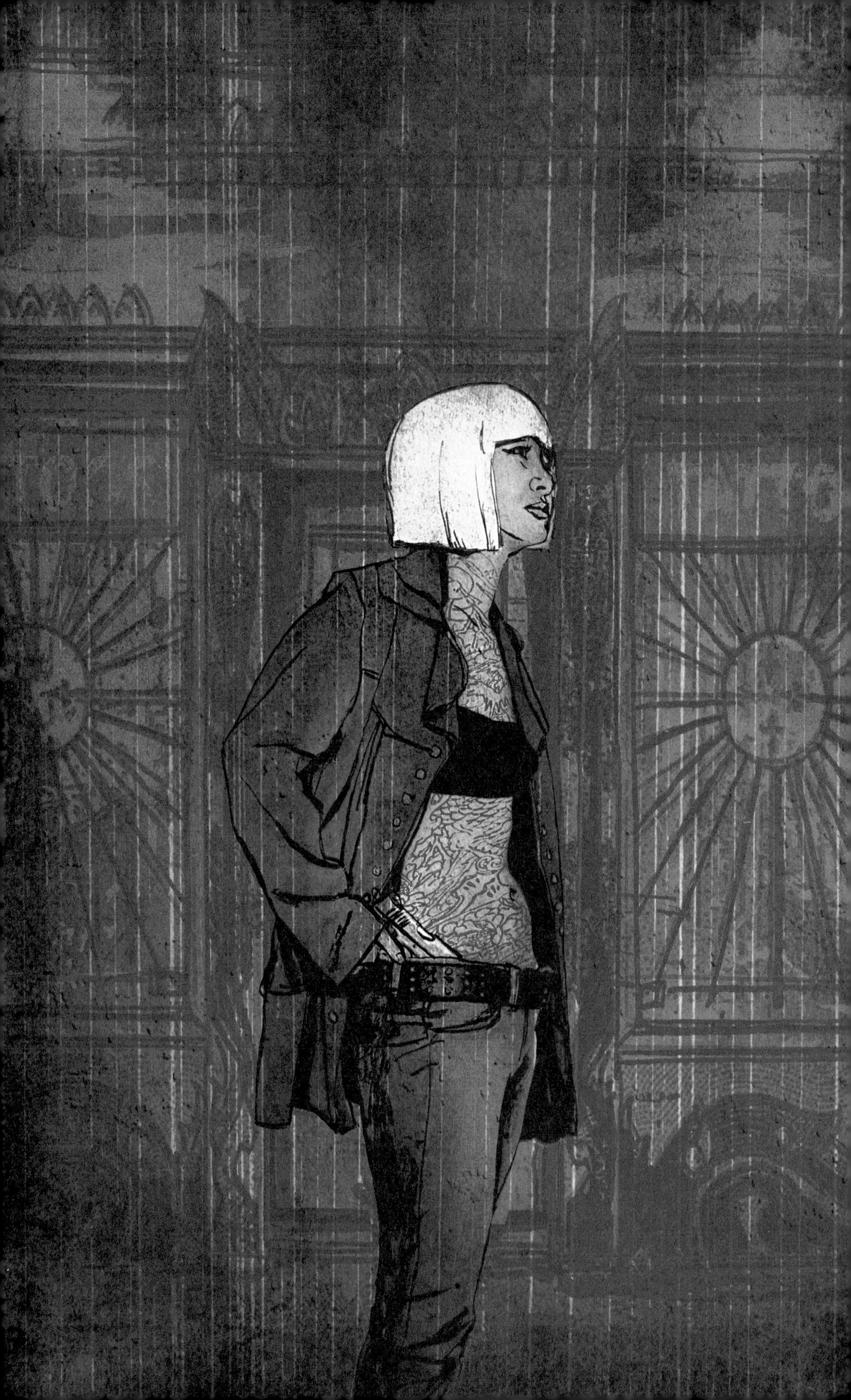

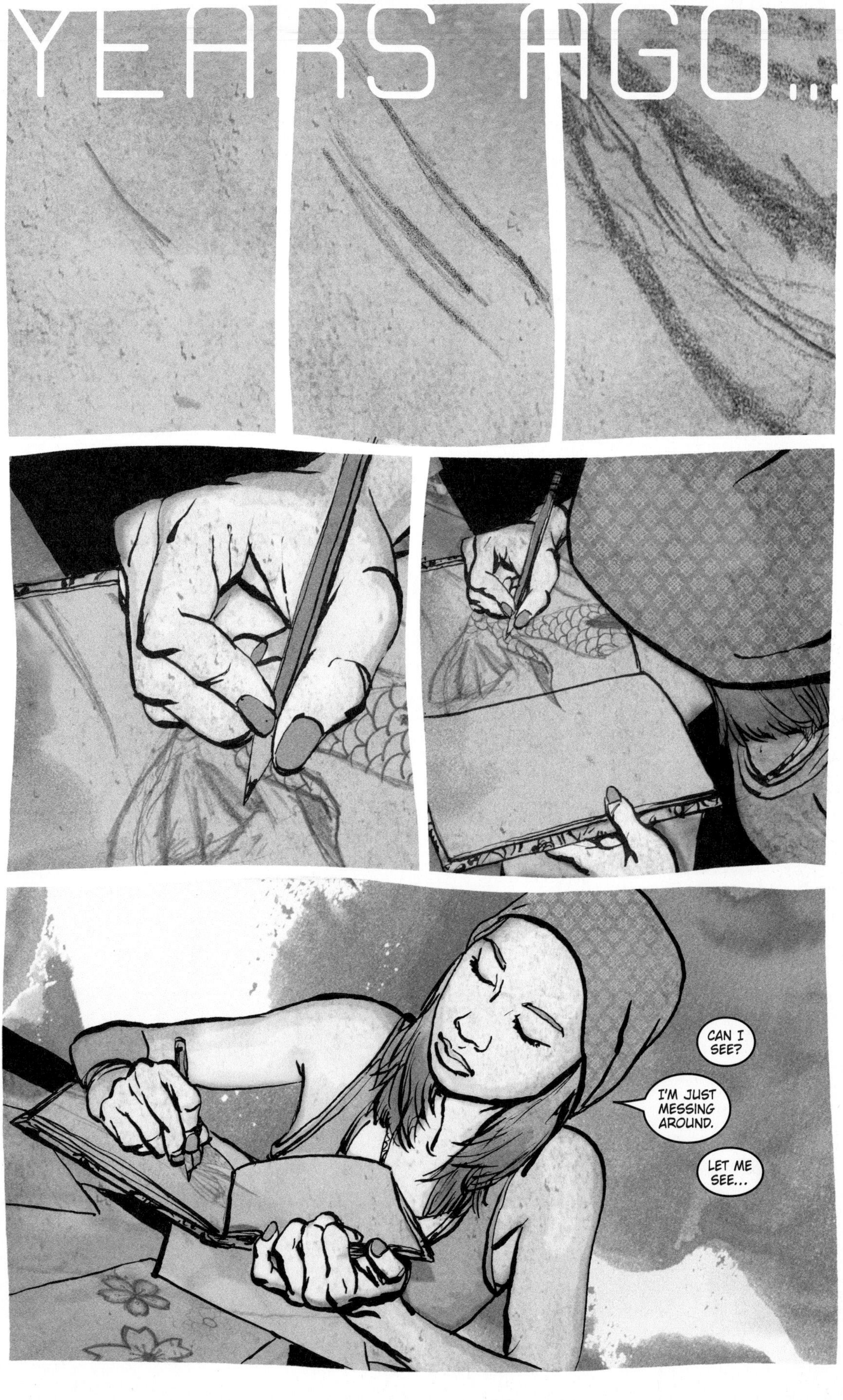
YEARS AGO...
CAN I SEE?
I'M JUST MESSING AROUND.
LET ME SEE...

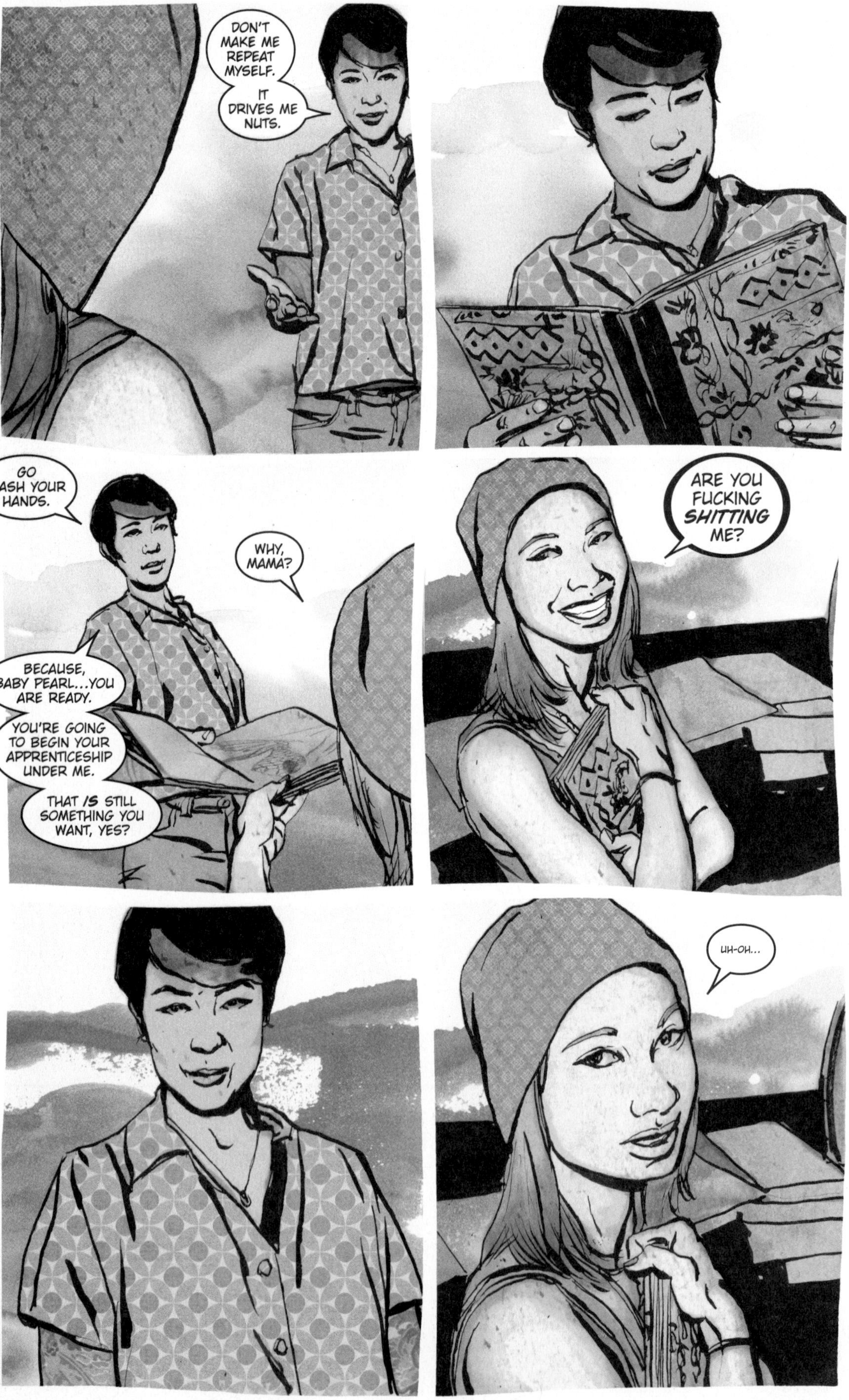
DON'T MAKE ME REPEAT MYSELF.
IT DRIVES ME NUTS.
GO WASH YOUR HANDS.
WHY, MAMA?
BECAUSE, BABY PEARL...YOU ARE READY.
YOU'RE GOING TO BEGIN YOUR APPRENTICESHIP UNDER ME.
THAT IS STILL SOMETHING YOU WANT, YES?
ARE YOU FUCKING SHITTING ME?
UH-OH...

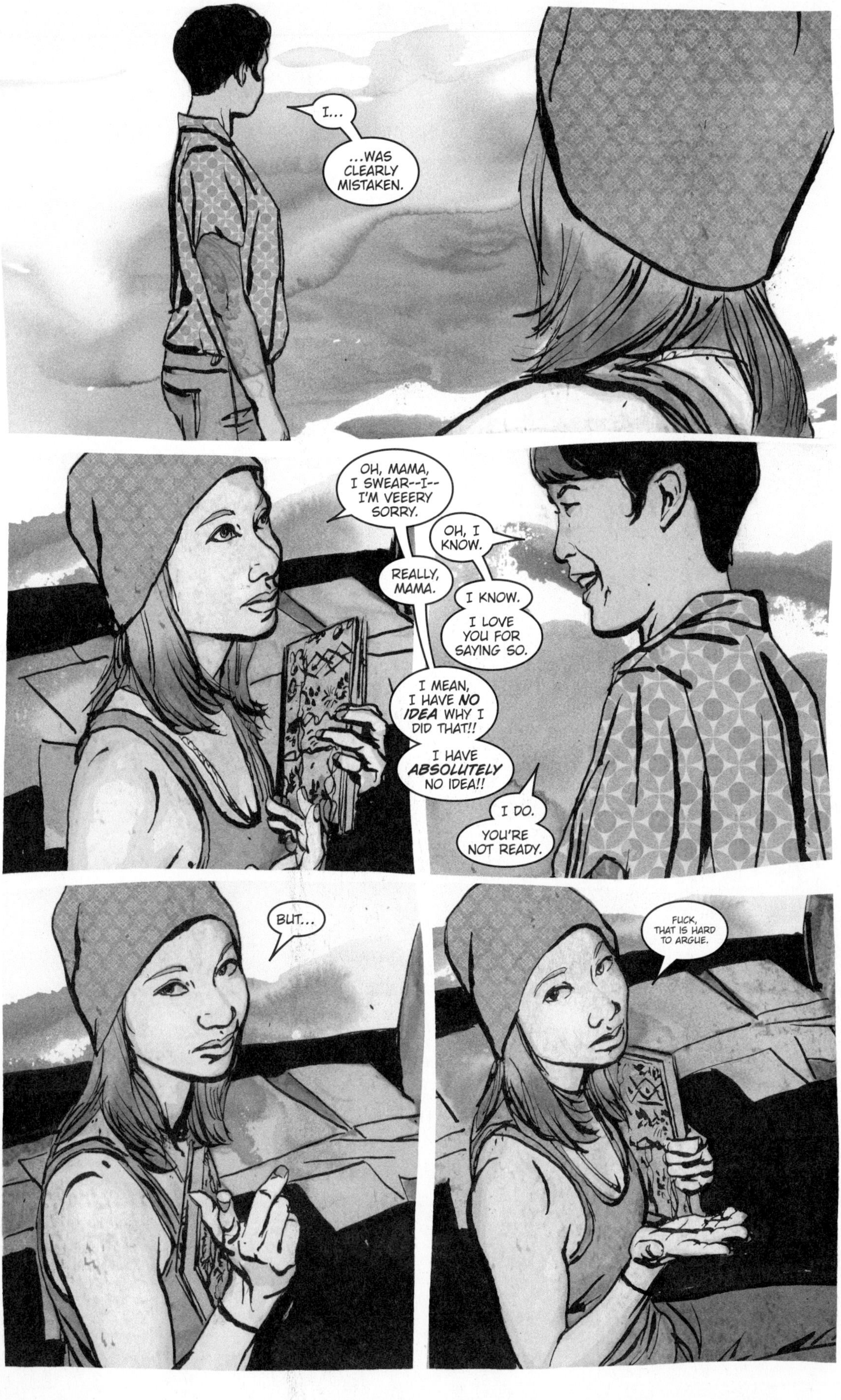
I...
...WAS CLEARLY MISTAKEN.
OH, MAMA, I SWEAR--I--I'M VEEERY SORRY.
REALLY, MAMA.
OH, I KNOW.
I KNOW.
I LOVE YOU FOR SAYING SO.
I MEAN, I HAVE NO IDEA WHY I DID THAT!!
I HAVE ABSOLUTELY NO IDEA!!
I DO.
YOU'RE NOT READY.
BUT...
FUCK, THAT IS HARD TO ARGUE.

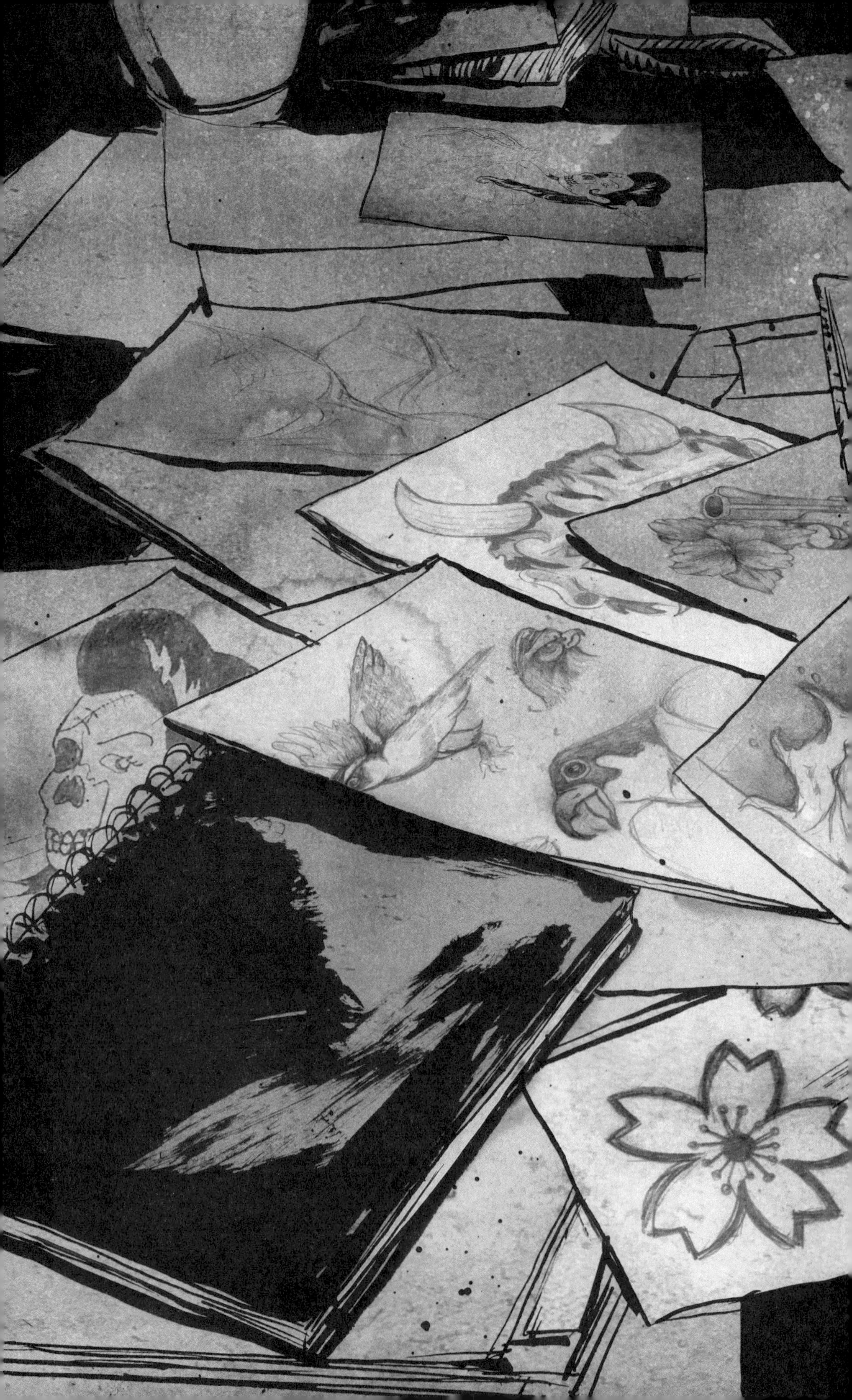

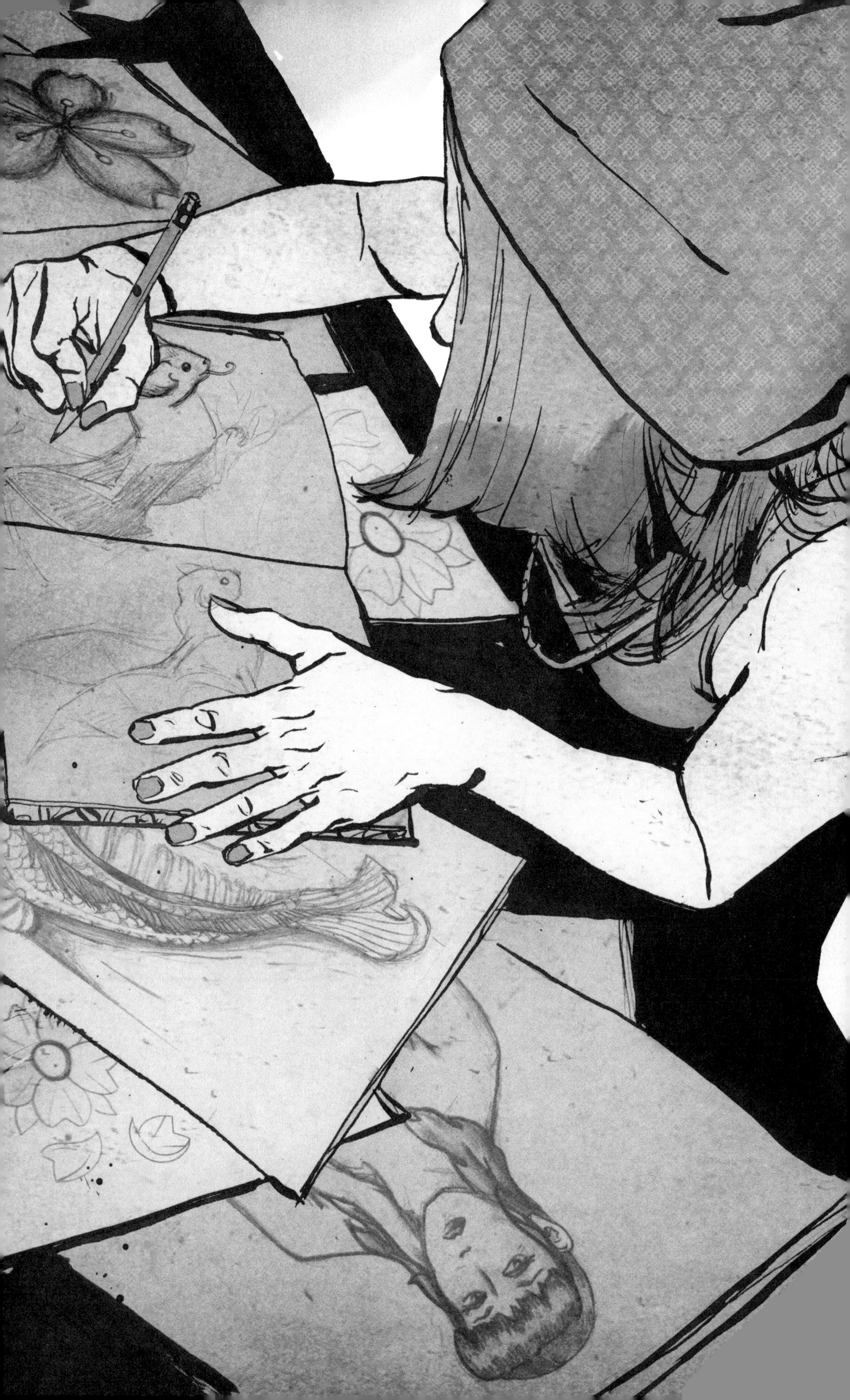

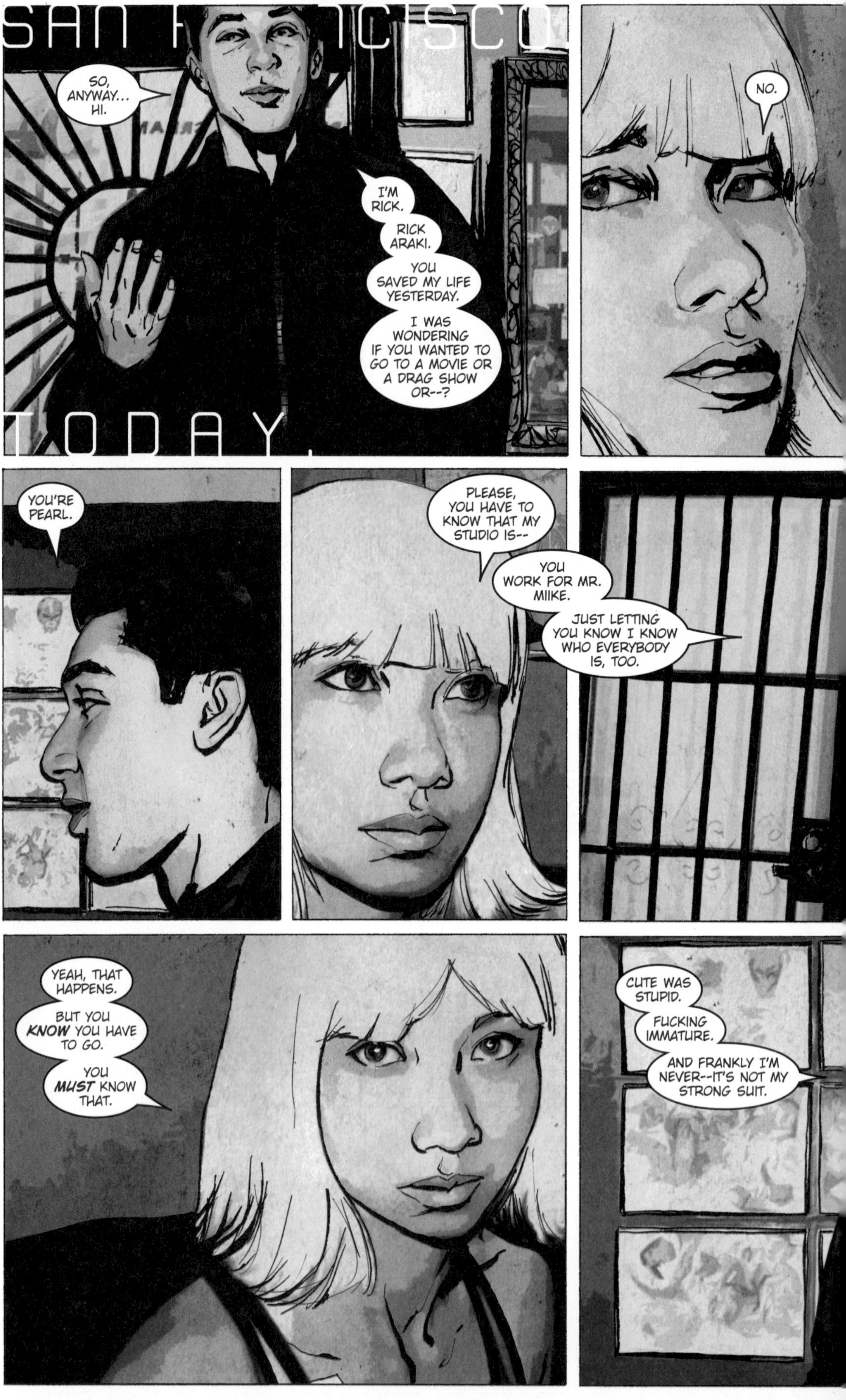
SAN FRANCISCO
SO, ANYWAY... HI.
I'M RICK.
RICK ARAKI.
YOU SAVED MY LIFE YESTERDAY.
I WAS WONDERING IF YOU WANTED TO GO TO A MOVIE OR A DRAG SHOW OR--?
TODAY.
NO.
YOU'RE PEARL.
PLEASE, YOU HAVE TO KNOW THAT MY STUDIO IS--
YOU WORK FOR MR. MIIKE.
JUST LETTING YOU KNOW I KNOW WHO EVERYBODY IS, TOO.
YEAH, THAT HAPPENS.
BUT YOU KNOW YOU HAVE TO GO.
YOU MUST KNOW THAT.
CUTE WAS STUPID.
FUCKING IMMATURE.
AND FRANKLY I'M NEVER--IT'S NOT MY STRONG SUIT.

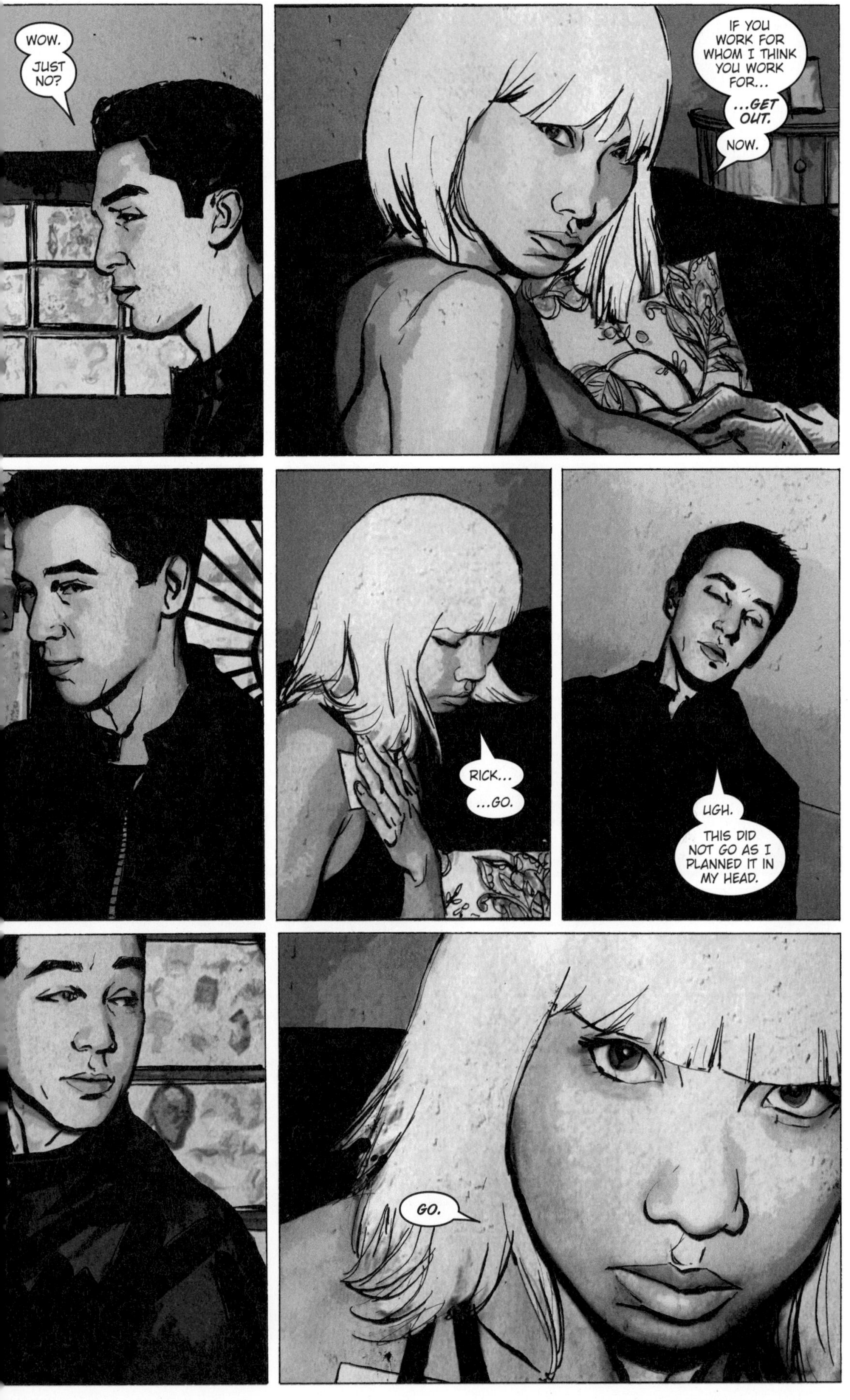
WOW.
JUST NO?
IF YOU WORK FOR WHOM I THINK YOU WORK FOR...
...GET OUT.
NOW.
RICK...
...GO.
UGH.
THIS DID NOT GO AS I PLANNED IT IN MY HEAD.
GO.

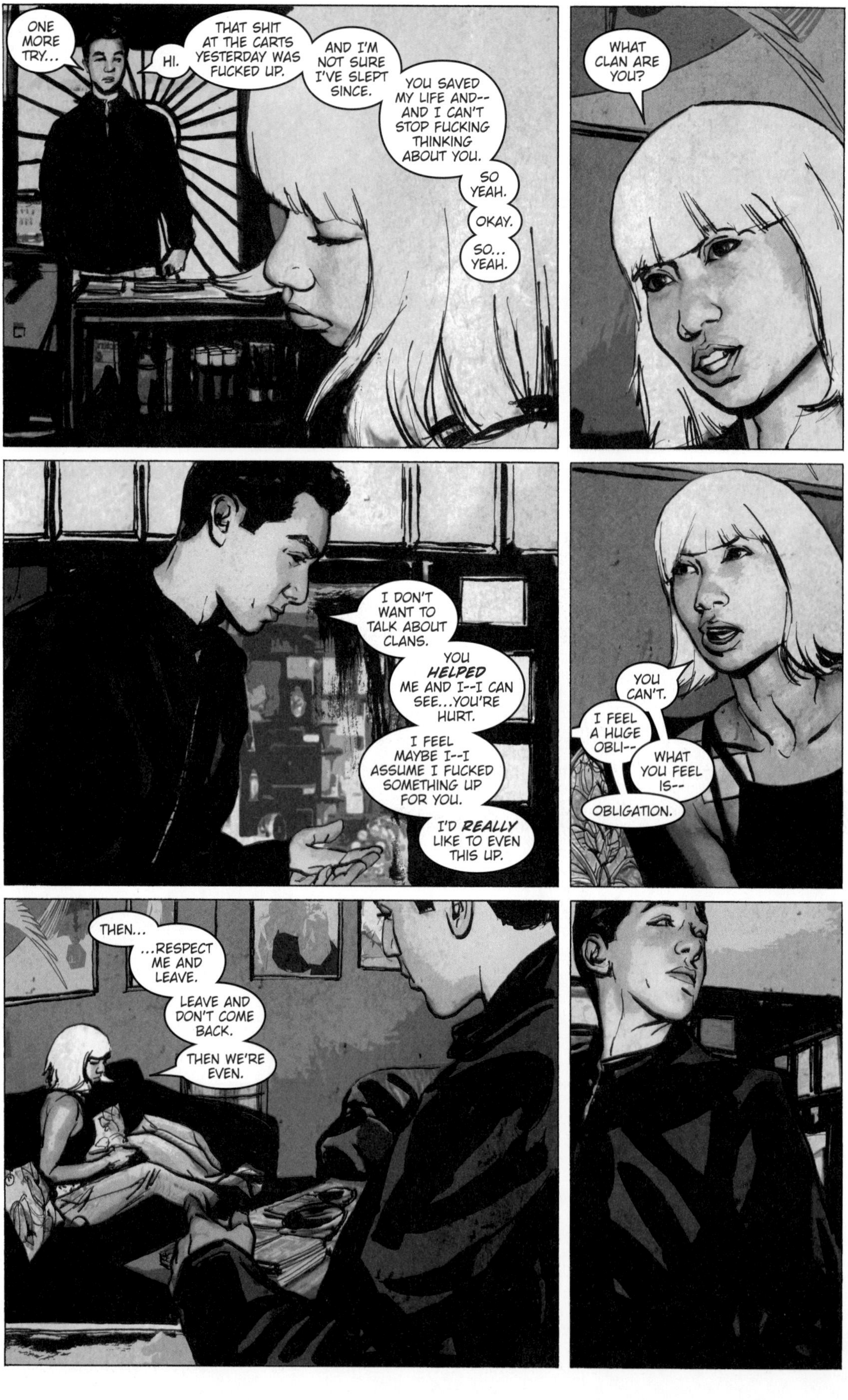
ONE MORE TRY...
HI.
THAT SHIT AT THE CARTS YESTERDAY WAS FUCKED UP.
AND I'M NOT SURE I'VE SLEPT SINCE.
YOU SAVED MY LIFE AND-- AND I CAN'T STOP FUCKING THINKING ABOUT YOU.
SO YEAH.
OKAY.
SO... YEAH.
WHAT CLAN ARE YOU?
I DON'T WANT TO TALK ABOUT CLANS.
YOU *HELPED* ME AND I--I CAN SEE...YOU'RE HURT.
I FEEL MAYBE I--I ASSUME I FUCKED SOMETHING UP FOR YOU.
I'D *REALLY* LIKE TO EVEN THIS UP.
YOU CAN'T.
I FEEL A HUGE OBLI--
WHAT YOU FEEL IS--
OBLIGATION.
THEN...
...RESPECT ME AND LEAVE.
LEAVE AND DON'T COME BACK.
THEN WE'RE EVEN.

REJECTED.
NO. NO. NO. STOP. STOP.

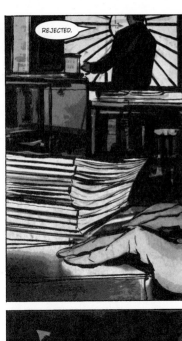

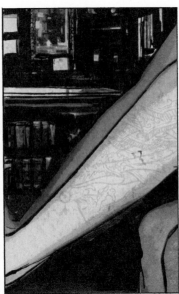

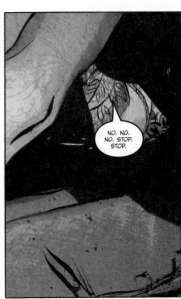

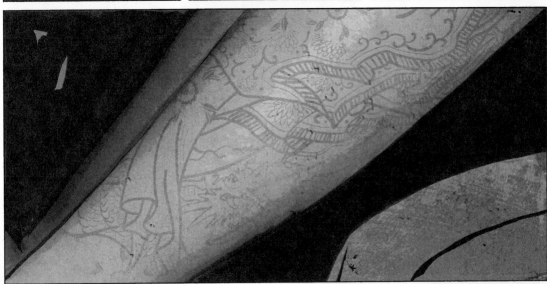

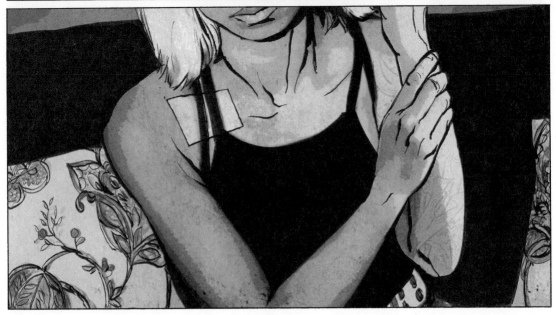

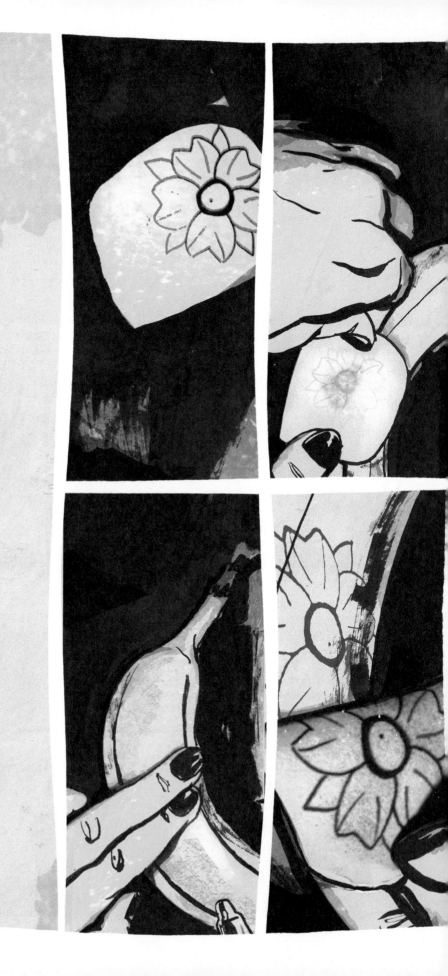

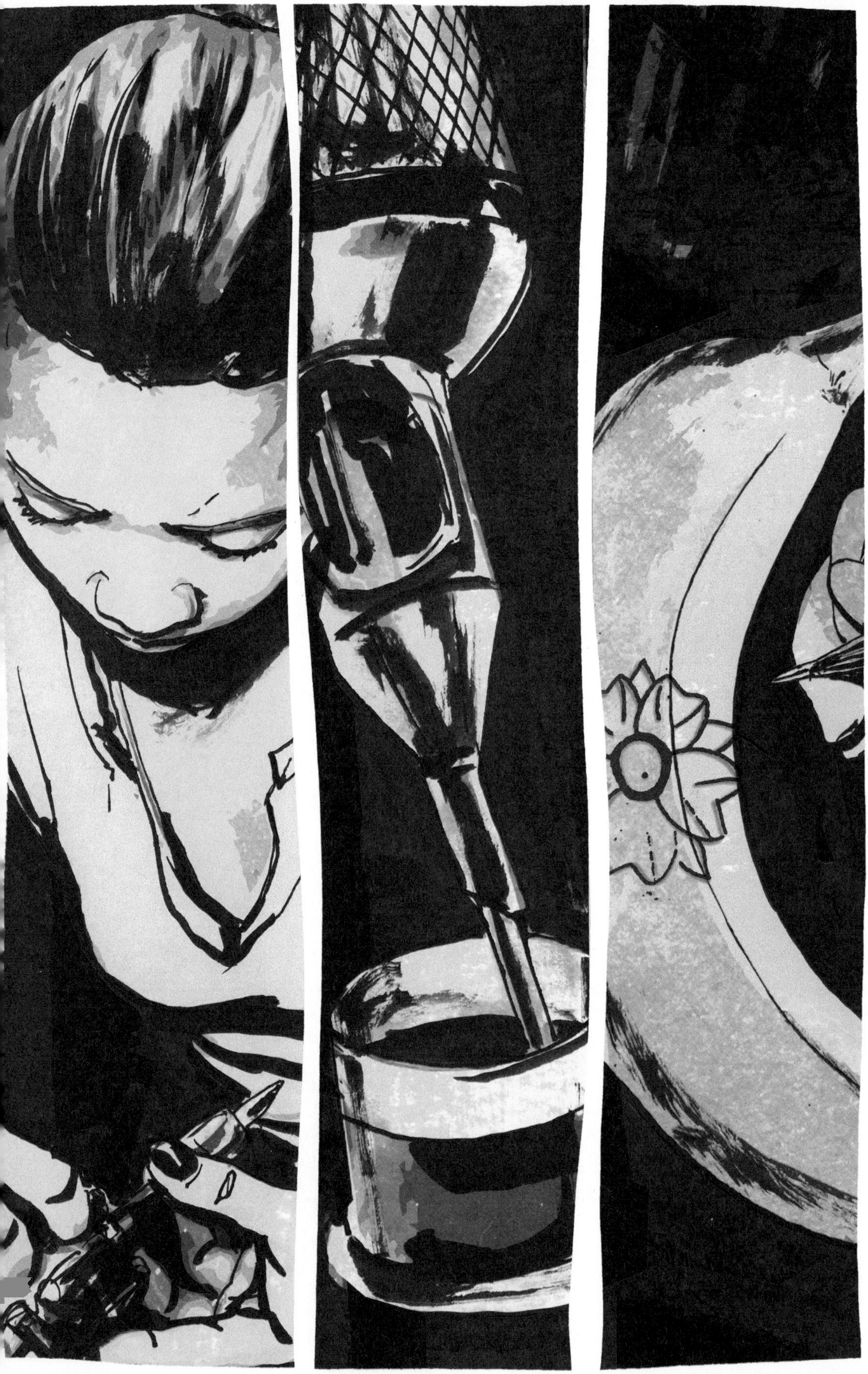

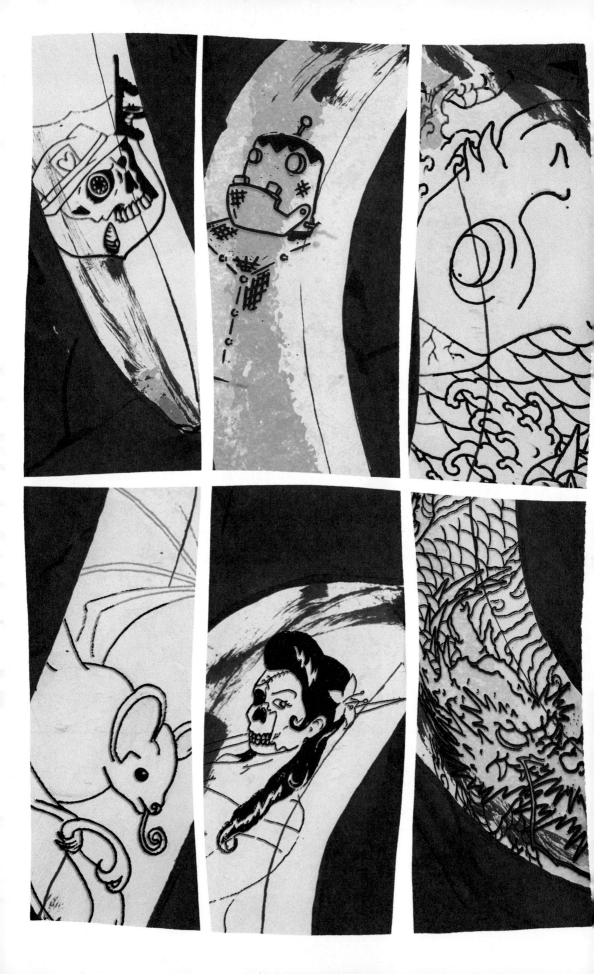

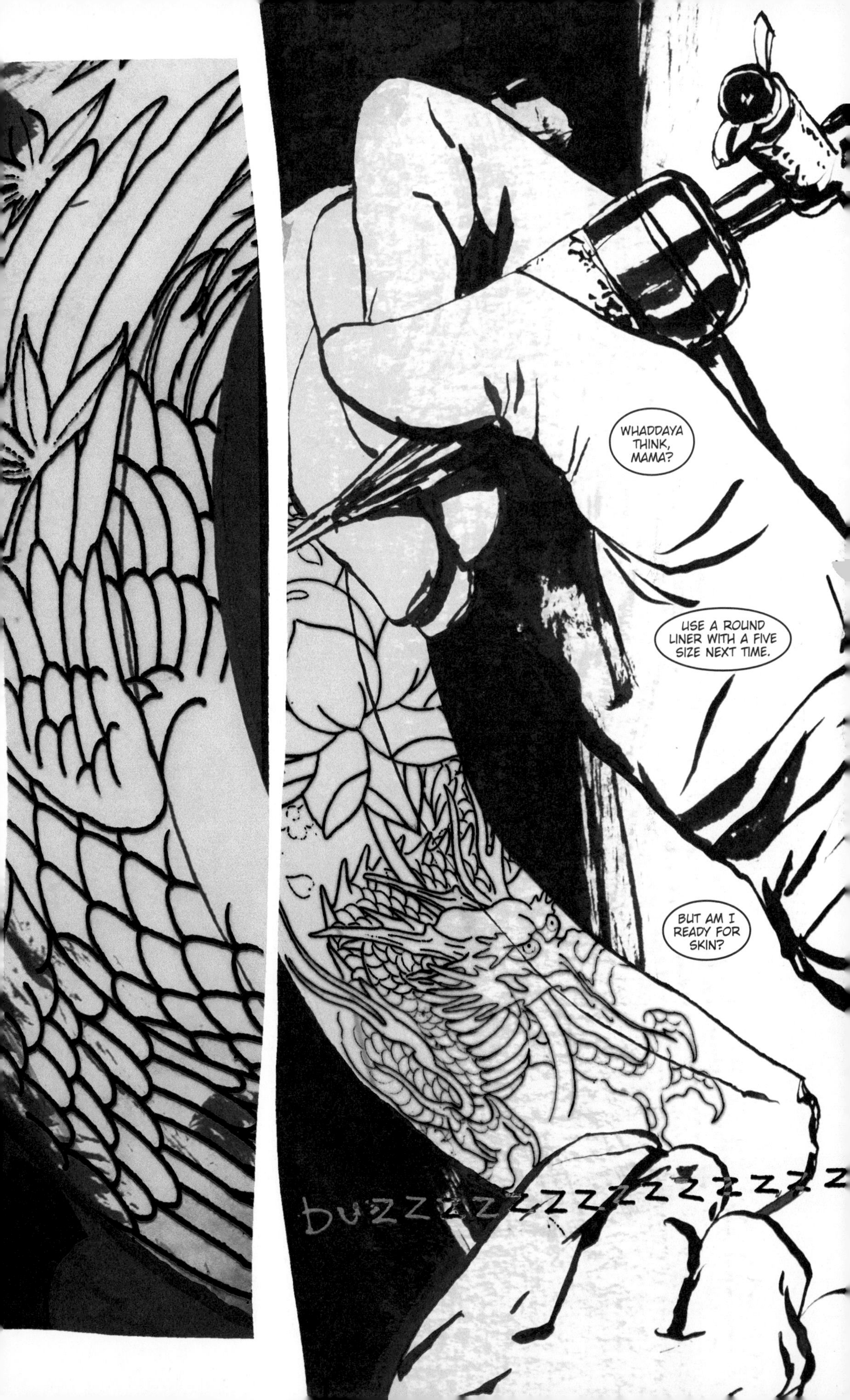
WHADDAYA THINK, MAMA?
USE A ROUND LINER WITH A FIVE SIZE NEXT TIME.
BUT AM I READY FOR SKIN?
buzzzzzzzzzzzzzzzz

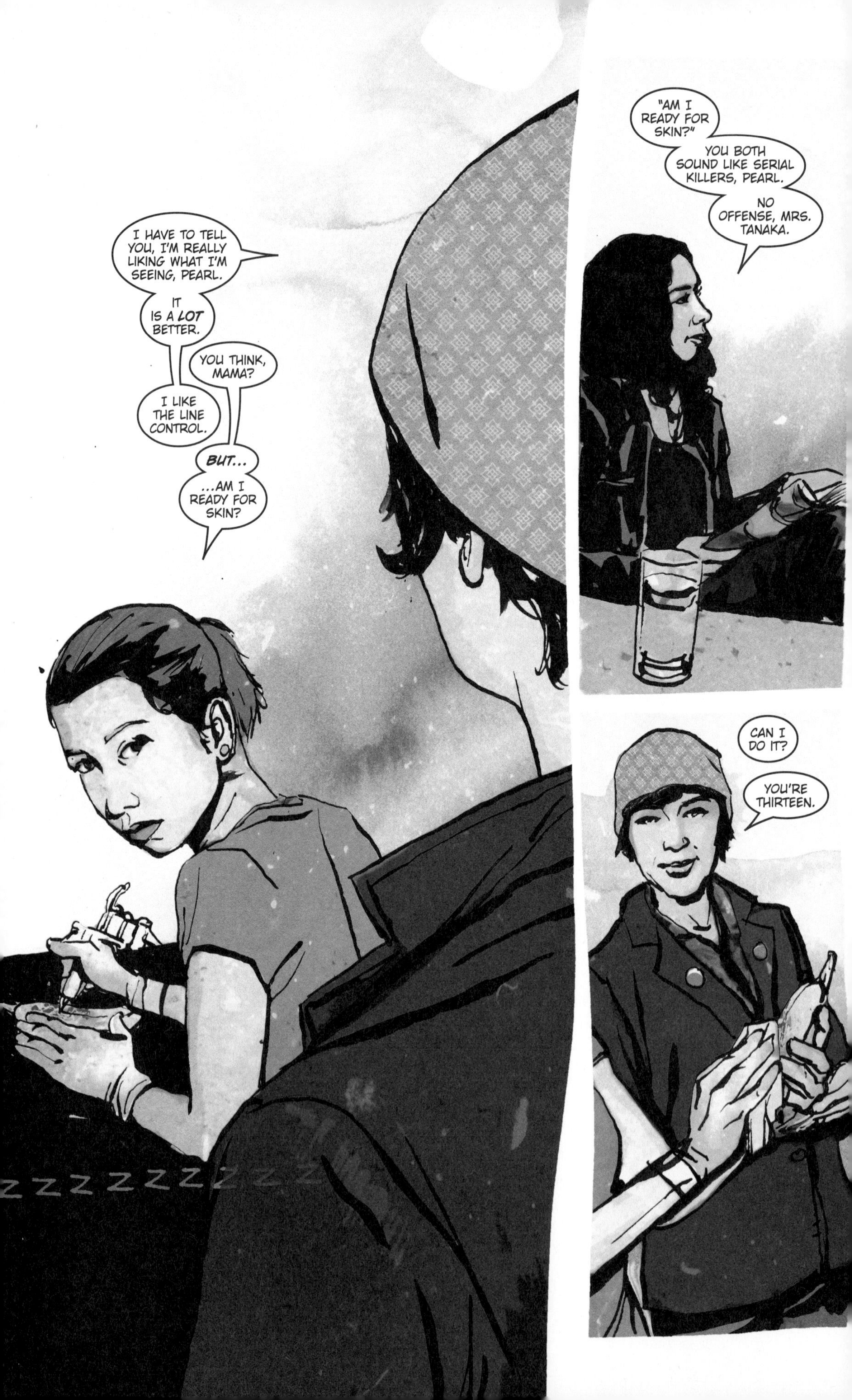
I HAVE TO TELL YOU, I'M REALLY LIKING WHAT I'M SEEING, PEARL.
IT IS A *LOT* BETTER.
YOU THINK, MAMA?
I LIKE THE LINE CONTROL.
BUT...
...AM I READY FOR SKIN?
ZZZZZZZZZ
"AM I READY FOR SKIN?"
YOU BOTH SOUND LIKE SERIAL KILLERS, PEARL.
NO OFFENSE, MRS. TANAKA.
CAN I DO IT?
YOU'RE THIRTEEN.

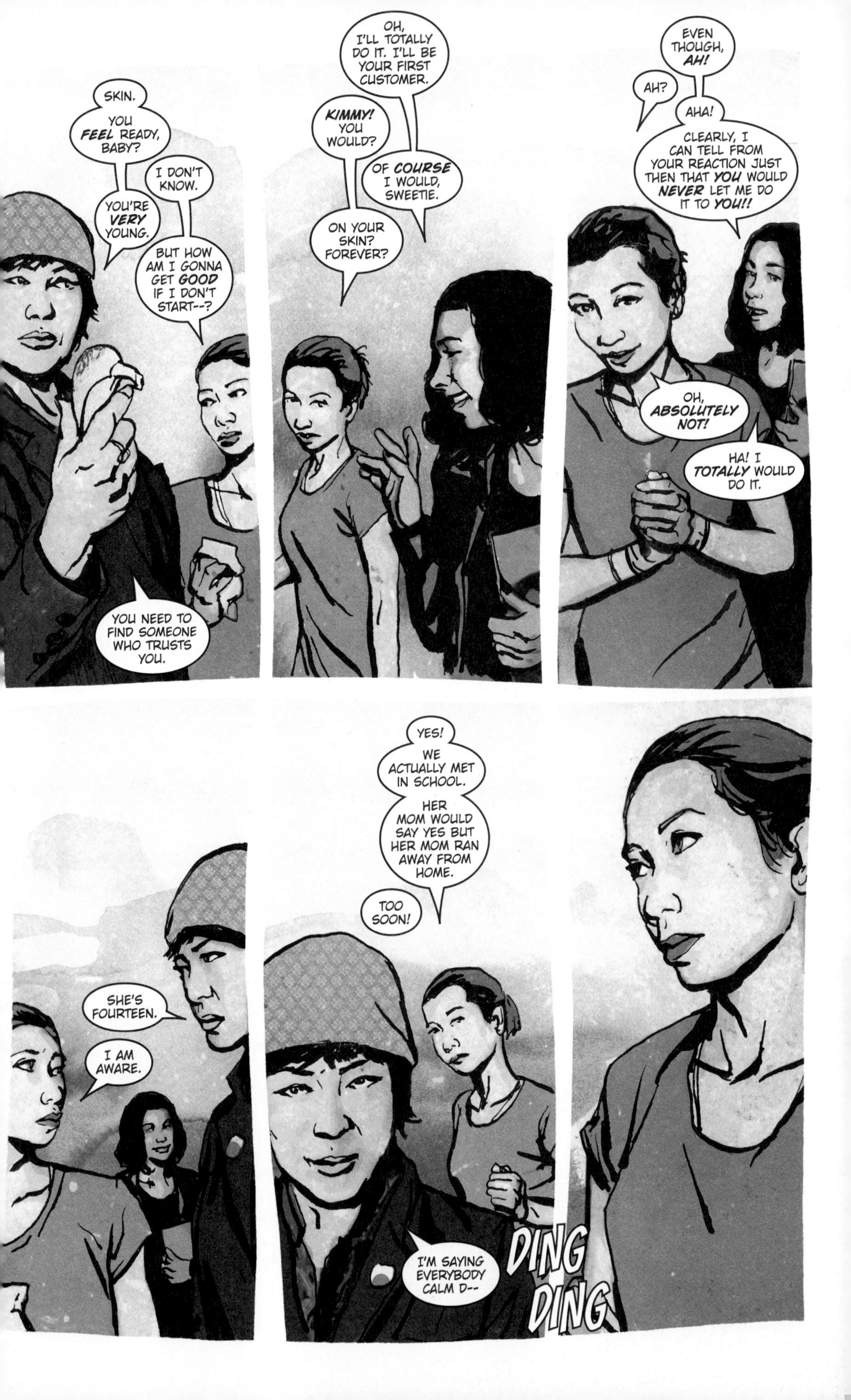
SKIN.
YOU FEEL READY, BABY?
YOU'RE VERY YOUNG.
I DON'T KNOW.
BUT HOW AM I GONNA GET GOOD IF I DON'T START--?
YOU NEED TO FIND SOMEONE WHO TRUSTS YOU.
OH, I'LL TOTALLY DO IT. I'LL BE YOUR FIRST CUSTOMER.
KIMMY! YOU WOULD?
OF COURSE I WOULD, SWEETIE.
ON YOUR SKIN? FOREVER?
EVEN THOUGH, AH!
AH?
AHA!
CLEARLY, I CAN TELL FROM YOUR REACTION JUST THEN THAT YOU WOULD NEVER LET ME DO IT TO YOU!!
OH, ABSOLUTELY NOT!
HA! I TOTALLY WOULD DO IT.
SHE'S FOURTEEN.
I AM AWARE.
YES!
WE ACTUALLY MET IN SCHOOL.
HER MOM WOULD SAY YES BUT HER MOM RAN AWAY FROM HOME.
TOO SOON!
I'M SAYING EVERYBODY CALM D--
DING
DING

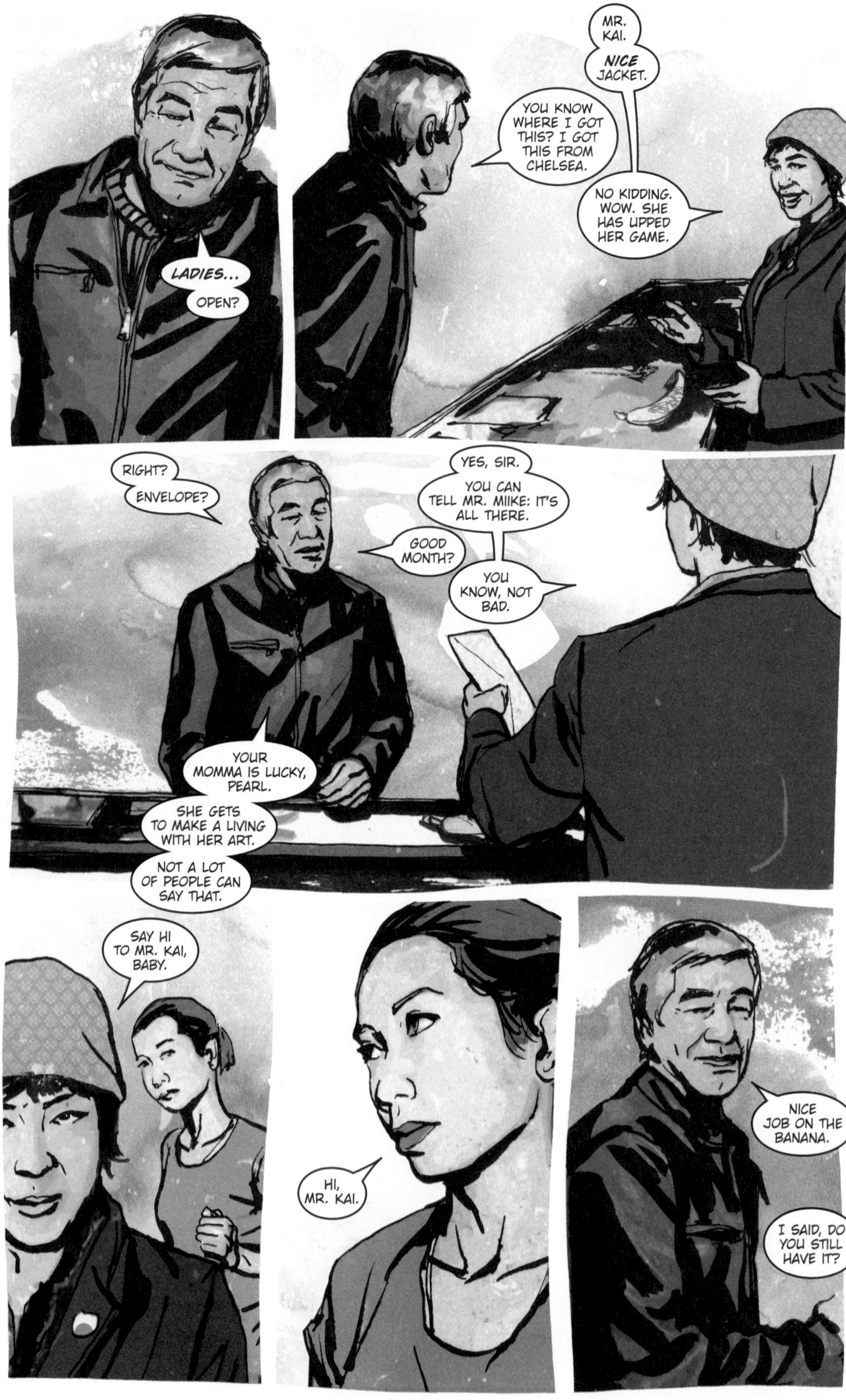
LADIES...
OPEN?
YOU KNOW WHERE I GOT THIS? I GOT THIS FROM CHELSEA.
MR. KAI.
NICE JACKET.
NO KIDDING. WOW. SHE HAS UPPED HER GAME.
RIGHT?
ENVELOPE?
YES, SIR.
YOU CAN TELL MR. MIIKE: IT'S ALL THERE.
GOOD MONTH?
YOU KNOW, NOT BAD.
YOUR MOMMA IS LUCKY, PEARL.
SHE GETS TO MAKE A LIVING WITH HER ART.
NOT A LOT OF PEOPLE CAN SAY THAT.
SAY HI TO MR. KAI, BABY.
HI, MR. KAI.
NICE JOB ON THE BANANA.
I SAID, DO YOU STILL HAVE IT?

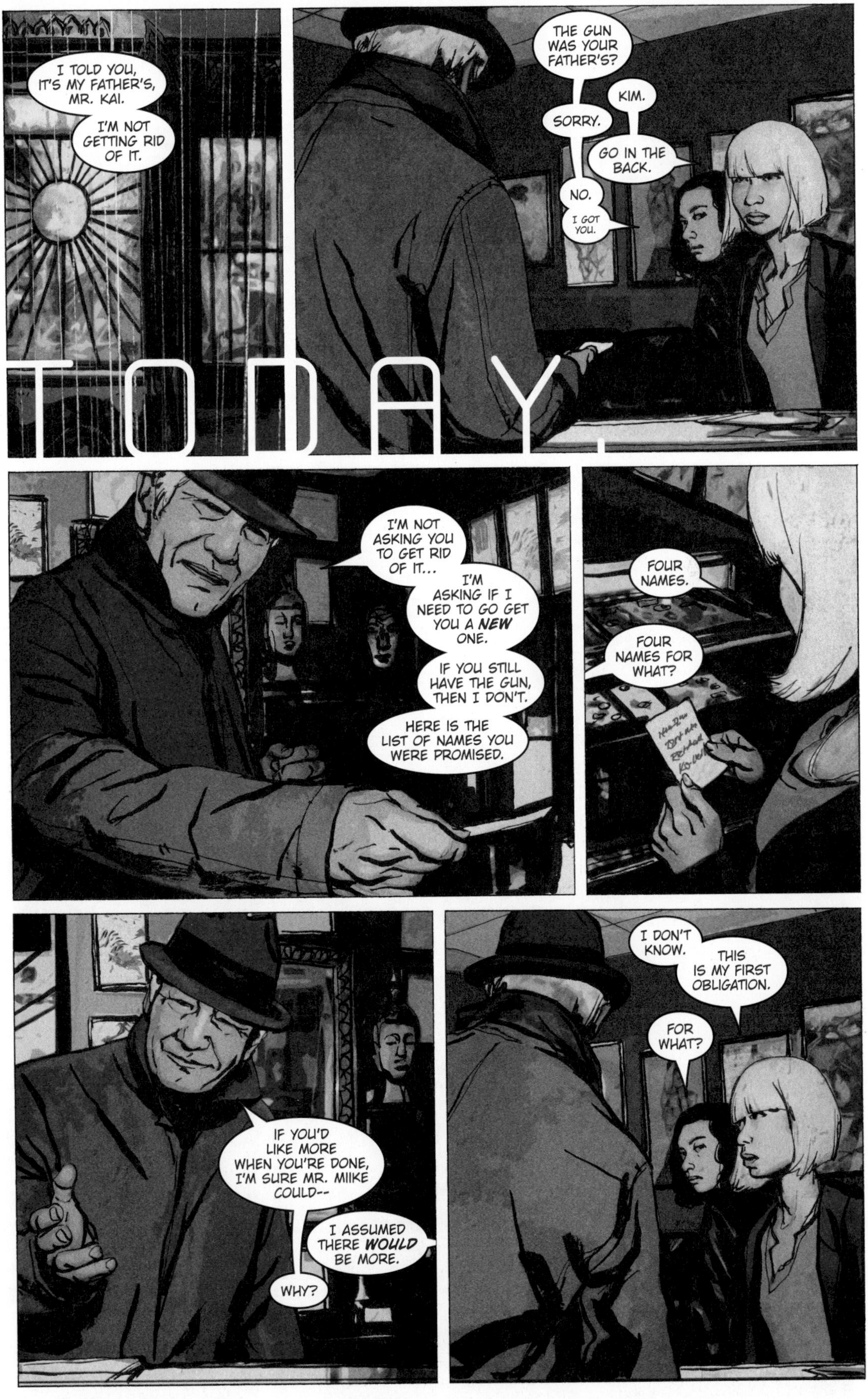
I TOLD YOU, IT'S MY FATHER'S, MR. KAI.
I'M NOT GETTING RID OF IT.
THE GUN WAS YOUR FATHER'S?
SORRY.
KIM.
GO IN THE BACK.
NO.
I GOT YOU.
TODAY.
I'M NOT ASKING YOU TO GET RID OF IT...
I'M ASKING IF I NEED TO GO GET YOU A **NEW** ONE.
IF YOU STILL HAVE THE GUN, THEN I DON'T.
HERE IS THE LIST OF NAMES YOU WERE PROMISED.
FOUR NAMES.
FOUR NAMES FOR WHAT?
IF YOU'D LIKE MORE WHEN YOU'RE DONE, I'M SURE MR. MIIKE COULD--
I ASSUMED THERE **WOULD** BE MORE.
WHY?
I DON'T KNOW.
THIS IS MY FIRST OBLIGATION.
FOR WHAT?

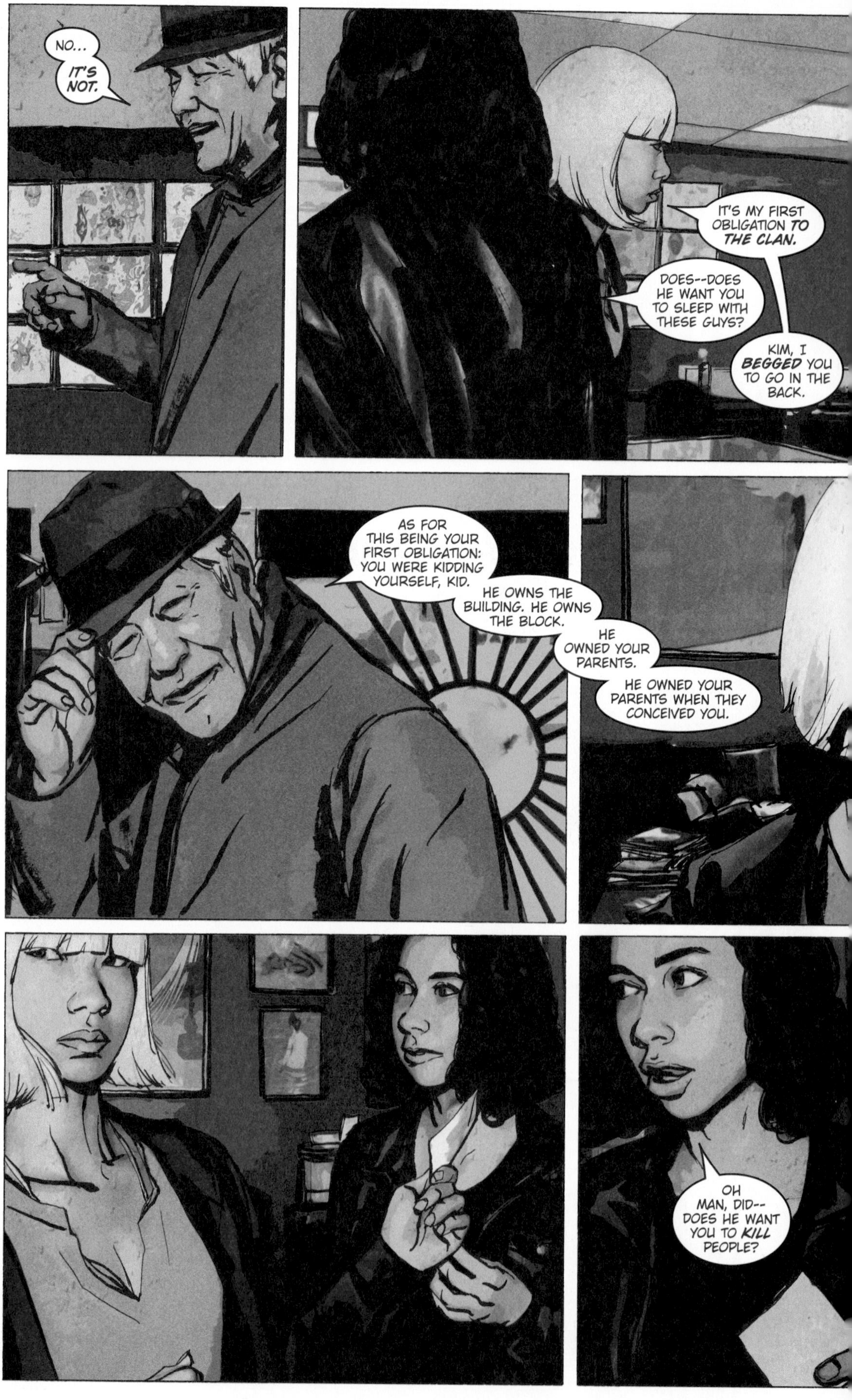
NO... IT'S NOT.
IT'S MY FIRST OBLIGATION TO THE CLAN.
DOES--DOES HE WANT YOU TO SLEEP WITH THESE GUYS?
KIM, I BEGGED YOU TO GO IN THE BACK.
AS FOR THIS BEING YOUR FIRST OBLIGATION: YOU WERE KIDDING YOURSELF, KID.
HE OWNS THE BUILDING. HE OWNS THE BLOCK.
HE OWNED YOUR PARENTS.
HE OWNED YOUR PARENTS WHEN THEY CONCEIVED YOU.
OH MAN, DID-- DOES HE WANT YOU TO KILL PEOPLE?

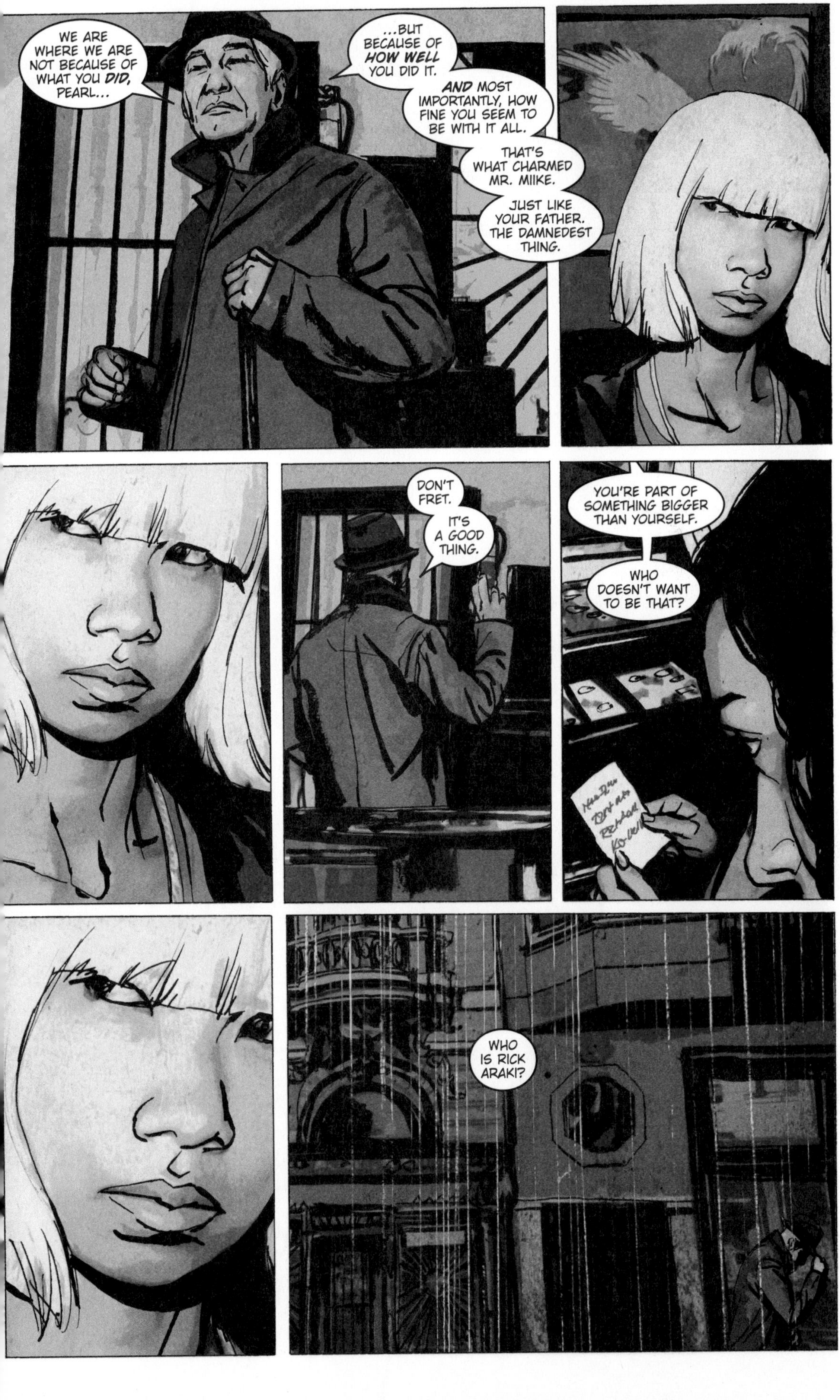
WE ARE WHERE WE ARE NOT BECAUSE OF WHAT YOU *DID,* PEARL...
...BUT BECAUSE OF ***HOW WELL*** YOU DID IT.
AND MOST IMPORTANTLY, HOW FINE YOU SEEM TO BE WITH IT ALL.
THAT'S WHAT CHARMED MR. MIIKE.
JUST LIKE YOUR FATHER. THE DAMNEDEST THING.
DON'T FRET.
IT'S A GOOD THING.
YOU'RE PART OF SOMETHING BIGGER THAN YOURSELF.
WHO DOESN'T WANT TO BE THAT?
WHO IS RICK ARAKI?

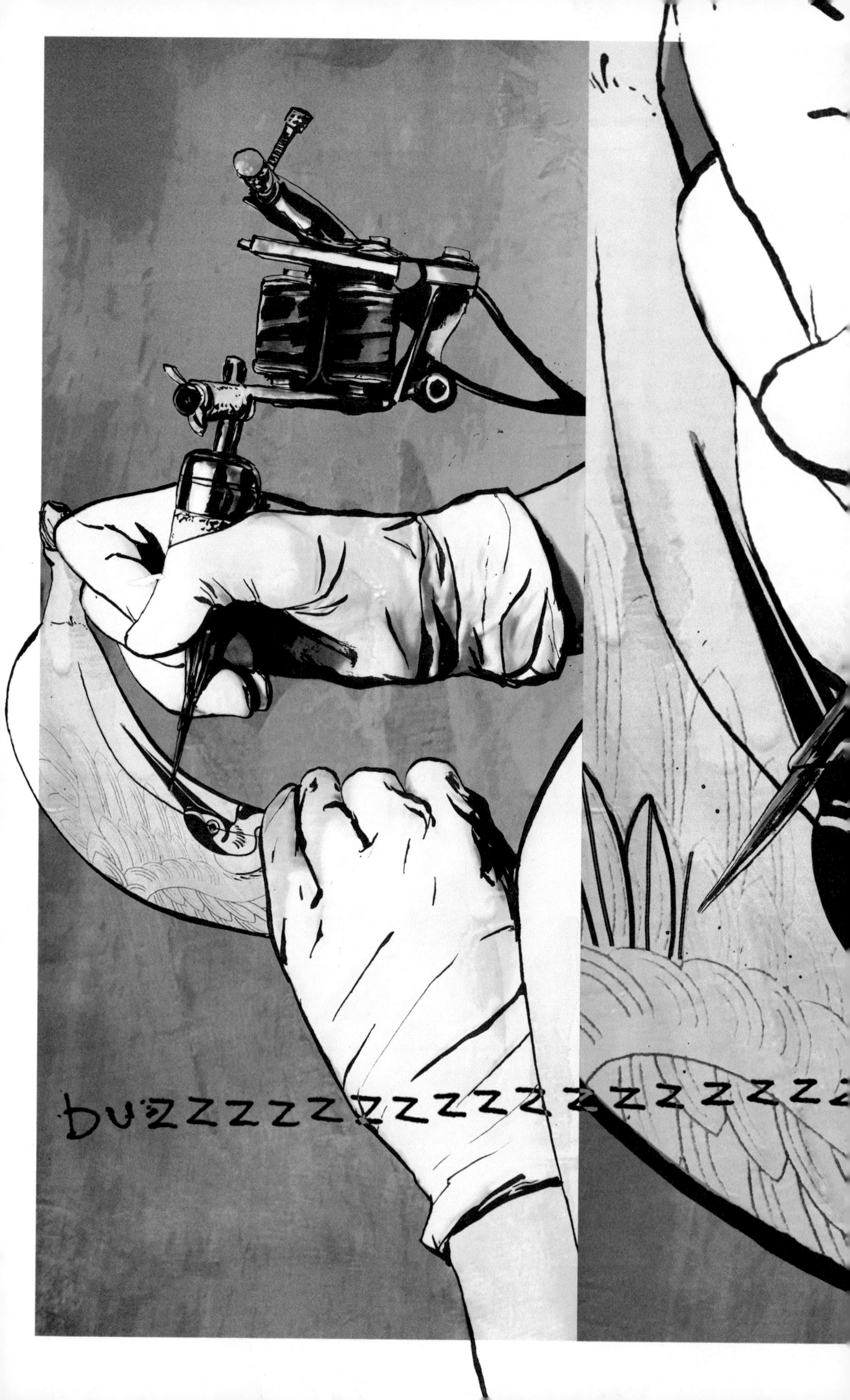
buzzzzzzzzzzzzzzzzzz

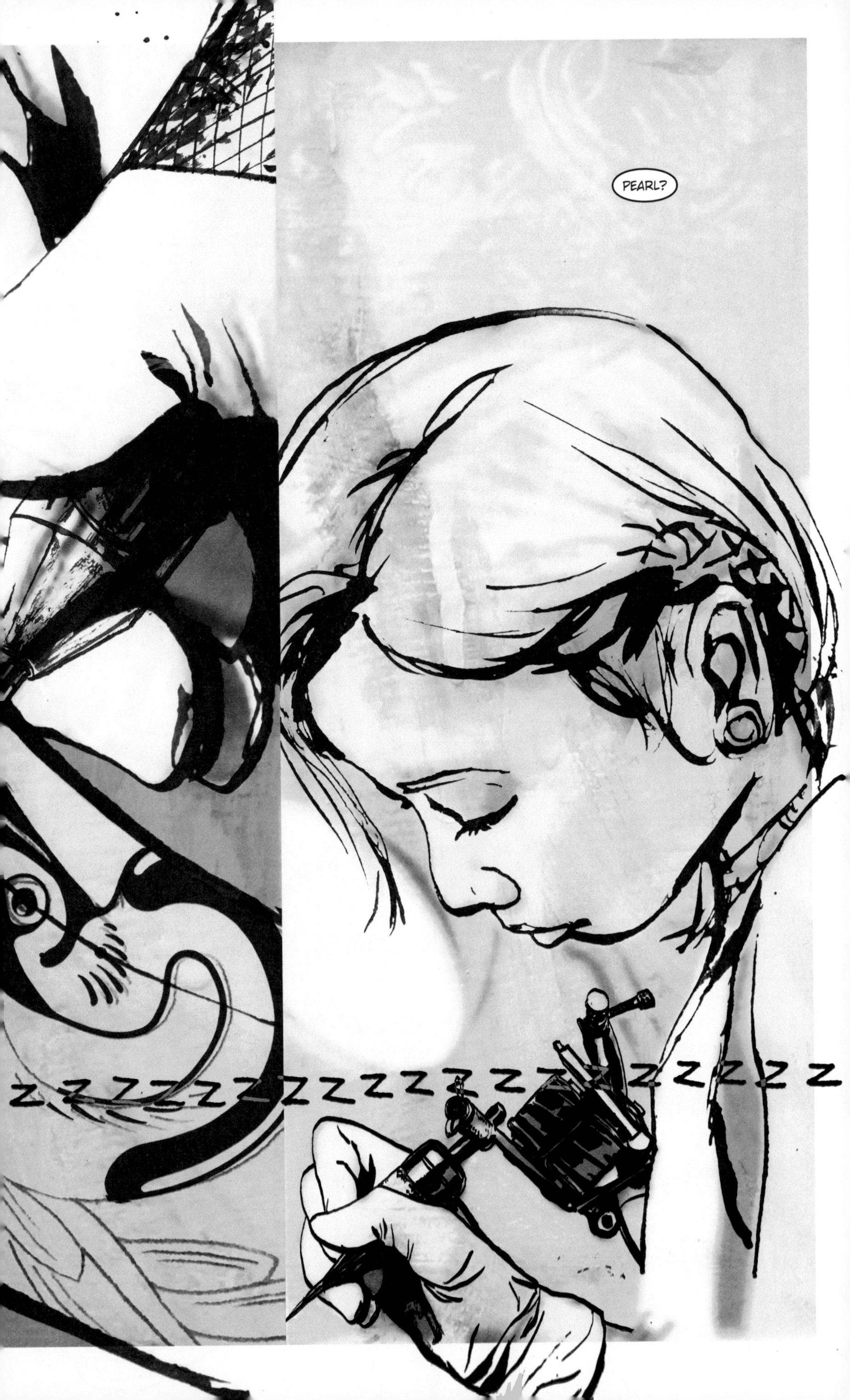
PEARL?
Z Z Z Z Z Z Z Z Z Z Z Z Z Z Z Z Z Z Z Z Z Z

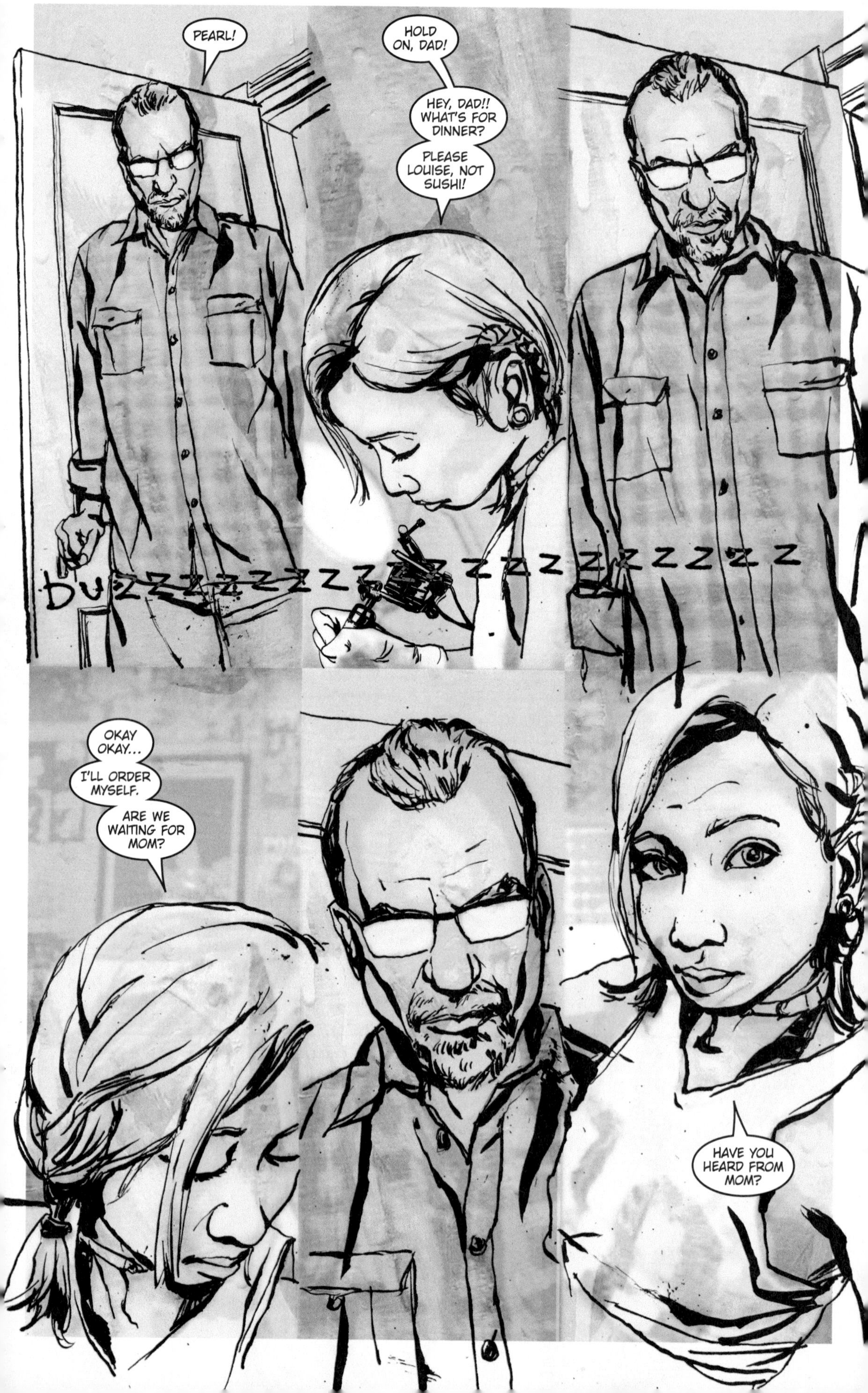
PEARL!
HOLD ON, DAD!
HEY, DAD!! WHAT'S FOR DINNER?
PLEASE LOUISE, NOT SUSHI!
BUZZZZZZZZZZZZZZZZZZZZZZ
OKAY OKAY...
I'LL ORDER MYSELF.
ARE WE WAITING FOR MOM?
HAVE YOU HEARD FROM MOM?

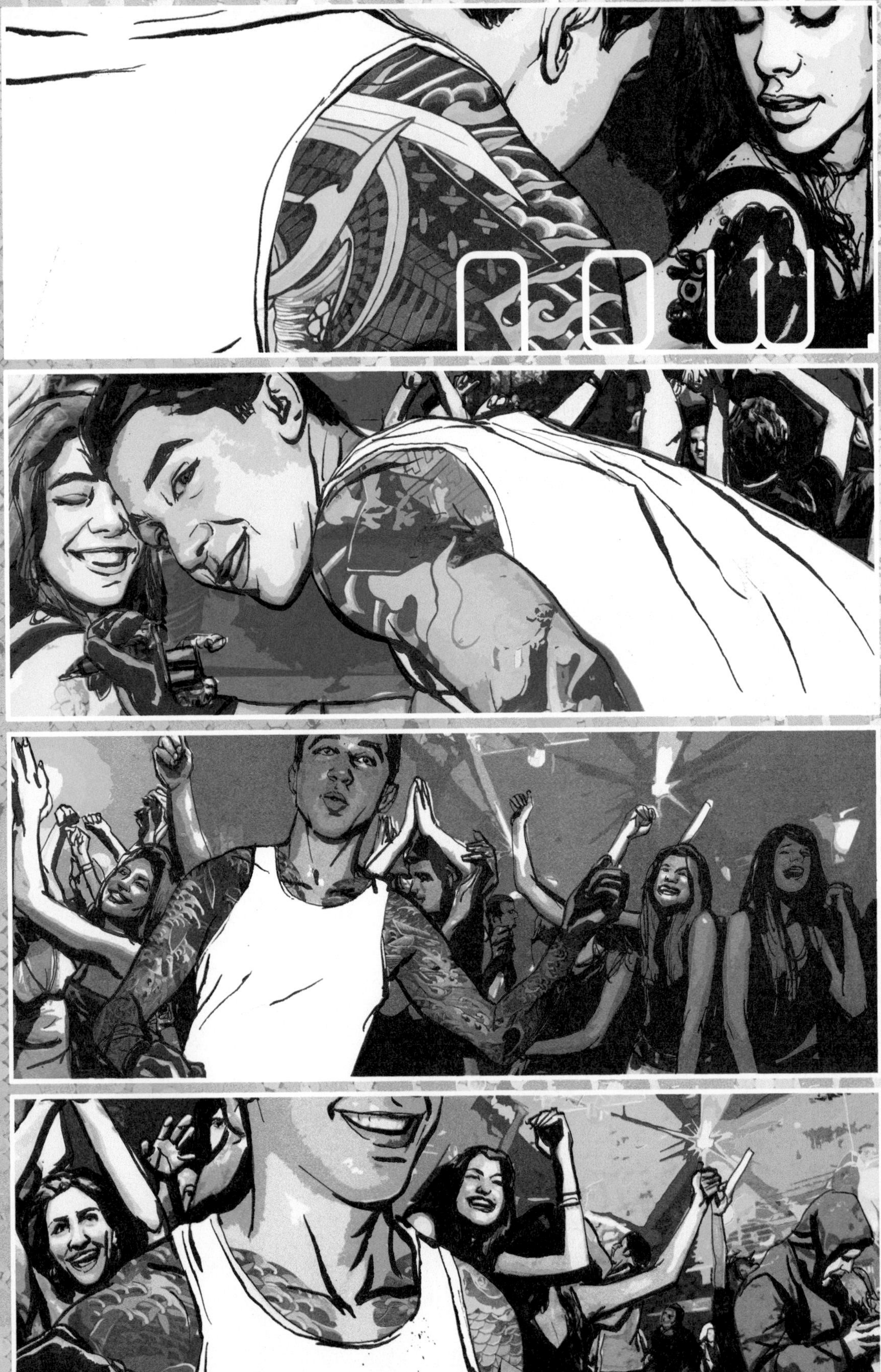
NOW

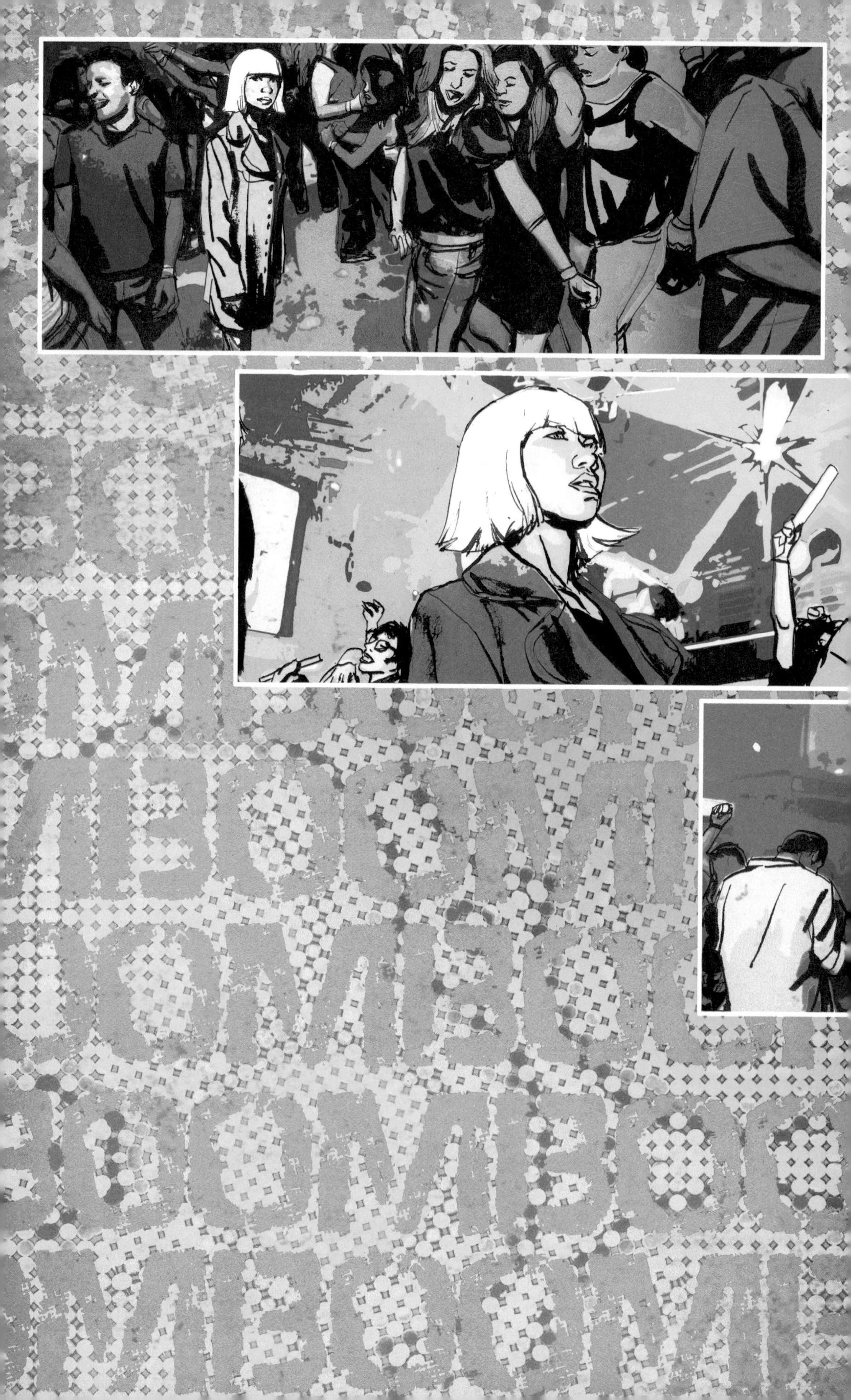

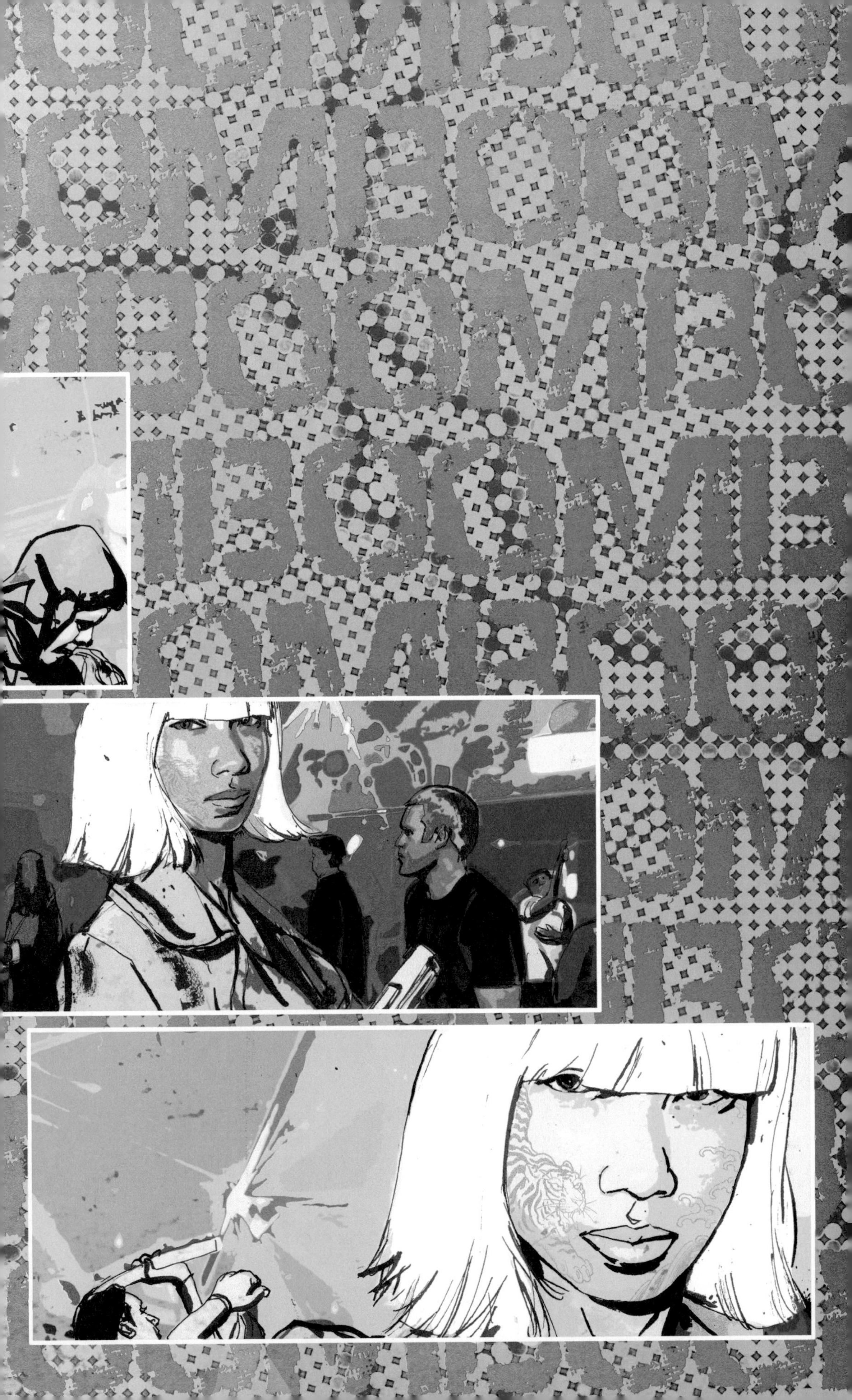

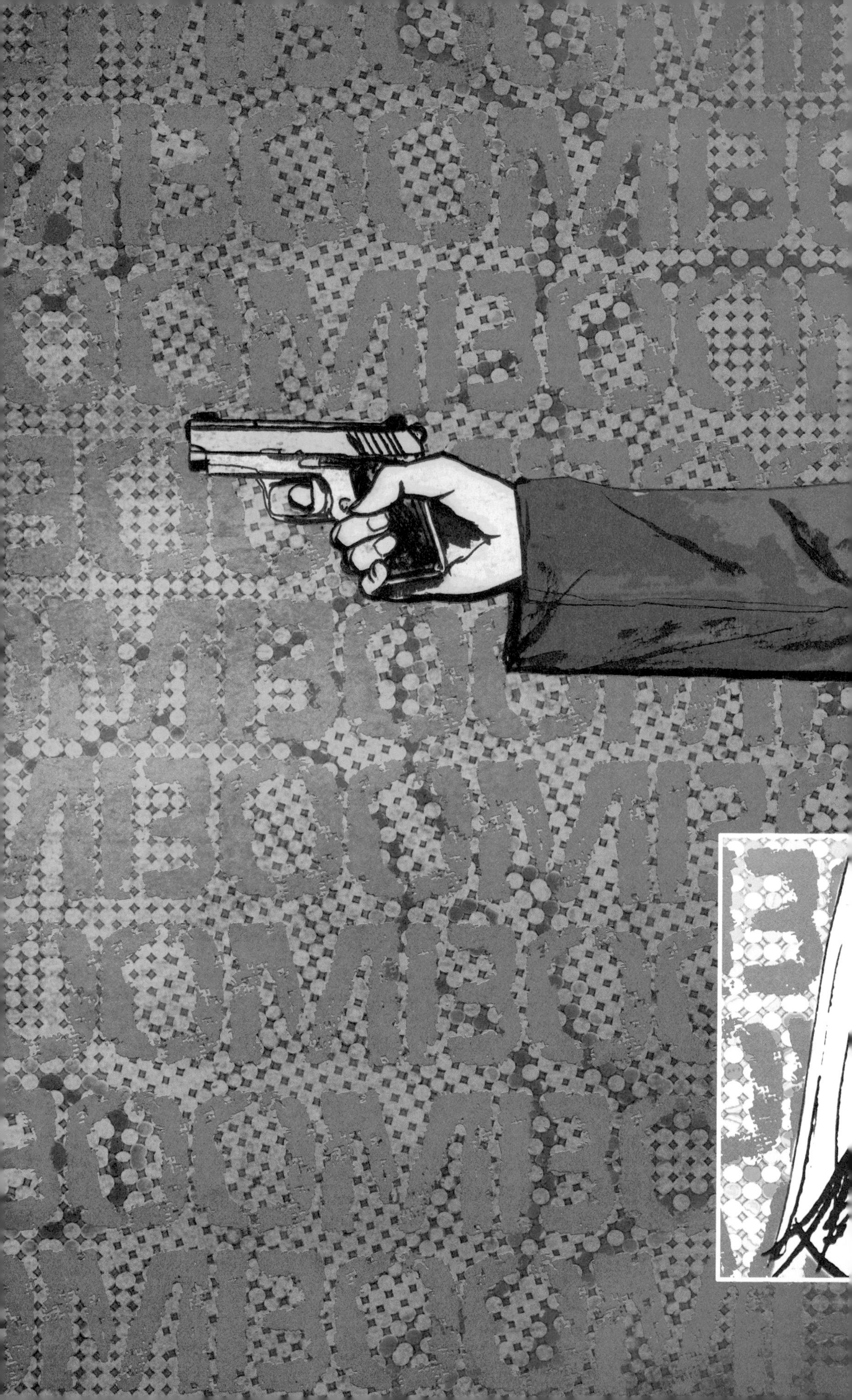

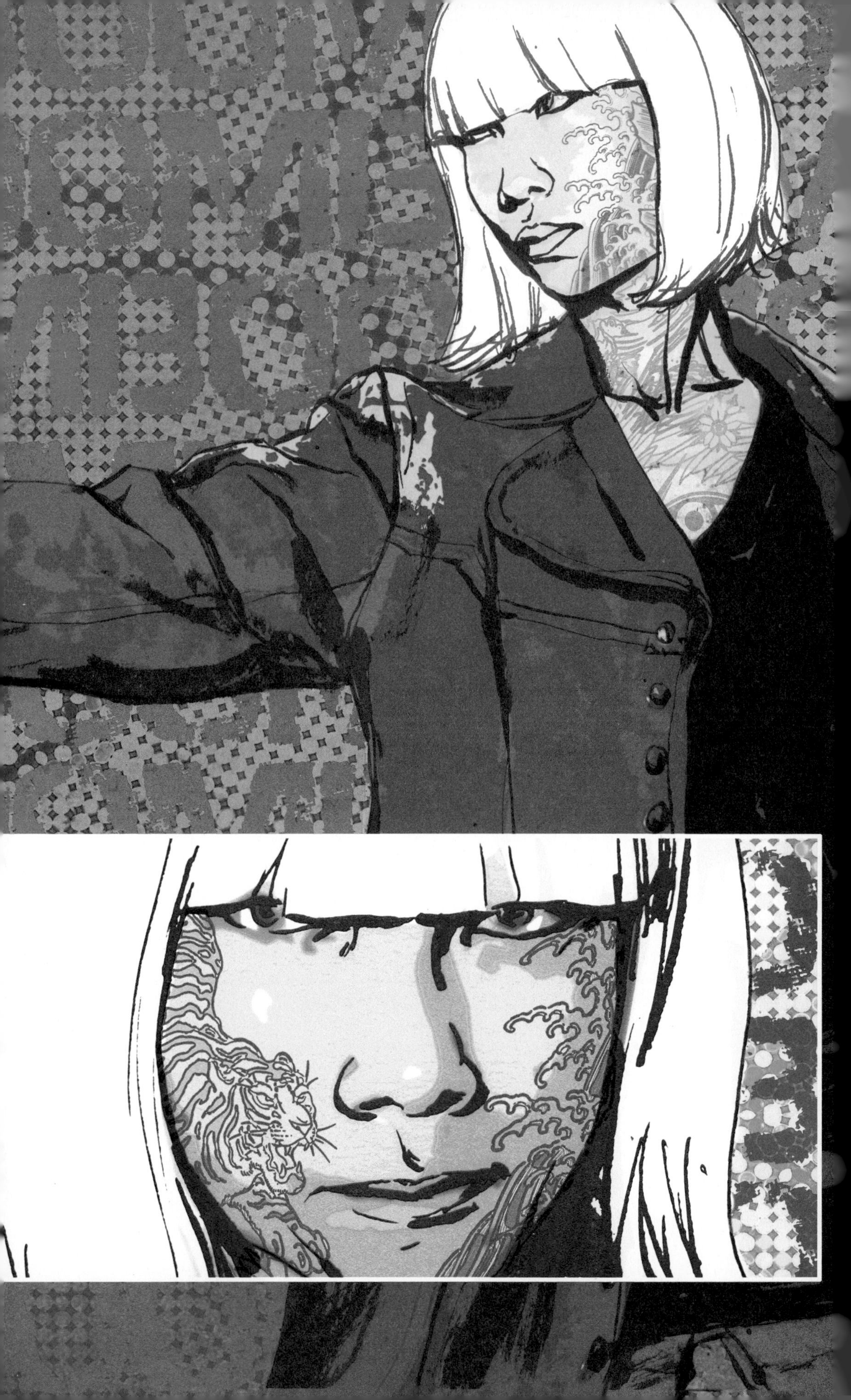

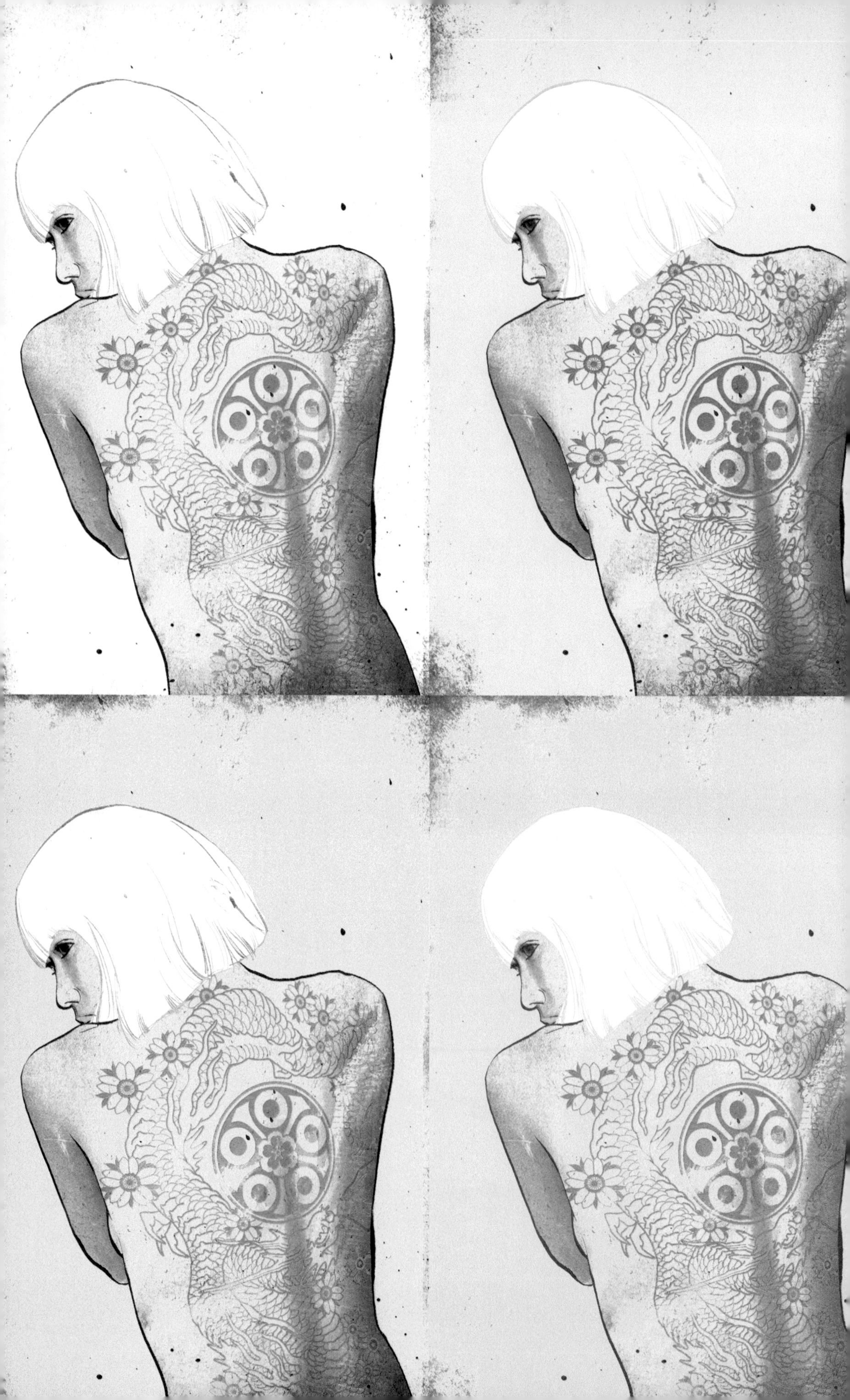

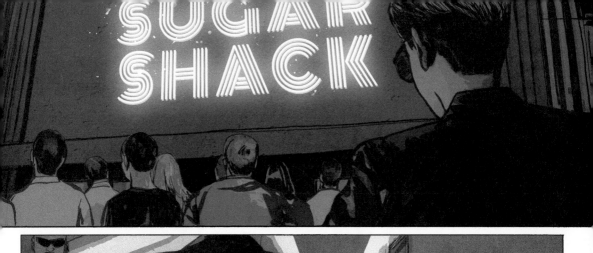

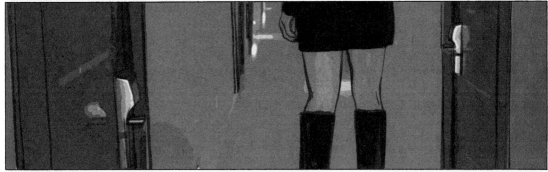

MS. ENDO!

ANY TROUBLE?

NOTHING *YOU* NEED WORRY ABOUT.

GOOD MAN.

WHAT THE ACTUAL FUCK, RYU?

HEY, SIS!

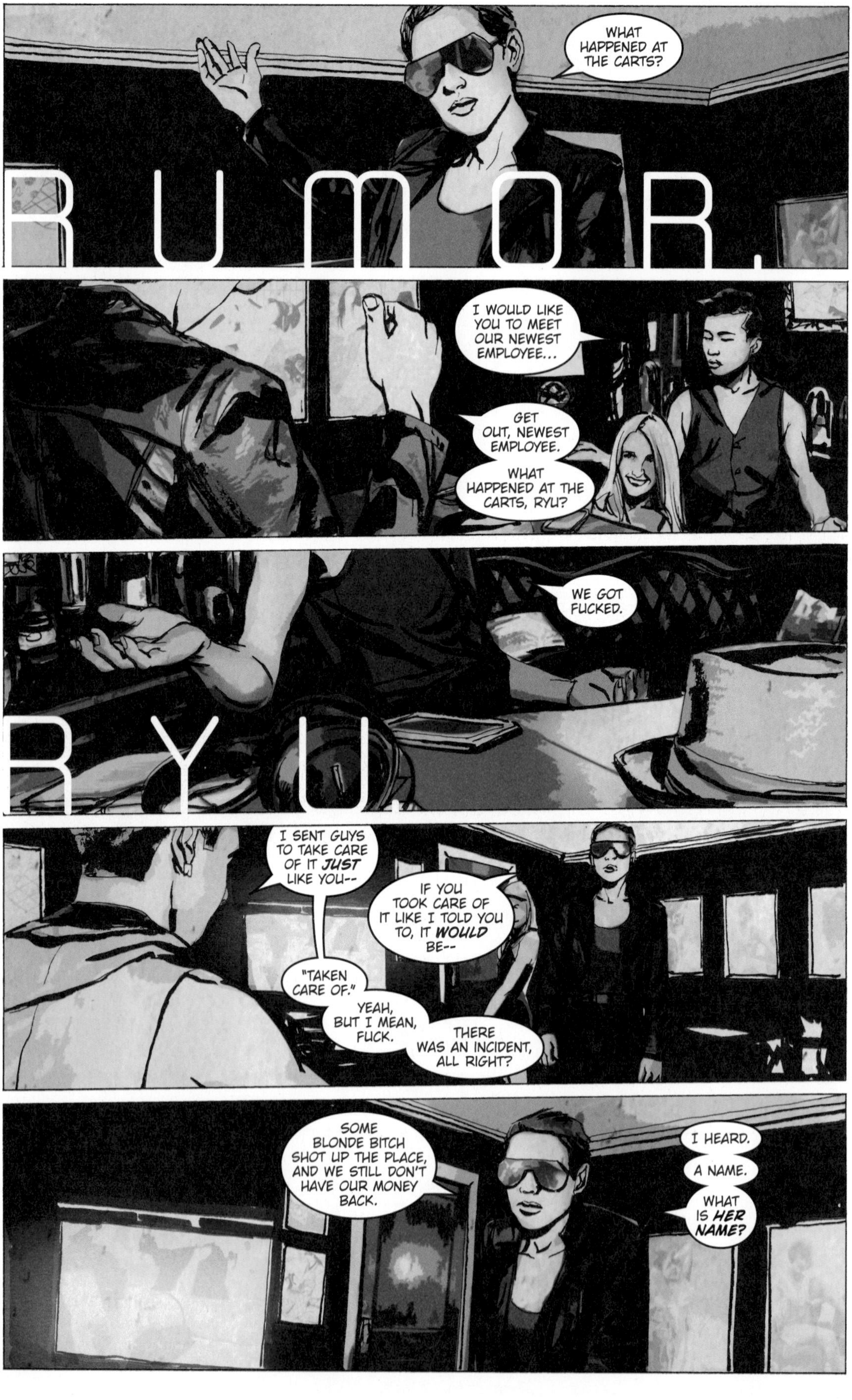
WHAT HAPPENED AT THE CARTS?
RUMOR.
I WOULD LIKE YOU TO MEET OUR NEWEST EMPLOYEE...
GET OUT, NEWEST EMPLOYEE.
WHAT HAPPENED AT THE CARTS, RYU?
WE GOT FUCKED.
RYU.
I SENT GUYS TO TAKE CARE OF IT **JUST** LIKE YOU--
IF YOU TOOK CARE OF IT LIKE I TOLD YOU TO, IT **WOULD** BE--
"TAKEN CARE OF."
YEAH, BUT I MEAN, FUCK.
THERE WAS AN INCIDENT, ALL RIGHT?
SOME BLONDE BITCH SHOT UP THE PLACE, AND WE STILL DON'T HAVE OUR MONEY BACK.
I HEARD.
A NAME.
WHAT IS **HER NAME?**

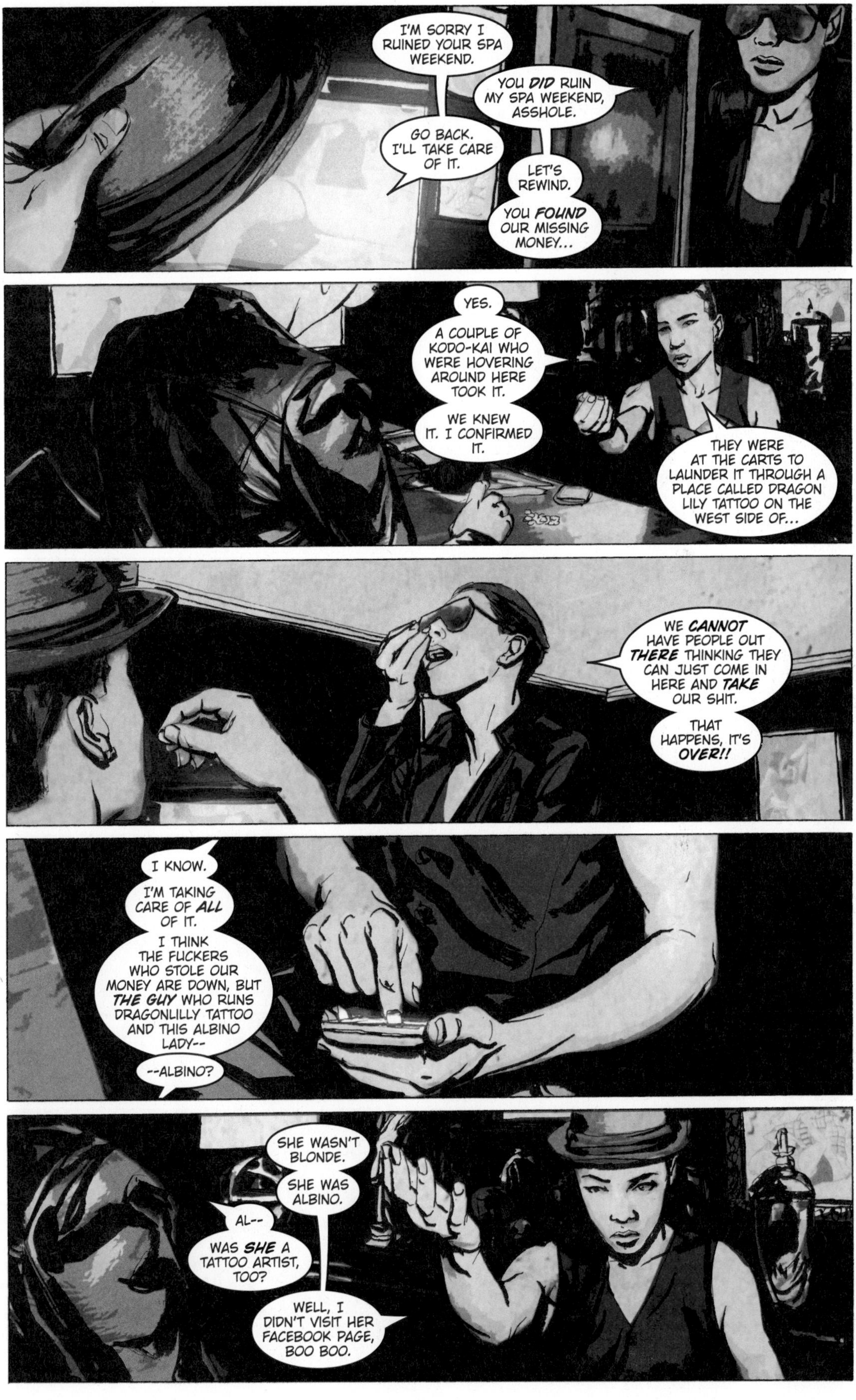
I'M SORRY I RUINED YOUR SPA WEEKEND.
YOU DID RUIN MY SPA WEEKEND, ASSHOLE.
GO BACK. I'LL TAKE CARE OF IT.
LET'S REWIND.
YOU FOUND OUR MISSING MONEY...
YES.
A COUPLE OF KODO-KAI WHO WERE HOVERING AROUND HERE TOOK IT.
WE KNEW IT. I CONFIRMED IT.
THEY WERE AT THE CARTS TO LAUNDER IT THROUGH A PLACE CALLED DRAGON LILY TATTOO ON THE WEST SIDE OF...
WE CANNOT HAVE PEOPLE OUT THERE THINKING THEY CAN JUST COME IN HERE AND TAKE OUR SHIT.
THAT HAPPENS, IT'S OVER!!
I KNOW.
I'M TAKING CARE OF ALL OF IT.
I THINK THE FUCKERS WHO STOLE OUR MONEY ARE DOWN, BUT THE GUY WHO RUNS DRAGONLILLY TATTOO AND THIS ALBINO LADY--
--ALBINO?
SHE WASN'T BLONDE.
SHE WAS ALBINO.
AL--
WAS SHE A TATTOO ARTIST, TOO?
WELL, I DIDN'T VISIT HER FACEBOOK PAGE, BOO BOO.

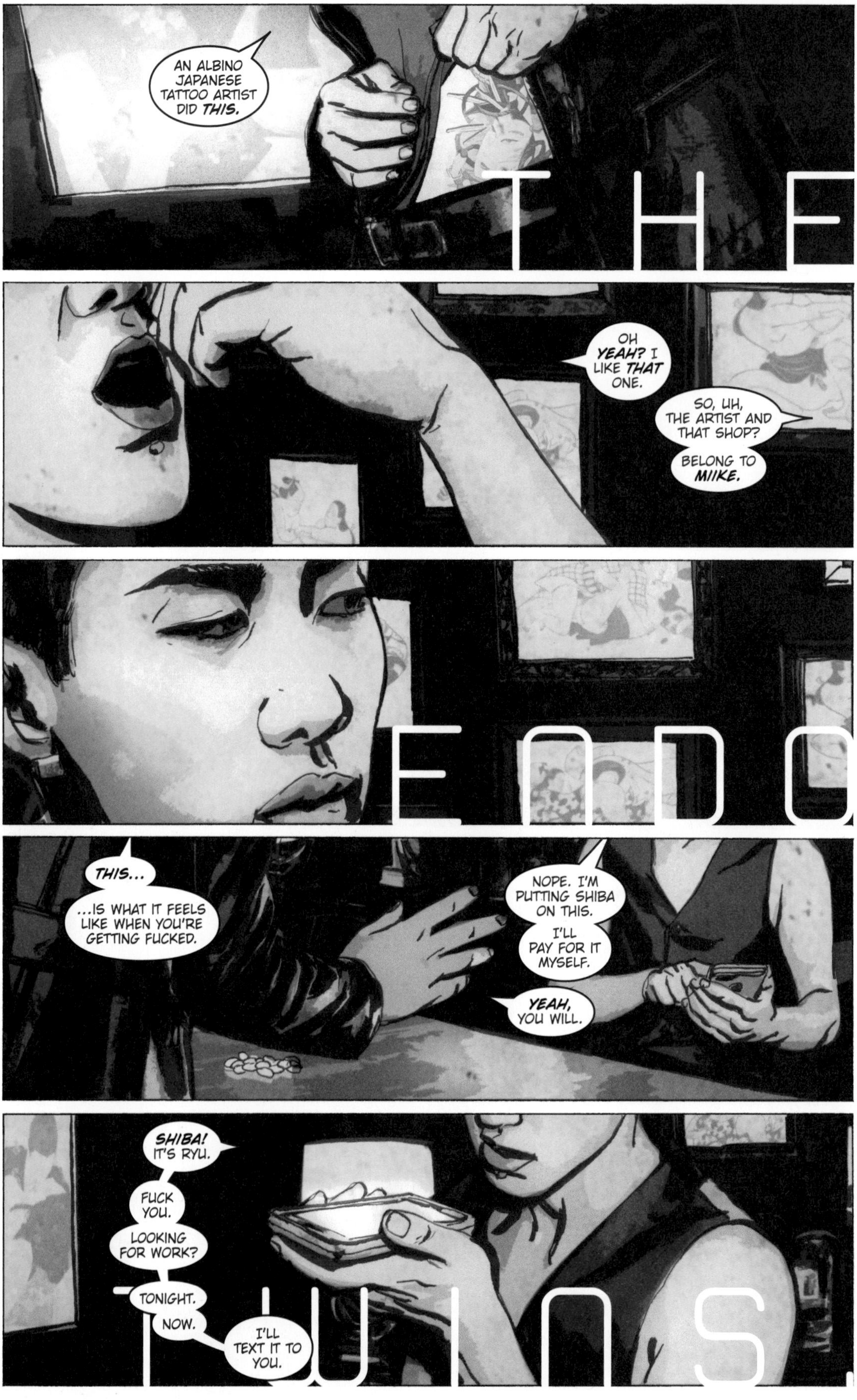
AN ALBINO JAPANESE TATTOO ARTIST DID THIS.
THE
OH YEAH? I LIKE THAT ONE.
SO, UH, THE ARTIST AND THAT SHOP?
BELONG TO MIIKE.
ENDO
THIS...
...IS WHAT IT FEELS LIKE WHEN YOU'RE GETTING FUCKED.
NOPE. I'M PUTTING SHIBA ON THIS.
I'LL PAY FOR IT MYSELF.
YEAH, YOU WILL.
SHIBA! IT'S RYU.
FUCK YOU.
LOOKING FOR WORK?
TONIGHT.
NOW.
I'LL TEXT IT TO YOU.
TWINS.

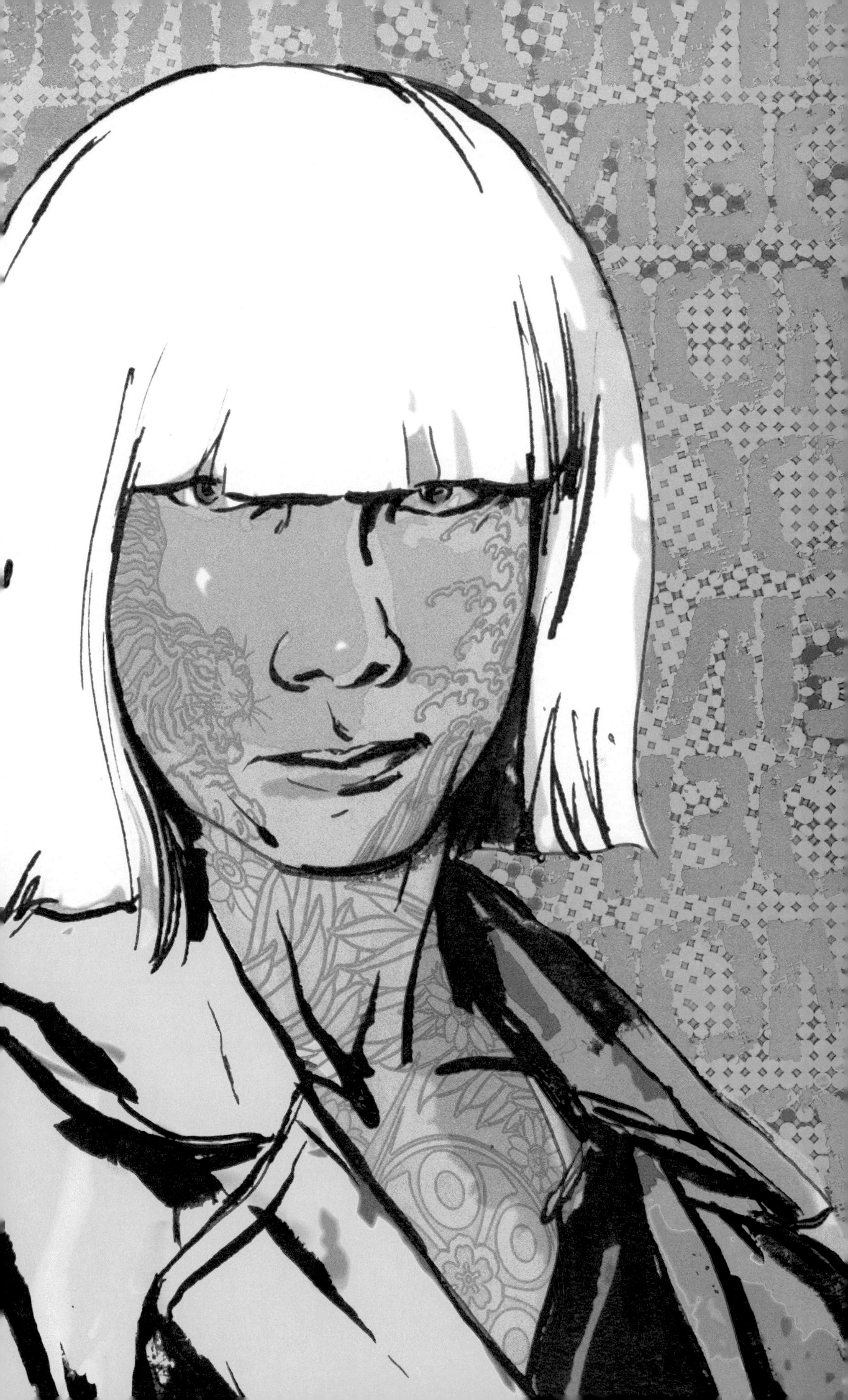

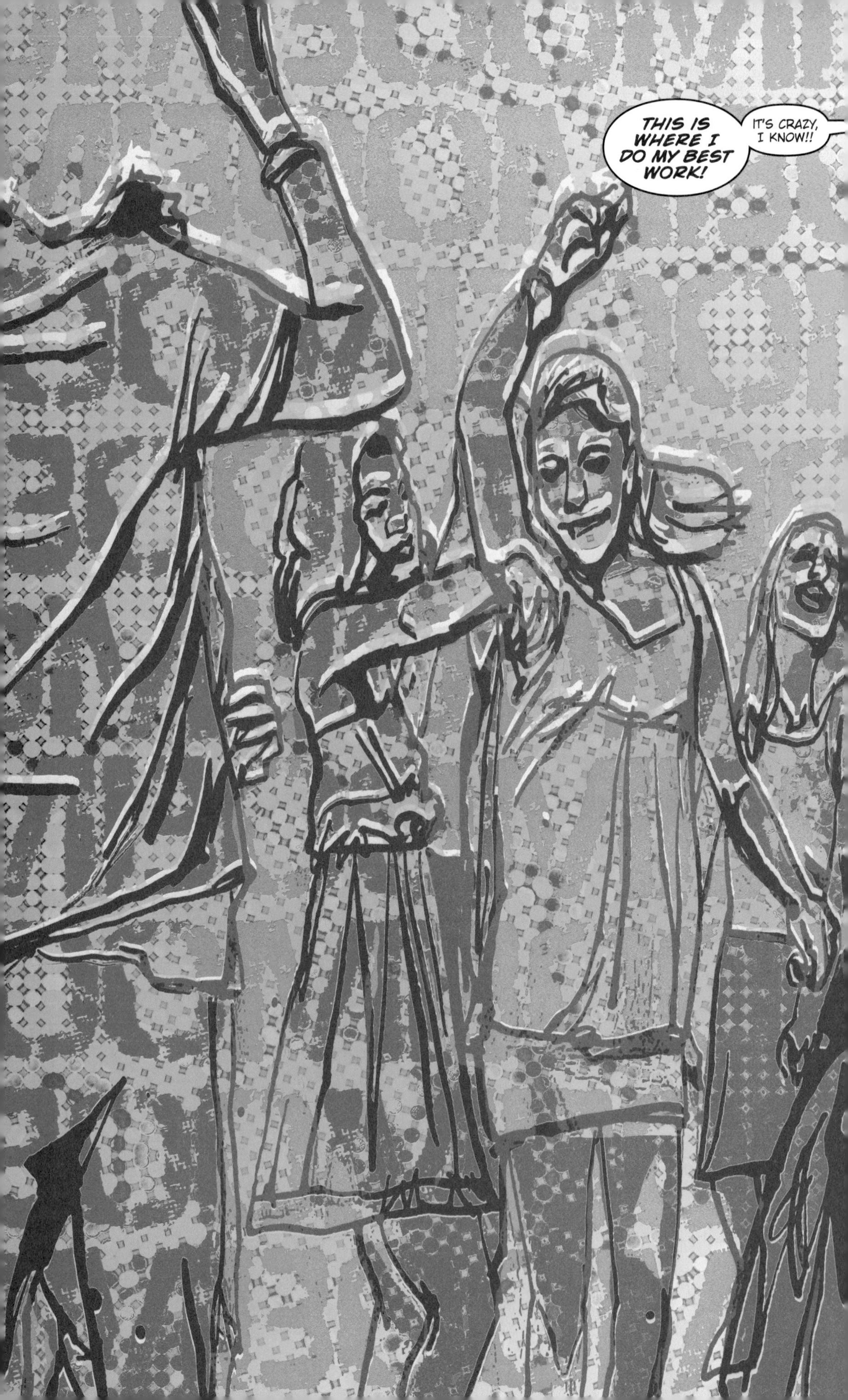
THIS IS WHERE I DO MY BEST WORK!
IT'S CRAZY, I KNOW!!

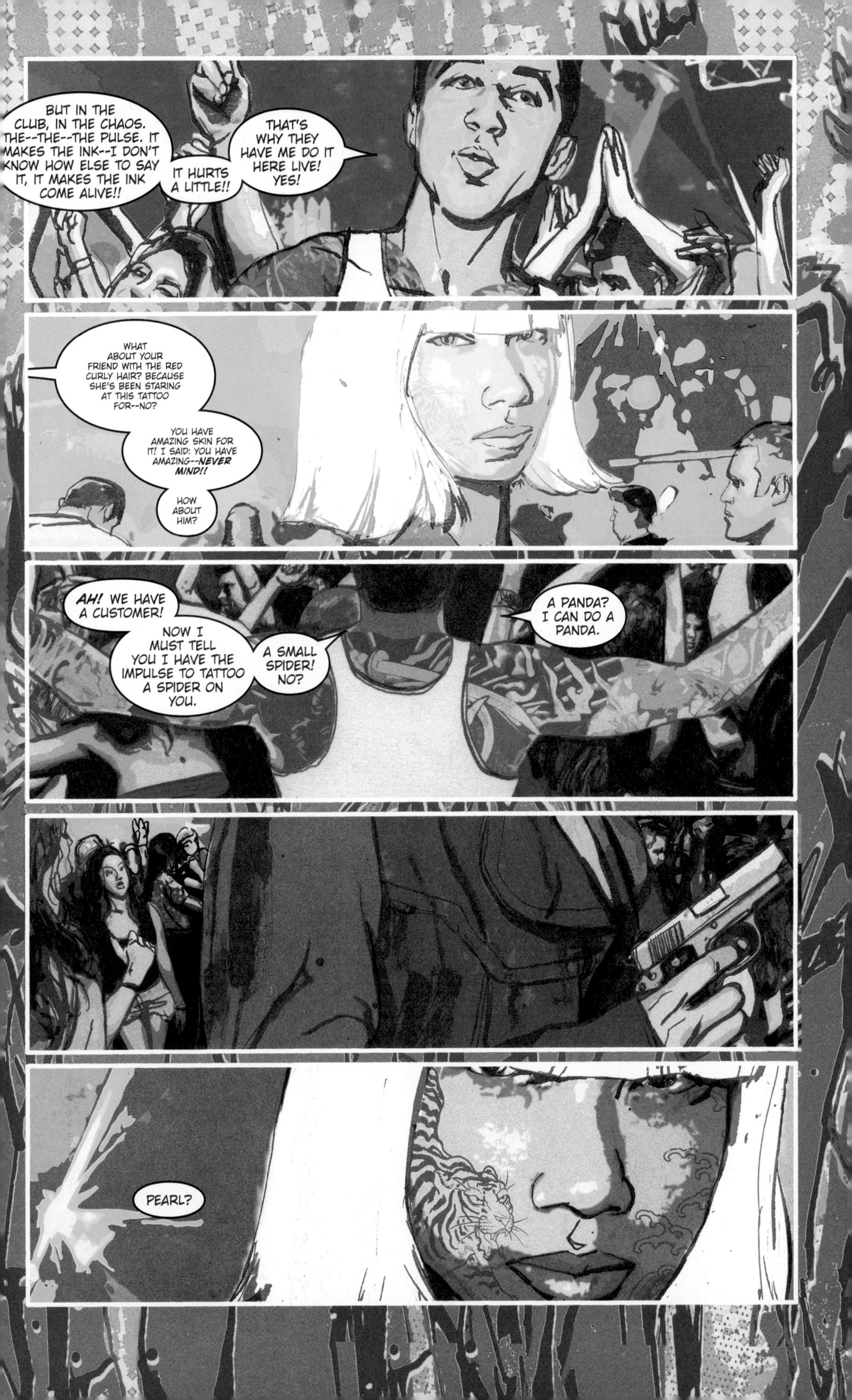
BUT IN THE CLUB, IN THE CHAOS. THE--THE--THE PULSE. IT MAKES THE INK--I DON'T KNOW HOW ELSE TO SAY IT, IT MAKES THE INK COME ALIVE!!
IT HURTS A LITTLE!!
THAT'S WHY THEY HAVE ME DO IT HERE LIVE! YES!
WHAT ABOUT YOUR FRIEND WITH THE RED CURLY HAIR? BECAUSE SHE'S BEEN STARING AT THIS TATTOO FOR--NO?
YOU HAVE AMAZING SKIN FOR IT! I SAID: YOU HAVE AMAZING--NEVER MIND!!
HOW ABOUT HIM?
AH! WE HAVE A CUSTOMER!
NOW I MUST TELL YOU I HAVE THE IMPULSE TO TATTOO A SPIDER ON YOU.
A SMALL SPIDER! NO?
A PANDA? I CAN DO A PANDA.
PEARL?

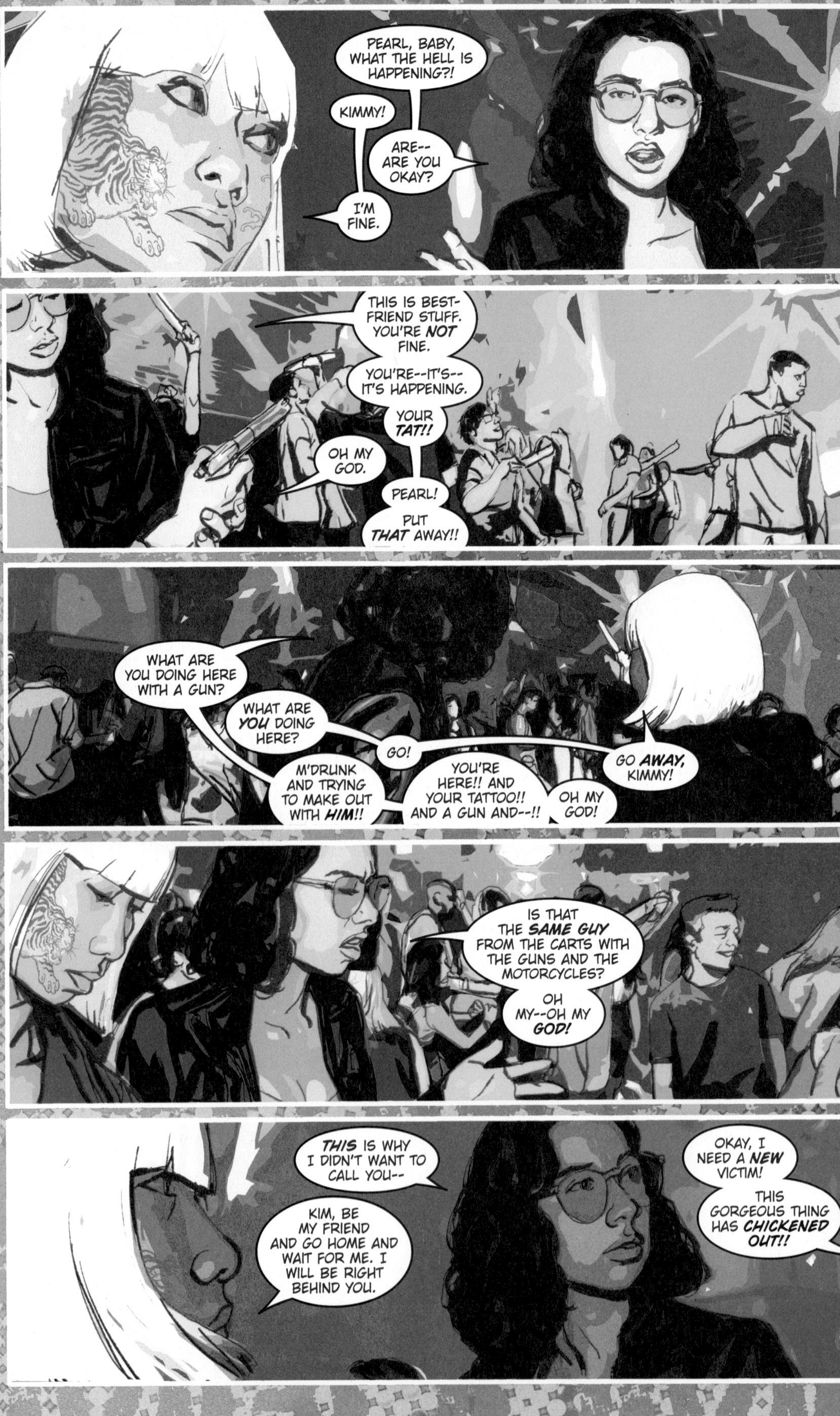
PEARL, BABY, WHAT THE HELL IS HAPPENING?!
KIMMY!
ARE-- ARE YOU OKAY?
I'M FINE.
THIS IS BEST-FRIEND STUFF. YOU'RE NOT FINE.
YOU'RE--IT'S-- IT'S HAPPENING.
YOUR TAT!!
OH MY GOD.
PEARL!
PUT THAT AWAY!!
WHAT ARE YOU DOING HERE WITH A GUN?
WHAT ARE YOU DOING HERE?
M'DRUNK AND TRYING TO MAKE OUT WITH HIM!!
GO!
YOU'RE HERE!! AND YOUR TATTOO!! AND A GUN AND--!!
GO AWAY, KIMMY!
OH MY GOD!
IS THAT THE SAME GUY FROM THE CARTS WITH THE GUNS AND THE MOTORCYCLES?
OH MY--OH MY GOD!
THIS IS WHY I DIDN'T WANT TO CALL YOU--
KIM, BE MY FRIEND AND GO HOME AND WAIT FOR ME. I WILL BE RIGHT BEHIND YOU.
OKAY, I NEED A NEW VICTIM!
THIS GORGEOUS THING HAS CHICKENED OUT!!

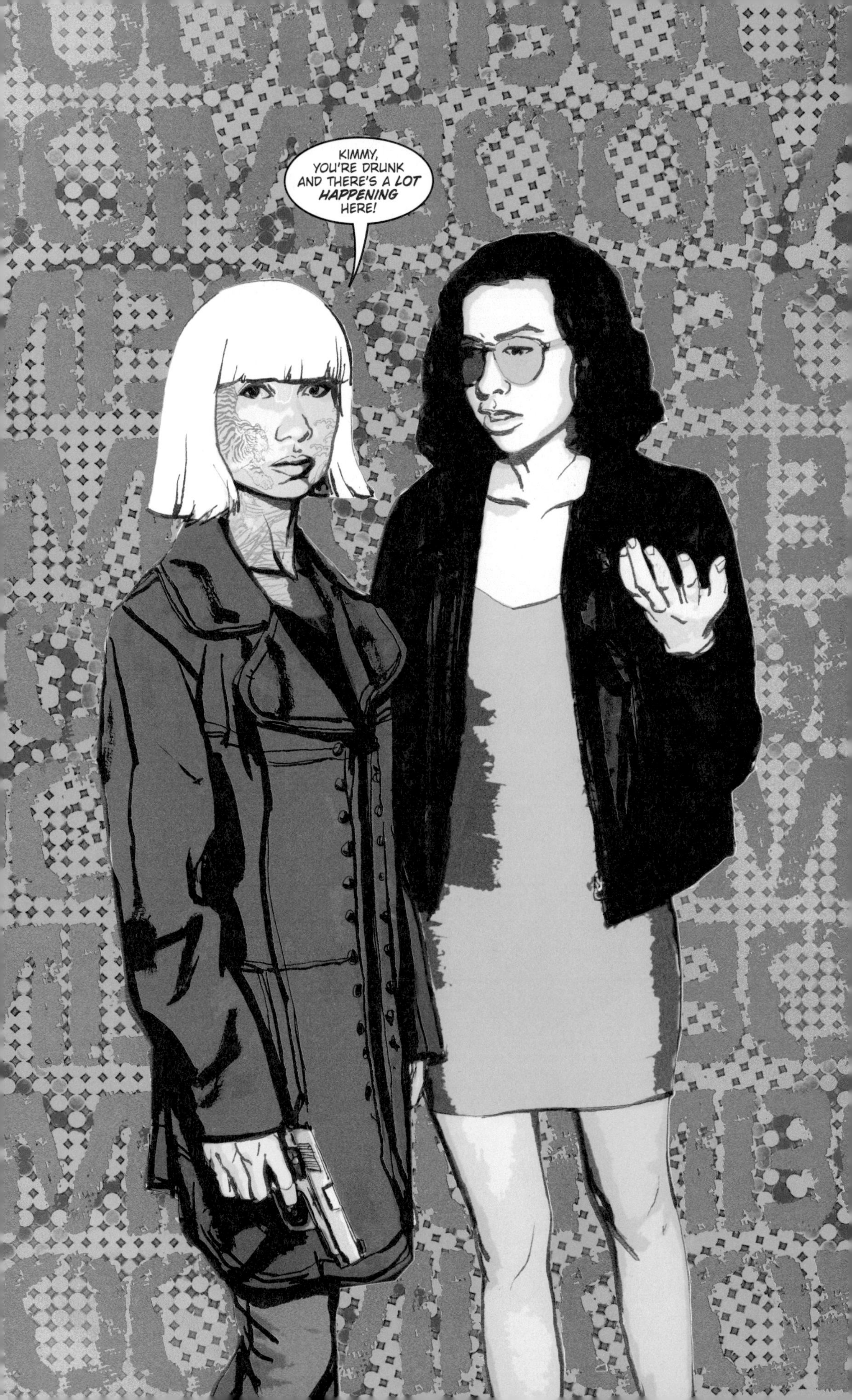
KIMMY, YOU'RE DRUNK AND THERE'S A LOT HAPPENING HERE!

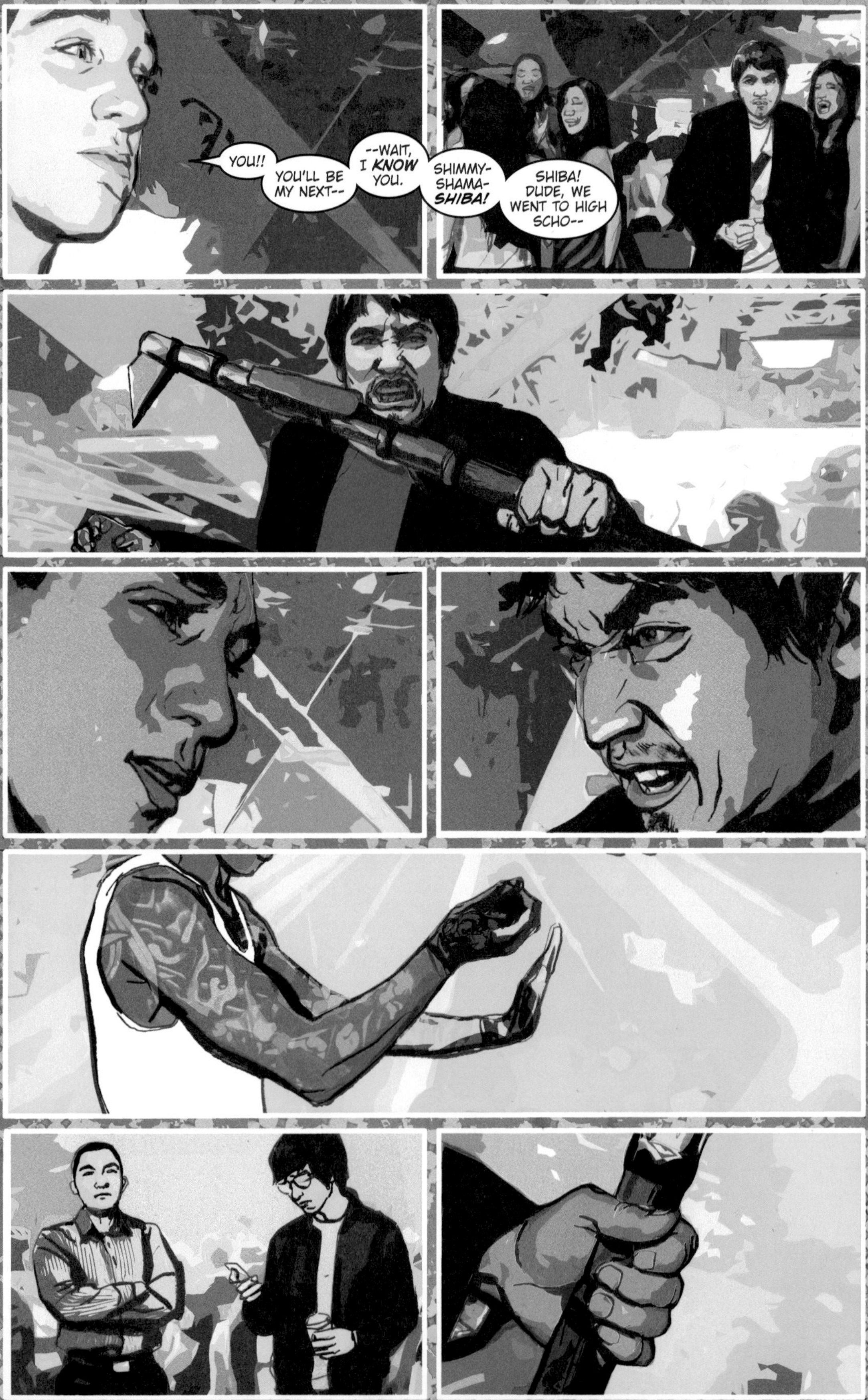
YOU!!
YOU'LL BE MY NEXT--
--WAIT, I KNOW YOU.
SHIMMY-SHAMA-SHIBA!
SHIBA! DUDE, WE WENT TO HIGH SCHO--

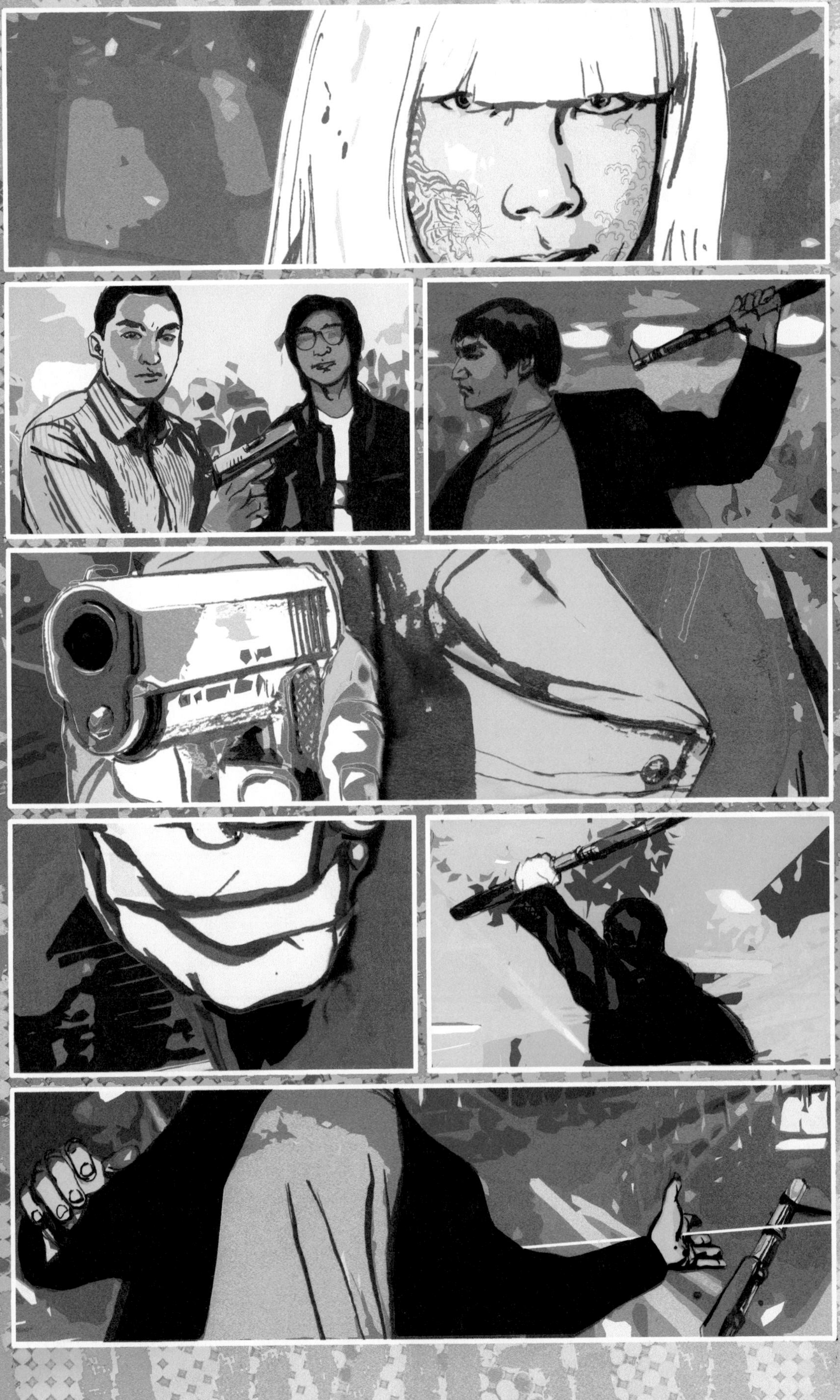

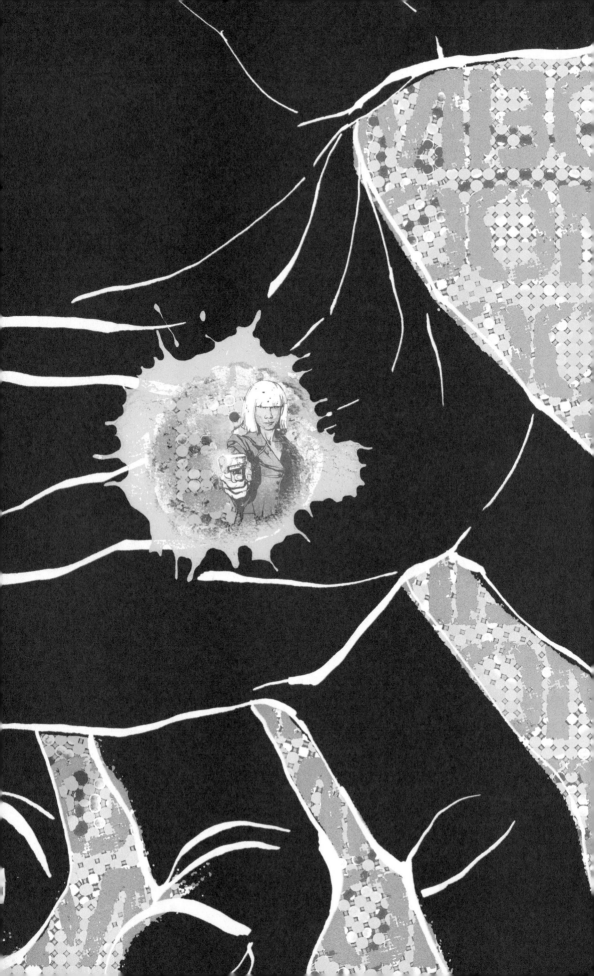

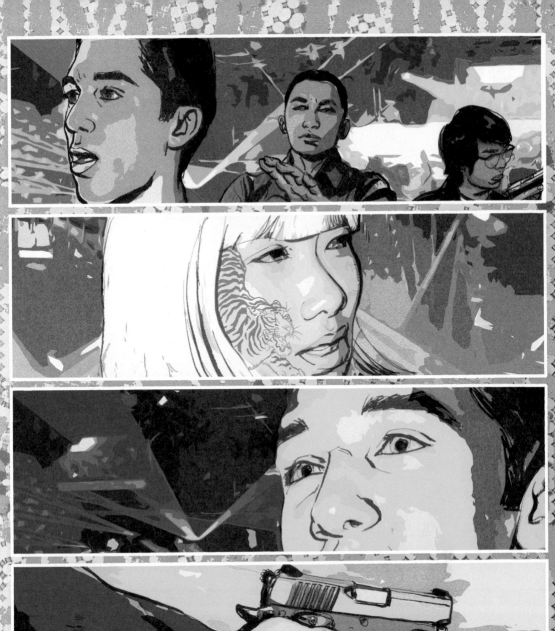

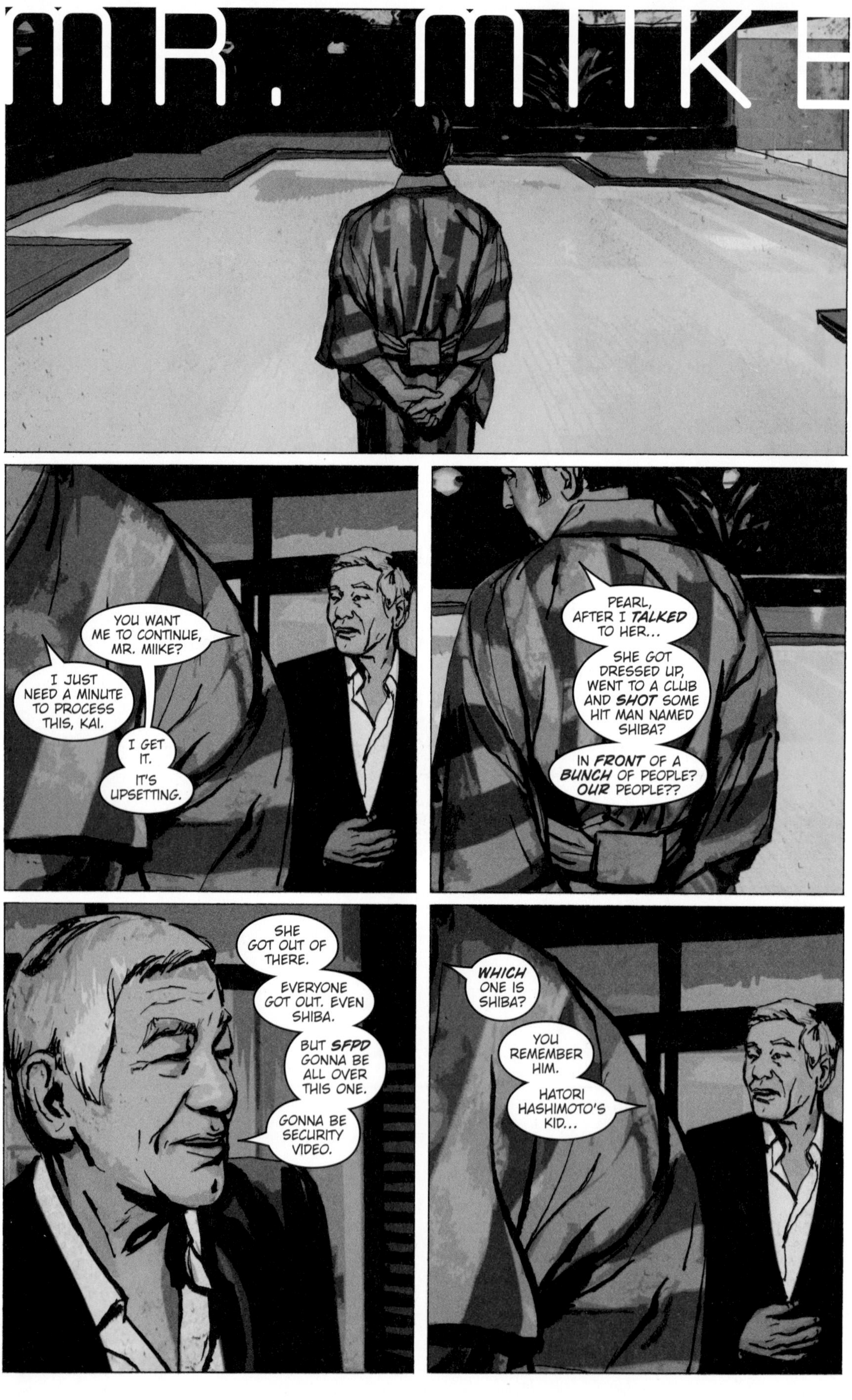
MR. MIIKE
YOU WANT ME TO CONTINUE, MR. MIIKE?
I JUST NEED A MINUTE TO PROCESS THIS, KAI.
I GET IT.
IT'S UPSETTING.
PEARL, AFTER I TALKED TO HER...
SHE GOT DRESSED UP, WENT TO A CLUB AND SHOT SOME HIT MAN NAMED SHIBA?
IN FRONT OF A BUNCH OF PEOPLE? OUR PEOPLE??
SHE GOT OUT OF THERE.
EVERYONE GOT OUT. EVEN SHIBA.
BUT SFPD GONNA BE ALL OVER THIS ONE.
GONNA BE SECURITY VIDEO.
WHICH ONE IS SHIBA?
YOU REMEMBER HIM.
HATORI HASHIMOTO'S KID...

SHIBA IN DADDY'S BOY ALL GROWED UP

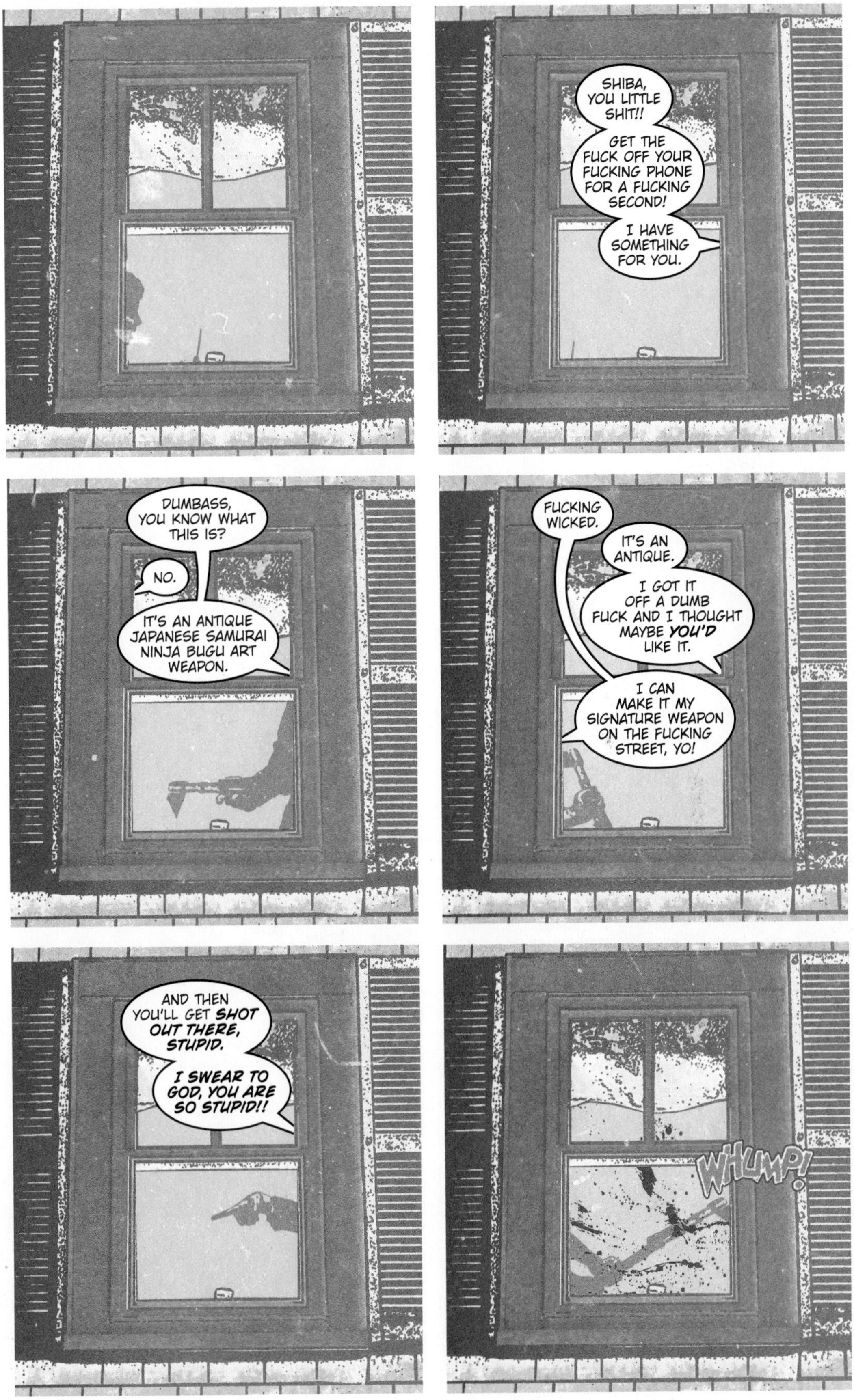
SHIBA, YOU LITTLE SHIT!!
GET THE FUCK OFF YOUR FUCKING PHONE FOR A FUCKING SECOND!
I HAVE SOMETHING FOR YOU.
DUMBASS, YOU KNOW WHAT THIS IS?
NO.
IT'S AN ANTIQUE JAPANESE SAMURAI NINJA BUGU ART WEAPON.
FUCKING WICKED.
IT'S AN ANTIQUE.
I GOT IT OFF A DUMB FUCK AND I THOUGHT MAYBE *YOU'D* LIKE IT.
I CAN MAKE IT MY SIGNATURE WEAPON ON THE FUCKING STREET, YO!
AND THEN YOU'LL GET *SHOT OUT THERE, STUPID.*
I SWEAR TO GOD, YOU ARE SO STUPID!!
WHUMP!

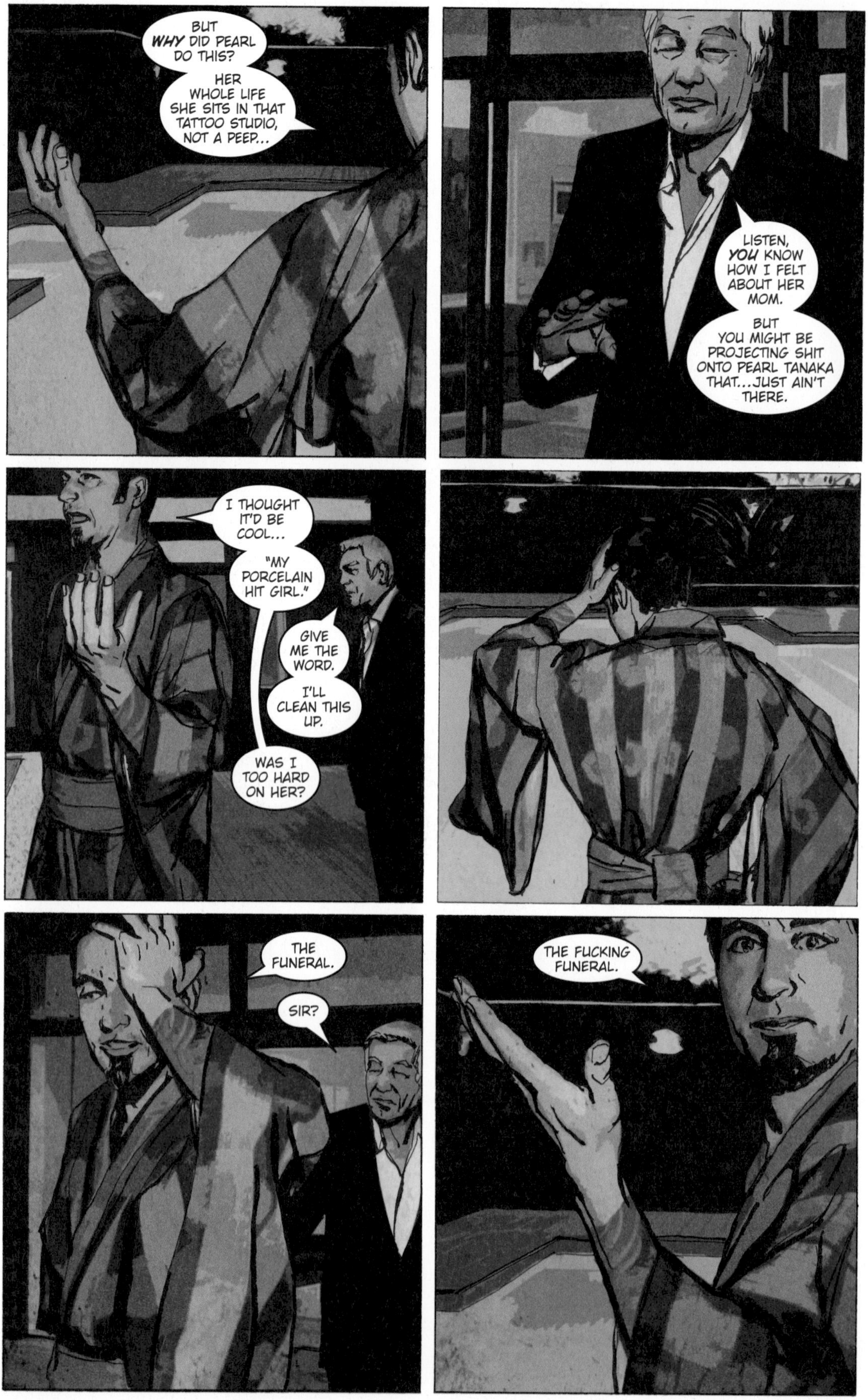

BUT WHY DID PEARL DO THIS?
HER WHOLE LIFE SHE SITS IN THAT TATTOO STUDIO, NOT A PEEP...
LISTEN, YOU KNOW HOW I FELT ABOUT HER MOM.
BUT YOU MIGHT BE PROJECTING SHIT ONTO PEARL TANAKA THAT...JUST AIN'T THERE.
I THOUGHT IT'D BE COOL...
"MY PORCELAIN HIT GIRL."
GIVE ME THE WORD.
I'LL CLEAN THIS UP.
WAS I TOO HARD ON HER?
THE FUNERAL.
SIR?
THE FUCKING FUNERAL.

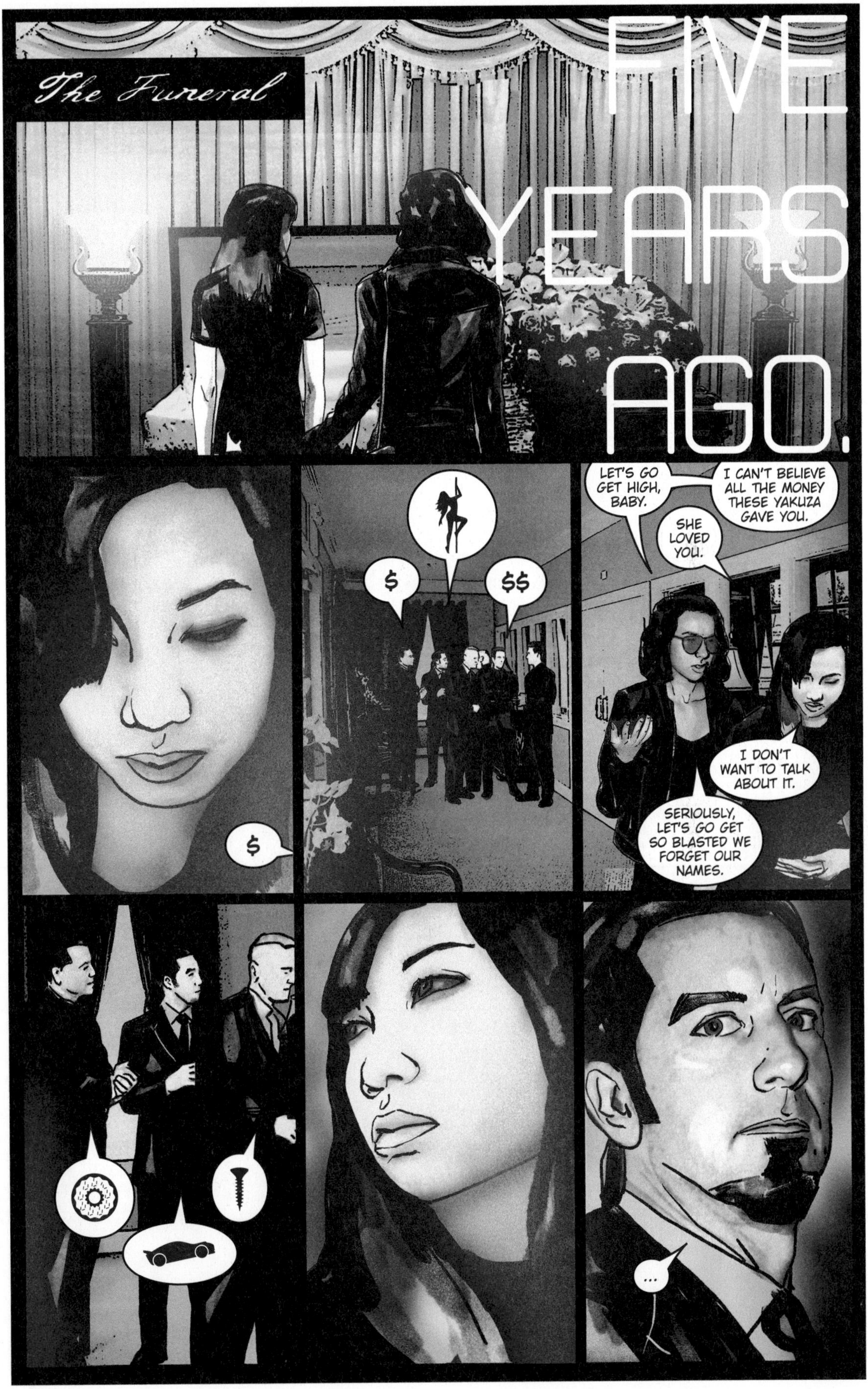
The Funeral
FIVE YEARS AGO.
$
$
$$
LET'S GO GET HIGH, BABY.
I CAN'T BELIEVE ALL THE MONEY THESE YAKUZA GAVE YOU.
SHE LOVED YOU.
I DON'T WANT TO TALK ABOUT IT.
SERIOUSLY, LET'S GO GET SO BLASTED WE FORGET OUR NAMES.
...

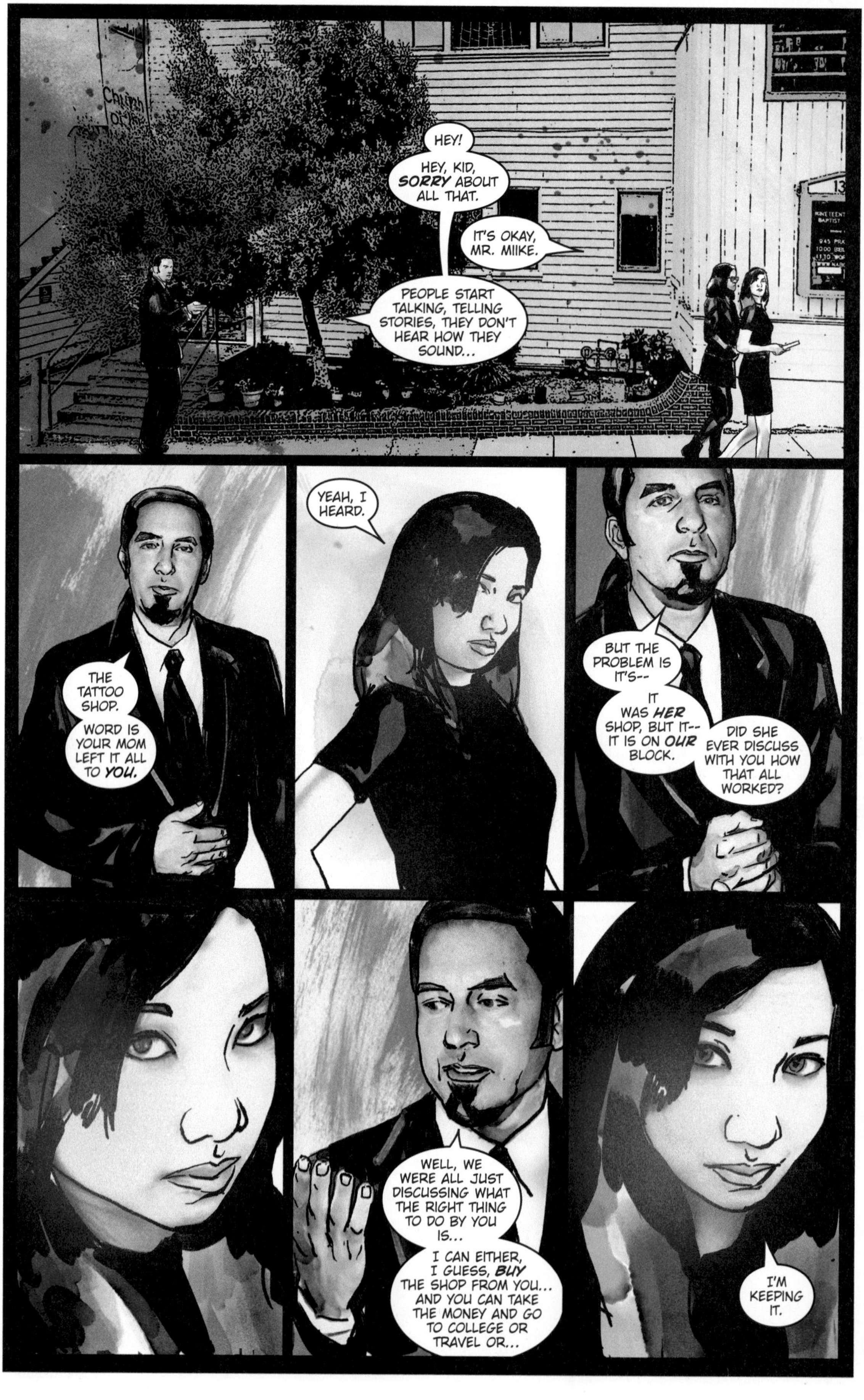
HEY!
HEY, KID, SORRY ABOUT ALL THAT.
IT'S OKAY, MR. MIIKE.
PEOPLE START TALKING, TELLING STORIES, THEY DON'T HEAR HOW THEY SOUND...
THE TATTOO SHOP.
WORD IS YOUR MOM LEFT IT ALL TO YOU.
YEAH, I HEARD.
BUT THE PROBLEM IS IT'S--
IT WAS HER SHOP, BUT IT-- IT IS ON OUR BLOCK.
DID SHE EVER DISCUSS WITH YOU HOW THAT ALL WORKED?
WELL, WE WERE ALL JUST DISCUSSING WHAT THE RIGHT THING TO DO BY YOU IS...
I CAN EITHER, I GUESS, BUY THE SHOP FROM YOU... AND YOU CAN TAKE THE MONEY AND GO TO COLLEGE OR TRAVEL OR...
I'M KEEPING IT.

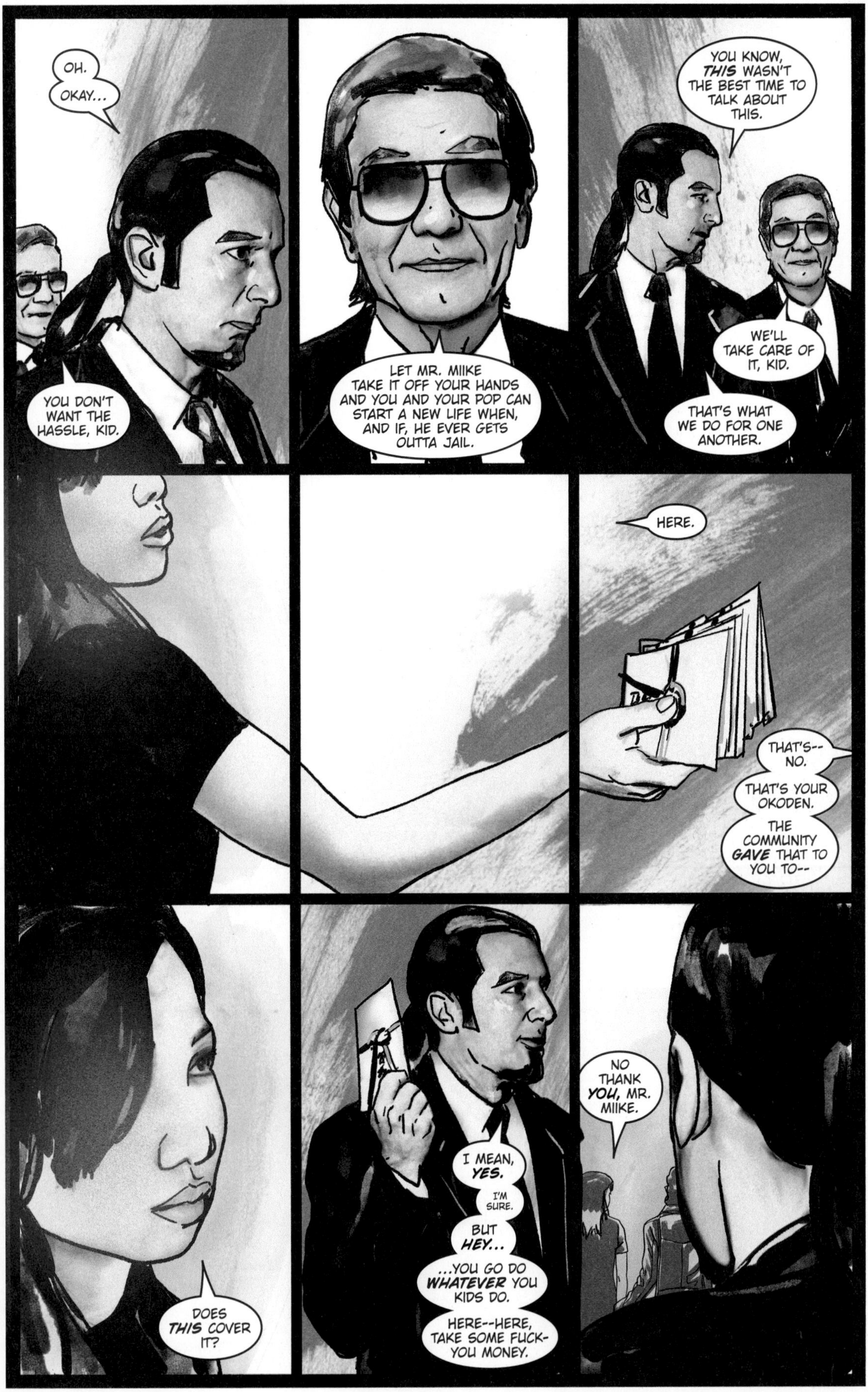
OH.
OKAY...
YOU DON'T WANT THE HASSLE, KID.
LET MR. MIIKE TAKE IT OFF YOUR HANDS AND YOU AND YOUR POP CAN START A NEW LIFE WHEN, AND IF, HE EVER GETS OUTTA JAIL.
YOU KNOW, THIS WASN'T THE BEST TIME TO TALK ABOUT THIS.
WE'LL TAKE CARE OF IT, KID.
THAT'S WHAT WE DO FOR ONE ANOTHER.
HERE.
THAT'S-- NO.
THAT'S YOUR OKODEN.
THE COMMUNITY GAVE THAT TO YOU TO--
DOES THIS COVER IT?
I MEAN, YES.
I'M SURE.
BUT HEY...
...YOU GO DO WHATEVER YOU KIDS DO.
HERE--HERE, TAKE SOME FUCK-YOU MONEY.
NO THANK YOU, MR. MIIKE.

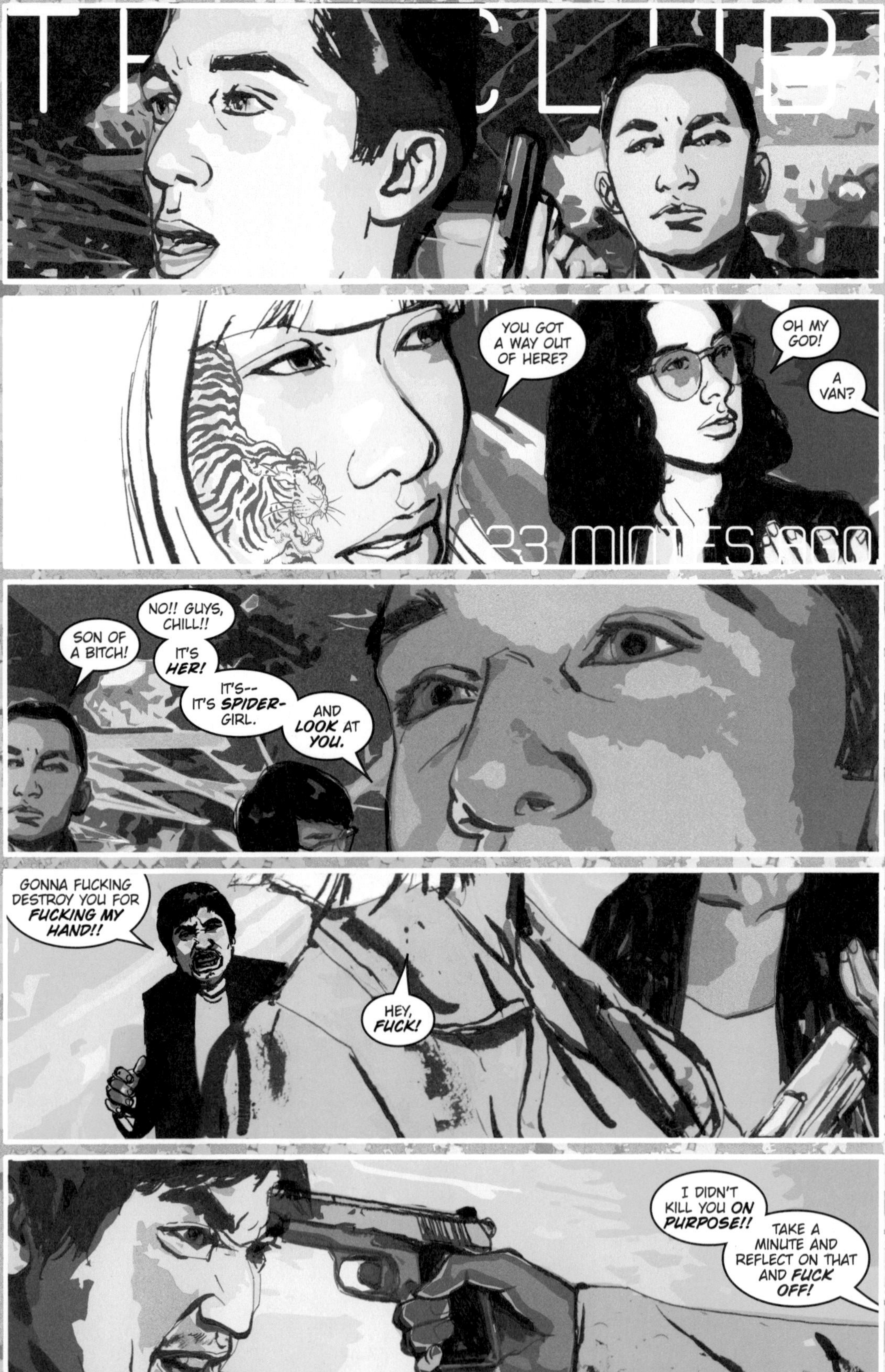
THE CLUB
YOU GOT A WAY OUT OF HERE?
OH MY GOD!
A VAN?
23 MINUTES AGO
SON OF A BITCH!
NO!! GUYS, CHILL!!
IT'S *HER!*
IT'S-- IT'S *SPIDER-GIRL.*
AND *LOOK* AT *YOU.*
GONNA FUCKING DESTROY YOU FOR *FUCKING MY HAND!!*
HEY, *FUCK!*
I DIDN'T KILL YOU *ON PURPOSE!!*
TAKE A MINUTE AND REFLECT ON THAT AND *FUCK OFF!*

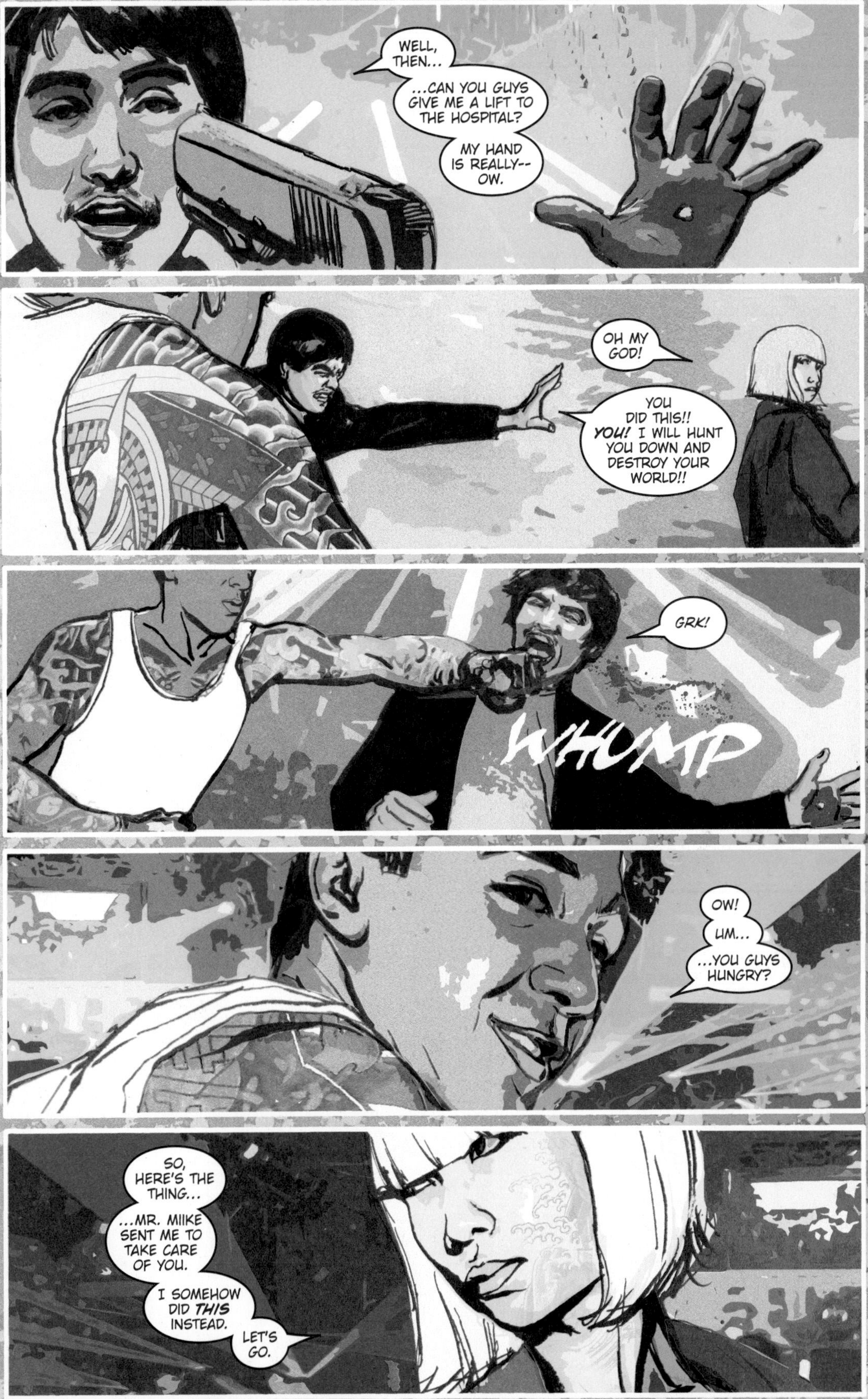
WELL, THEN...
...CAN YOU GUYS GIVE ME A LIFT TO THE HOSPITAL?
MY HAND IS REALLY-- OW.
OH MY GOD!
YOU DID THIS!! YOU! I WILL HUNT YOU DOWN AND DESTROY YOUR WORLD!!
GRK!
WHUMP
OW!
UM...
...YOU GUYS HUNGRY?
SO, HERE'S THE THING...
...MR. MIIKE SENT ME TO TAKE CARE OF YOU.
I SOMEHOW DID THIS INSTEAD.
LET'S GO.

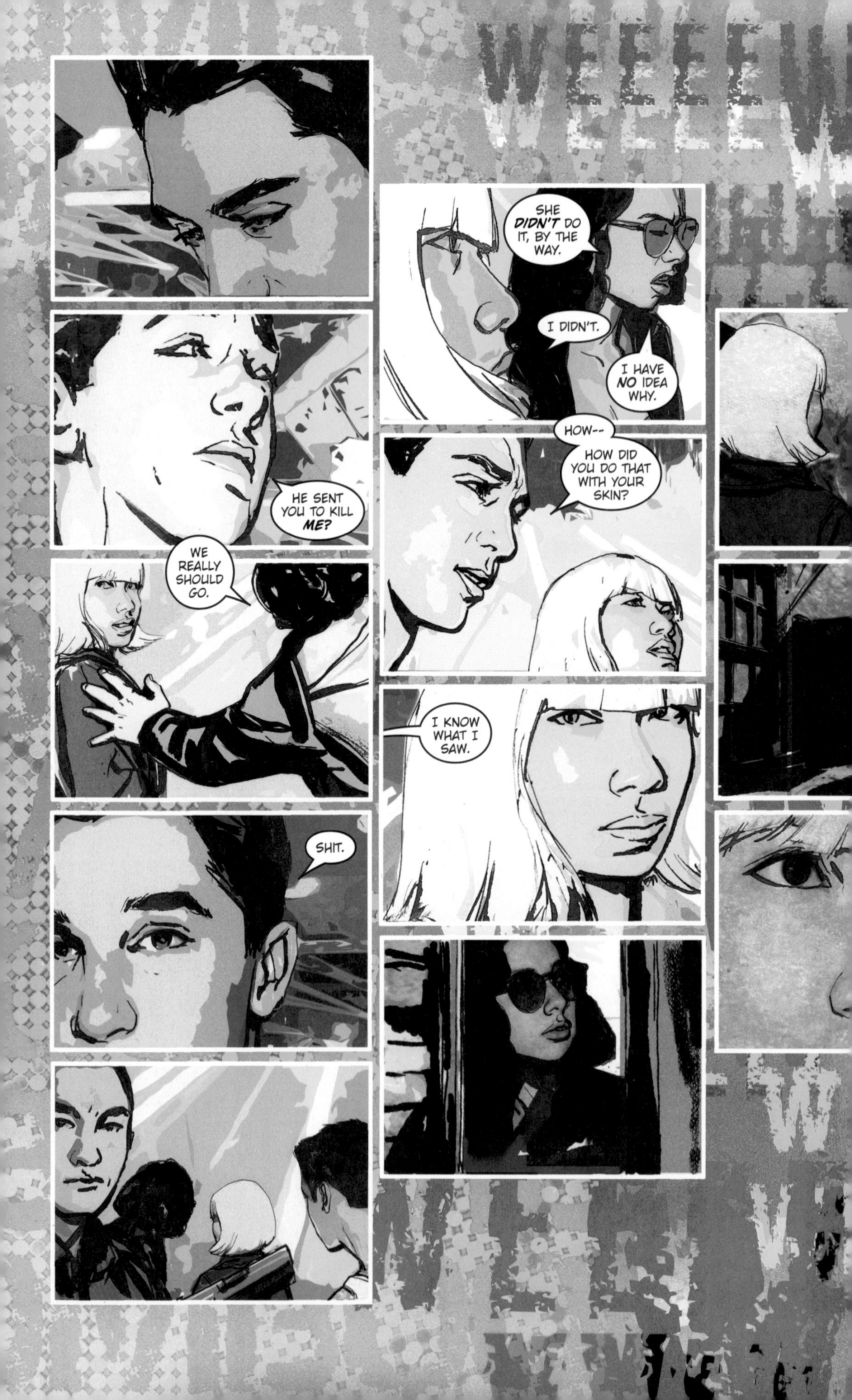
HE SENT YOU TO KILL **ME?**
SHE **DIDN'T** DO IT, BY THE WAY.
I DIDN'T.
I HAVE **NO** IDEA WHY.
HOW--
HOW DID YOU DO THAT WITH YOUR SKIN?
I KNOW WHAT I SAW.
WE REALLY SHOULD GO.
SHIT.

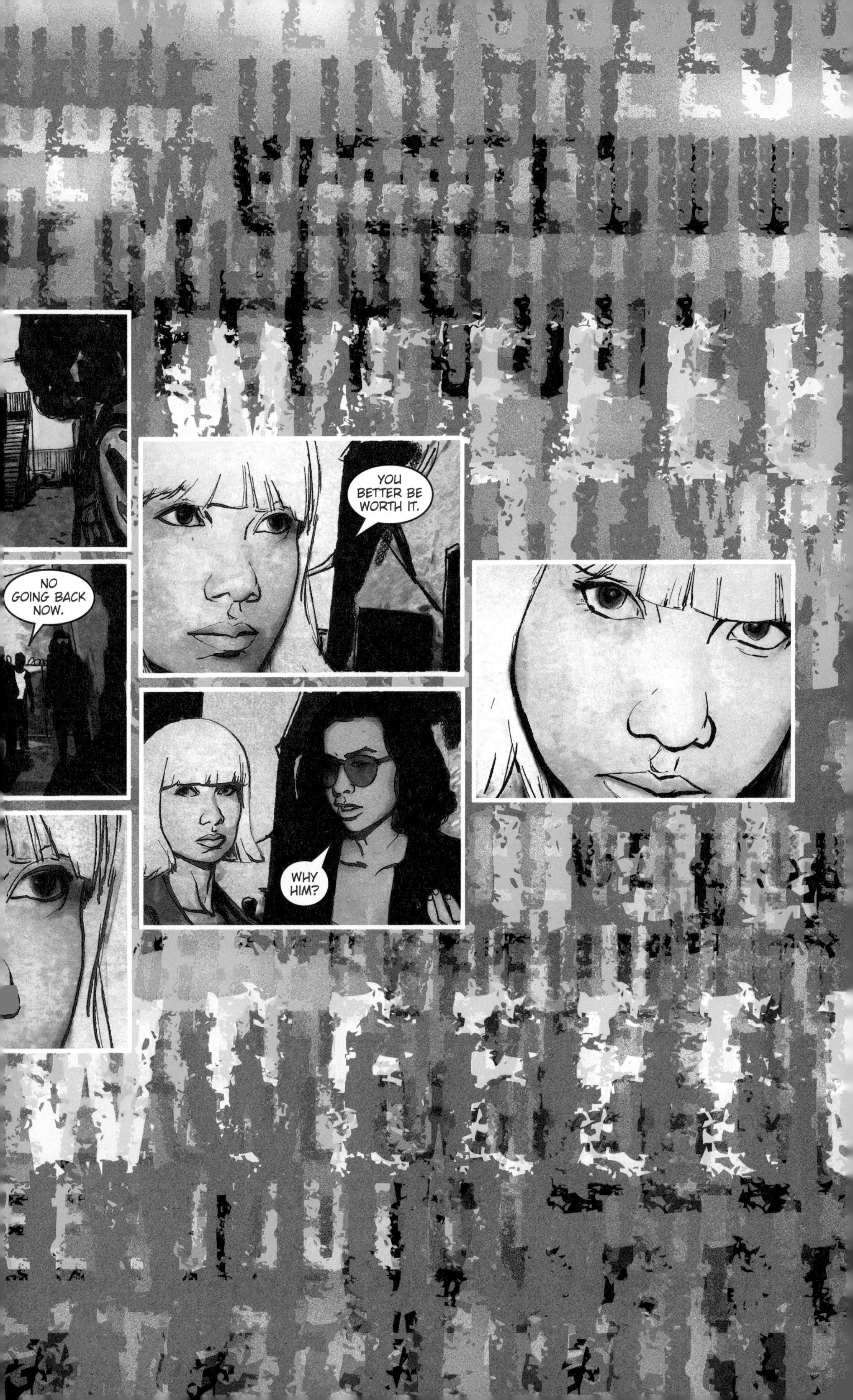
NO GOING BACK NOW.
YOU BETTER BE WORTH IT.
WHY HIM?

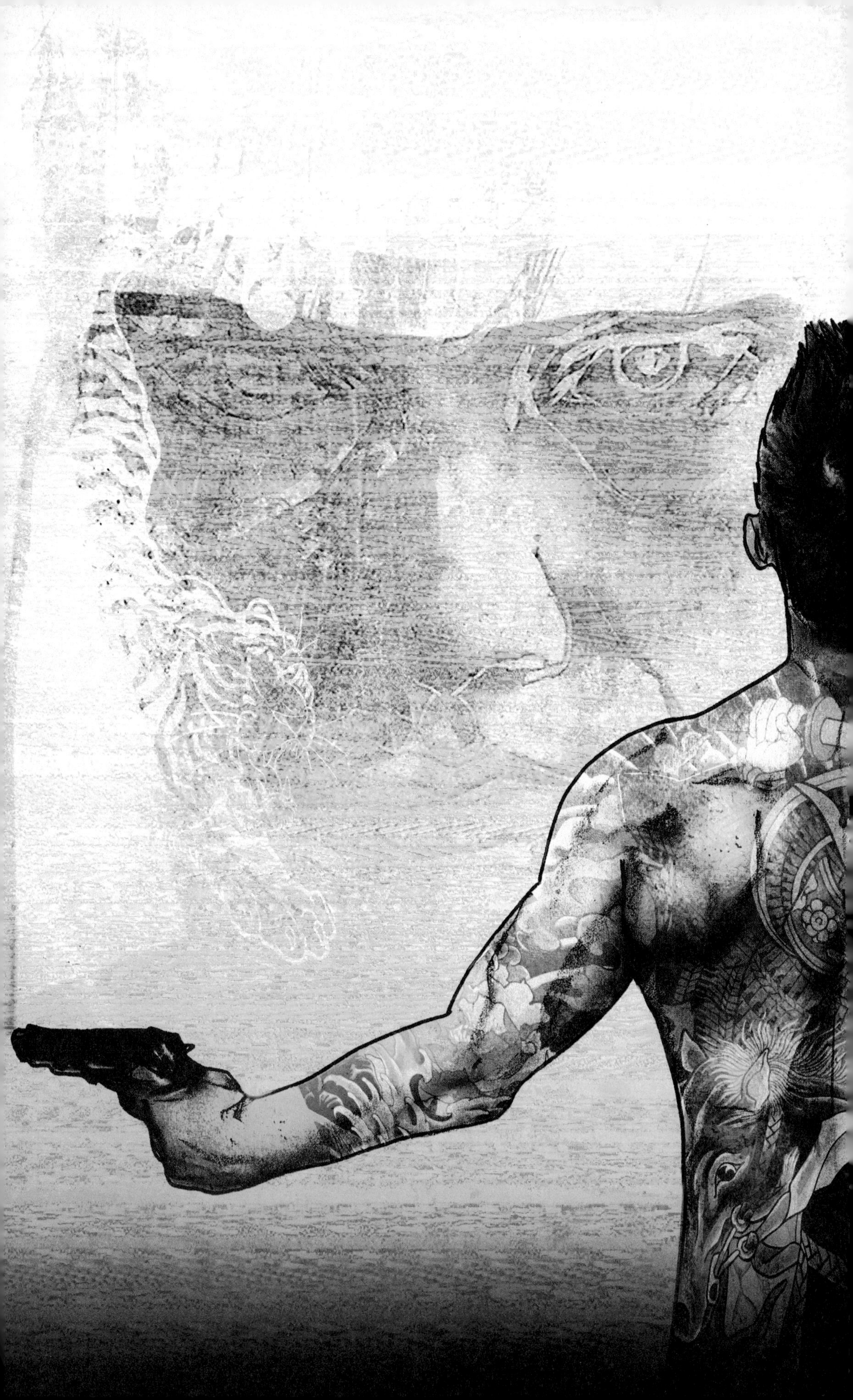

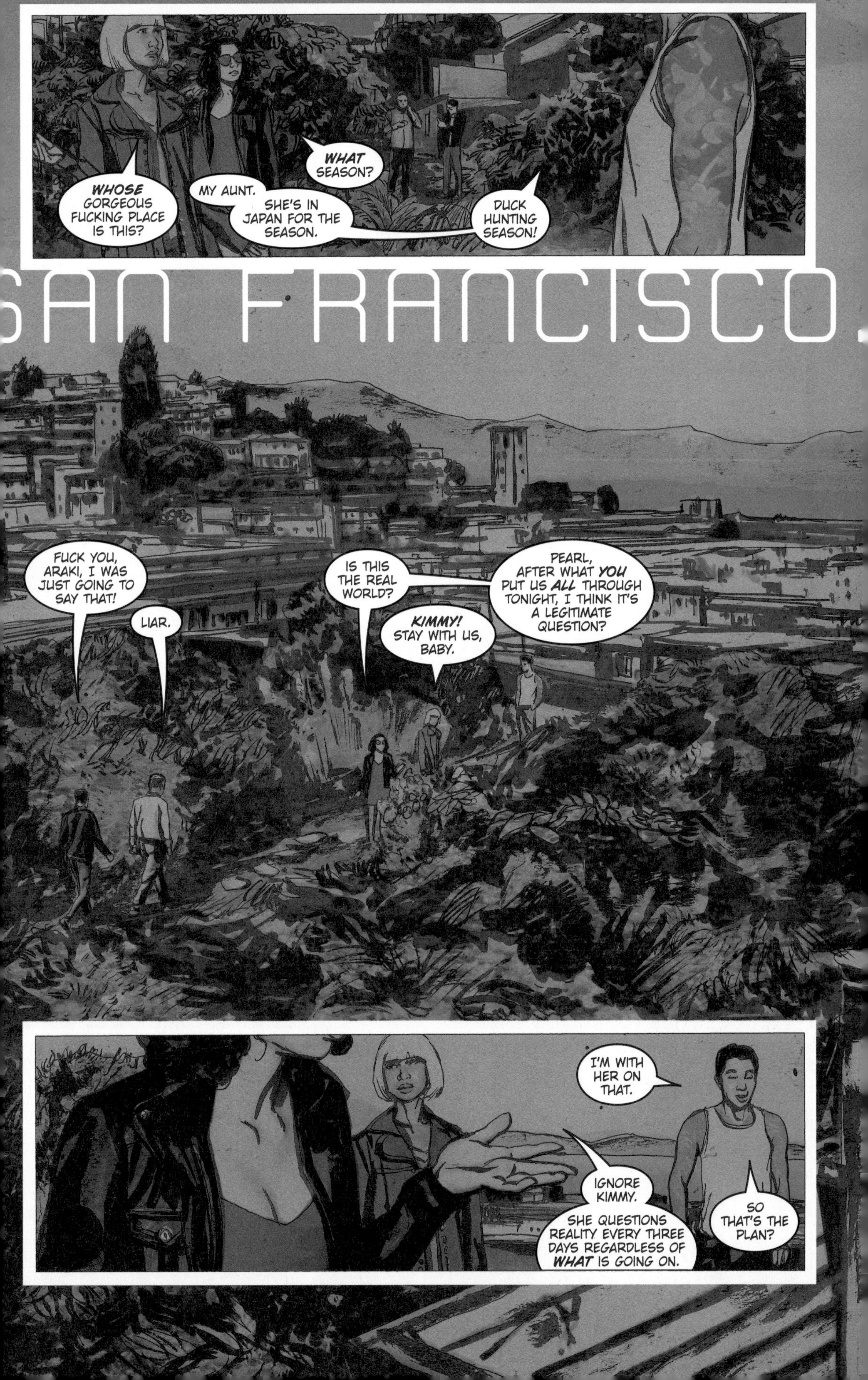
WHOSE GORGEOUS FUCKING PLACE IS THIS?
MY AUNT.
SHE'S IN JAPAN FOR THE SEASON.
WHAT SEASON?
DUCK HUNTING SEASON!
SAN FRANCISCO.
FUCK YOU, ARAKI, I WAS JUST GOING TO SAY THAT!
LIAR.
IS THIS THE REAL WORLD?
KIMMY! STAY WITH US, BABY.
PEARL, AFTER WHAT YOU PUT US ALL THROUGH TONIGHT, I THINK IT'S A LEGITIMATE QUESTION?
I'M WITH HER ON THAT.
IGNORE KIMMY.
SHE QUESTIONS REALITY EVERY THREE DAYS REGARDLESS OF WHAT IS GOING ON.
SO THAT'S THE PLAN?

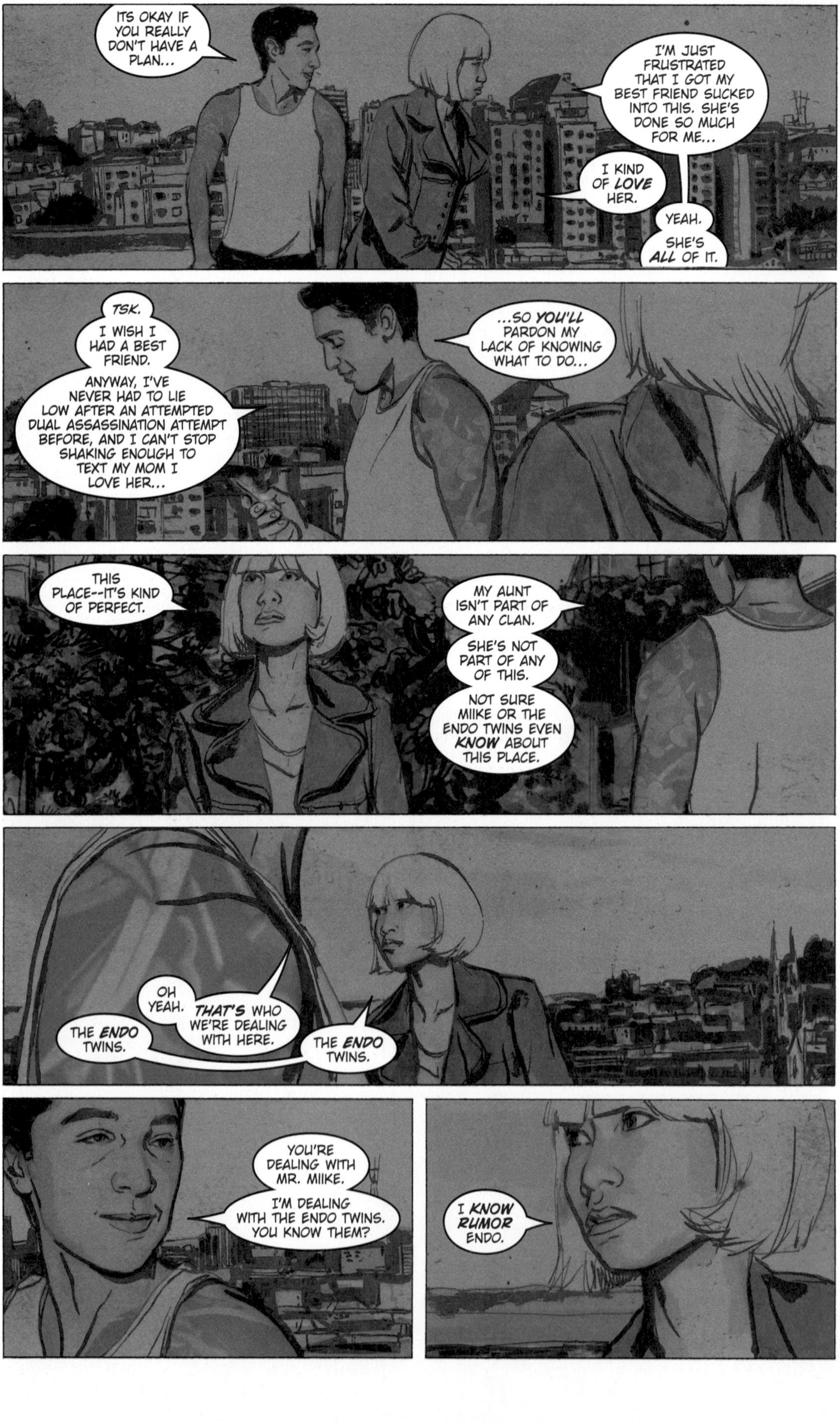

ITS OKAY IF YOU REALLY DON'T HAVE A PLAN...
I'M JUST FRUSTRATED THAT I GOT MY BEST FRIEND SUCKED INTO THIS. SHE'S DONE SO MUCH FOR ME...
I KIND OF LOVE HER.
YEAH.
SHE'S ALL OF IT.
TSK.
I WISH I HAD A BEST FRIEND.
ANYWAY, I'VE NEVER HAD TO LIE LOW AFTER AN ATTEMPTED DUAL ASSASSINATION ATTEMPT BEFORE, AND I CAN'T STOP SHAKING ENOUGH TO TEXT MY MOM I LOVE HER...
...SO YOU'LL PARDON MY LACK OF KNOWING WHAT TO DO...
THIS PLACE--IT'S KIND OF PERFECT.
MY AUNT ISN'T PART OF ANY CLAN.
SHE'S NOT PART OF ANY OF THIS.
NOT SURE MIIKE OR THE ENDO TWINS EVEN KNOW ABOUT THIS PLACE.
OH YEAH.
THE ENDO TWINS.
THAT'S WHO WE'RE DEALING WITH HERE.
THE ENDO TWINS.
YOU'RE DEALING WITH MR. MIIKE.
I'M DEALING WITH THE ENDO TWINS. YOU KNOW THEM?
I KNOW RUMOR ENDO.

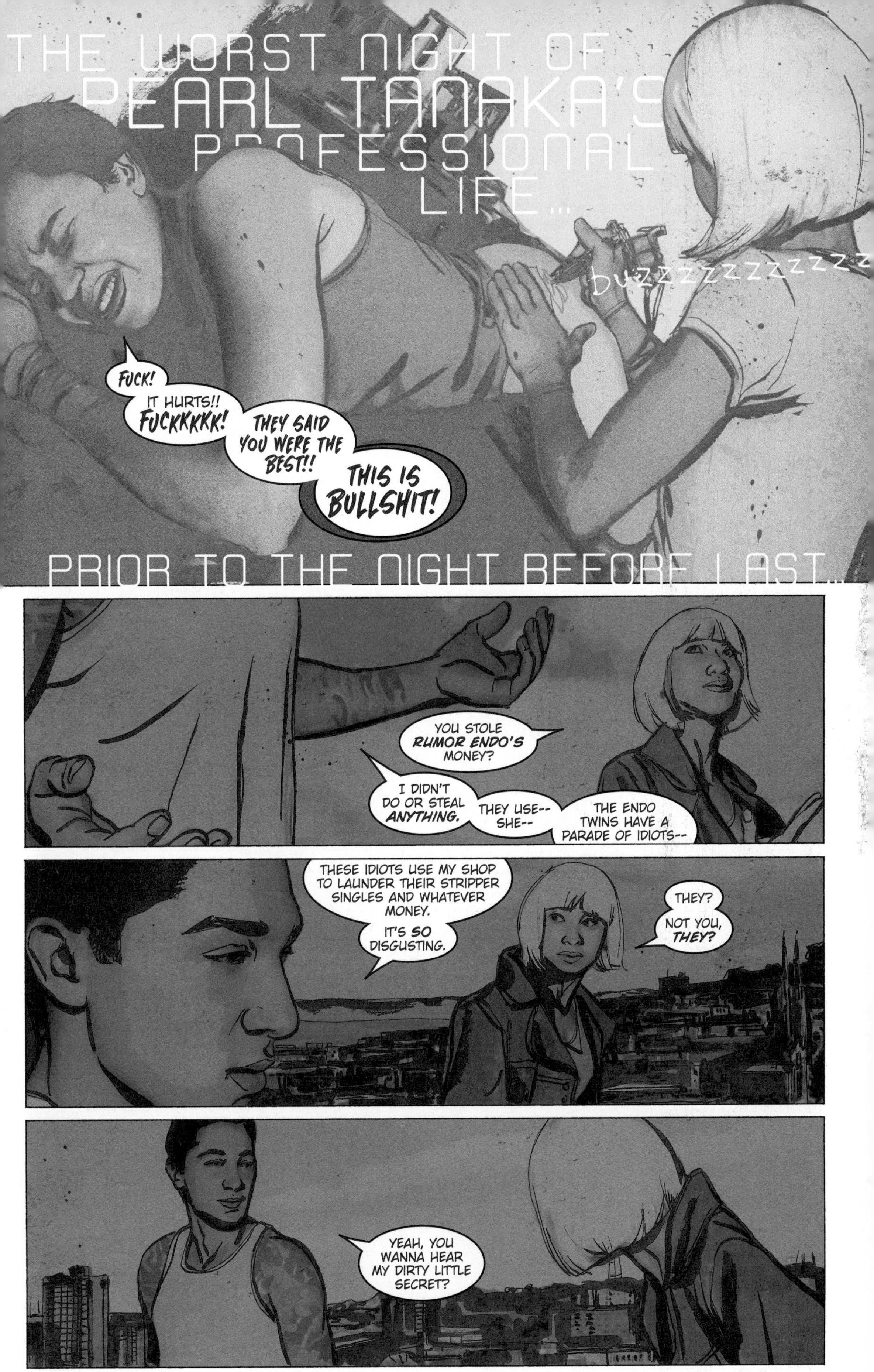
THE WORST NIGHT OF
PEARL TANAKA'S
PROFESSIONAL
LIFE...
buzzzzzzzzzzz
FUCK!
IT HURTS!! FUCKKKKK!
THEY SAID YOU WERE THE BEST!!
THIS IS BULLSHIT!
PRIOR TO THE NIGHT BEFORE LAST...
YOU STOLE RUMOR ENDO'S MONEY?
I DIDN'T DO OR STEAL ANYTHING.
THEY USE-- SHE--
THE ENDO TWINS HAVE A PARADE OF IDIOTS--
THESE IDIOTS USE MY SHOP TO LAUNDER THEIR STRIPPER SINGLES AND WHATEVER MONEY.
IT'S SO DISGUSTING.
THEY? NOT YOU, THEY?
YEAH, YOU WANNA HEAR MY DIRTY LITTLE SECRET?

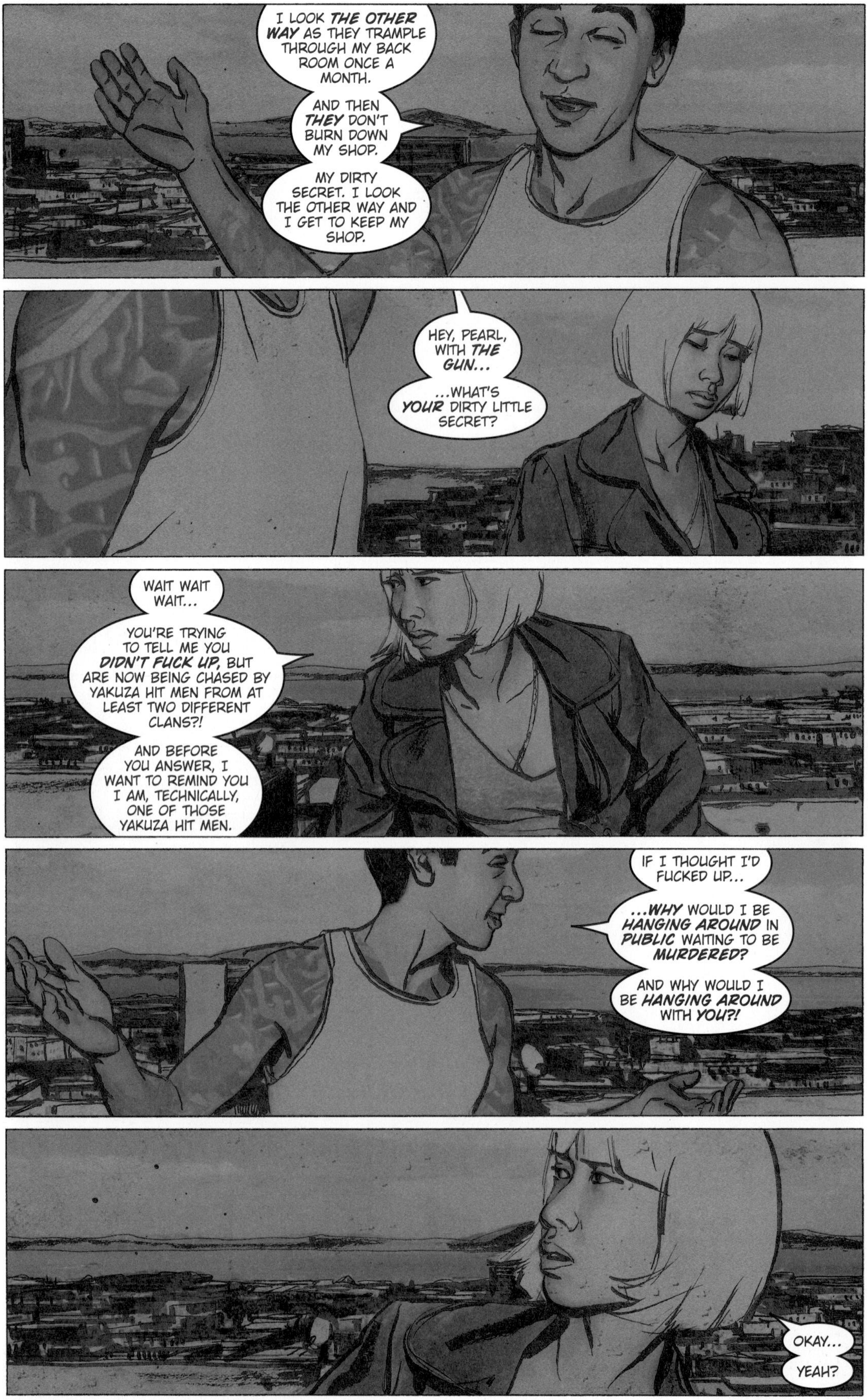
I LOOK THE OTHER WAY AS THEY TRAMPLE THROUGH MY BACK ROOM ONCE A MONTH.
AND THEN THEY DON'T BURN DOWN MY SHOP.
MY DIRTY SECRET. I LOOK THE OTHER WAY AND I GET TO KEEP MY SHOP.
HEY, PEARL, WITH THE GUN...
...WHAT'S YOUR DIRTY LITTLE SECRET?
WAIT WAIT WAIT...
YOU'RE TRYING TO TELL ME YOU DIDN'T FUCK UP, BUT ARE NOW BEING CHASED BY YAKUZA HIT MEN FROM AT LEAST TWO DIFFERENT CLANS?!
AND BEFORE YOU ANSWER, I WANT TO REMIND YOU I AM, TECHNICALLY, ONE OF THOSE YAKUZA HIT MEN.
IF I THOUGHT I'D FUCKED UP...
...WHY WOULD I BE HANGING AROUND IN PUBLIC WAITING TO BE MURDERED?
AND WHY WOULD I BE HANGING AROUND WITH YOU?!
OKAY...
YEAH?

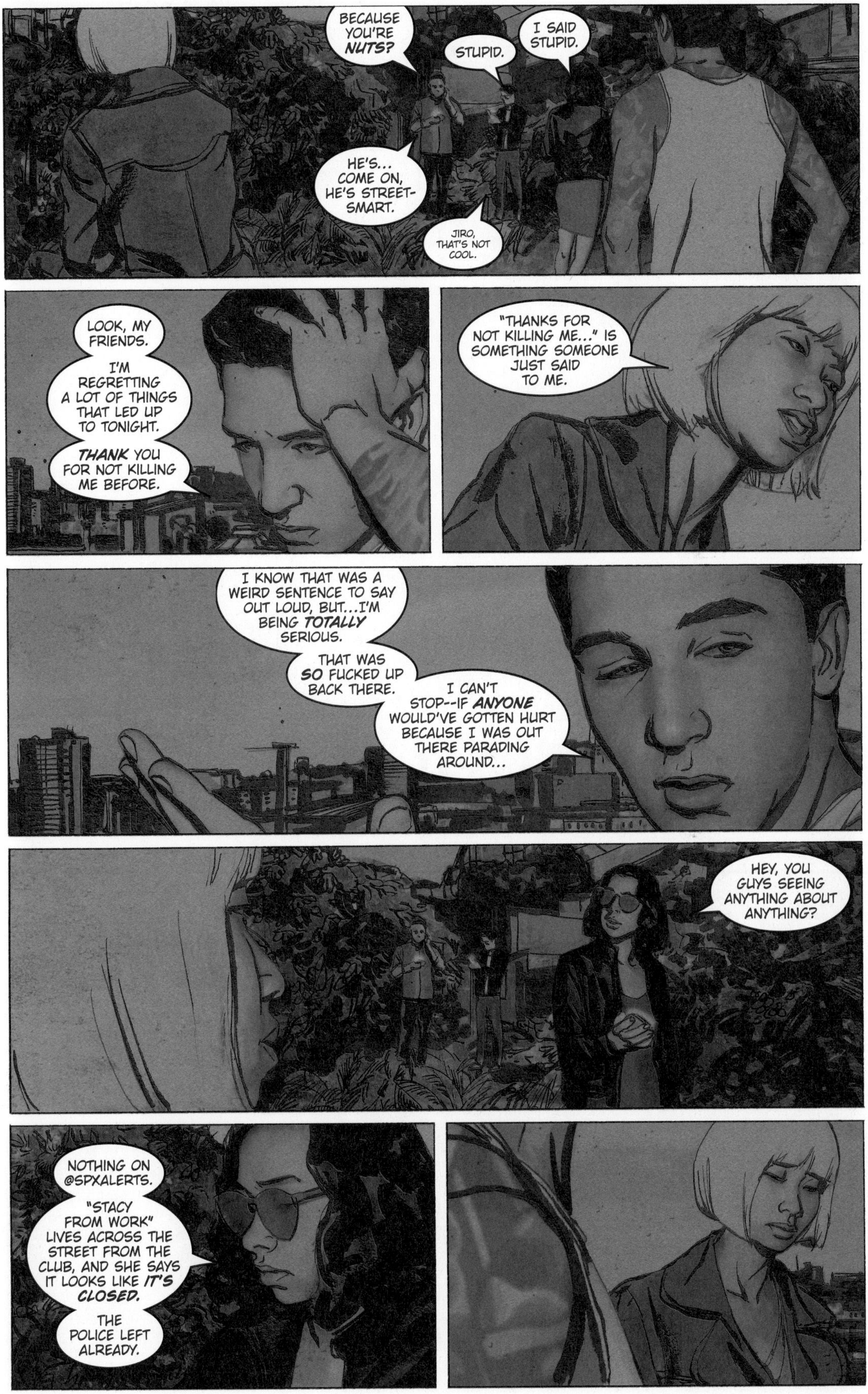

BECAUSE YOU'RE NUTS?
STUPID.
I SAID STUPID.
HE'S... COME ON, HE'S STREET-SMART.
JIRO, THAT'S NOT COOL.
LOOK, MY FRIENDS.
I'M REGRETTING A LOT OF THINGS THAT LED UP TO TONIGHT.
THANK YOU FOR NOT KILLING ME BEFORE.
"THANKS FOR NOT KILLING ME..." IS SOMETHING SOMEONE JUST SAID TO ME.
I KNOW THAT WAS A WEIRD SENTENCE TO SAY OUT LOUD, BUT...I'M BEING TOTALLY SERIOUS.
THAT WAS SO FUCKED UP BACK THERE.
I CAN'T STOP--IF ANYONE WOULD'VE GOTTEN HURT BECAUSE I WAS OUT THERE PARADING AROUND...
HEY, YOU GUYS SEEING ANYTHING ABOUT ANYTHING?
NOTHING ON @SPXALERTS.
"STACY FROM WORK" LIVES ACROSS THE STREET FROM THE CLUB, AND SHE SAYS IT LOOKS LIKE IT'S CLOSED.
THE POLICE LEFT ALREADY.

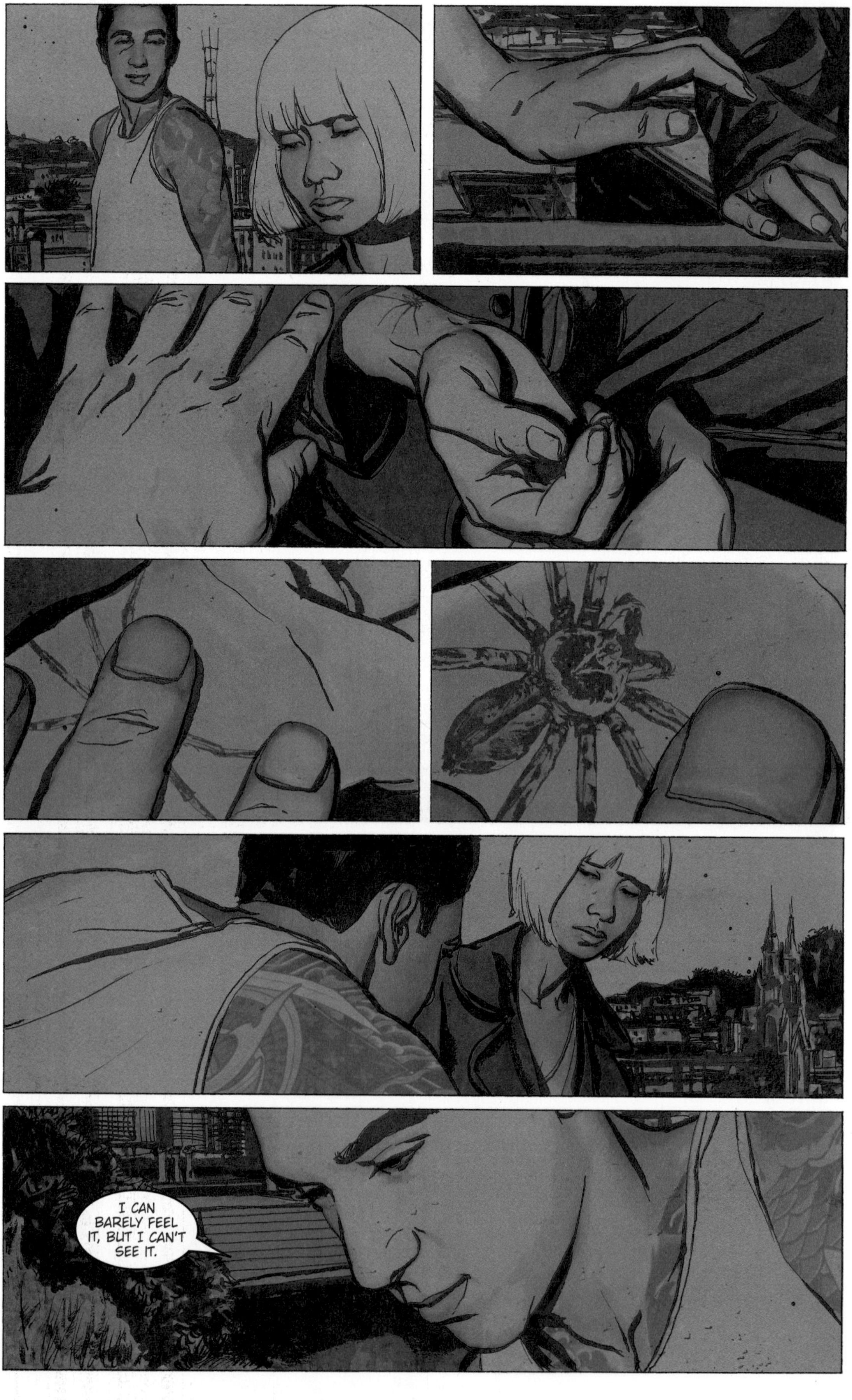
I CAN BARELY FEEL IT, BUT I CAN'T SEE IT.

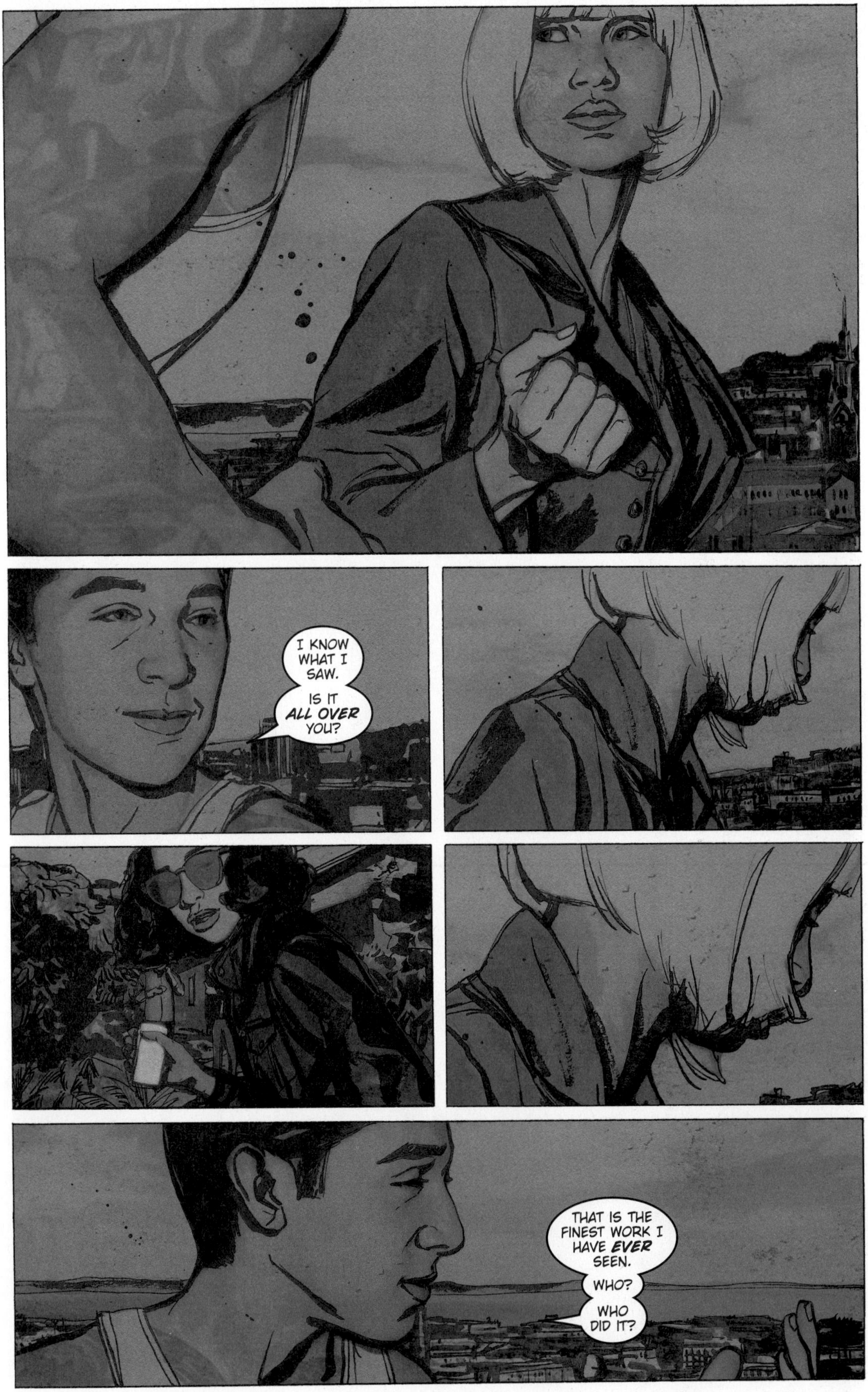
I KNOW WHAT I SAW.
IS IT ALL OVER YOU?
THAT IS THE FINEST WORK I HAVE EVER SEEN.
WHO?
WHO DID IT?

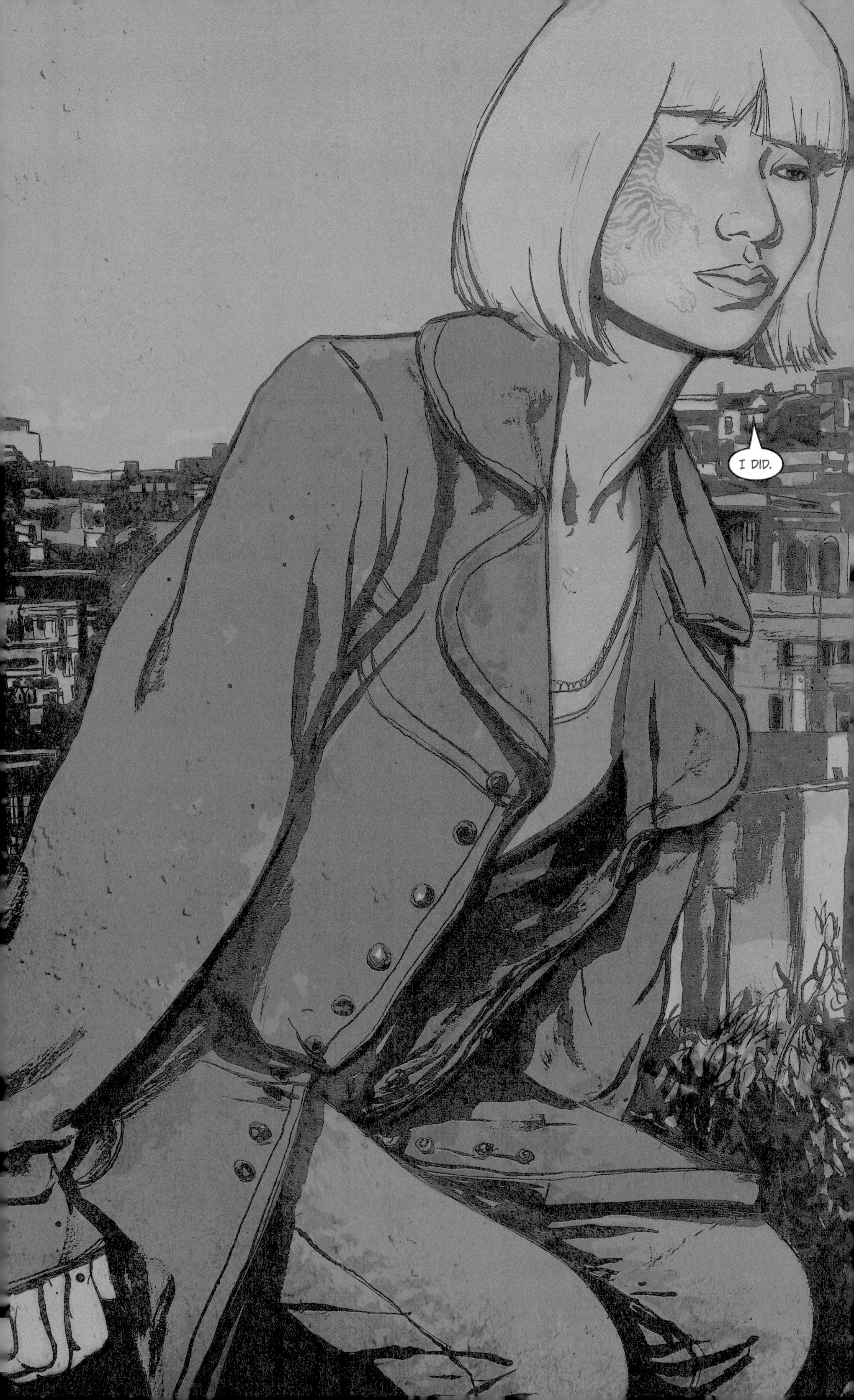
I DID.

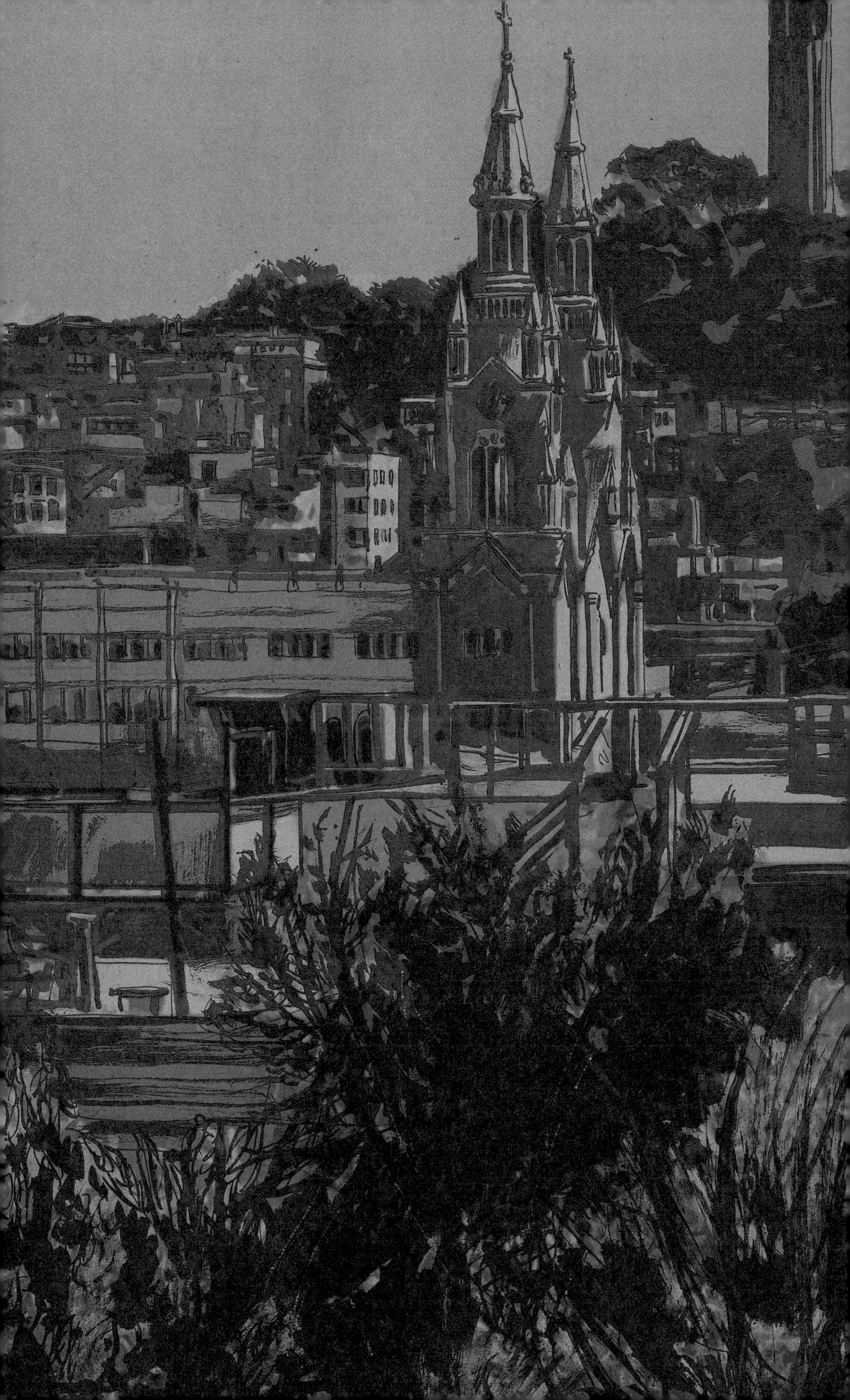

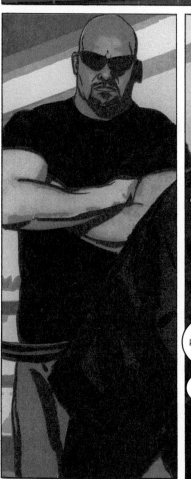

I.D., PLEASE.

TELL *RYU ENDO* SHIBA IS HERE.

I NEED AN *I.D.*

I'M EXPECTED.

THEN YOU SHOULD HAVE EXPECTED TO BRING AN I.D.

TAKE CARE. BRUSH YOUR--

WHUMP

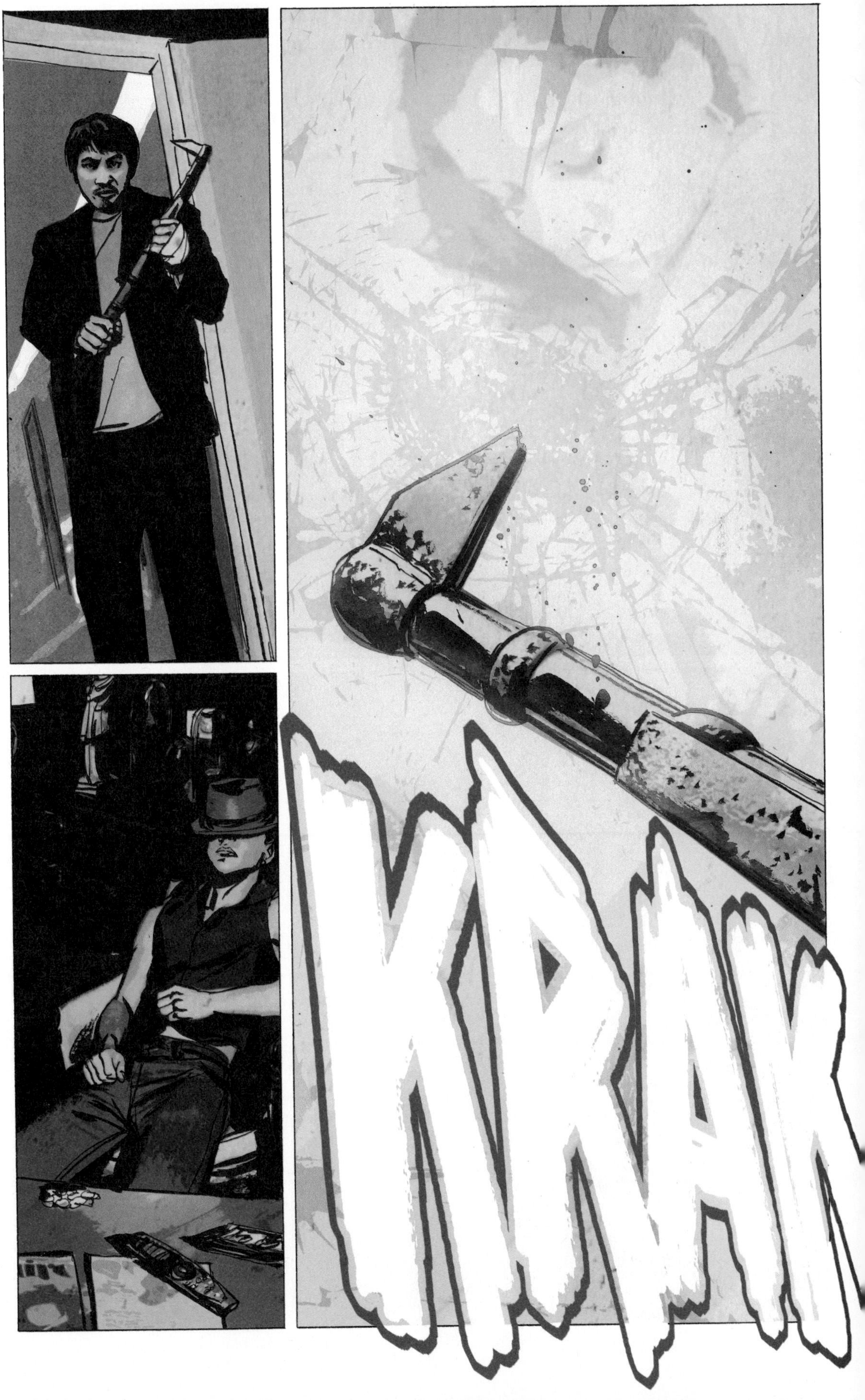
KRAK

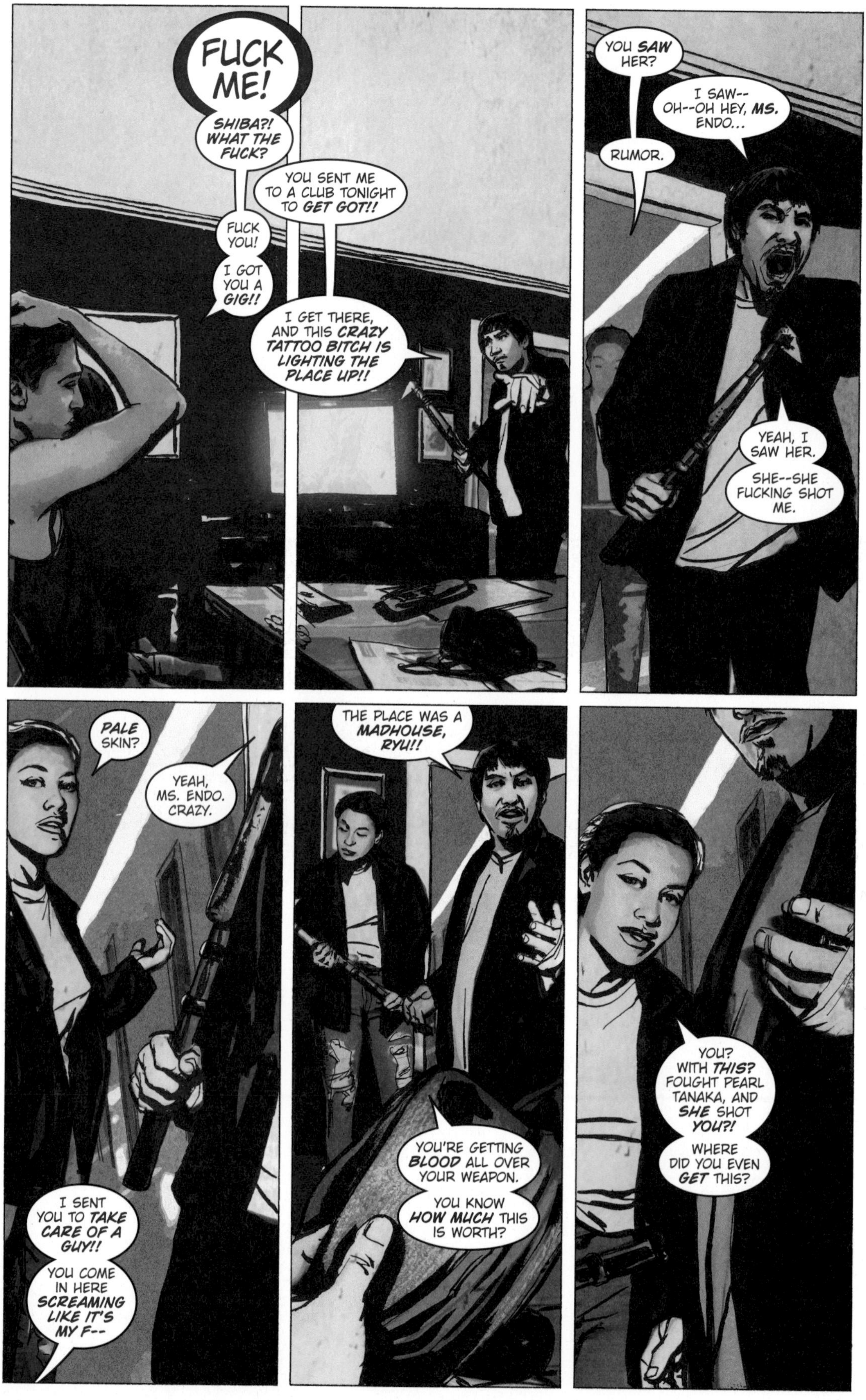
FUCK ME!
SHIBA?! WHAT THE FUCK?
YOU SENT ME TO A CLUB TONIGHT TO GET GOT!!
FUCK YOU!
I GOT YOU A GIG!!
I GET THERE, AND THIS CRAZY TATTOO BITCH IS LIGHTING THE PLACE UP!!
YOU SAW HER?
I SAW-- OH--OH HEY, MS. ENDO...
RUMOR.
YEAH, I SAW HER.
SHE--SHE FUCKING SHOT ME.
PALE SKIN?
YEAH, MS. ENDO. CRAZY.
I SENT YOU TO TAKE CARE OF A GUY!!
YOU COME IN HERE SCREAMING LIKE IT'S MY F--
THE PLACE WAS A MADHOUSE, RYU!!
YOU'RE GETTING BLOOD ALL OVER YOUR WEAPON.
YOU KNOW HOW MUCH THIS IS WORTH?
YOU? WITH THIS? FOUGHT PEARL TANAKA, AND SHE SHOT YOU?!
WHERE DID YOU EVEN GET THIS?

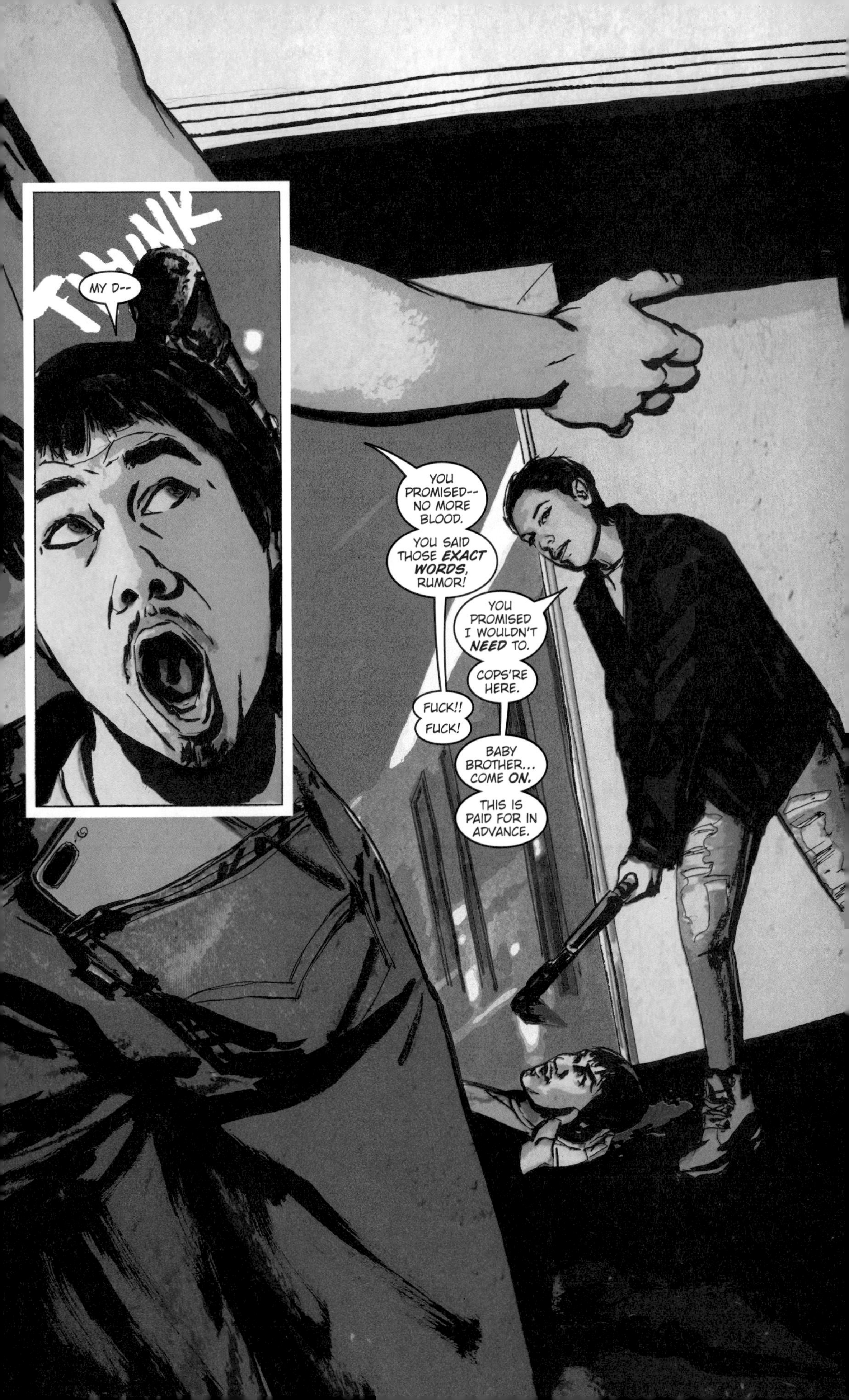
THUNK
MY D--
YOU PROMISED-- NO MORE BLOOD.
YOU SAID THOSE EXACT WORDS, RUMOR!
YOU PROMISED I WOULDN'T NEED TO.
COPS'RE HERE.
FUCK!!
FUCK!
BABY BROTHER... COME ON.
THIS IS PAID FOR IN ADVANCE.

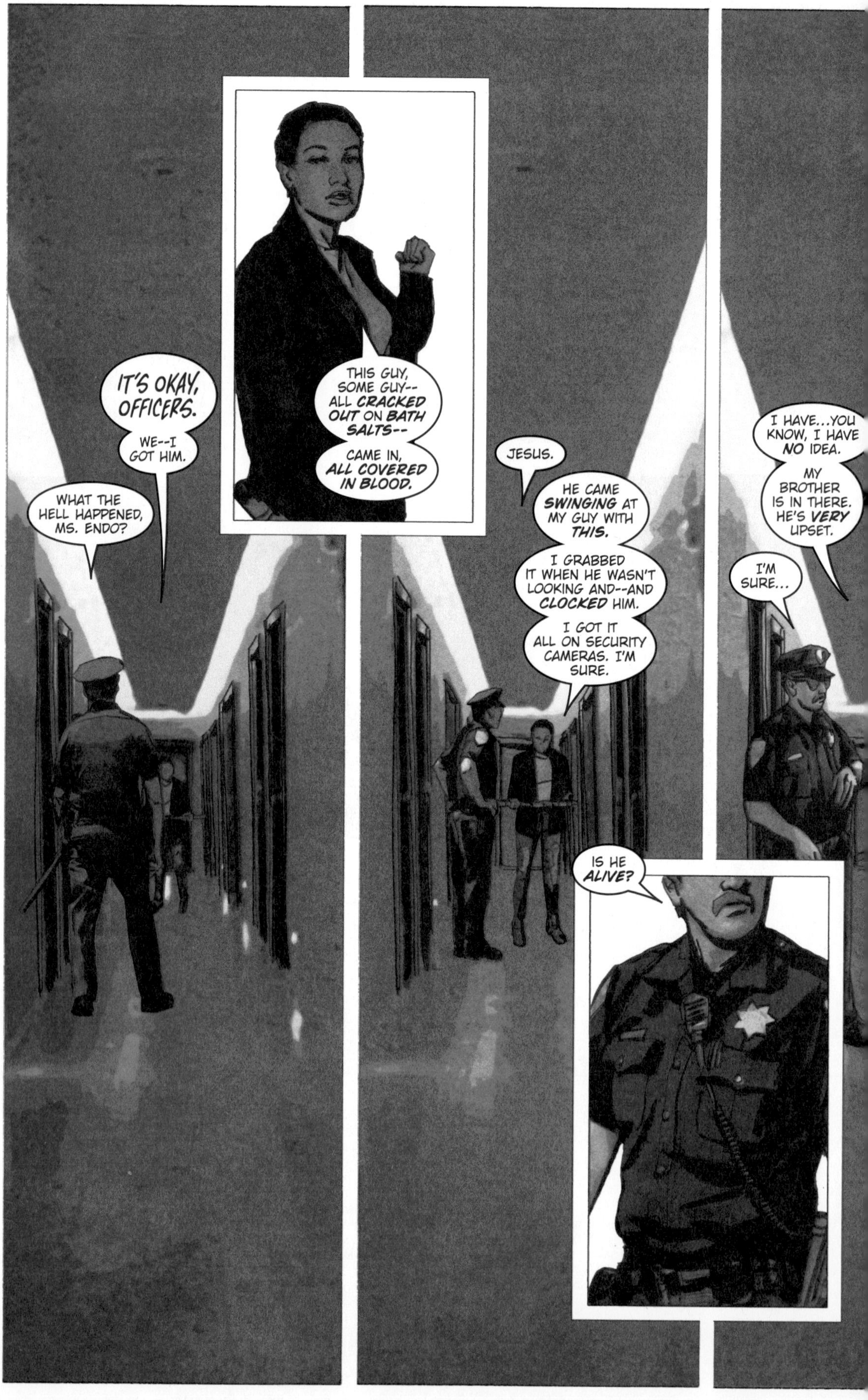

THIS GUY, SOME GUY-- ALL CRACKED OUT ON BATH SALTS--
CAME IN, ALL COVERED IN BLOOD.
IT'S OKAY, OFFICERS.
WE--I GOT HIM.
WHAT THE HELL HAPPENED, MS. ENDO?
JESUS.
HE CAME SWINGING AT MY GUY WITH THIS.
I GRABBED IT WHEN HE WASN'T LOOKING AND--AND CLOCKED HIM.
I GOT IT ALL ON SECURITY CAMERAS. I'M SURE.
I HAVE...YOU KNOW, I HAVE NO IDEA.
MY BROTHER IS IN THERE. HE'S VERY UPSET.
I'M SURE...
IS HE ALIVE?

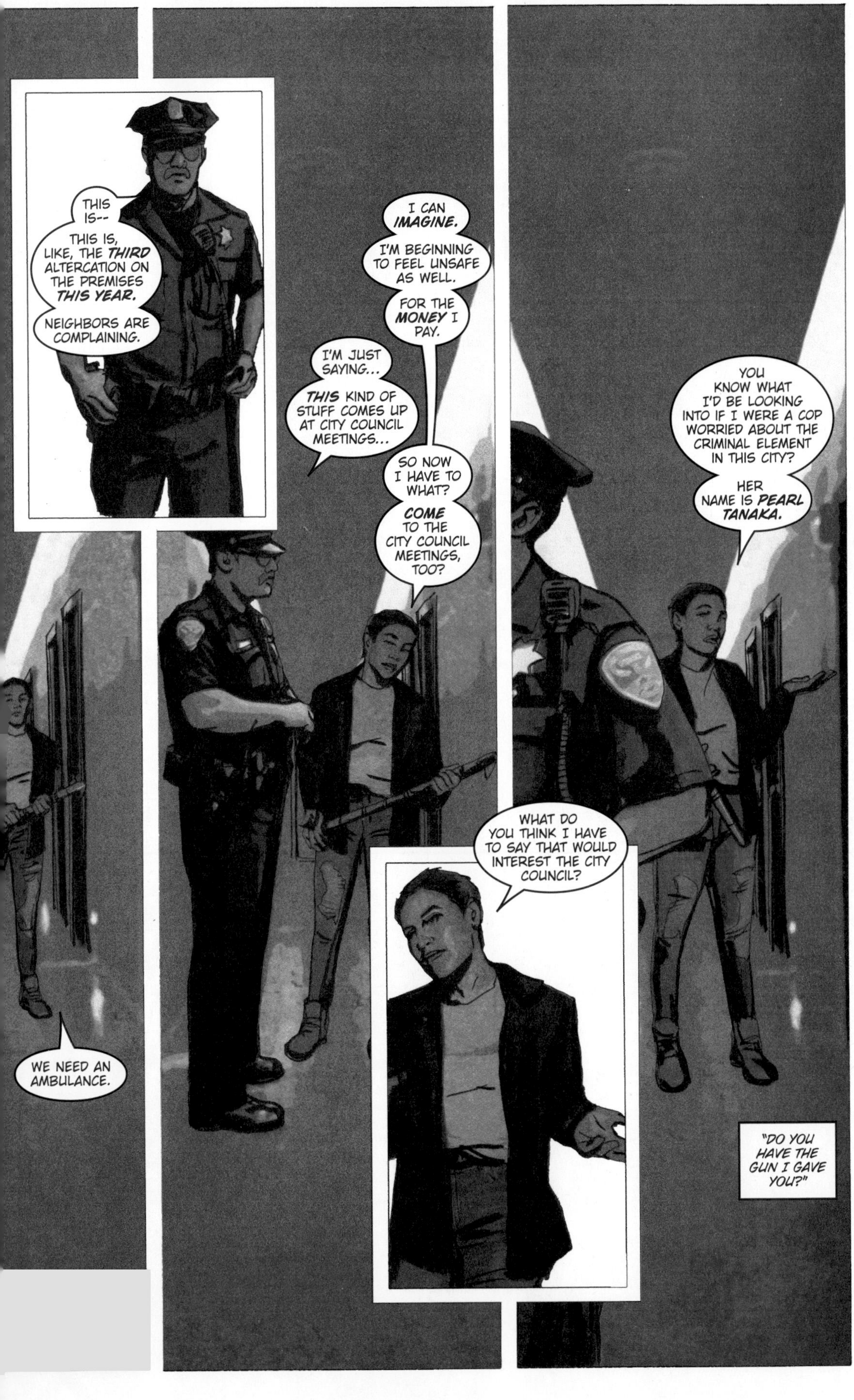
THIS IS--
THIS IS, LIKE, THE THIRD ALTERCATION ON THE PREMISES THIS YEAR.
NEIGHBORS ARE COMPLAINING.
WE NEED AN AMBULANCE.
I'M JUST SAYING...
THIS KIND OF STUFF COMES UP AT CITY COUNCIL MEETINGS...
I CAN IMAGINE.
I'M BEGINNING TO FEEL UNSAFE AS WELL.
FOR THE MONEY I PAY.
SO NOW I HAVE TO WHAT?
COME TO THE CITY COUNCIL MEETINGS, TOO?
WHAT DO YOU THINK I HAVE TO SAY THAT WOULD INTEREST THE CITY COUNCIL?
YOU KNOW WHAT I'D BE LOOKING INTO IF I WERE A COP WORRIED ABOUT THE CRIMINAL ELEMENT IN THIS CITY?
HER NAME IS PEARL TANAKA.
"DO YOU HAVE THE GUN I GAVE YOU?"

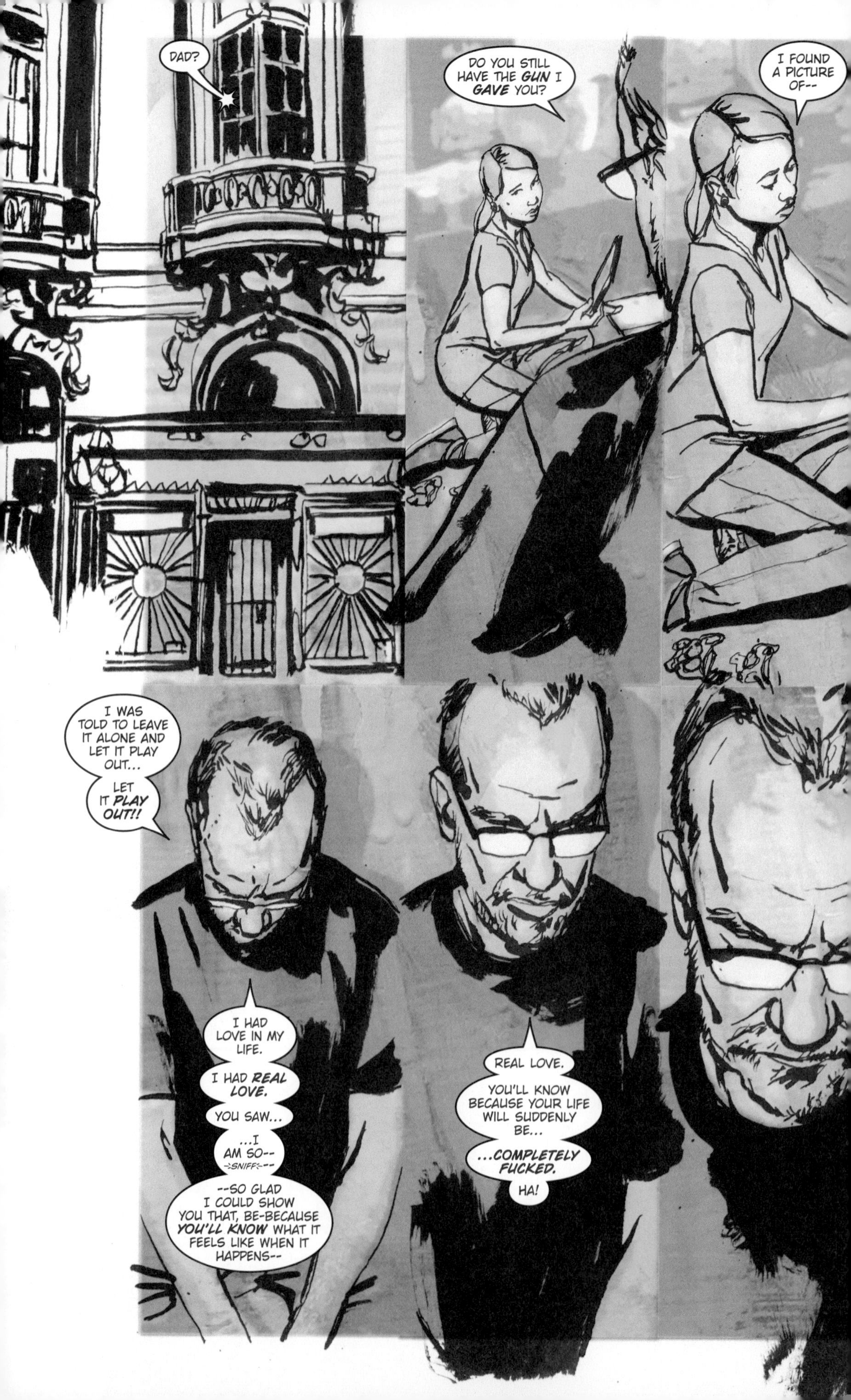
DAD?
DO YOU STILL HAVE THE GUN I GAVE YOU?
I FOUND A PICTURE OF--
I WAS TOLD TO LEAVE IT ALONE AND LET IT PLAY OUT...
LET IT PLAY OUT!!
I HAD LOVE IN MY LIFE.
I HAD REAL LOVE.
YOU SAW...
...I AM SO--
SNIFF
--SO GLAD I COULD SHOW YOU THAT, BE-BECAUSE YOU'LL KNOW WHAT IT FEELS LIKE WHEN IT HAPPENS--
REAL LOVE.
YOU'LL KNOW BECAUSE YOUR LIFE WILL SUDDENLY BE...
...COMPLETELY FUCKED.
HA!

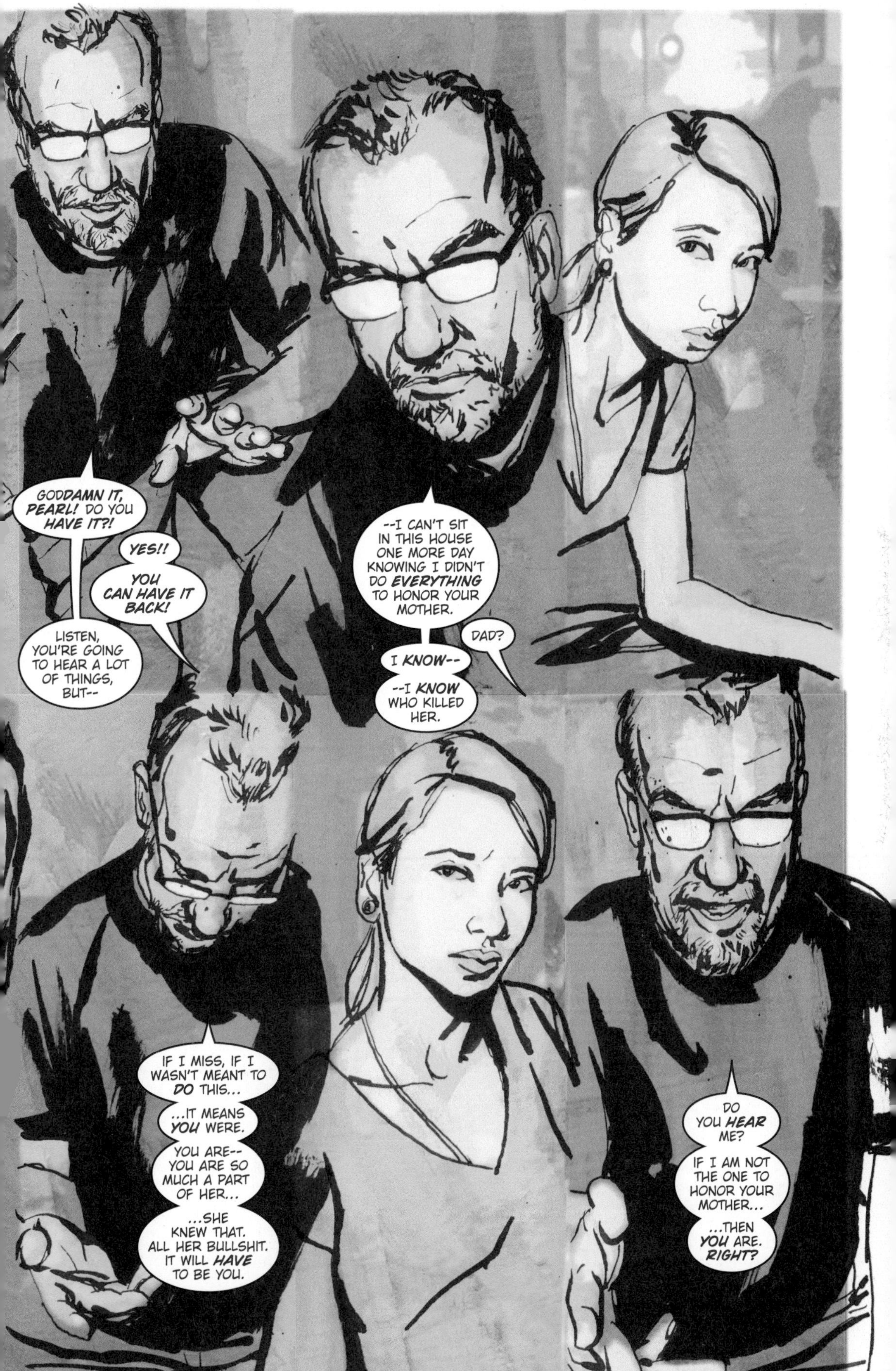
GODDAMN IT, PEARL! DO YOU HAVE IT?!
YES!! YOU CAN HAVE IT BACK!
LISTEN, YOU'RE GOING TO HEAR A LOT OF THINGS, BUT--
--I CAN'T SIT IN THIS HOUSE ONE MORE DAY KNOWING I DIDN'T DO EVERYTHING TO HONOR YOUR MOTHER.
DAD?
I KNOW--
--I KNOW WHO KILLED HER.
IF I MISS, IF I WASN'T MEANT TO DO THIS...
...IT MEANS YOU WERE.
YOU ARE-- YOU ARE SO MUCH A PART OF HER...
...SHE KNEW THAT. ALL HER BULLSHIT. IT WILL HAVE TO BE YOU.
DO YOU HEAR ME?
IF I AM NOT THE ONE TO HONOR YOUR MOTHER...
...THEN YOU ARE. RIGHT?

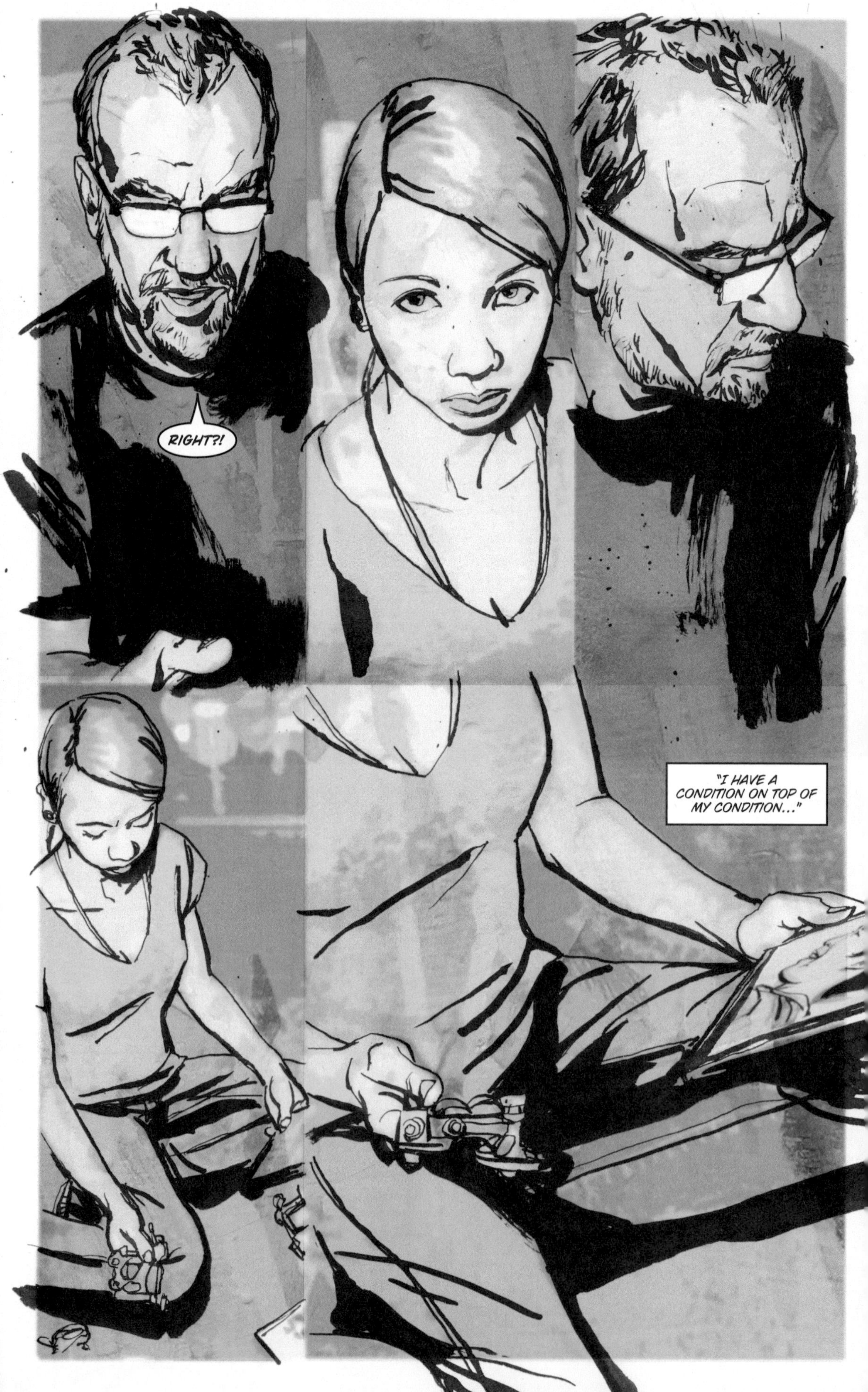
RIGHT?!
"I HAVE A CONDITION ON TOP OF MY CONDITION..."

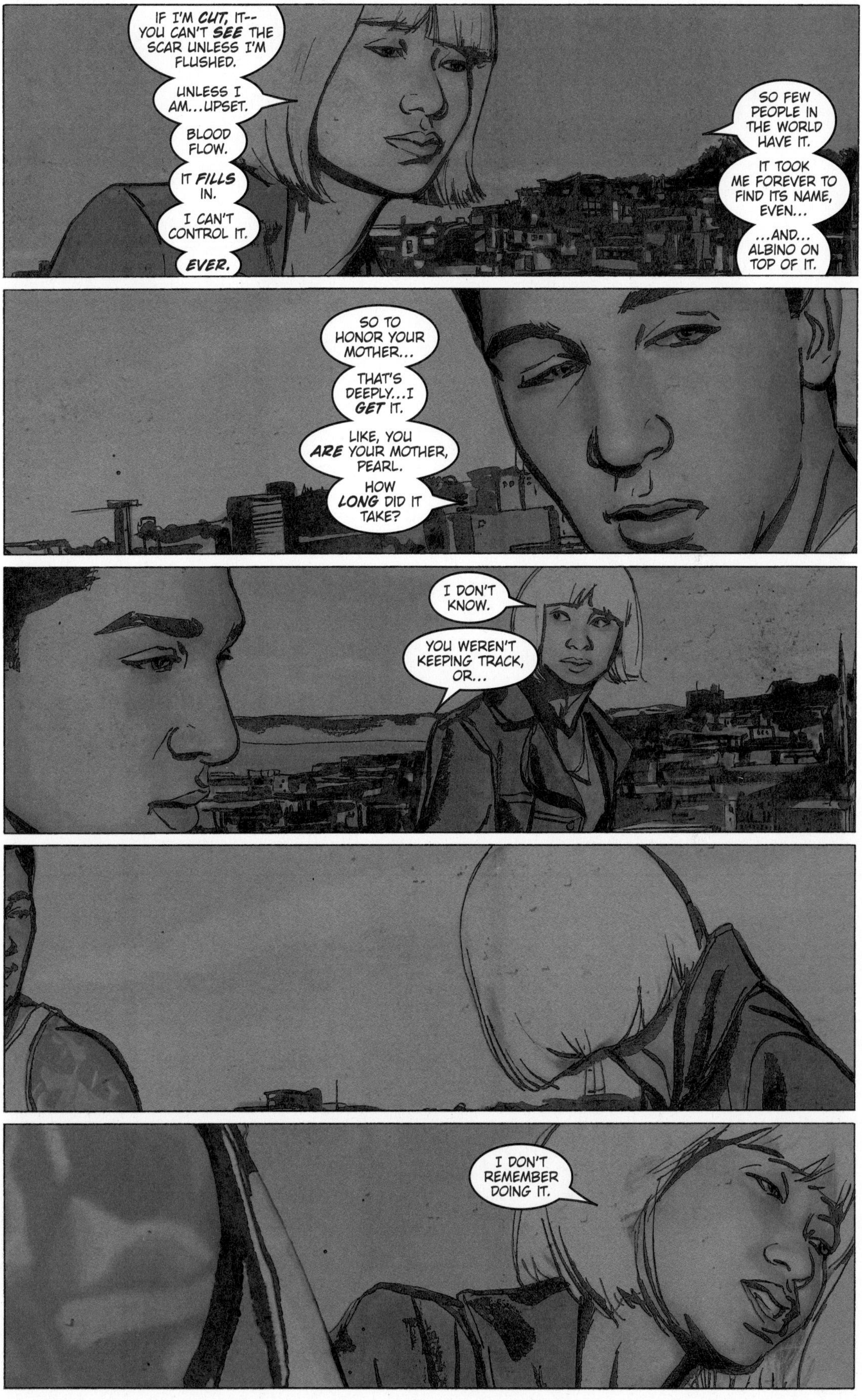
IF I'M CUT, IT-- YOU CAN'T SEE THE SCAR UNLESS I'M FLUSHED.
UNLESS I AM...UPSET.
BLOOD FLOW.
IT FILLS IN.
I CAN'T CONTROL IT.
EVER.
SO FEW PEOPLE IN THE WORLD HAVE IT.
IT TOOK ME FOREVER TO FIND ITS NAME, EVEN...
...AND... ALBINO ON TOP OF IT.
SO TO HONOR YOUR MOTHER...
THAT'S DEEPLY...I GET IT.
LIKE, YOU ARE YOUR MOTHER, PEARL.
HOW LONG DID IT TAKE?
I DON'T KNOW.
YOU WEREN'T KEEPING TRACK, OR...
I DON'T REMEMBER DOING IT.

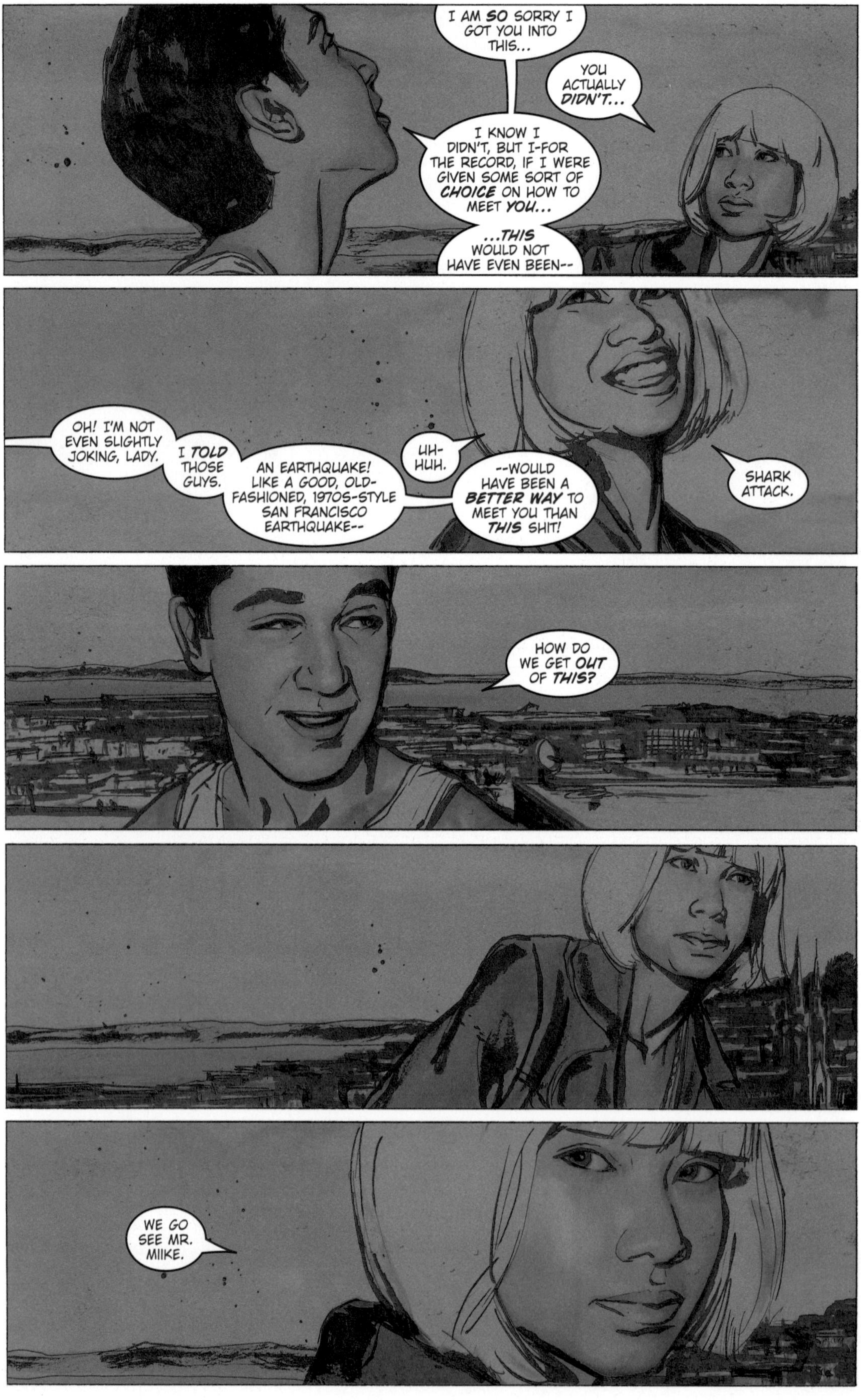
I AM SO SORRY I GOT YOU INTO THIS...
YOU ACTUALLY DIDN'T...
I KNOW I DIDN'T, BUT I-FOR THE RECORD, IF I WERE GIVEN SOME SORT OF CHOICE ON HOW TO MEET YOU...
...THIS WOULD NOT HAVE EVEN BEEN--
SHARK ATTACK.
UH-HUH.
OH! I'M NOT EVEN SLIGHTLY JOKING, LADY.
I TOLD THOSE GUYS.
AN EARTHQUAKE! LIKE A GOOD, OLD-FASHIONED, 1970S-STYLE SAN FRANCISCO EARTHQUAKE--
--WOULD HAVE BEEN A BETTER WAY TO MEET YOU THAN THIS SHIT!
HOW DO WE GET OUT OF THIS?
WE GO SEE MR. MIIKE.

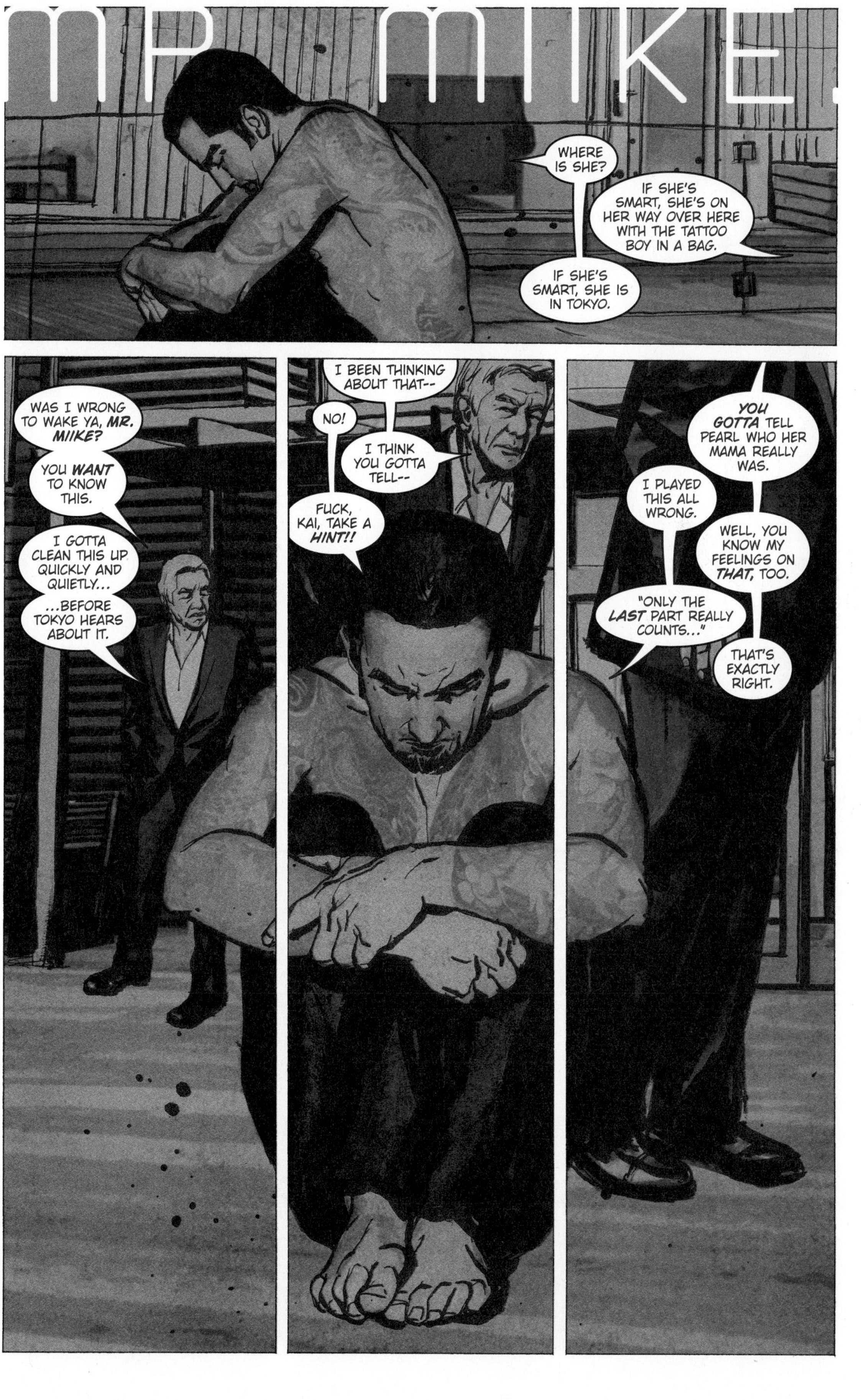
MR. MIIKE.
WHERE IS SHE?
IF SHE'S SMART, SHE'S ON HER WAY OVER HERE WITH THE TATTOO BOY IN A BAG.
IF SHE'S SMART, SHE IS IN TOKYO.
WAS I WRONG TO WAKE YA, **MR. MIIKE?**
YOU **WANT** TO KNOW THIS.
I GOTTA CLEAN THIS UP QUICKLY AND QUIETLY...
...BEFORE TOKYO HEARS ABOUT IT.
I BEEN THINKING ABOUT THAT--
NO!
I THINK YOU GOTTA TELL--
FUCK, KAI, TAKE A **HINT!!**
YOU GOTTA TELL PEARL WHO HER MAMA REALLY WAS.
I PLAYED THIS ALL WRONG.
WELL, YOU KNOW MY FEELINGS ON **THAT,** TOO.
"ONLY THE **LAST** PART REALLY COUNTS..."
THAT'S EXACTLY RIGHT.

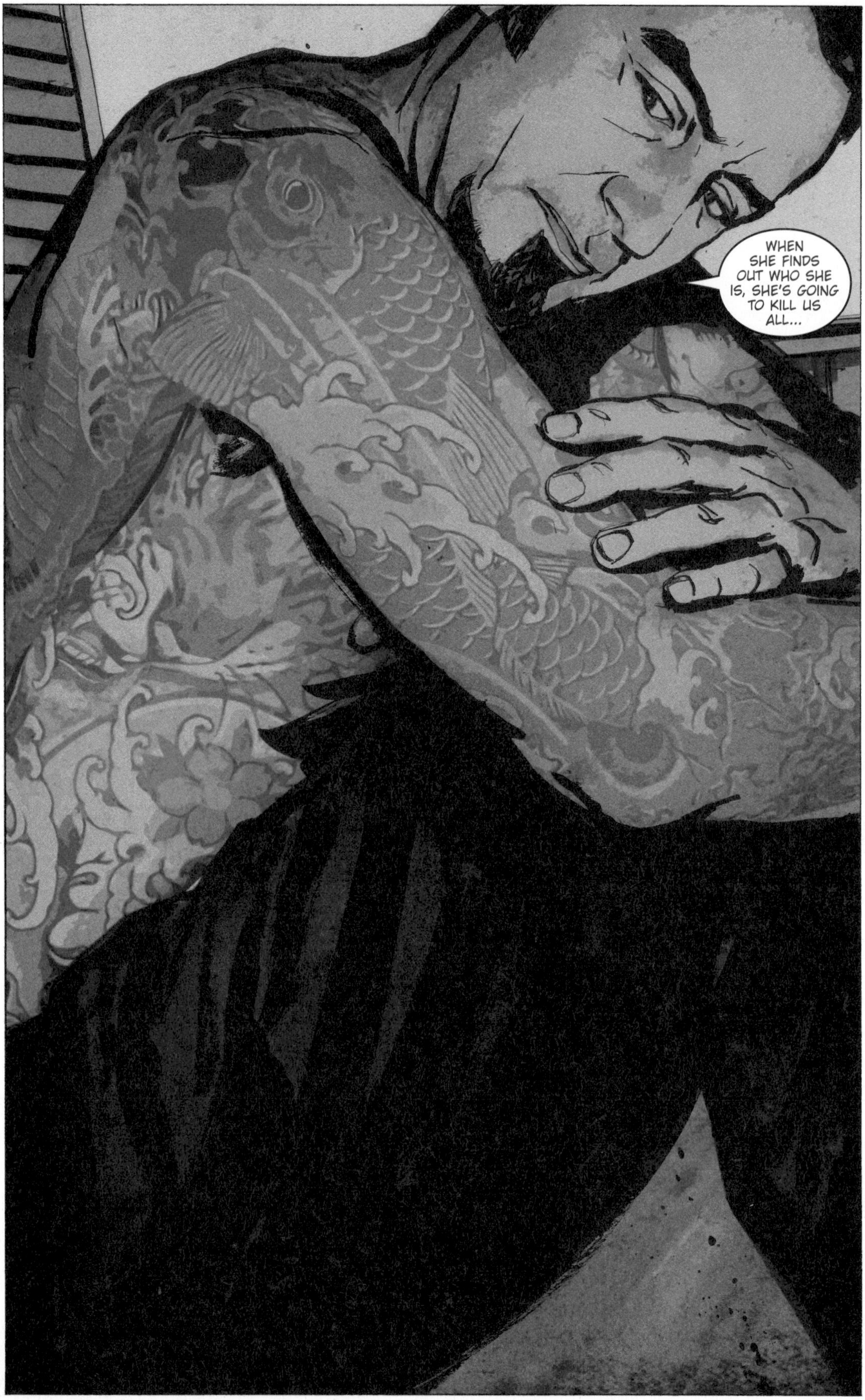
WHEN SHE FINDS OUT WHO SHE IS, SHE'S GOING TO KILL US ALL...

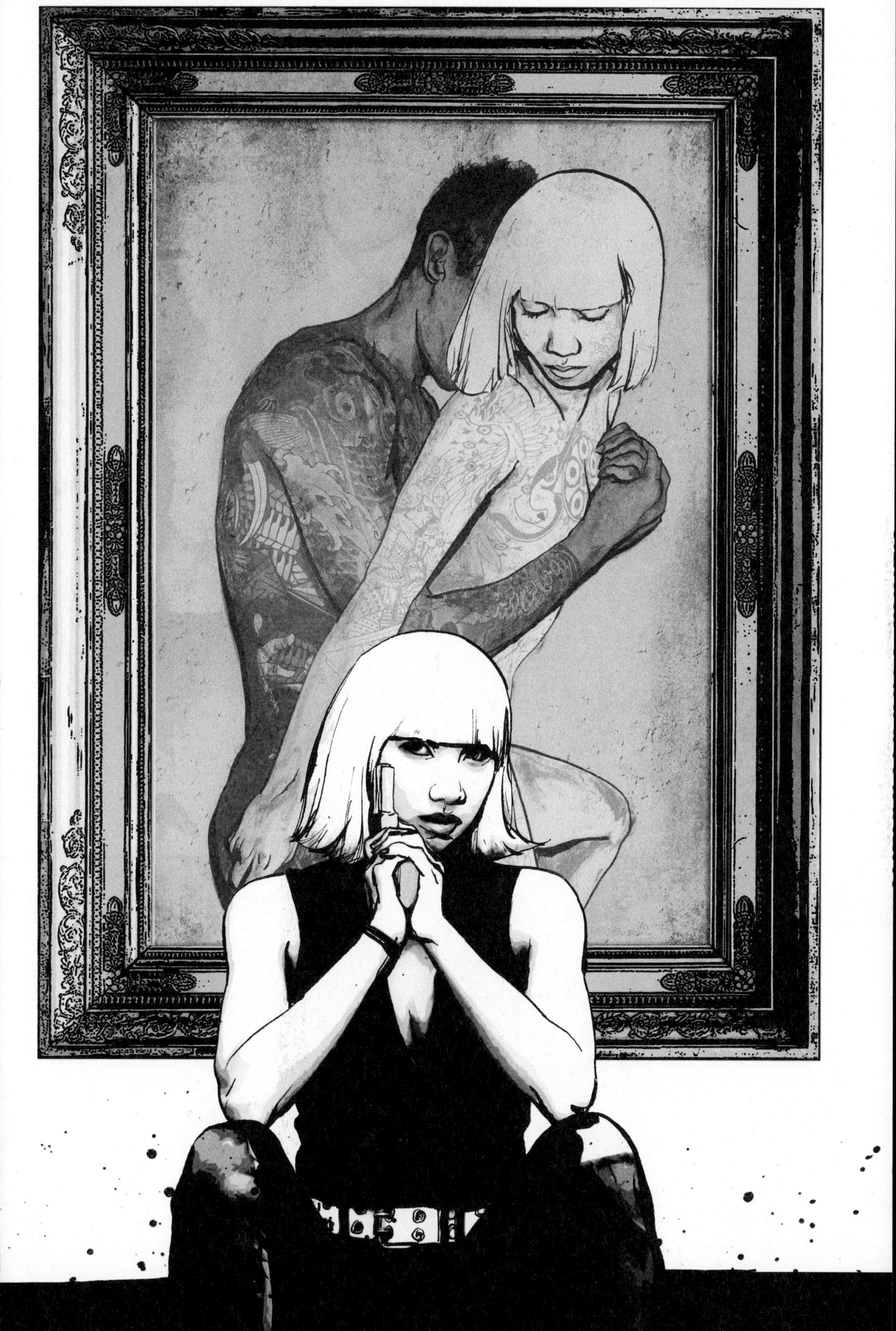

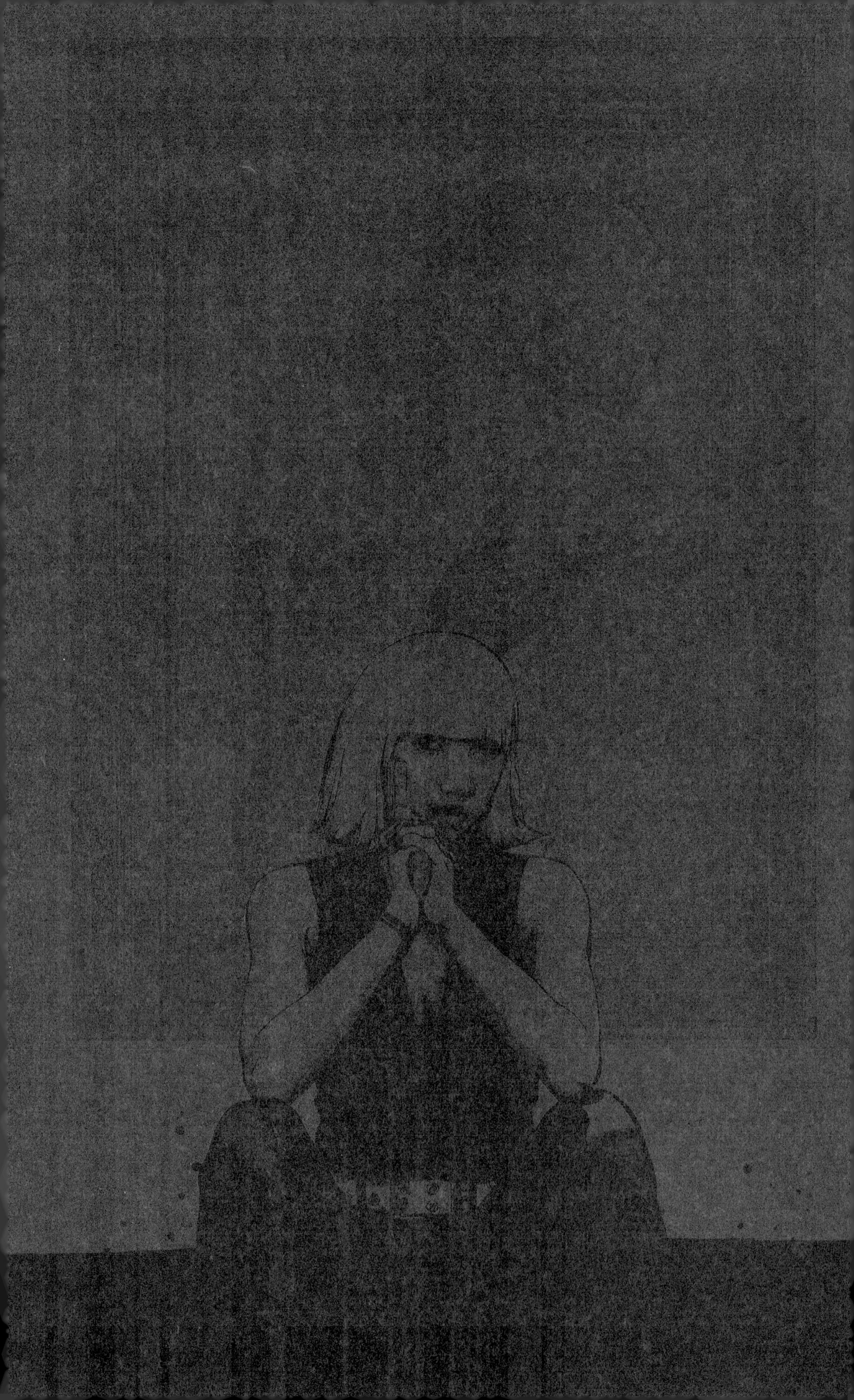

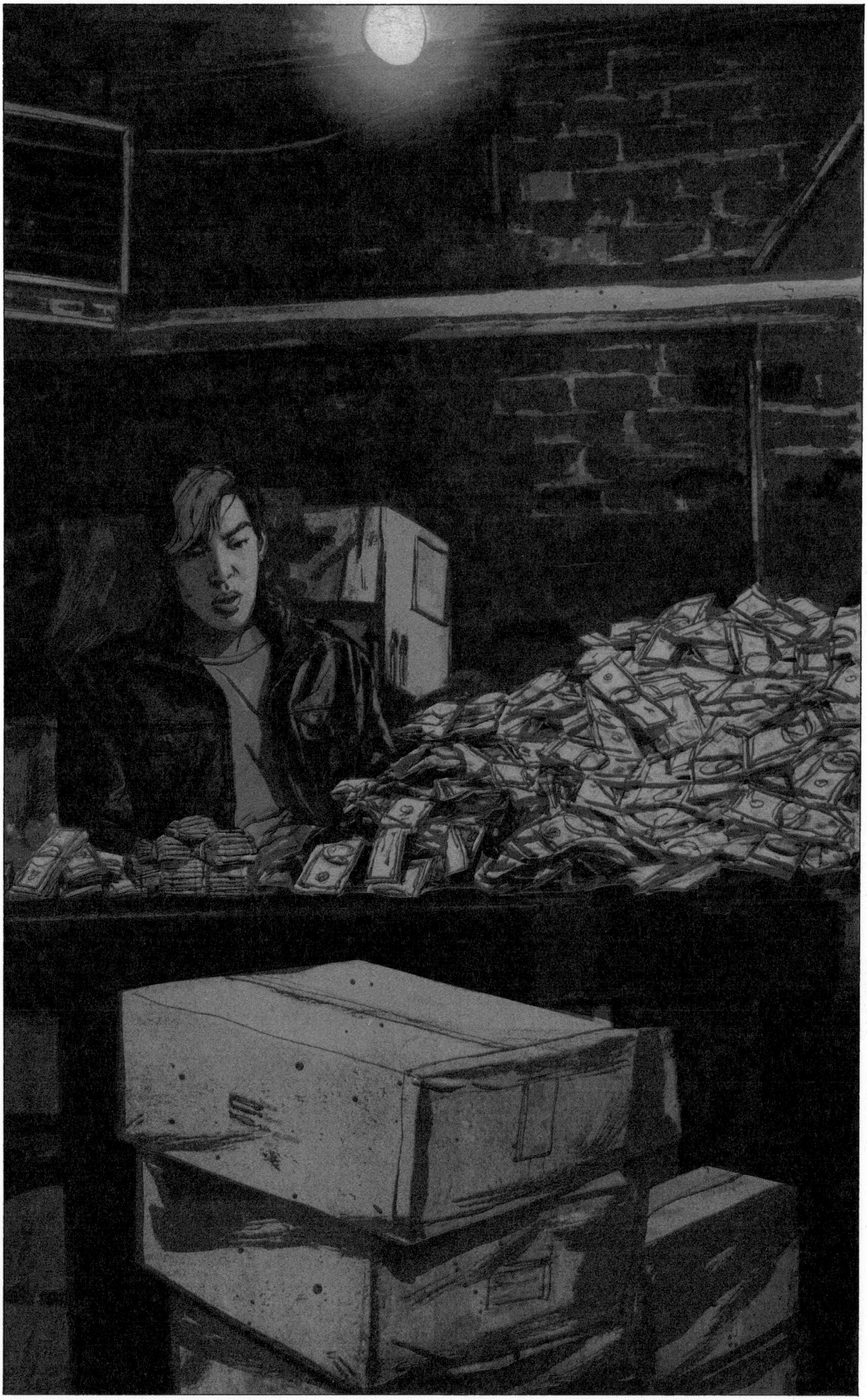

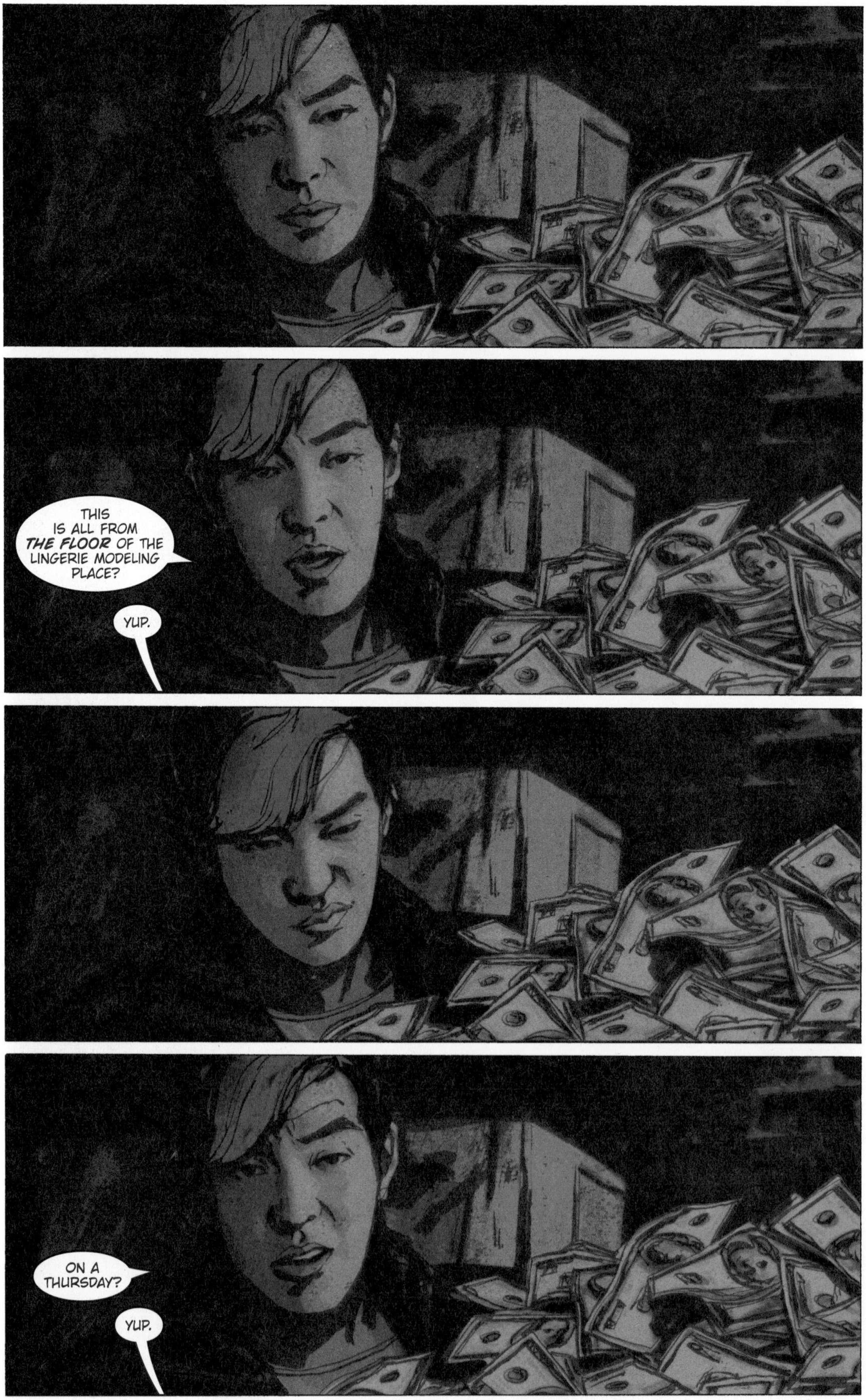
THIS IS ALL FROM ***THE FLOOR*** OF THE LINGERIE MODELING PLACE?
YUP.
ON A THURSDAY?
YUP.

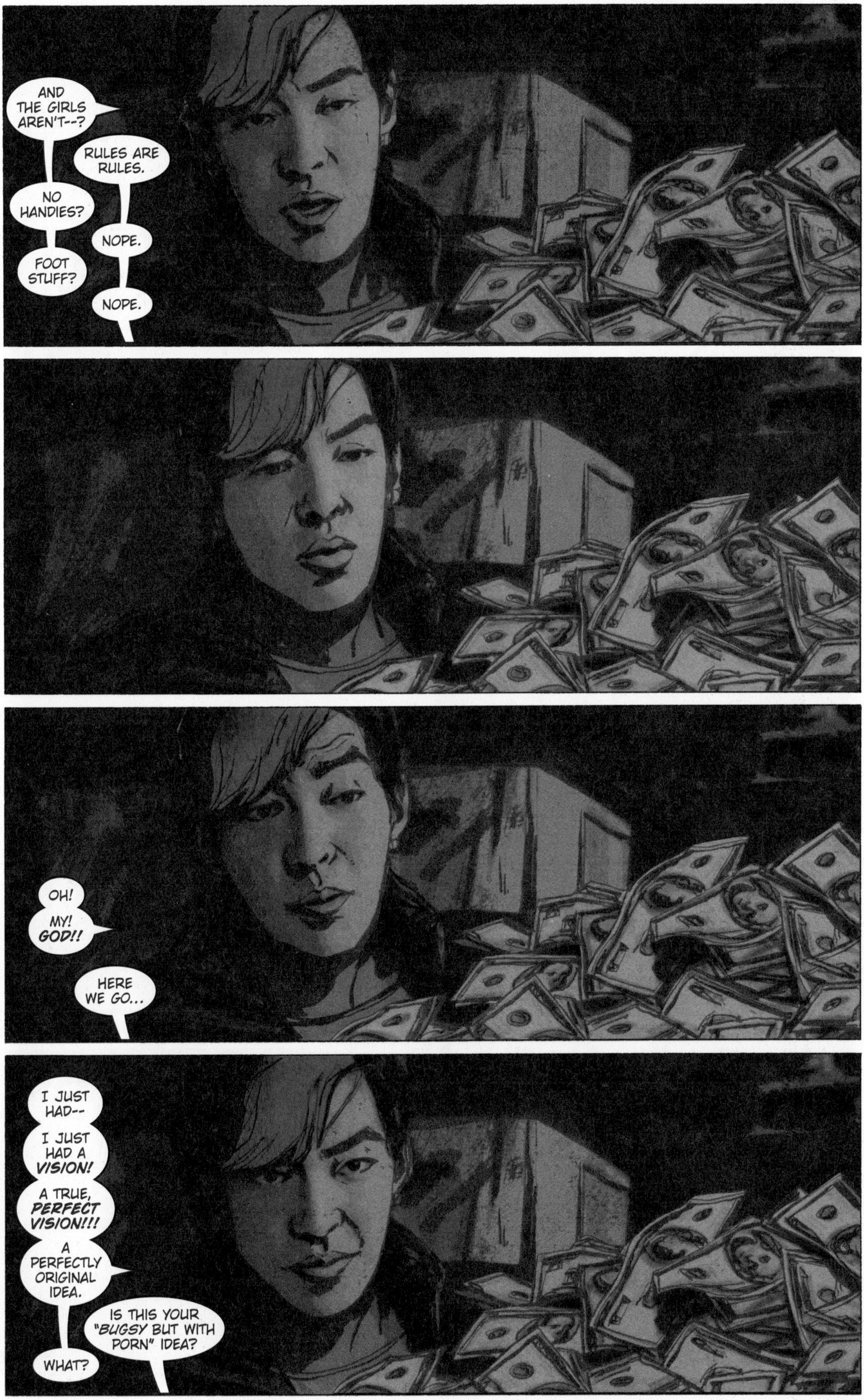
AND THE GIRLS AREN'T--?
RULES ARE RULES.
NO HANDIES?
NOPE.
FOOT STUFF?
NOPE.
OH!
MY!
GOD!!
HERE WE GO...
I JUST HAD--
I JUST HAD A VISION!
A TRUE, PERFECT VISION!!!
A PERFECTLY ORIGINAL IDEA.
IS THIS YOUR "BUGSY BUT WITH PORN" IDEA?
WHAT?

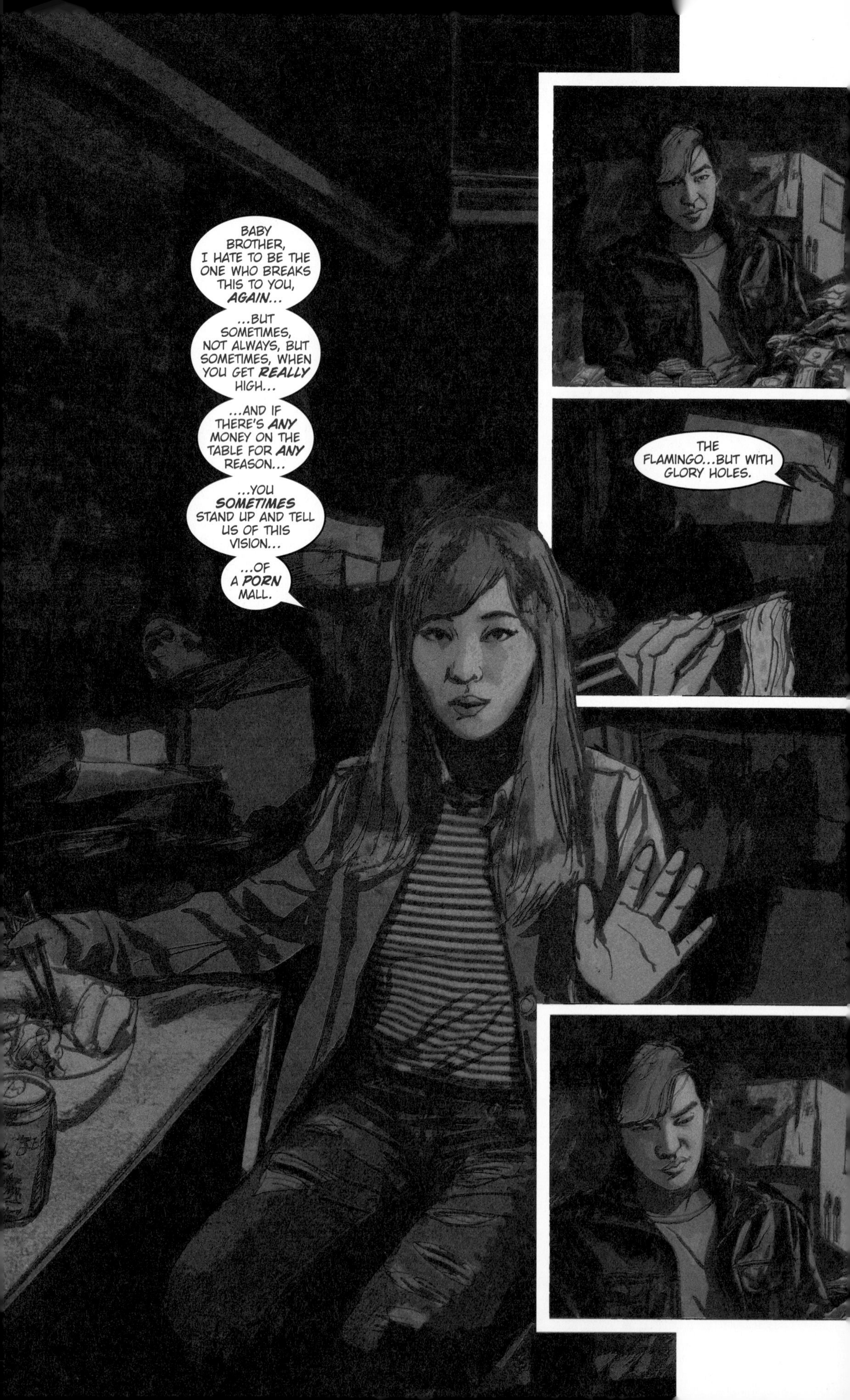

BABY BROTHER, I HATE TO BE THE ONE WHO BREAKS THIS TO YOU, AGAIN...
...BUT SOMETIMES, NOT ALWAYS, BUT SOMETIMES, WHEN YOU GET REALLY HIGH...
...AND IF THERE'S ANY MONEY ON THE TABLE FOR ANY REASON...
...YOU SOMETIMES STAND UP AND TELL US OF THIS VISION...
...OF A PORN MALL.
THE FLAMINGO...BUT WITH GLORY HOLES.

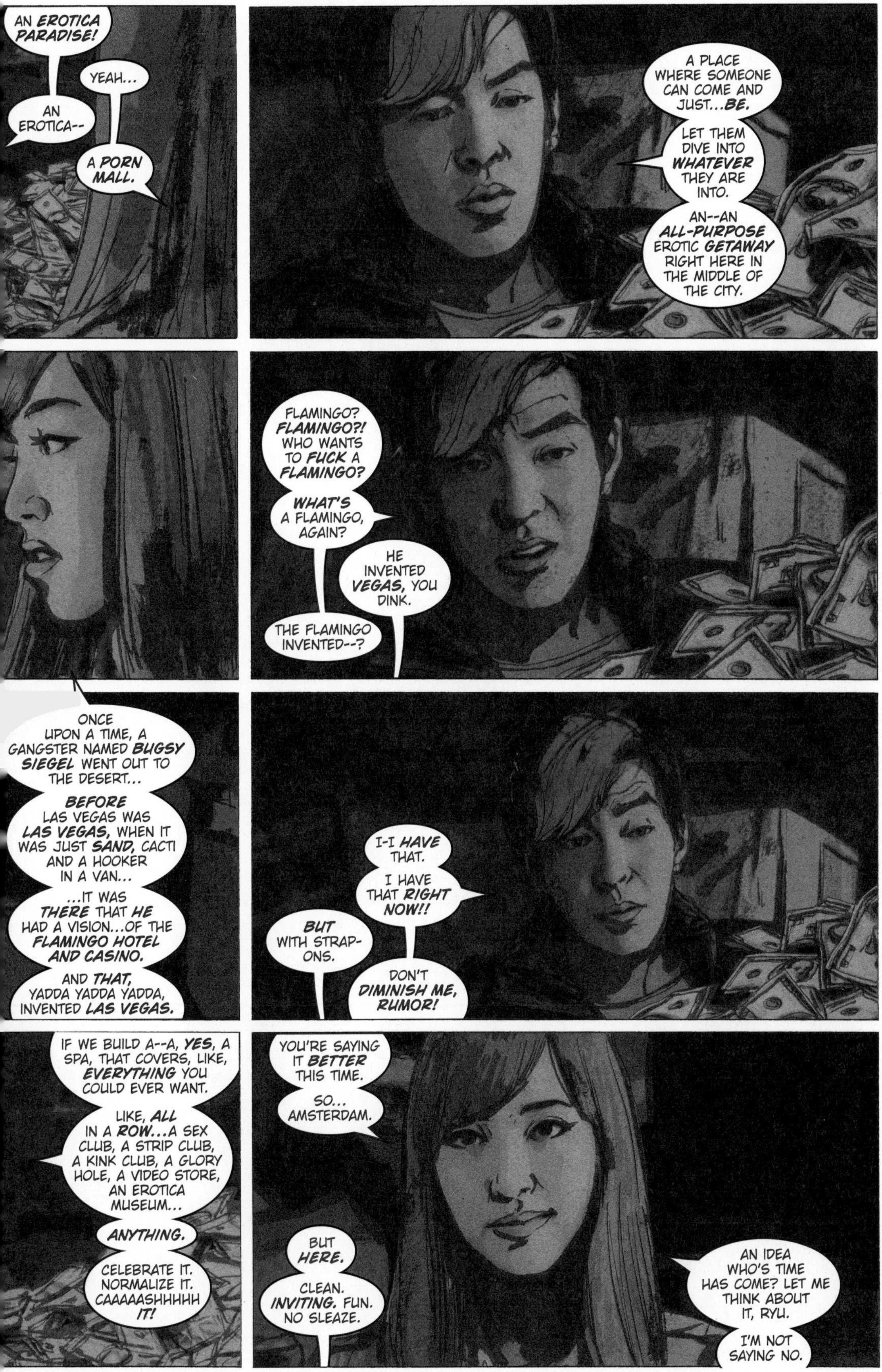

AN EROTICA PARADISE!
YEAH...
AN EROTICA--
A PORN MALL.
A PLACE WHERE SOMEONE CAN COME AND JUST...BE.
LET THEM DIVE INTO WHATEVER THEY ARE INTO.
AN--AN ALL-PURPOSE EROTIC GETAWAY RIGHT HERE IN THE MIDDLE OF THE CITY.
FLAMINGO? FLAMINGO?! WHO WANTS TO FUCK A FLAMINGO?
WHAT'S A FLAMINGO, AGAIN?
HE INVENTED VEGAS, YOU DINK.
THE FLAMINGO INVENTED--?
ONCE UPON A TIME, A GANGSTER NAMED BUGSY SIEGEL WENT OUT TO THE DESERT...
BEFORE LAS VEGAS WAS LAS VEGAS, WHEN IT WAS JUST SAND, CACTI AND A HOOKER IN A VAN...
...IT WAS THERE THAT HE HAD A VISION...OF THE FLAMINGO HOTEL AND CASINO.
AND THAT, YADDA YADDA YADDA, INVENTED LAS VEGAS.
I-I HAVE THAT.
I HAVE THAT RIGHT NOW!!
BUT WITH STRAP-ONS.
DON'T DIMINISH ME, RUMOR!
IF WE BUILD A--A, YES, A SPA, THAT COVERS, LIKE, EVERYTHING YOU COULD EVER WANT.
LIKE, ALL IN A ROW...A SEX CLUB, A STRIP CLUB, A KINK CLUB, A GLORY HOLE, A VIDEO STORE, AN EROTICA MUSEUM...
ANYTHING.
CELEBRATE IT. NORMALIZE IT. CAAAAASHHHHH IT!
YOU'RE SAYING IT BETTER THIS TIME.
SO... AMSTERDAM.
BUT HERE.
CLEAN. INVITING. FUN. NO SLEAZE.
AN IDEA WHO'S TIME HAS COME? LET ME THINK ABOUT IT, RYU.
I'M NOT SAYING NO.

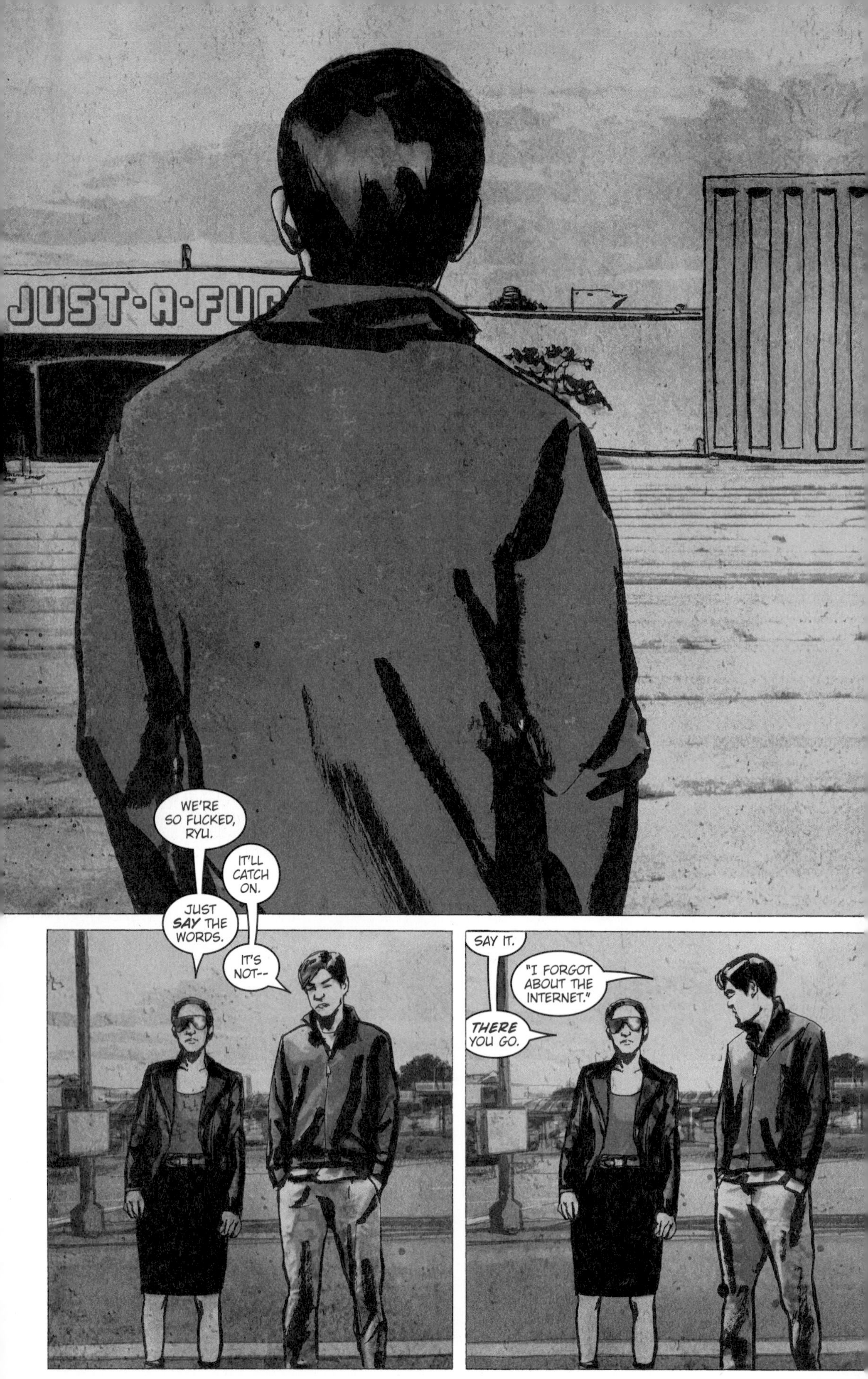
JUST-A-FUC
WE'RE SO FUCKED, RYU.
IT'LL CATCH ON.
JUST SAY THE WORDS.
IT'S NOT--
SAY IT.
"I FORGOT ABOUT THE INTERNET."
THERE YOU GO.

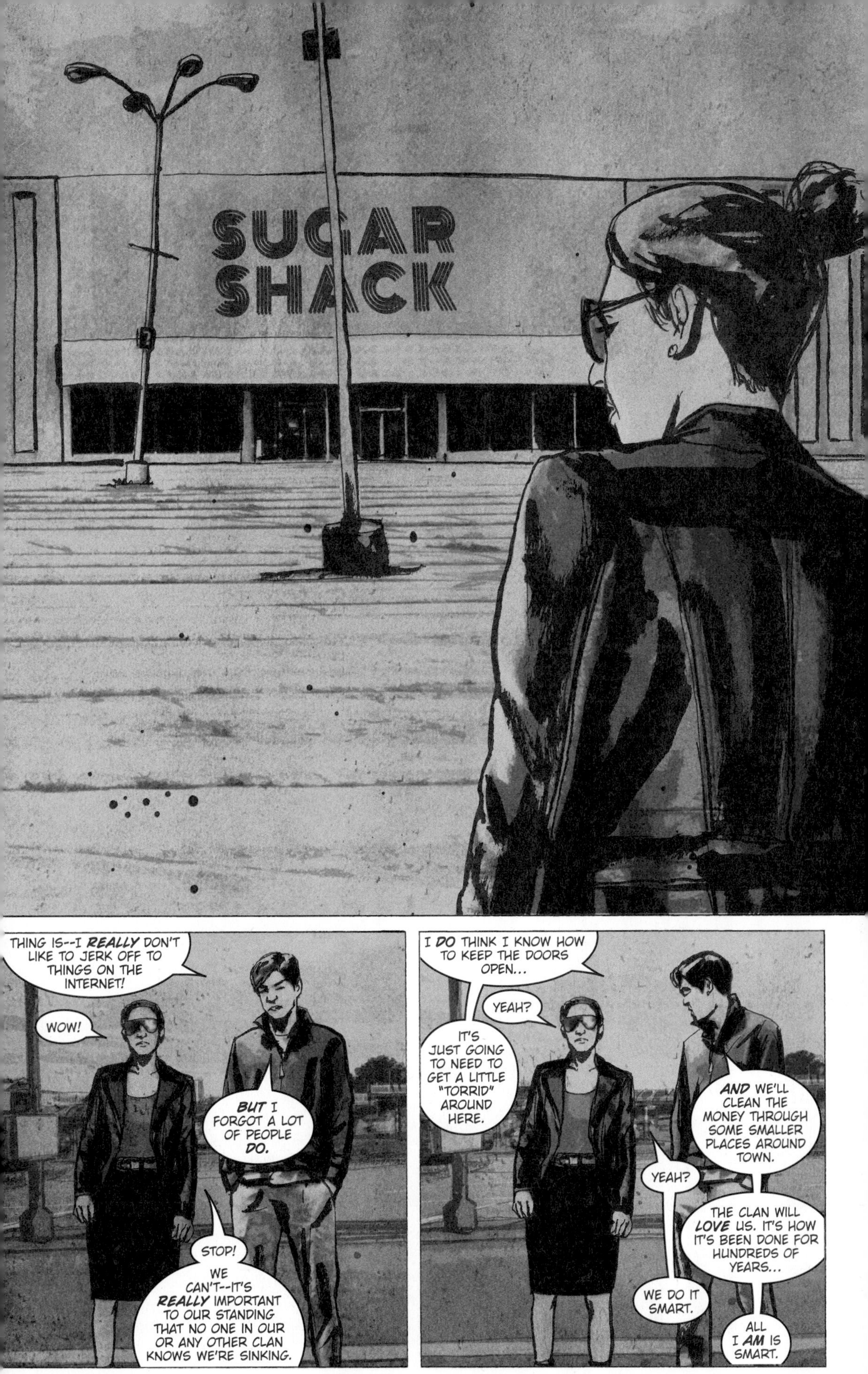
SUGAR SHACK
THING IS--I *REALLY* DON'T LIKE TO JERK OFF TO THINGS ON THE INTERNET!
WOW!
BUT I FORGOT A LOT OF PEOPLE *DO.*
STOP!
WE CAN'T--IT'S *REALLY* IMPORTANT TO OUR STANDING THAT NO ONE IN OUR OR ANY OTHER CLAN KNOWS WE'RE SINKING.
I *DO* THINK I KNOW HOW TO KEEP THE DOORS OPEN...
YEAH?
IT'S JUST GOING TO NEED TO GET A LITTLE "TORRID" AROUND HERE.
AND WE'LL CLEAN THE MONEY THROUGH SOME SMALLER PLACES AROUND TOWN.
YEAH?
THE CLAN WILL *LOVE* US. IT'S HOW IT'S BEEN DONE FOR HUNDREDS OF YEARS...
WE DO IT SMART.
ALL I *AM* IS SMART.

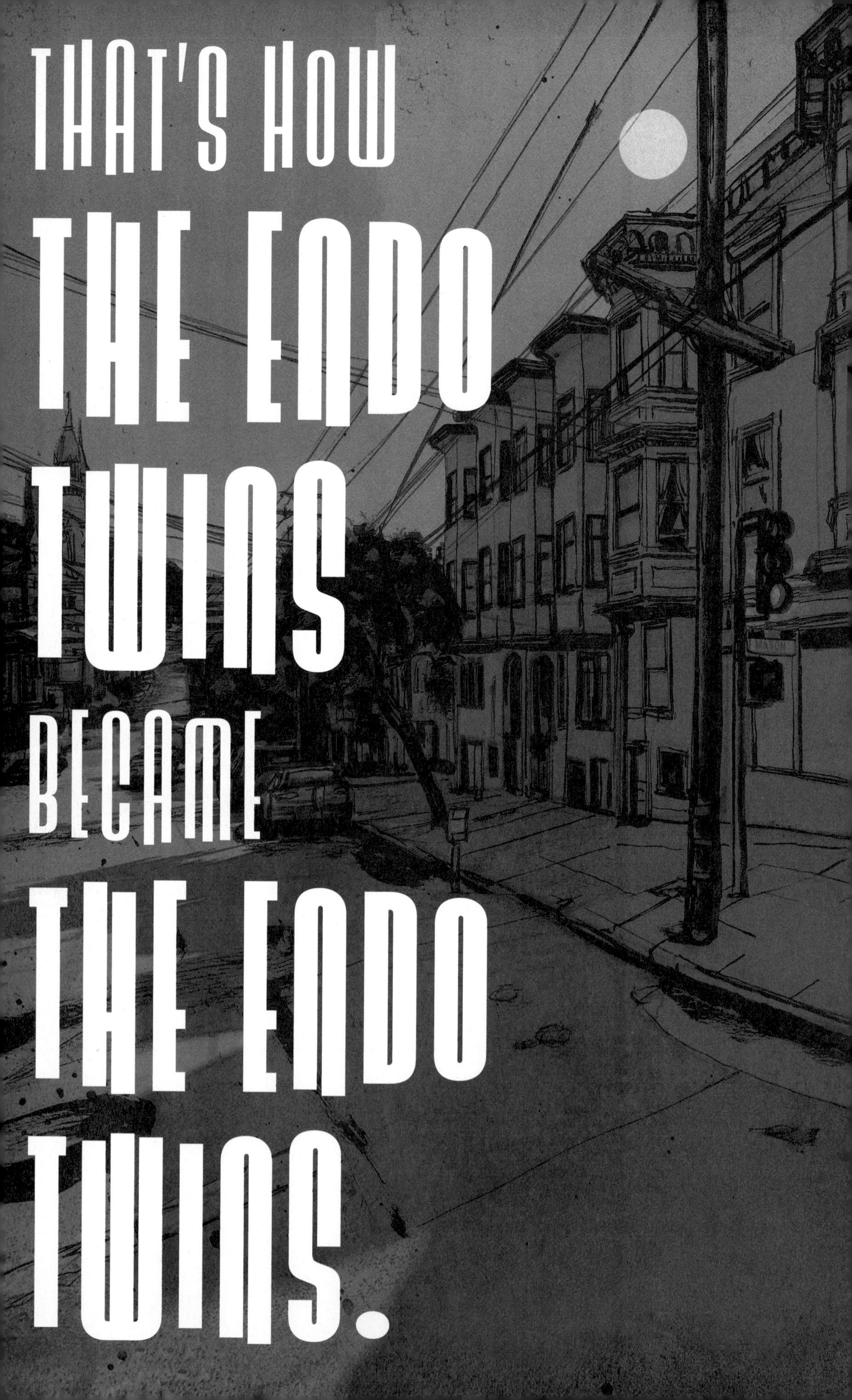
THAT'S HOW THE ENDO TWINS BECAME THE ENDO TWINS.

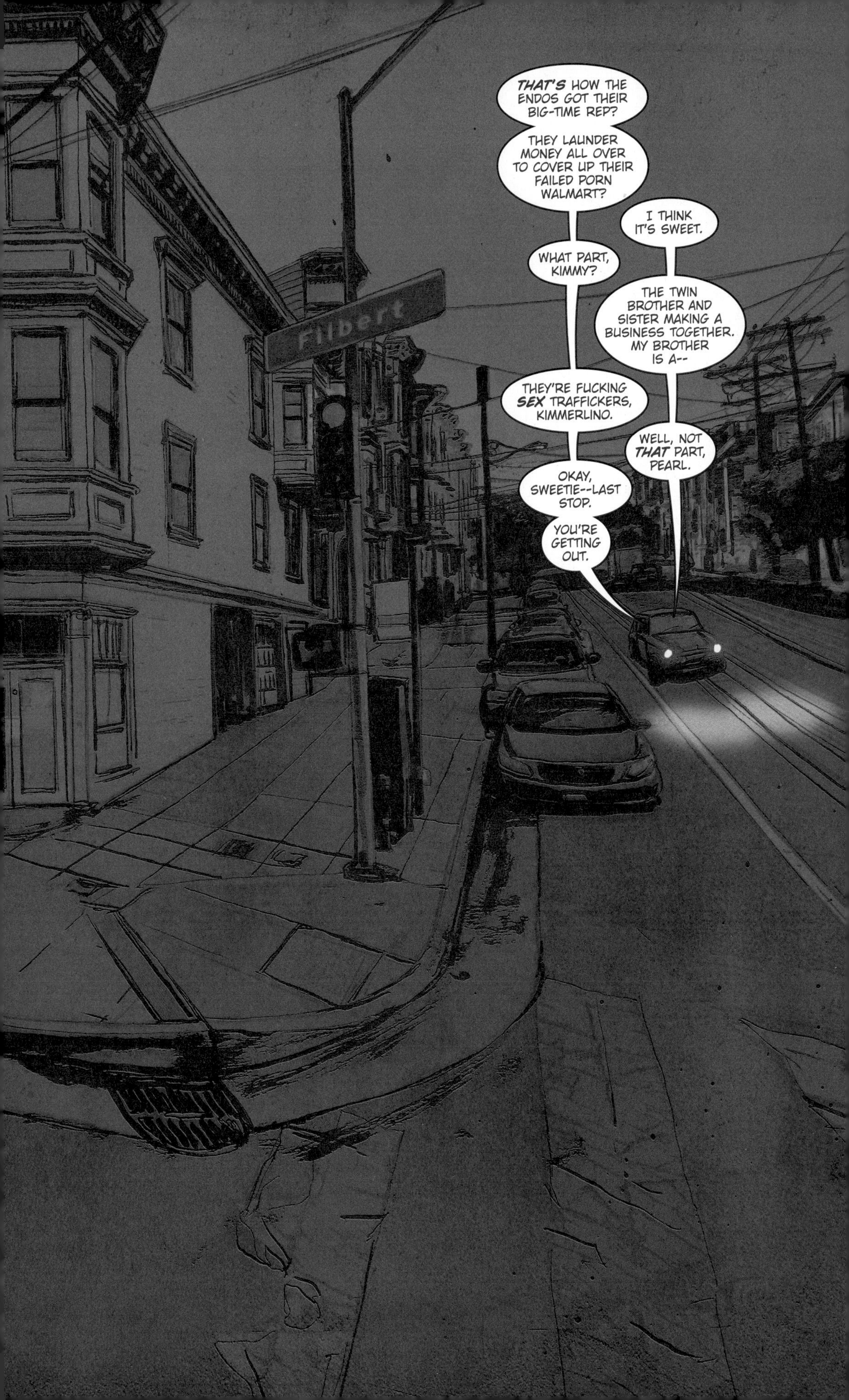
Filbert
THAT'S HOW THE ENDOS GOT THEIR BIG-TIME REP?
THEY LAUNDER MONEY ALL OVER TO COVER UP THEIR FAILED PORN WALMART?
I THINK IT'S SWEET.
WHAT PART, KIMMY?
THE TWIN BROTHER AND SISTER MAKING A BUSINESS TOGETHER. MY BROTHER IS A--
THEY'RE FUCKING SEX TRAFFICKERS, KIMMERLINO.
WELL, NOT THAT PART, PEARL.
OKAY, SWEETIE--LAST STOP.
YOU'RE GETTING OUT.

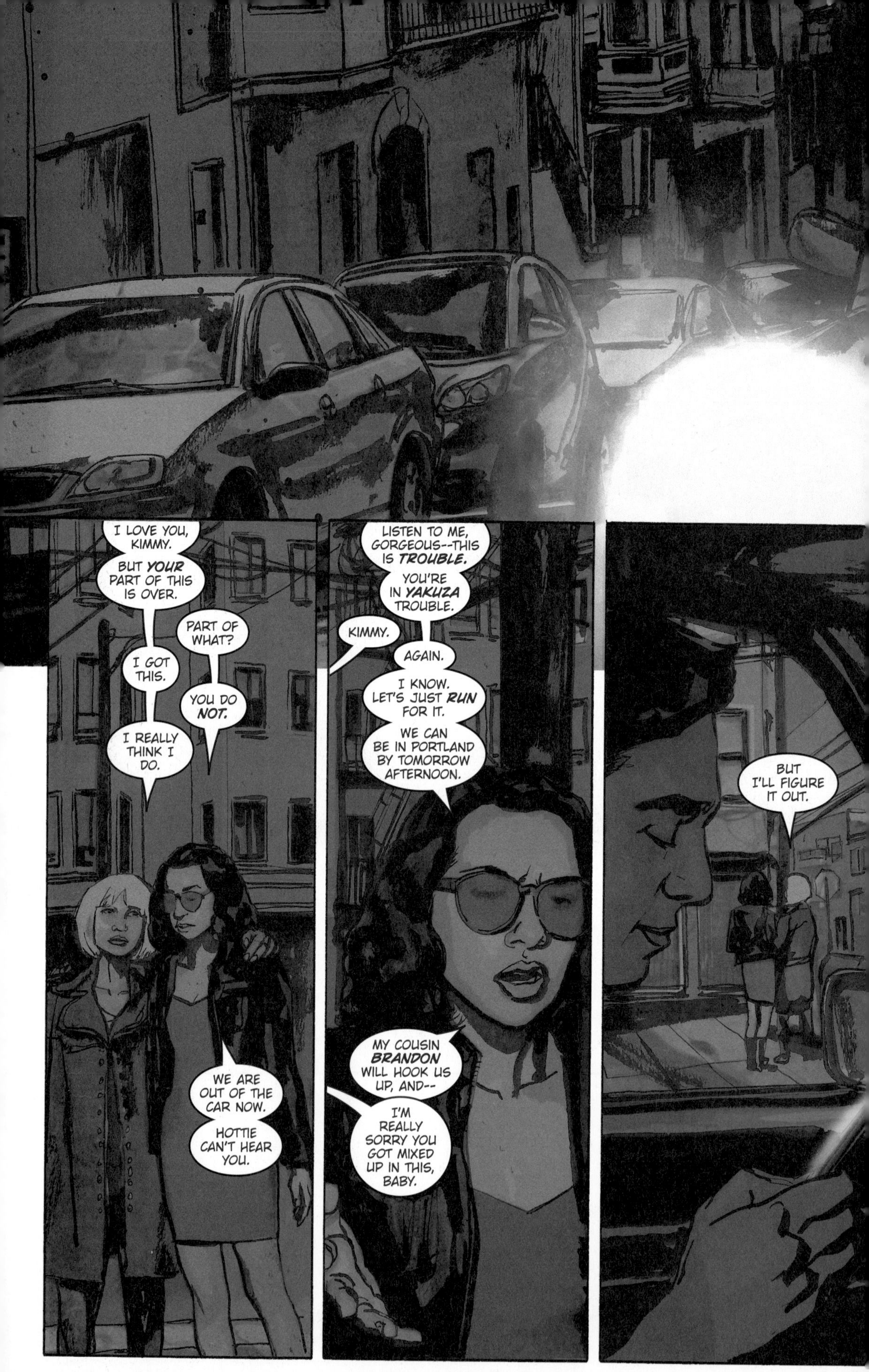
I LOVE YOU, KIMMY.
BUT YOUR PART OF THIS IS OVER.
PART OF WHAT?
I GOT THIS.
YOU DO NOT.
I REALLY THINK I DO.
WE ARE OUT OF THE CAR NOW.
HOTTIE CAN'T HEAR YOU.
LISTEN TO ME, GORGEOUS--THIS IS TROUBLE.
YOU'RE IN YAKUZA TROUBLE.
KIMMY.
AGAIN.
I KNOW. LET'S JUST RUN FOR IT.
WE CAN BE IN PORTLAND BY TOMORROW AFTERNOON.
MY COUSIN BRANDON WILL HOOK US UP, AND--
I'M REALLY SORRY YOU GOT MIXED UP IN THIS, BABY.
BUT I'LL FIGURE IT OUT.

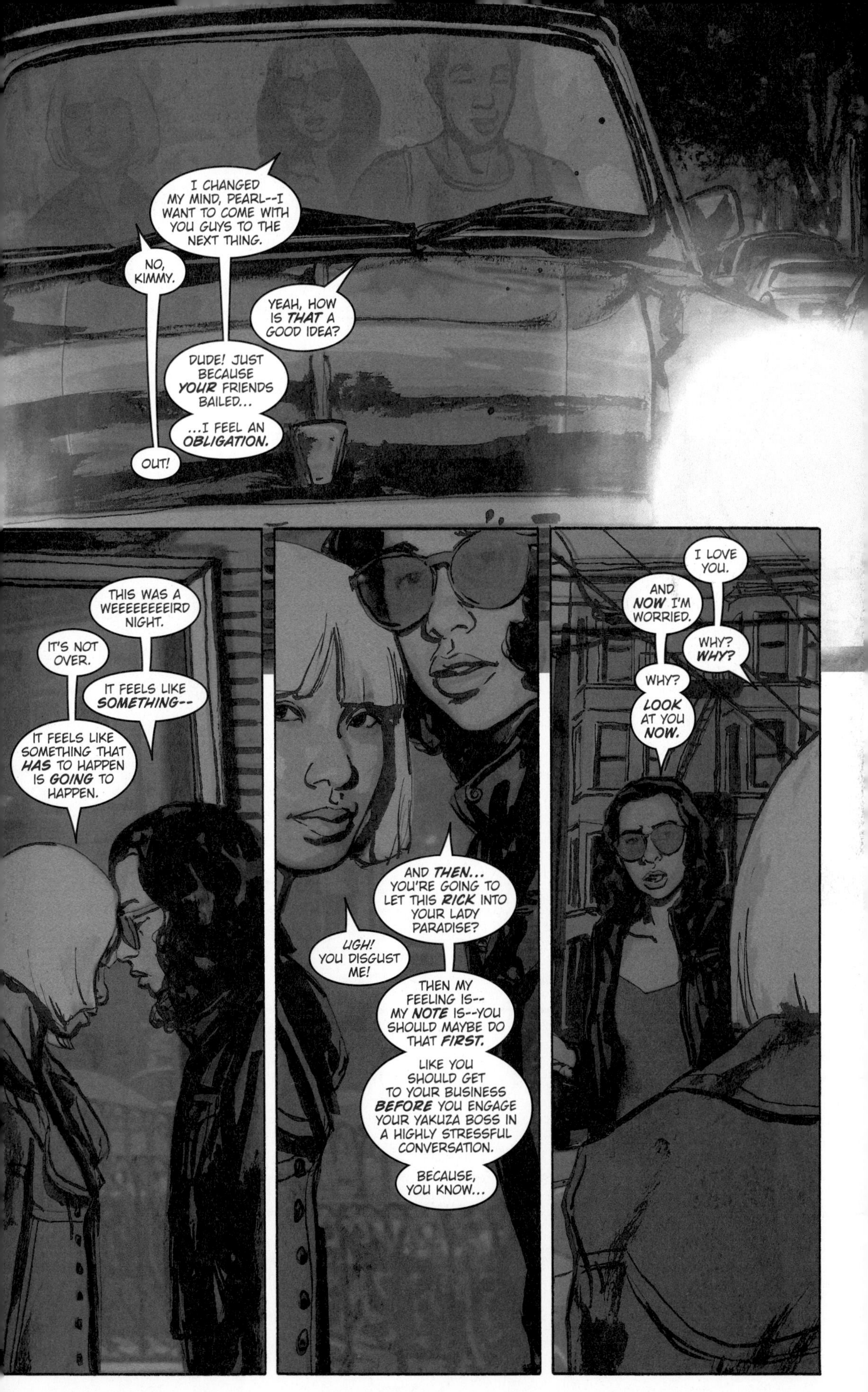
I CHANGED MY MIND, PEARL--I WANT TO COME WITH YOU GUYS TO THE NEXT THING.
NO, KIMMY.
YEAH, HOW IS THAT A GOOD IDEA?
DUDE! JUST BECAUSE YOUR FRIENDS BAILED...
...I FEEL AN OBLIGATION.
OUT!
THIS WAS A WEEEEEEEEIRD NIGHT.
IT'S NOT OVER.
IT FEELS LIKE SOMETHING--
IT FEELS LIKE SOMETHING THAT HAS TO HAPPEN IS GOING TO HAPPEN.
AND THEN... YOU'RE GOING TO LET THIS RICK INTO YOUR LADY PARADISE?
UGH! YOU DISGUST ME!
THEN MY FEELING IS--MY NOTE IS--YOU SHOULD MAYBE DO THAT FIRST.
LIKE YOU SHOULD GET TO YOUR BUSINESS BEFORE YOU ENGAGE YOUR YAKUZA BOSS IN A HIGHLY STRESSFUL CONVERSATION.
BECAUSE, YOU KNOW...
I LOVE YOU.
AND NOW I'M WORRIED.
WHY? WHY?
WHY? LOOK AT YOU NOW.

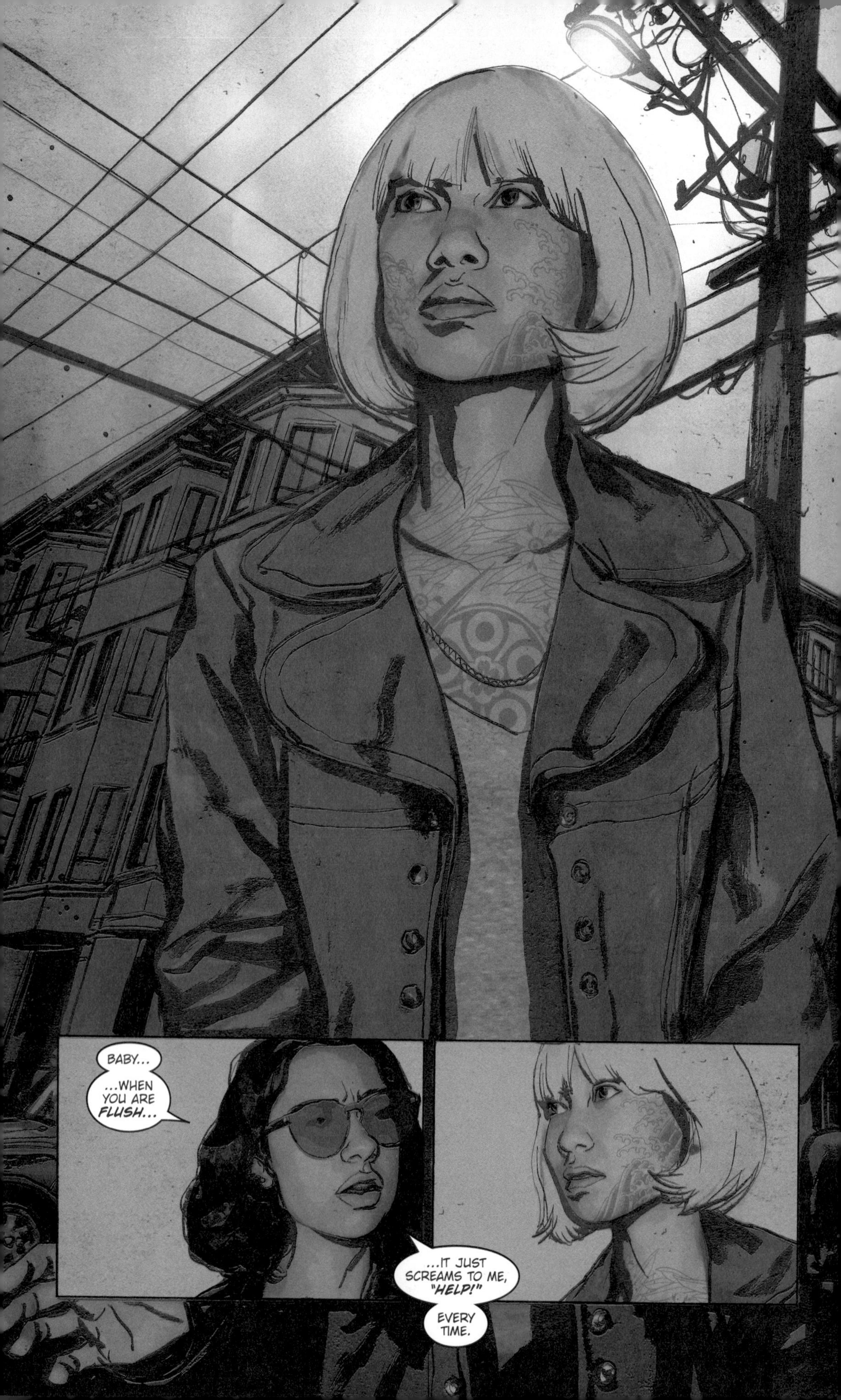
BABY...
...WHEN YOU ARE *FLUSH*...
...IT JUST SCREAMS TO ME, *"HELP!"*
EVERY TIME.

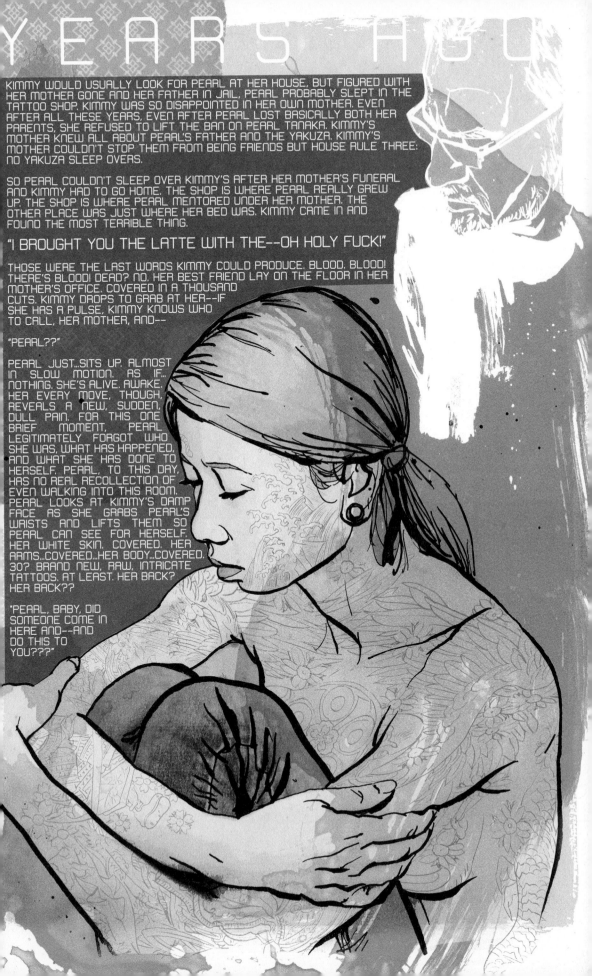

KIMMY WOULD USUALLY LOOK FOR PEARL AT HER HOUSE, BUT FIGURED WITH HER MOTHER GONE AND HER FATHER IN JAIL, PEARL PROBABLY SLEPT IN THE TATTOO SHOP. KIMMY WAS SO DISAPPOINTED IN HER OWN MOTHER. EVEN AFTER ALL THESE YEARS, EVEN AFTER PEARL LOST BASICALLY BOTH HER PARENTS, SHE REFUSED TO LIFT THE BAN ON PEARL TANAKA. KIMMY'S MOTHER KNEW ALL ABOUT PEARL'S FATHER AND THE YAKUZA. KIMMY'S MOTHER COULDN'T STOP THEM FROM BEING FRIENDS BUT HOUSE RULE THREE: NO YAKUZA SLEEP OVERS.

SO PEARL COULDN'T SLEEP OVER KIMMY'S AFTER HER MOTHER'S FUNERAL AND KIMMY HAD TO GO HOME. THE SHOP IS WHERE PEARL REALLY GREW UP. THE SHOP IS WHERE PEARL MENTORED UNDER HER MOTHER. THE OTHER PLACE WAS JUST WHERE HER BED WAS. KIMMY CAME IN AND FOUND THE MOST TERRIBLE THING.

"I BROUGHT YOU THE LATTE WITH THE--OH HOLY FUCK!"

THOSE WERE THE LAST WORDS KIMMY COULD PRODUCE. BLOOD. BLOOD! THERE'S BLOOD! DEAD? NO. HER BEST FRIEND LAY ON THE FLOOR IN HER MOTHER'S OFFICE. COVERED IN A THOUSAND CUTS. KIMMY DROPS TO GRAB AT HER--IF SHE HAS A PULSE, KIMMY KNOWS WHO TO CALL. HER MOTHER, AND--

"PEARL??"

PEARL JUST...SITS UP. ALMOST IN SLOW MOTION. AS IF... NOTHING. SHE'S ALIVE. AWAKE. HER EVERY MOVE, THOUGH, REVEALS A NEW, SUDDEN, DULL PAIN. FOR THIS ONE BRIEF MOMENT, PEARL LEGITIMATELY FORGOT WHO SHE WAS, WHAT HAS HAPPENED, AND WHAT SHE HAS DONE TO HERSELF. PEARL, TO THIS DAY, HAS NO REAL RECOLLECTION OF EVEN WALKING INTO THIS ROOM. PEARL LOOKS AT KIMMY'S DAMP FACE AS SHE GRABS PEARL'S WRISTS AND LIFTS THEM SO PEARL CAN SEE FOR HERSELF. HER WHITE SKIN. COVERED. HER ARMS...COVERED...HER BODY...COVERED. 30? BRAND NEW, RAW, INTRICATE TATTOOS. AT LEAST. HER BACK? HER BACK??

"PEARL, BABY, DID SOMEONE COME IN HERE AND--AND DO THIS TO YOU???"

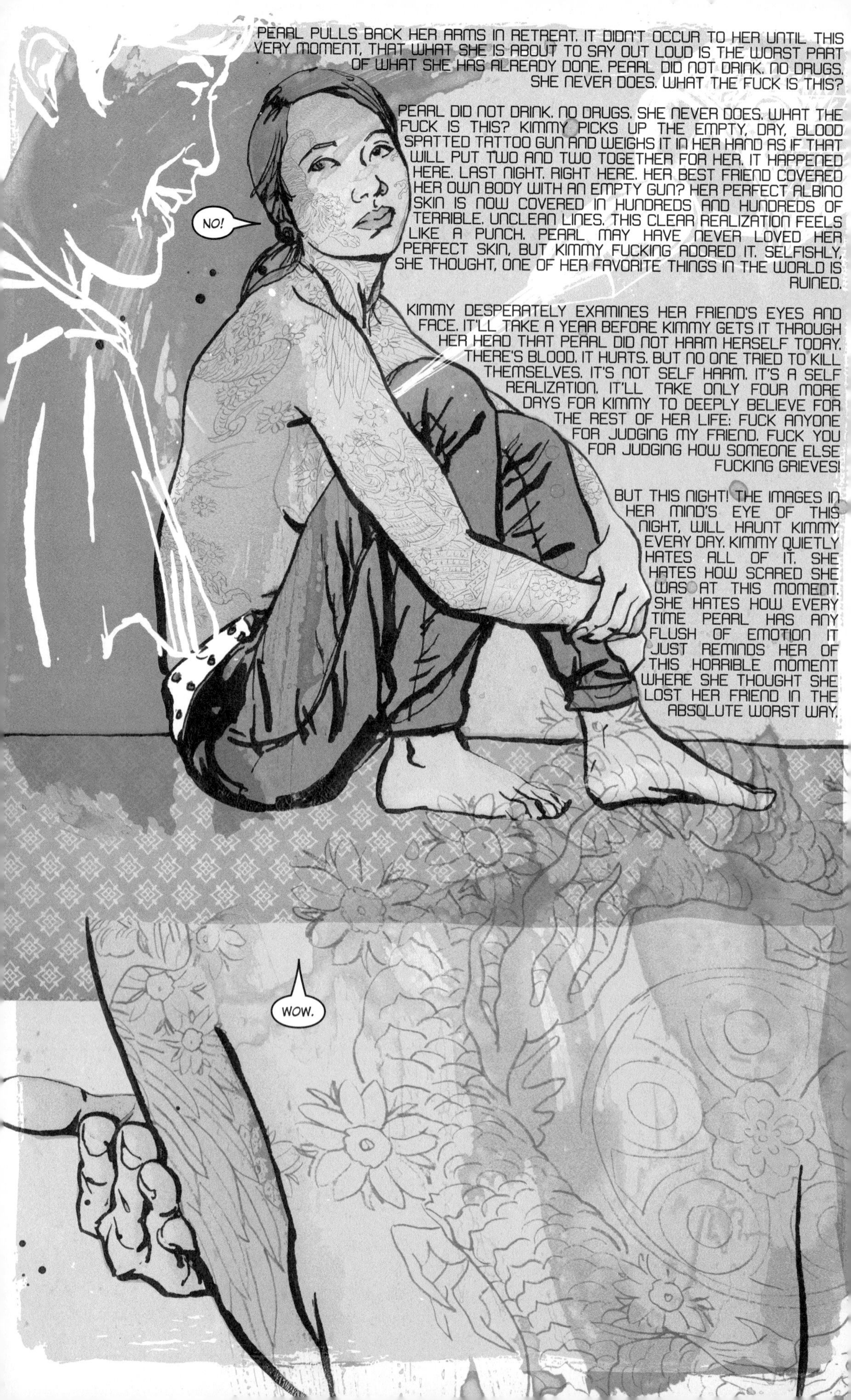
PEARL PULLS BACK HER ARMS IN RETREAT. IT DIDN'T OCCUR TO HER UNTIL THIS VERY MOMENT, THAT WHAT SHE IS ABOUT TO SAY OUT LOUD IS THE WORST PART OF WHAT SHE HAS ALREADY DONE. PEARL DID NOT DRINK. NO DRUGS. SHE NEVER DOES. WHAT THE FUCK IS THIS?
PEARL DID NOT DRINK. NO DRUGS. SHE NEVER DOES. WHAT THE FUCK IS THIS? KIMMY PICKS UP THE EMPTY, DRY, BLOOD SPATTED TATTOO GUN AND WEIGHS IT IN HER HAND AS IF THAT WILL PUT TWO AND TWO TOGETHER FOR HER. IT HAPPENED HERE. LAST NIGHT. RIGHT HERE. HER BEST FRIEND COVERED HER OWN BODY WITH AN EMPTY GUN? HER PERFECT ALBINO SKIN IS NOW COVERED IN HUNDREDS AND HUNDREDS OF TERRIBLE, UNCLEAN LINES. THIS CLEAR REALIZATION FEELS LIKE A PUNCH. PEARL MAY HAVE NEVER LOVED HER PERFECT SKIN, BUT KIMMY FUCKING ADORED IT. SELFISHLY, SHE THOUGHT, ONE OF HER FAVORITE THINGS IN THE WORLD IS RUINED.
NO!
KIMMY DESPERATELY EXAMINES HER FRIEND'S EYES AND FACE. IT'LL TAKE A YEAR BEFORE KIMMY GETS IT THROUGH HER HEAD THAT PEARL DID NOT HARM HERSELF TODAY. THERE'S BLOOD. IT HURTS. BUT NO ONE TRIED TO KILL THEMSELVES. IT'S NOT SELF HARM. IT'S A SELF REALIZATION. IT'LL TAKE ONLY FOUR MORE DAYS FOR KIMMY TO DEEPLY BELIEVE FOR THE REST OF HER LIFE: FUCK ANYONE FOR JUDGING MY FRIEND. FUCK YOU FOR JUDGING HOW SOMEONE ELSE FUCKING GRIEVES!
BUT THIS NIGHT! THE IMAGES IN HER MIND'S EYE OF THIS NIGHT, WILL HAUNT KIMMY EVERY DAY. KIMMY QUIETLY HATES ALL OF IT. SHE HATES HOW SCARED SHE WAS AT THIS MOMENT. SHE HATES HOW EVERY TIME PEARL HAS ANY FLUSH OF EMOTION IT JUST REMINDS HER OF THIS HORRIBLE MOMENT WHERE SHE THOUGHT SHE LOST HER FRIEND IN THE ABSOLUTE WORST WAY.
WOW.

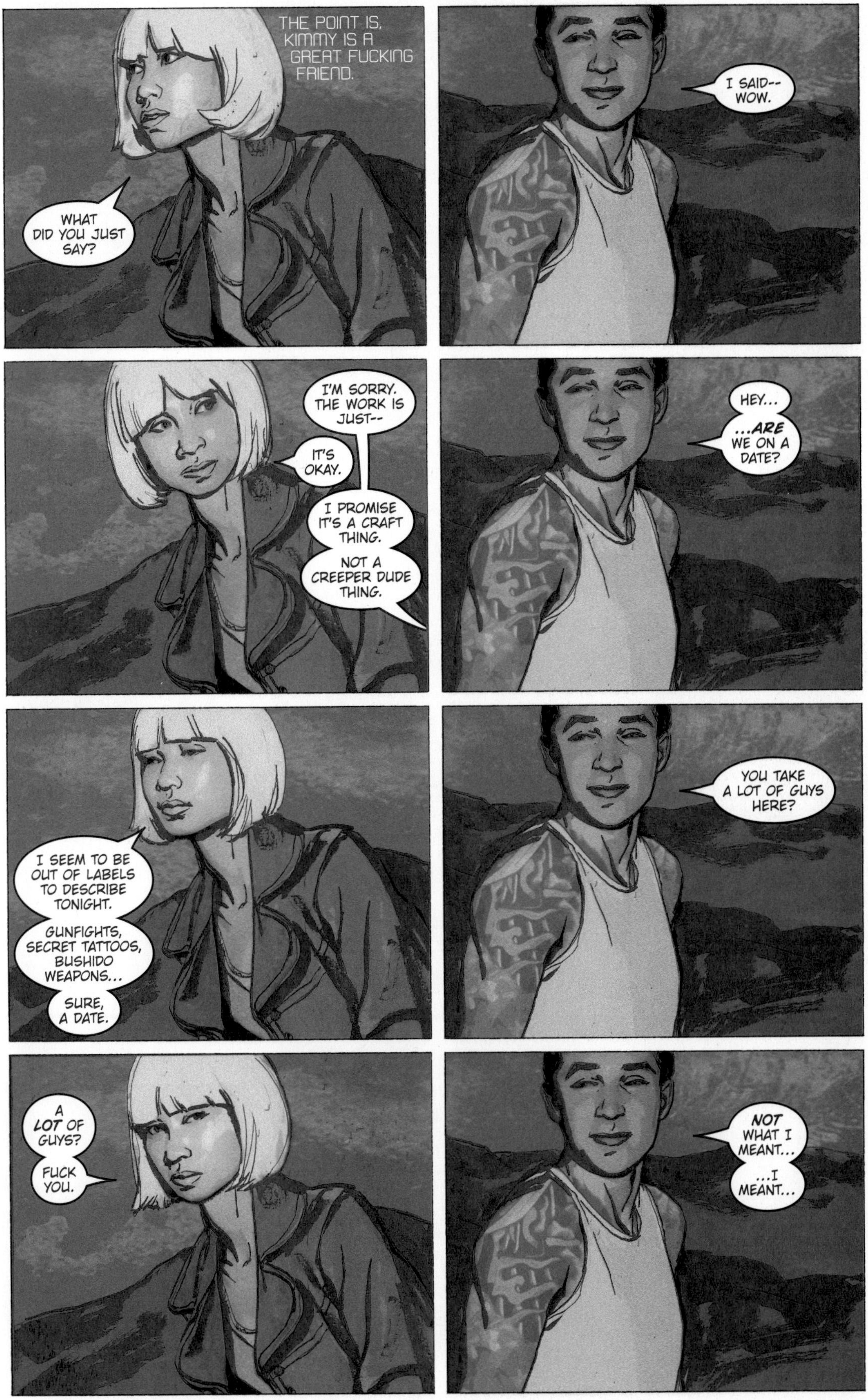
THE POINT IS, KIMMY IS A GREAT FUCKING FRIEND.
WHAT DID YOU JUST SAY?
I SAID-- WOW.
I'M SORRY. THE WORK IS JUST--
IT'S OKAY.
I PROMISE IT'S A CRAFT THING.
NOT A CREEPER DUDE THING.
HEY...
...ARE WE ON A DATE?
I SEEM TO BE OUT OF LABELS TO DESCRIBE TONIGHT.
GUNFIGHTS, SECRET TATTOOS, BUSHIDO WEAPONS...
SURE, A DATE.
YOU TAKE A LOT OF GUYS HERE?
A LOT OF GUYS?
FUCK YOU.
NOT WHAT I MEANT...
...I MEANT...

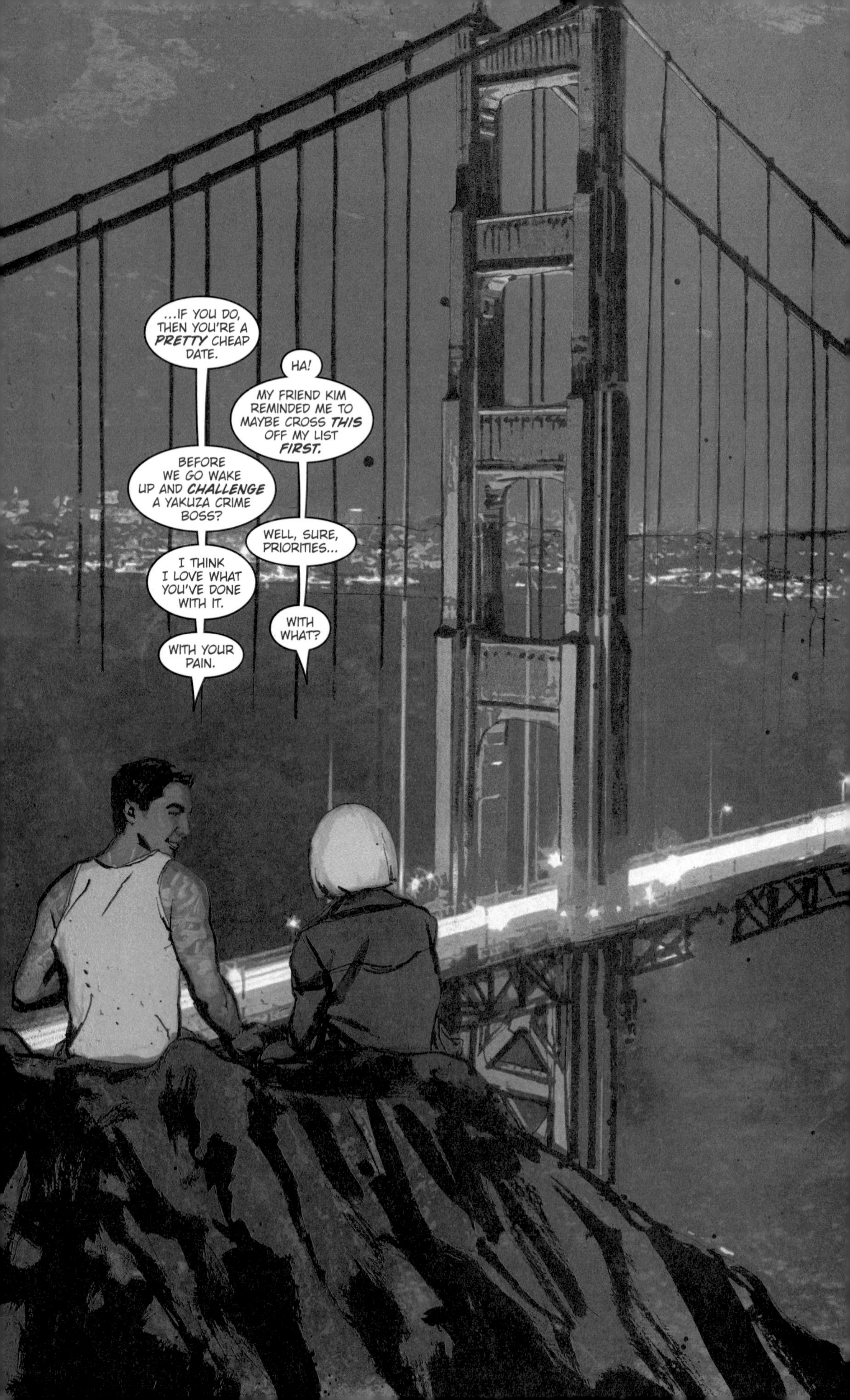
...IF YOU DO, THEN YOU'RE A PRETTY CHEAP DATE.
HA!
MY FRIEND KIM REMINDED ME TO MAYBE CROSS THIS OFF MY LIST FIRST.
BEFORE WE GO WAKE UP AND CHALLENGE A YAKUZA CRIME BOSS?
WELL, SURE, PRIORITIES...
I THINK I LOVE WHAT YOU'VE DONE WITH IT.
WITH WHAT?
WITH YOUR PAIN.

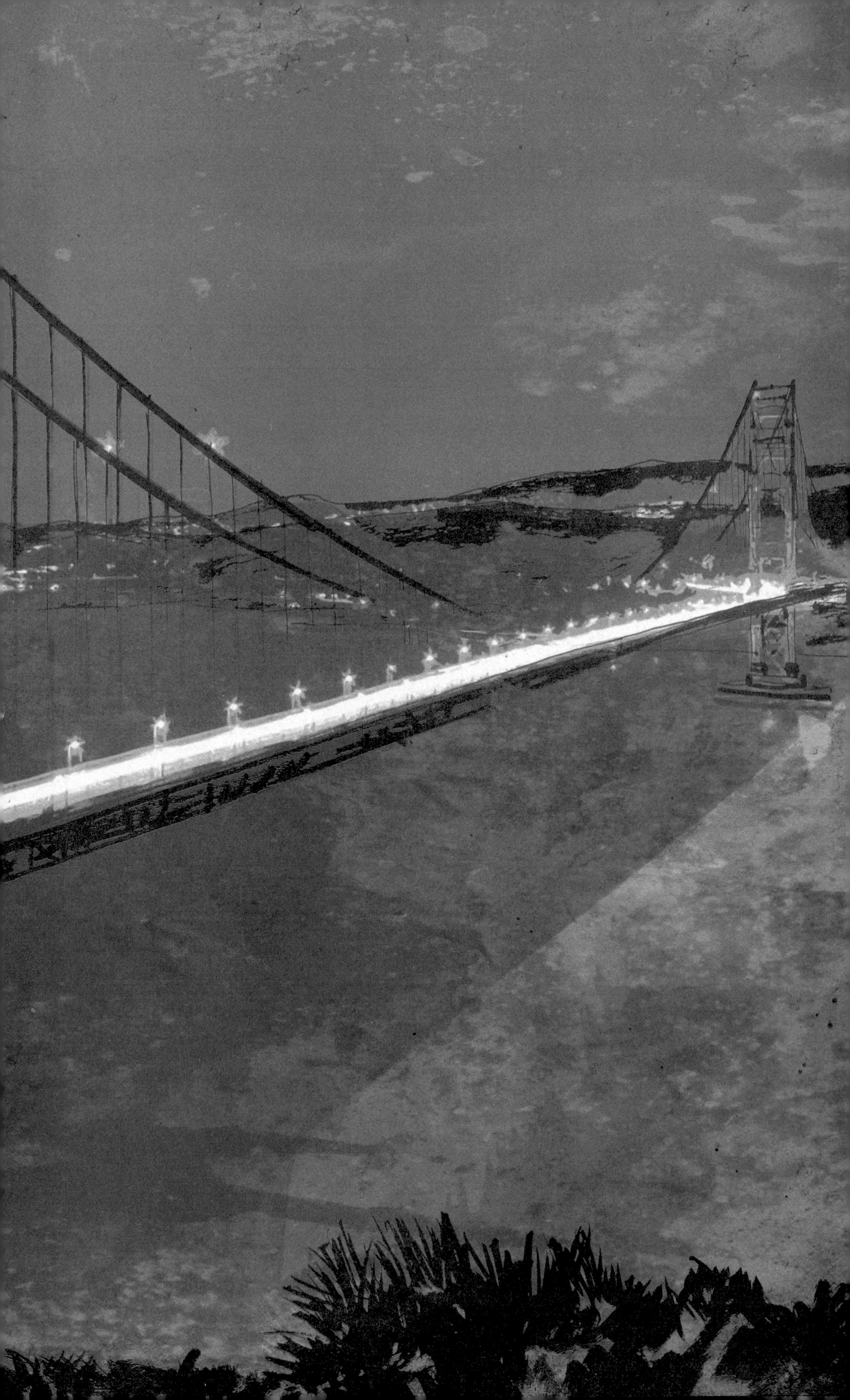

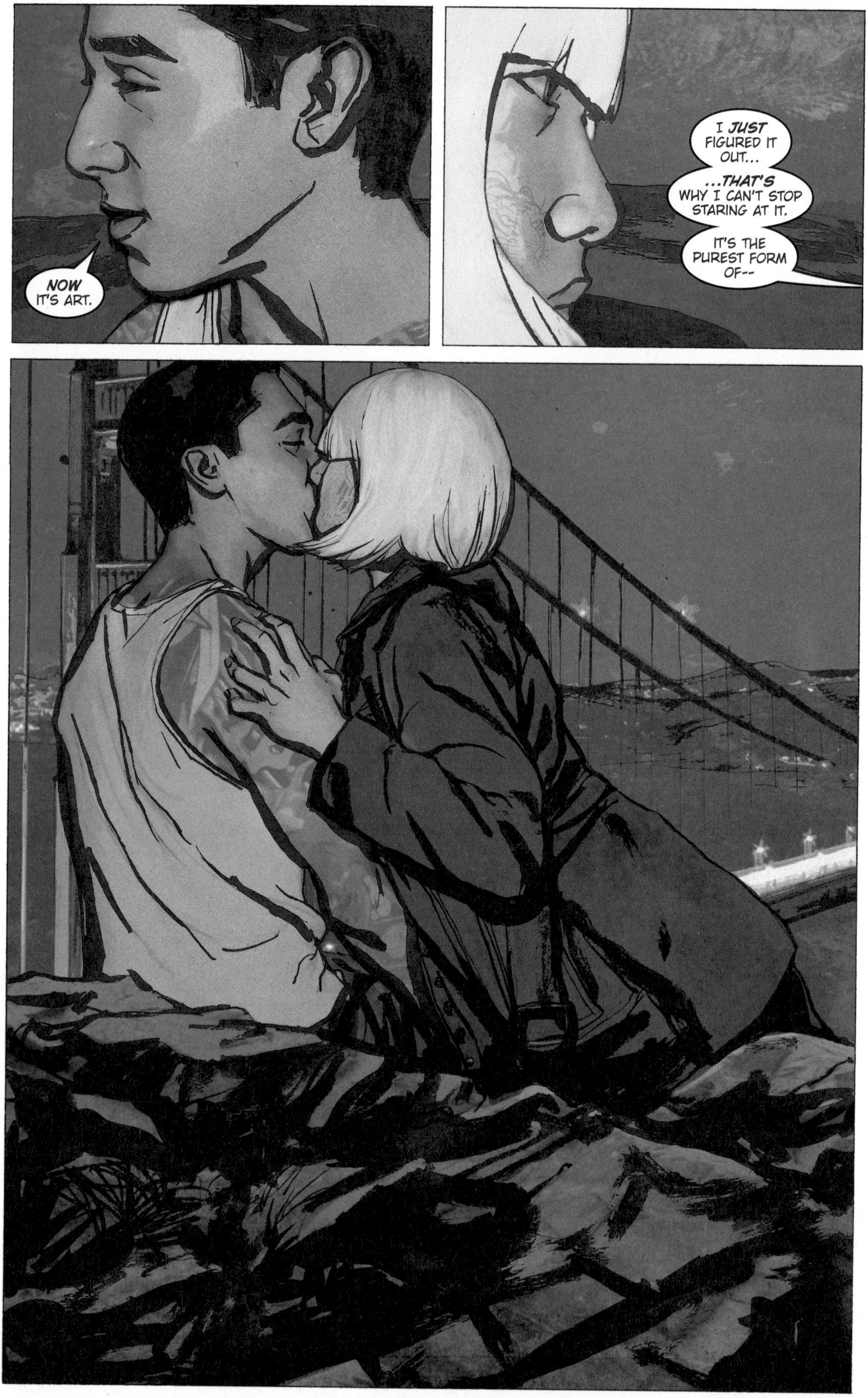
NOW IT'S ART.
I JUST FIGURED IT OUT...
...THAT'S WHY I CAN'T STOP STARING AT IT.
IT'S THE PUREST FORM OF--

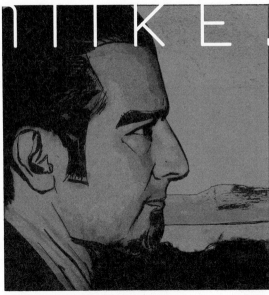

THEY'RE HERE, MR. MIIKE.

PEARL TANAKA AND...SOME DUDE. TO BE SPECIFIC.

OF *COURSE* THEY ARE.

PUT THEM IN THE LIVING ROOM.

ALL HANDS ON DECK, MR. KAI.

TURN OFF THE CAMERA.

PEARL, "DUDE", MR. MIIKE SAYS TAKE A SEAT. YOU KNOW THE BOYS...

HEY, ANDY...

HEY, PEARL.

YOU KNOW THE MUSCLE?

WE WENT TO HIGH SCHOOL TOGETHER.

AND IT CONTINUES TO BE A SMALL FUCKING WORLD...

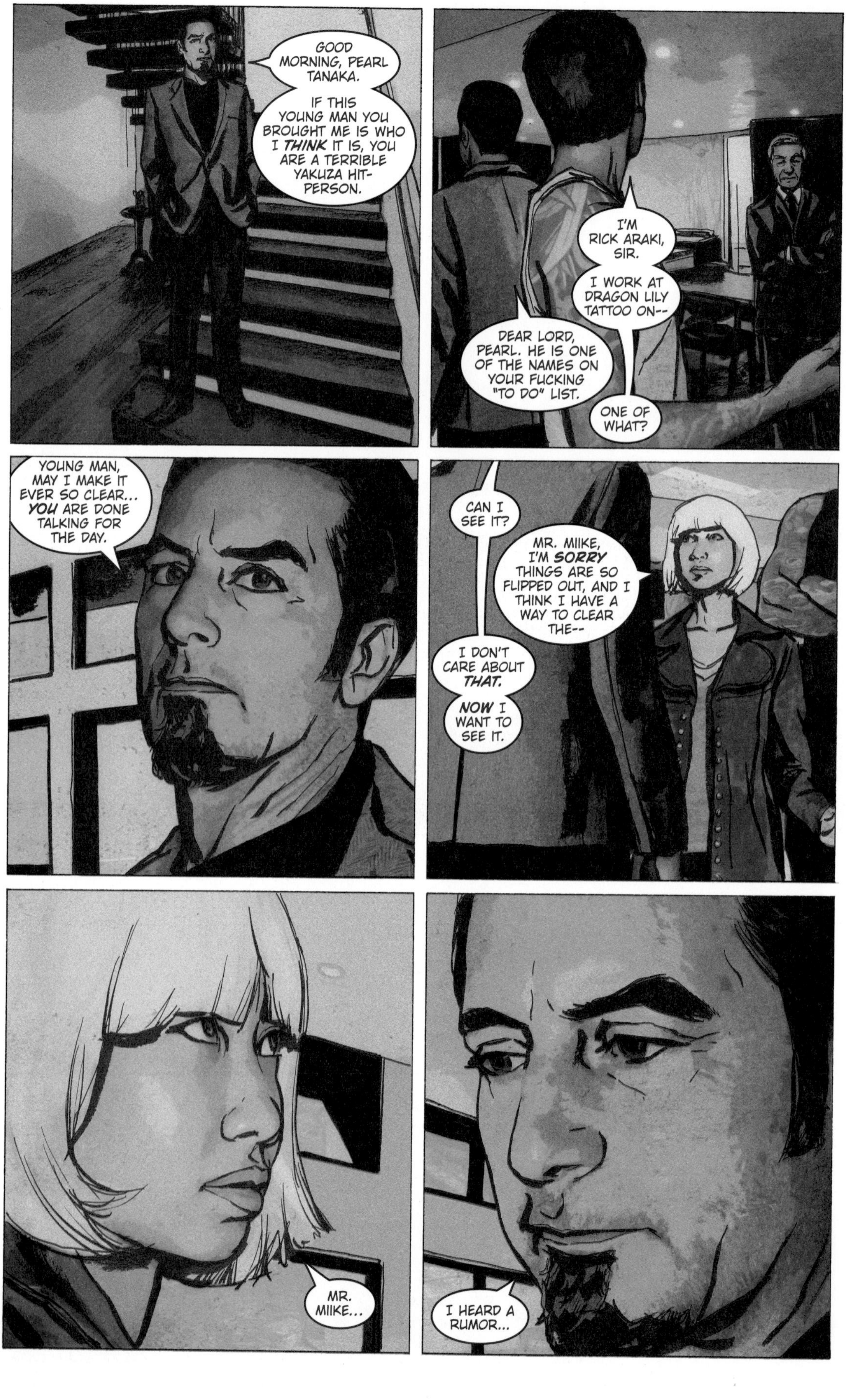
GOOD MORNING, PEARL TANAKA.
IF THIS YOUNG MAN YOU BROUGHT ME IS WHO I *THINK* IT IS, YOU ARE A TERRIBLE YAKUZA HIT-PERSON.
I'M RICK ARAKI, SIR.
I WORK AT DRAGON LILY TATTOO ON--
DEAR LORD, PEARL. HE IS ONE OF THE NAMES ON YOUR FUCKING "TO DO" LIST.
ONE OF WHAT?
YOUNG MAN, MAY I MAKE IT EVER SO CLEAR... *YOU* ARE DONE TALKING FOR THE DAY.
MR. MIIKE, I'M *SORRY* THINGS ARE SO FLIPPED OUT, AND I THINK I HAVE A WAY TO CLEAR THE--
I DON'T CARE ABOUT *THAT.*
CAN I SEE IT?
NOW I WANT TO SEE IT.
MR. MIIKE...
I HEARD A RUMOR...

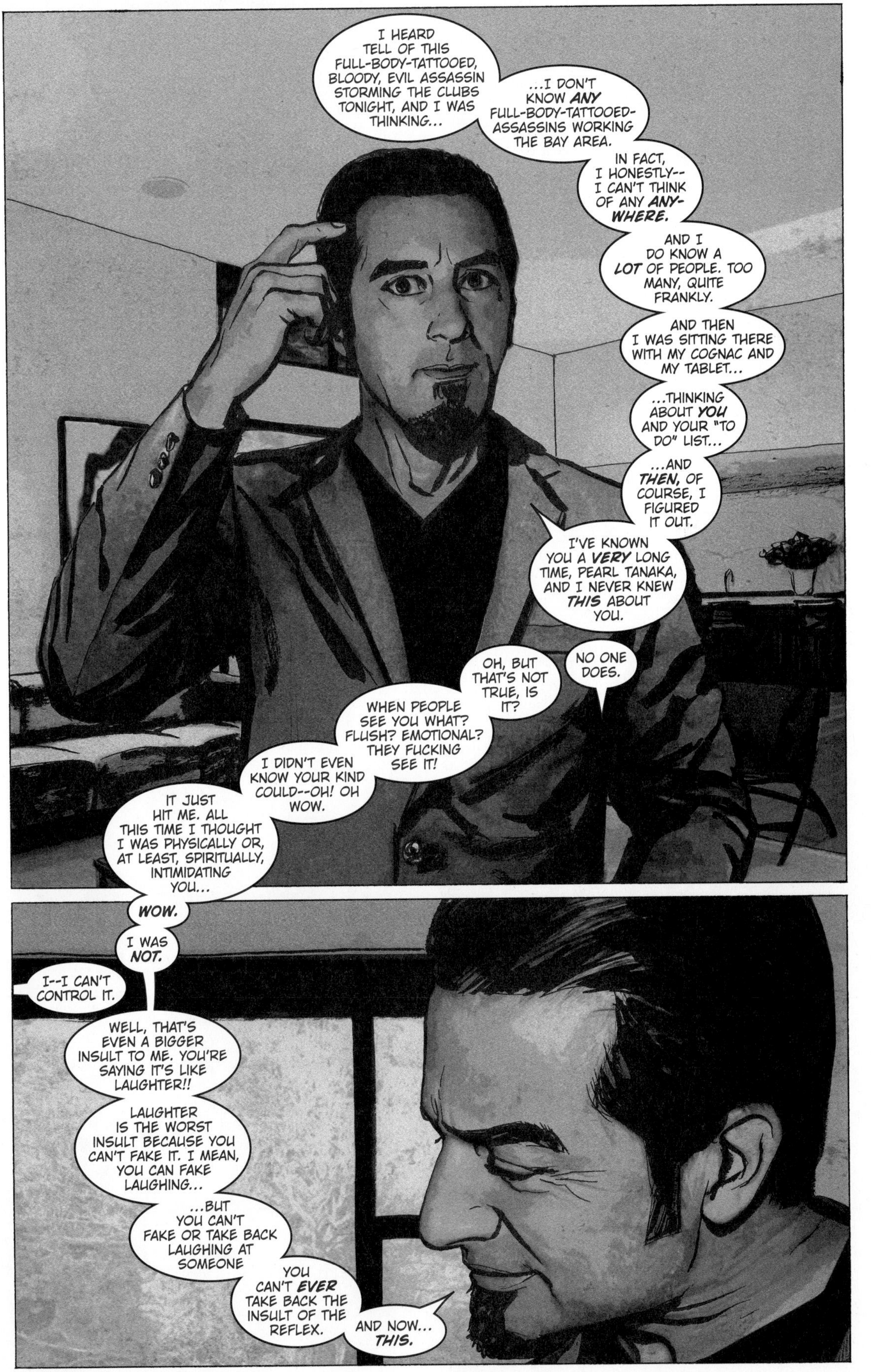
I HEARD TELL OF THIS FULL-BODY-TATTOOED, BLOODY, EVIL ASSASSIN STORMING THE CLUBS TONIGHT, AND I WAS THINKING...
...I DON'T KNOW **ANY** FULL-BODY-TATTOOED-ASSASSINS WORKING THE BAY AREA.
IN FACT, I HONESTLY-- I CAN'T THINK OF ANY **ANY-WHERE.**
AND I DO KNOW A **LOT** OF PEOPLE. TOO MANY, QUITE FRANKLY.
AND THEN I WAS SITTING THERE WITH MY COGNAC AND MY TABLET...
...THINKING ABOUT **YOU** AND YOUR "TO DO" LIST...
...AND **THEN,** OF COURSE, I FIGURED IT OUT.
I'VE KNOWN YOU A **VERY** LONG TIME, PEARL TANAKA, AND I NEVER KNEW **THIS** ABOUT YOU.
NO ONE DOES.
OH, BUT THAT'S NOT TRUE, IS IT?
WHEN PEOPLE SEE YOU WHAT? FLUSH? EMOTIONAL? THEY FUCKING SEE IT!
I DIDN'T EVEN KNOW YOUR KIND COULD--OH! OH WOW.
IT JUST HIT ME. ALL THIS TIME I THOUGHT I WAS PHYSICALLY OR, AT LEAST, SPIRITUALLY, INTIMIDATING YOU...
WOW.
I WAS **NOT.**
I--I CAN'T CONTROL IT.
WELL, THAT'S EVEN A BIGGER INSULT TO ME. YOU'RE SAYING IT'S LIKE LAUGHTER!!
LAUGHTER IS THE WORST INSULT BECAUSE YOU CAN'T FAKE IT. I MEAN, YOU CAN FAKE LAUGHING...
...BUT YOU CAN'T FAKE OR TAKE BACK LAUGHING AT SOMEONE
YOU CAN'T **EVER** TAKE BACK THE INSULT OF THE REFLEX.
AND NOW... **THIS.**

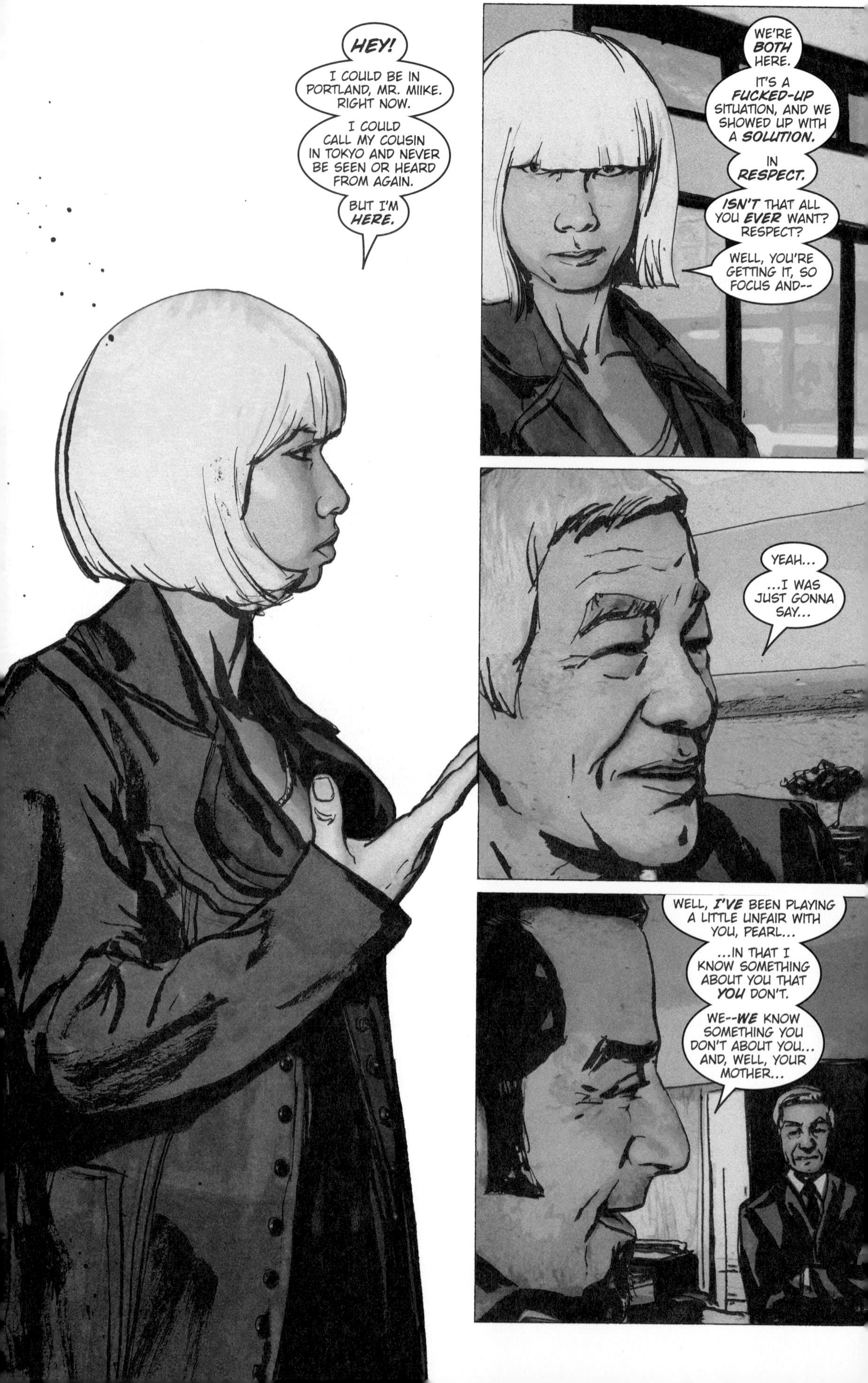
HEY!
I COULD BE IN PORTLAND, MR. MIIKE. RIGHT NOW.
I COULD CALL MY COUSIN IN TOKYO AND NEVER BE SEEN OR HEARD FROM AGAIN.
BUT I'M HERE.
WE'RE BOTH HERE.
IT'S A FUCKED-UP SITUATION, AND WE SHOWED UP WITH A SOLUTION.
IN RESPECT.
ISN'T THAT ALL YOU EVER WANT? RESPECT?
WELL, YOU'RE GETTING IT, SO FOCUS AND--
YEAH...
...I WAS JUST GONNA SAY...
WELL, I'VE BEEN PLAYING A LITTLE UNFAIR WITH YOU, PEARL...
...IN THAT I KNOW SOMETHING ABOUT YOU THAT YOU DON'T.
WE--WE KNOW SOMETHING YOU DON'T ABOUT YOU... AND, WELL, YOUR MOTHER...

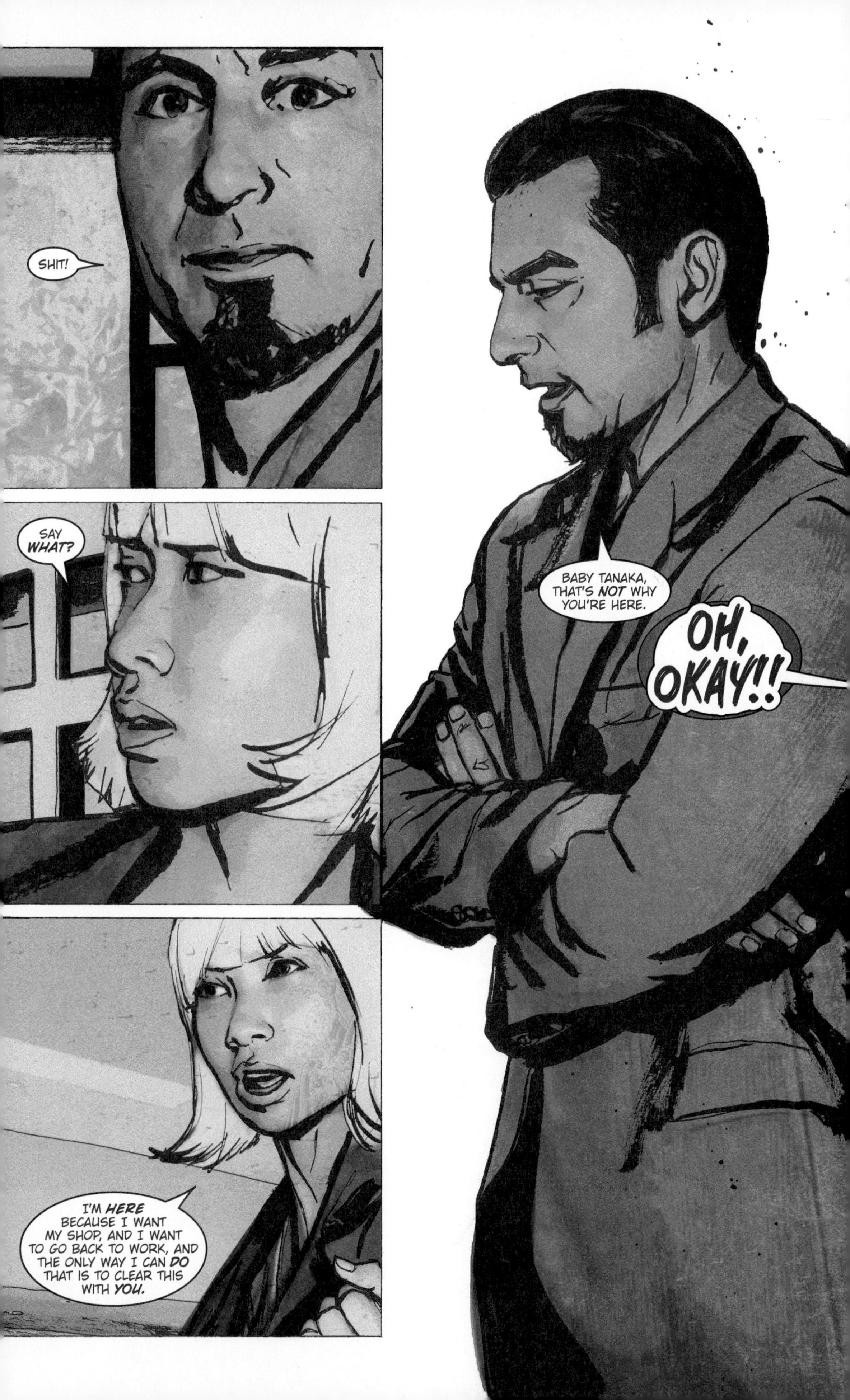
SHIT!
SAY WHAT?
BABY TANAKA, THAT'S NOT WHY YOU'RE HERE.
OH, OKAY!!
I'M HERE BECAUSE I WANT MY SHOP, AND I WANT TO GO BACK TO WORK, AND THE ONLY WAY I CAN DO THAT IS TO CLEAR THIS WITH YOU.

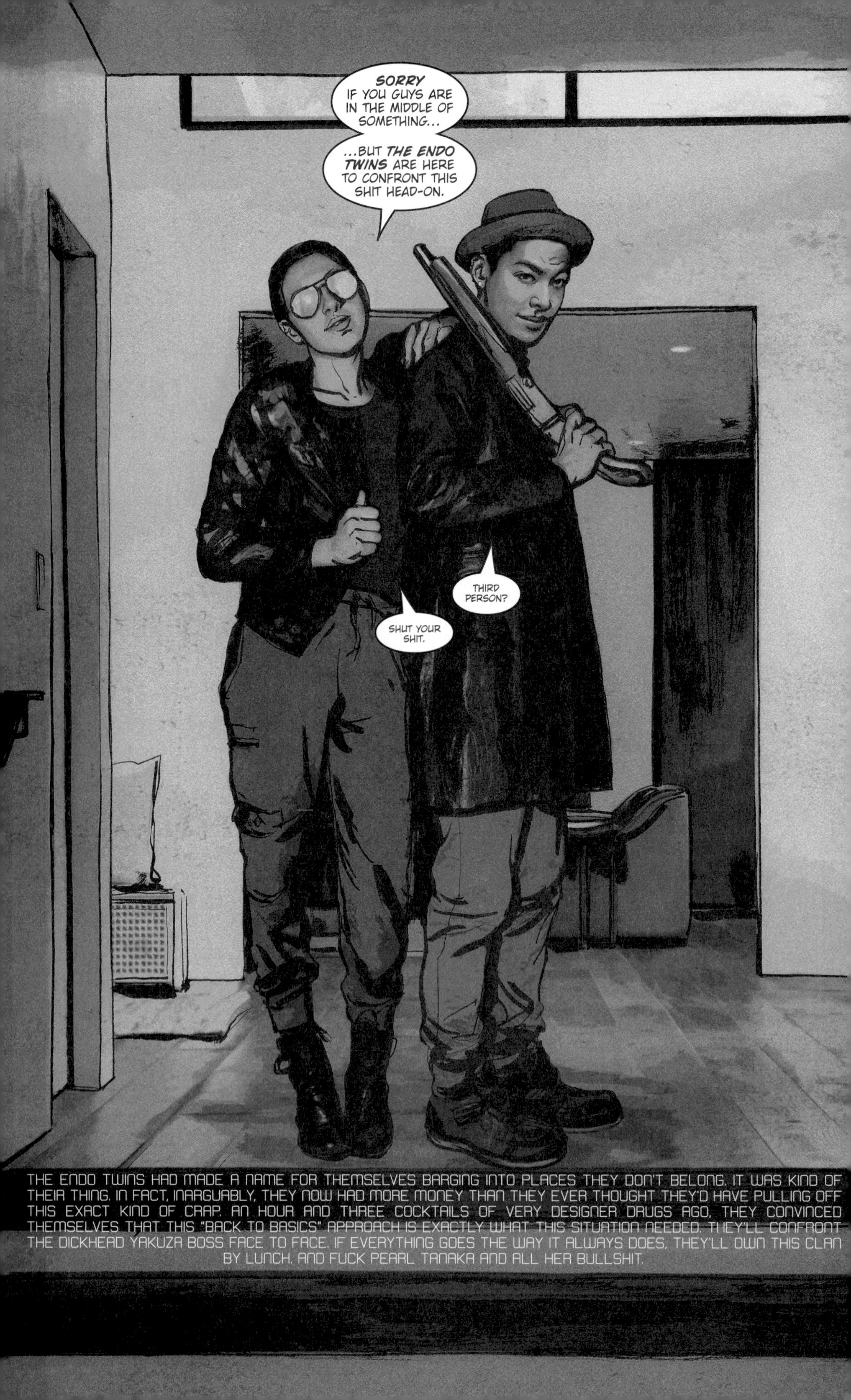
SORRY IF YOU GUYS ARE IN THE MIDDLE OF SOMETHING...
...BUT THE ENDO TWINS ARE HERE TO CONFRONT THIS SHIT HEAD-ON.
THIRD PERSON?
SHUT YOUR SHIT.
THE ENDO TWINS HAD MADE A NAME FOR THEMSELVES BARGING INTO PLACES THEY DON'T BELONG. IT WAS KIND OF THEIR THING. IN FACT, INARGUABLY, THEY NOW HAD MORE MONEY THAN THEY EVER THOUGHT THEY'D HAVE PULLING OFF THIS EXACT KIND OF CRAP. AN HOUR AND THREE COCKTAILS OF VERY DESIGNER DRUGS AGO, THEY CONVINCED THEMSELVES THAT THIS "BACK TO BASICS" APPROACH IS EXACTLY WHAT THIS SITUATION NEEDED. THEY'LL CONFRONT THE DICKHEAD YAKUZA BOSS FACE TO FACE. IF EVERYTHING GOES THE WAY IT ALWAYS DOES, THEY'LL OWN THIS CLAN BY LUNCH. AND FUCK PEARL TANAKA AND ALL HER BULLSHIT.

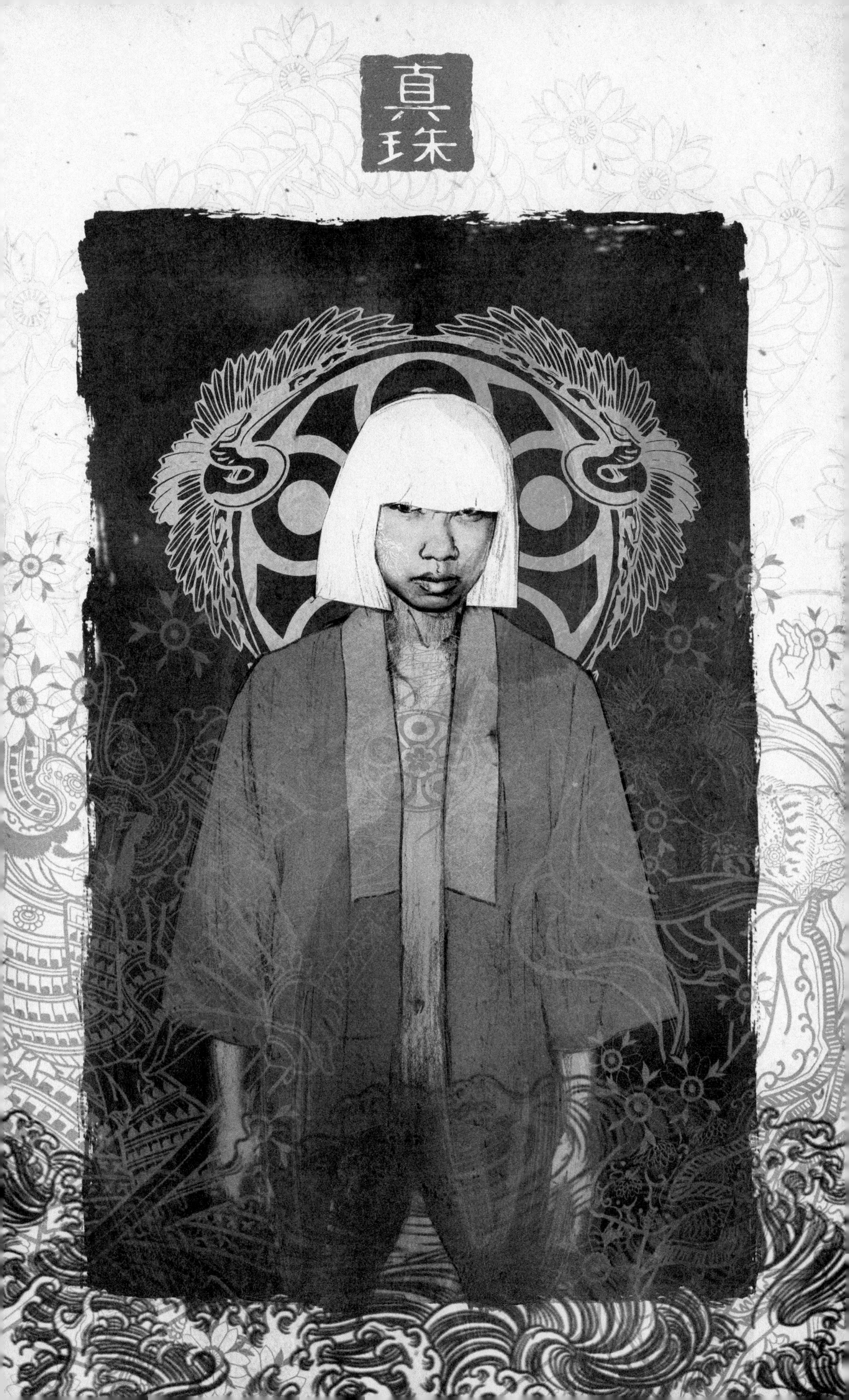
真珠

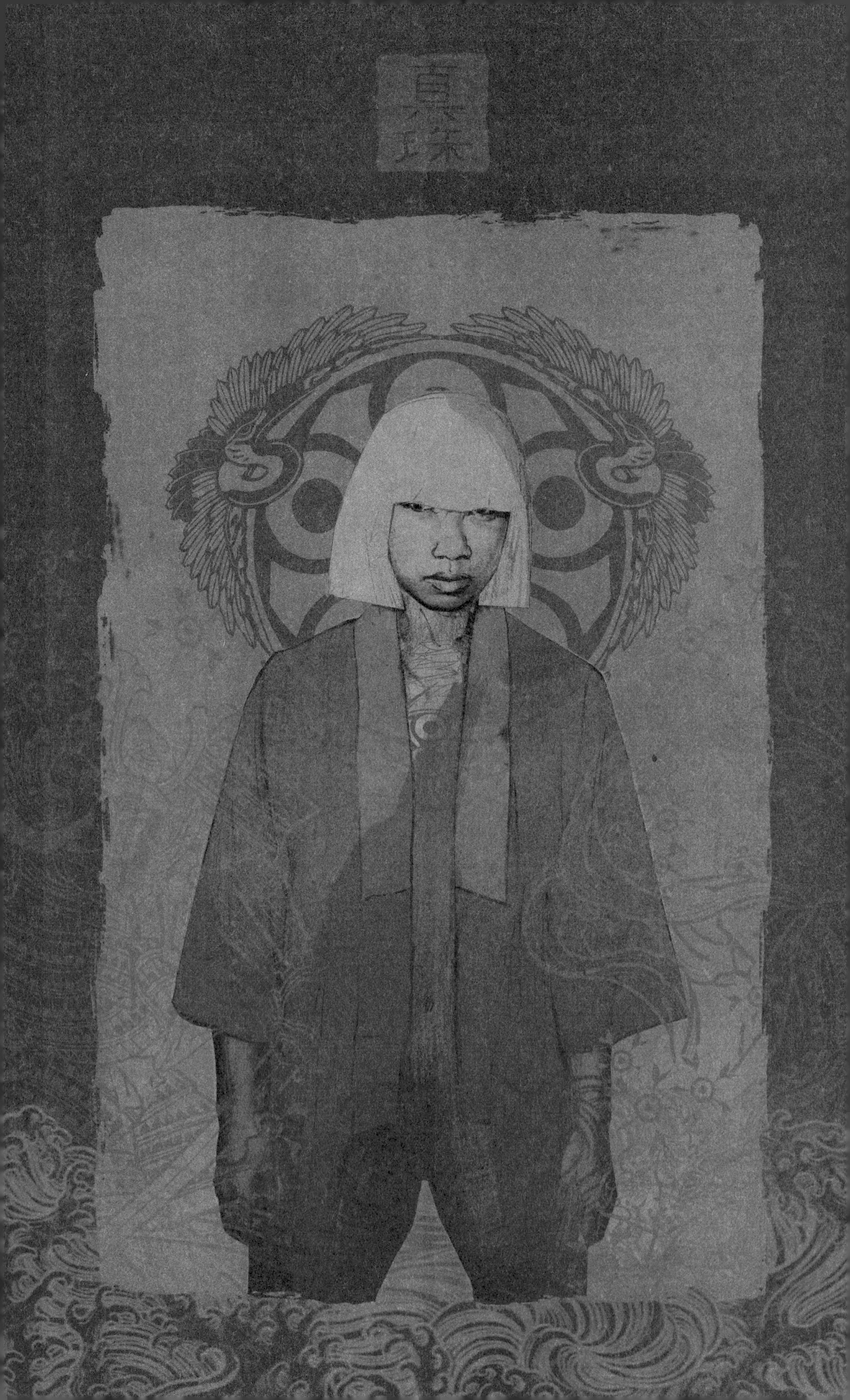

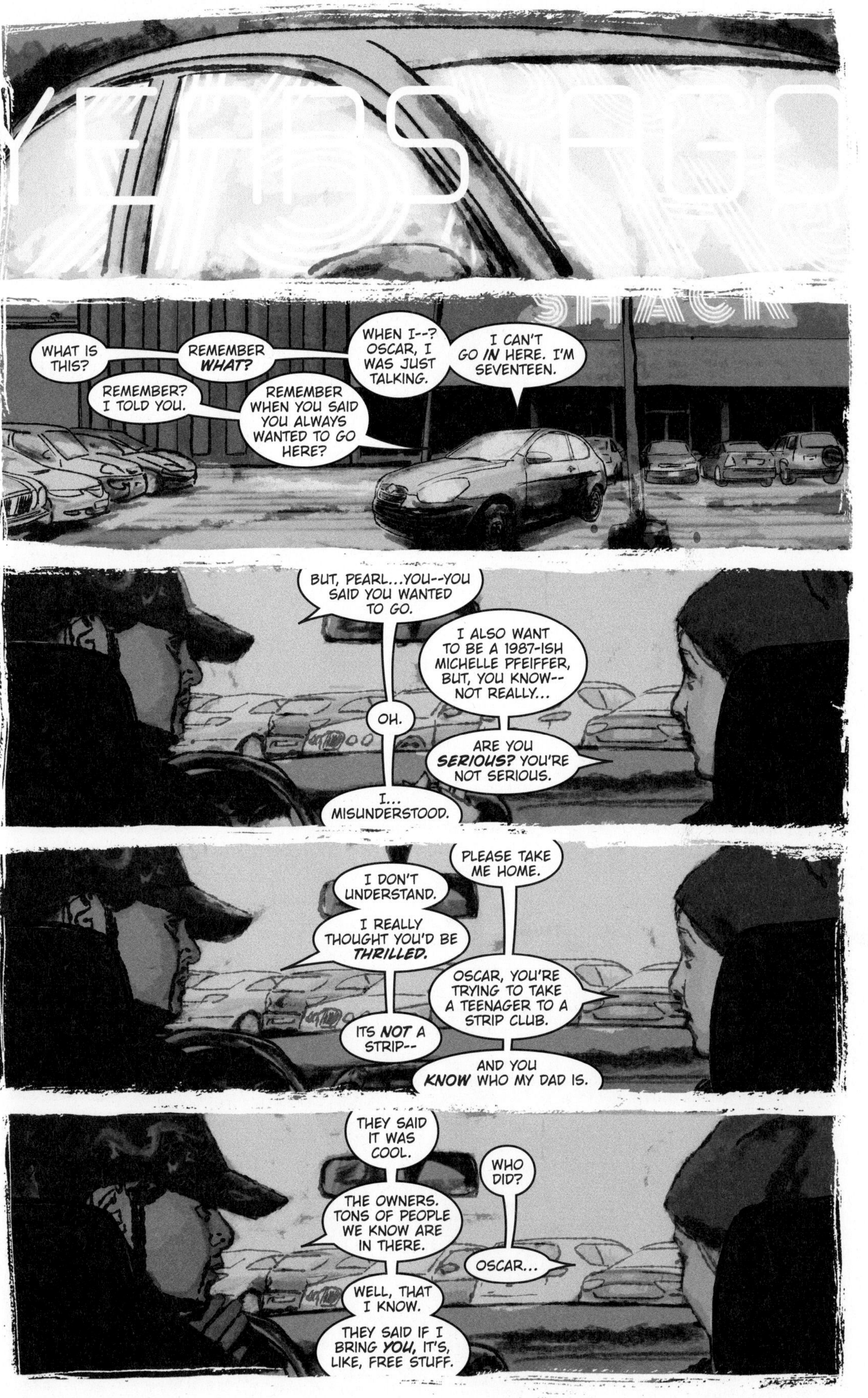
WHAT IS THIS?
REMEMBER? I TOLD YOU.
REMEMBER WHAT?
REMEMBER WHEN YOU SAID YOU ALWAYS WANTED TO GO HERE?
WHEN I--? OSCAR, I WAS JUST TALKING.
I CAN'T GO IN HERE. I'M SEVENTEEN.
BUT, PEARL...YOU--YOU SAID YOU WANTED TO GO.
I ALSO WANT TO BE A 1987-ISH MICHELLE PFEIFFER, BUT, YOU KNOW--NOT REALLY...
OH.
ARE YOU SERIOUS? YOU'RE NOT SERIOUS.
I... MISUNDERSTOOD.
PLEASE TAKE ME HOME.
I DON'T UNDERSTAND.
I REALLY THOUGHT YOU'D BE THRILLED.
OSCAR, YOU'RE TRYING TO TAKE A TEENAGER TO A STRIP CLUB.
ITS NOT A STRIP--
AND YOU KNOW WHO MY DAD IS.
THEY SAID IT WAS COOL.
WHO DID?
THE OWNERS. TONS OF PEOPLE WE KNOW ARE IN THERE.
OSCAR...
WELL, THAT I KNOW.
THEY SAID IF I BRING YOU, IT'S, LIKE, FREE STUFF.

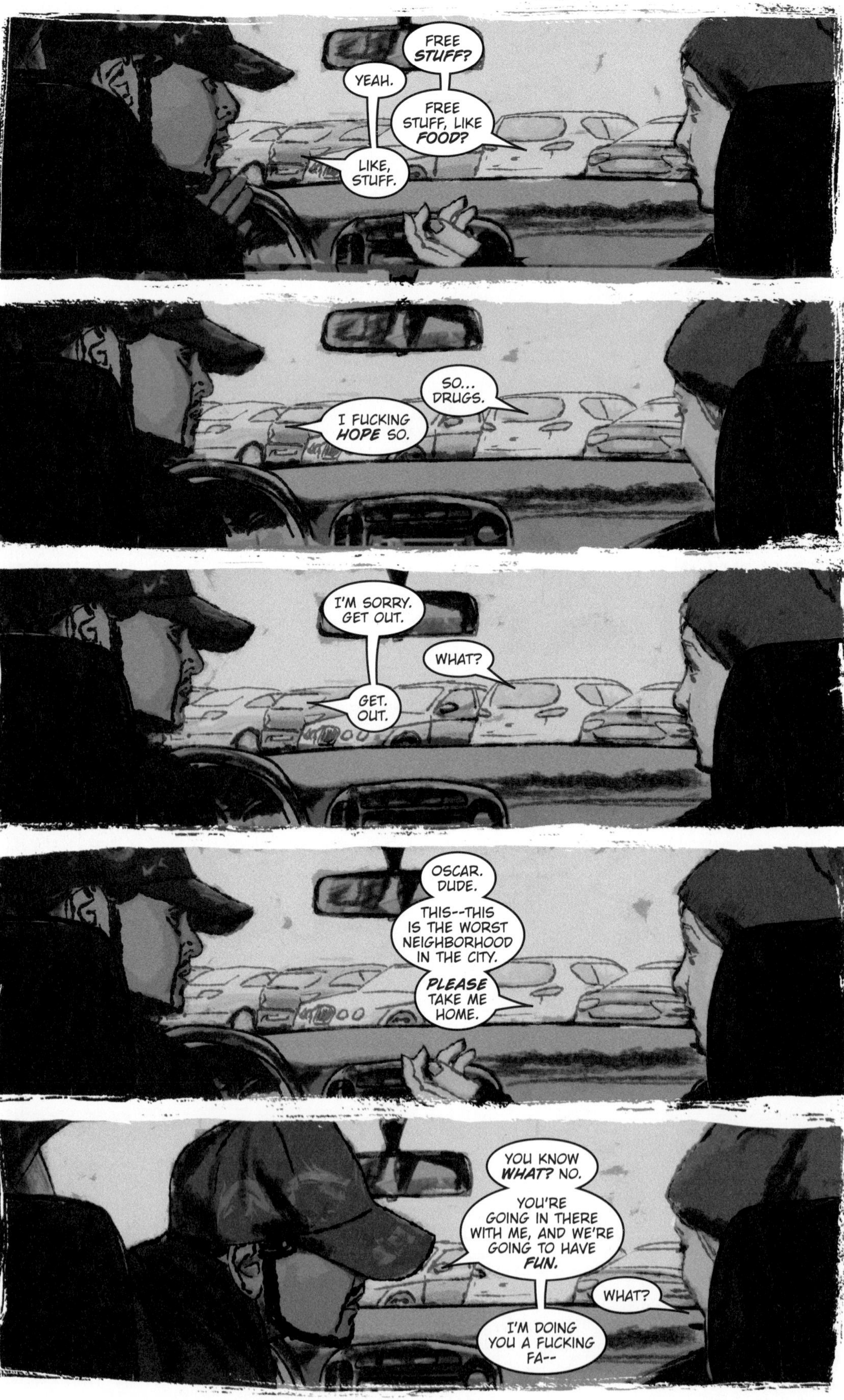
FREE STUFF?
YEAH.
FREE STUFF, LIKE FOOD?
LIKE, STUFF.
SO... DRUGS.
I FUCKING HOPE SO.
I'M SORRY. GET OUT.
WHAT?
GET. OUT.
OSCAR. DUDE.
THIS--THIS IS THE WORST NEIGHBORHOOD IN THE CITY.
PLEASE TAKE ME HOME.
YOU KNOW WHAT? NO.
YOU'RE GOING IN THERE WITH ME, AND WE'RE GOING TO HAVE FUN.
WHAT?
I'M DOING YOU A FUCKING FA--

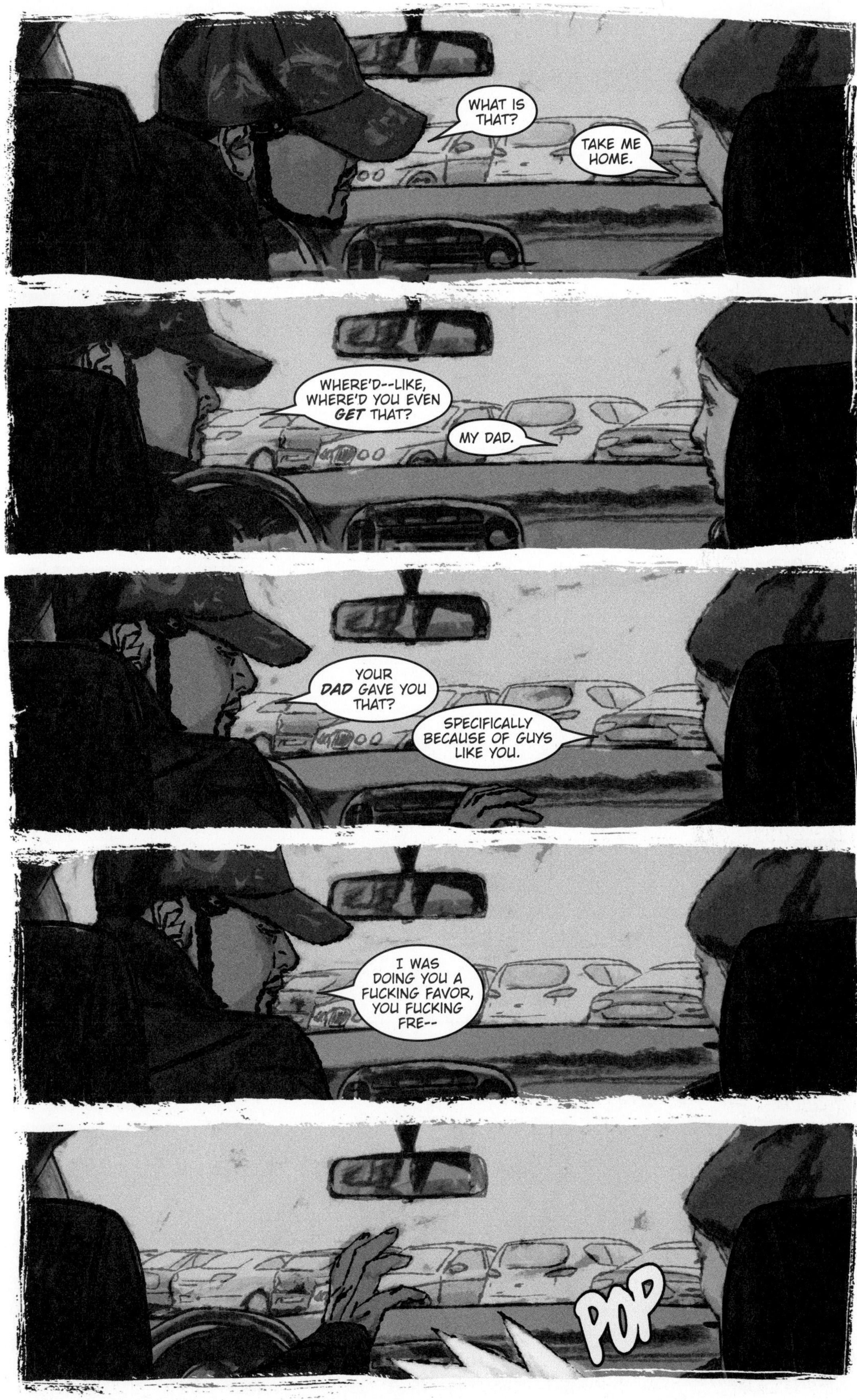
WHAT IS THAT?
TAKE ME HOME.
WHERE'D--LIKE, WHERE'D YOU EVEN GET THAT?
MY DAD.
YOUR DAD GAVE YOU THAT?
SPECIFICALLY BECAUSE OF GUYS LIKE YOU.
I WAS DOING YOU A FUCKING FAVOR, YOU FUCKING FRE--
POP

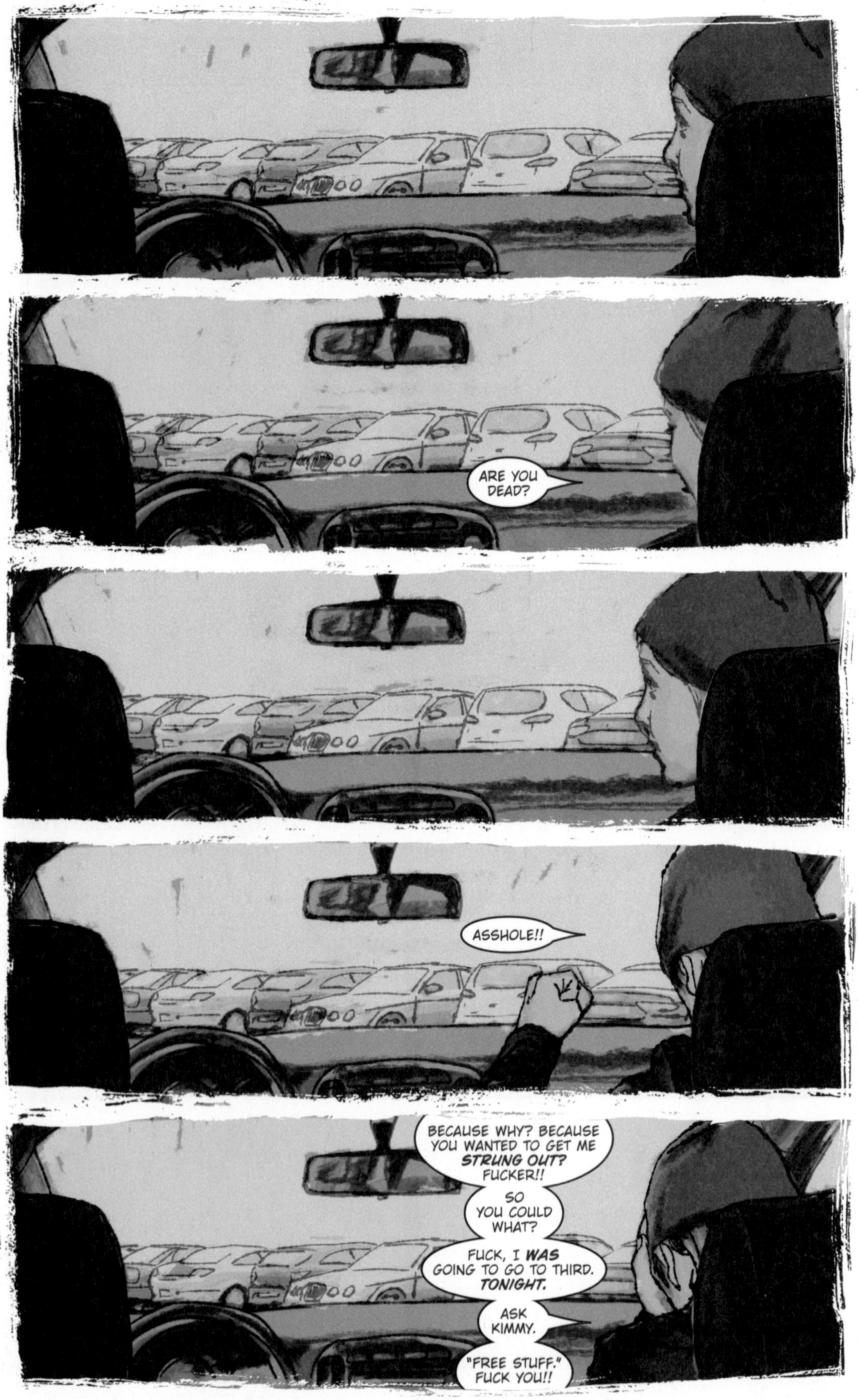
ARE YOU DEAD?
ASSHOLE!!
BECAUSE WHY? BECAUSE YOU WANTED TO GET ME STRUNG OUT? FUCKER!!
SO YOU COULD WHAT?
FUCK, I WAS GOING TO GO TO THIRD. TONIGHT.
ASK KIMMY.
"FREE STUFF." FUCK YOU!!

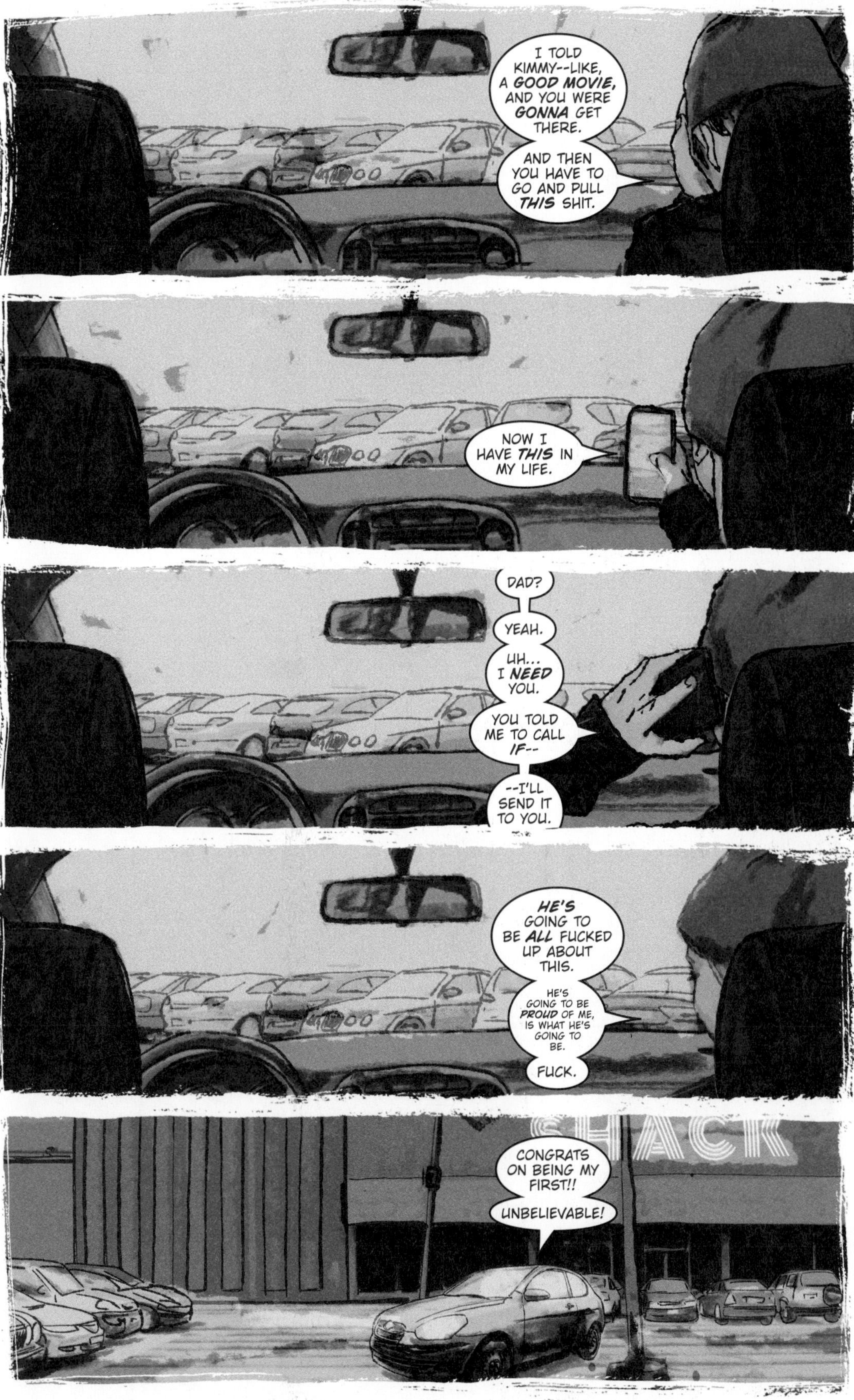
I TOLD KIMMY--LIKE, A GOOD MOVIE, AND YOU WERE GONNA GET THERE.
AND THEN YOU HAVE TO GO AND PULL THIS SHIT.
NOW I HAVE THIS IN MY LIFE.
DAD?
YEAH.
UH... I NEED YOU.
YOU TOLD ME TO CALL IF--
--I'LL SEND IT TO YOU.
HE'S GOING TO BE ALL FUCKED UP ABOUT THIS.
HE'S GOING TO BE PROUD OF ME, IS WHAT HE'S GOING TO BE.
FUCK.
HACK
CONGRATS ON BEING MY FIRST!!
UNBELIEVABLE!

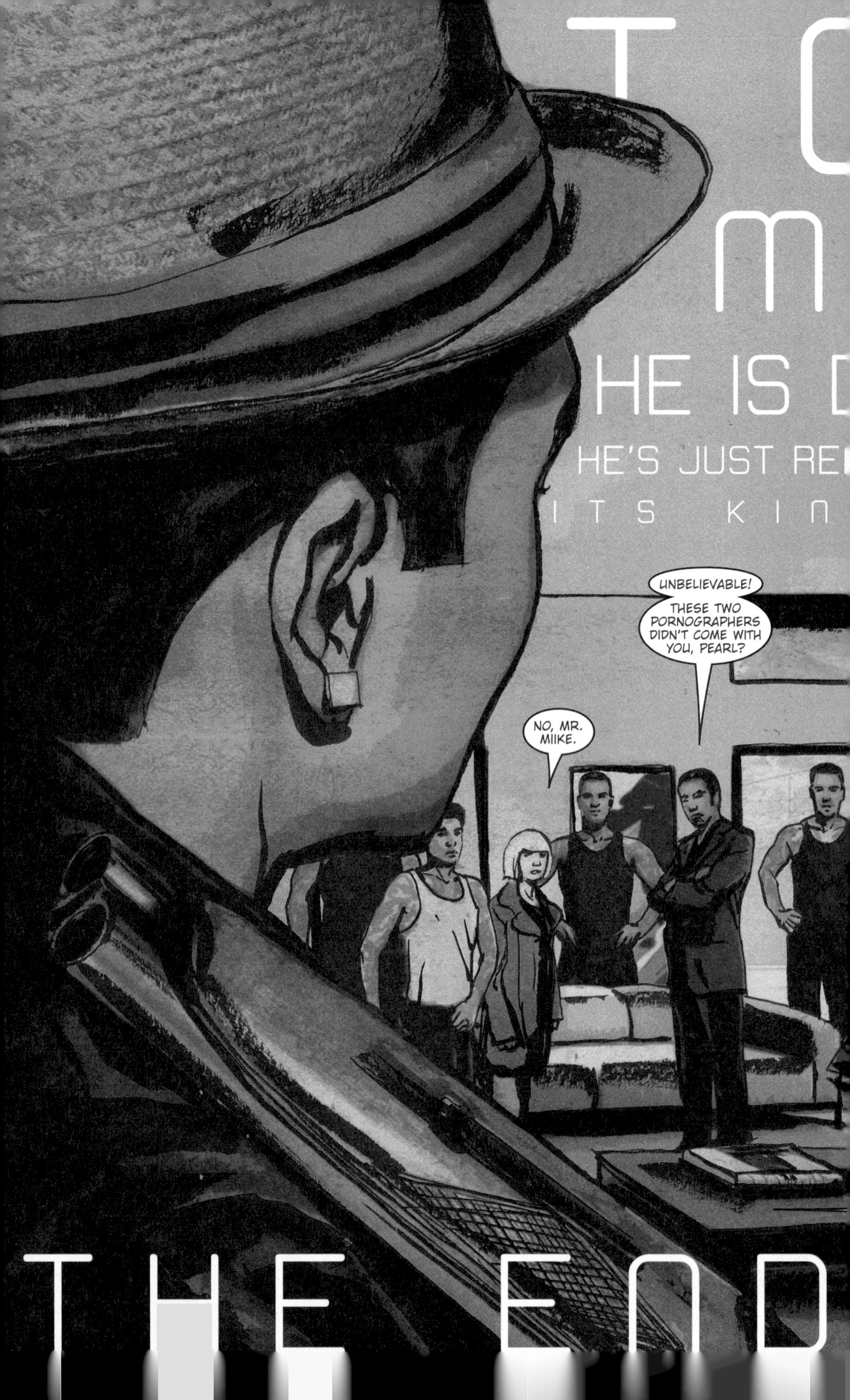
T O
M
HE IS D
HE'S JUST RE
ITS KIN
UNBELIEVABLE!
THESE TWO PORNOGRAPHERS DIDN'T COME WITH YOU, PEARL?
NO, MR. MIIKE.
THE END

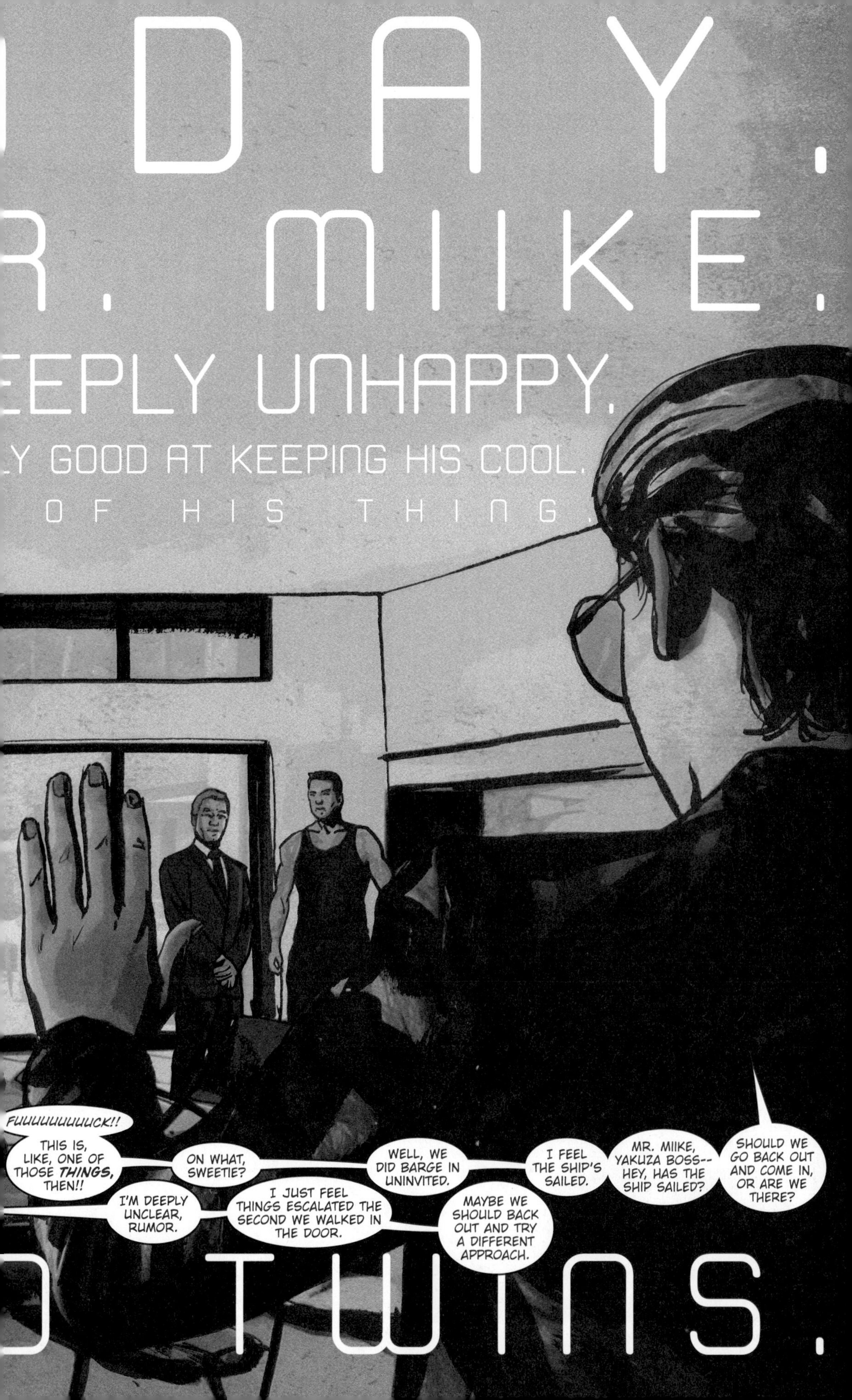

DAY.
R. MIIKE.
EEPLY UNHAPPY.
Y GOOD AT KEEPING HIS COOL.
OF HIS THING
FUUUUUUUUUCK!!
THIS IS, LIKE, ONE OF THOSE *THINGS,* THEN!!
ON WHAT, SWEETIE?
WELL, WE DID BARGE IN UNINVITED.
I FEEL THE SHIP'S SAILED.
MR. MIIKE, YAKUZA BOSS-- HEY, HAS THE SHIP SAILED?
SHOULD WE GO BACK OUT AND COME IN, OR ARE WE THERE?
I'M DEEPLY UNCLEAR, RUMOR.
I JUST FEEL THINGS ESCALATED THE SECOND WE WALKED IN THE DOOR.
MAYBE WE SHOULD BACK OUT AND TRY A DIFFERENT APPROACH.
TWINS.

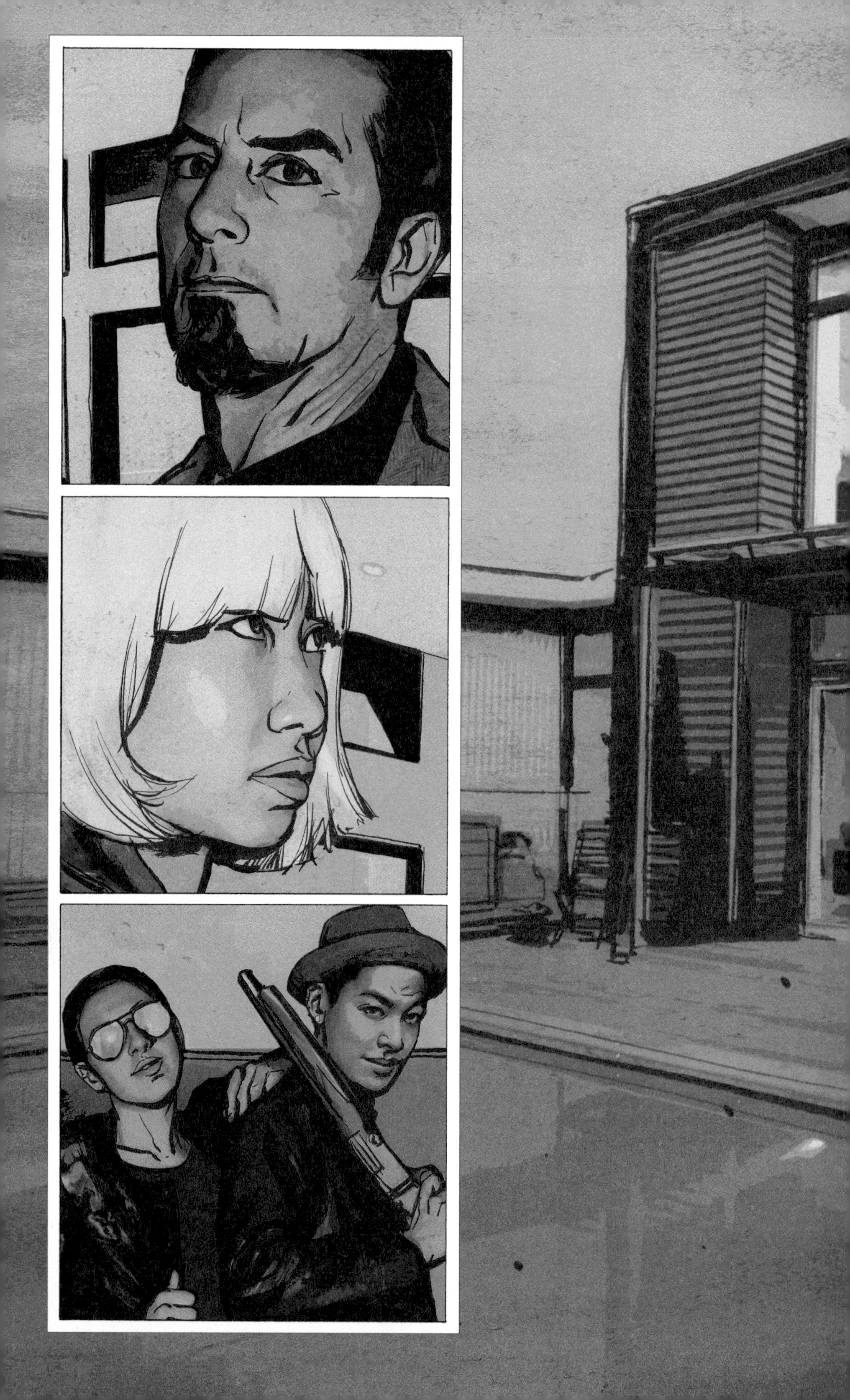

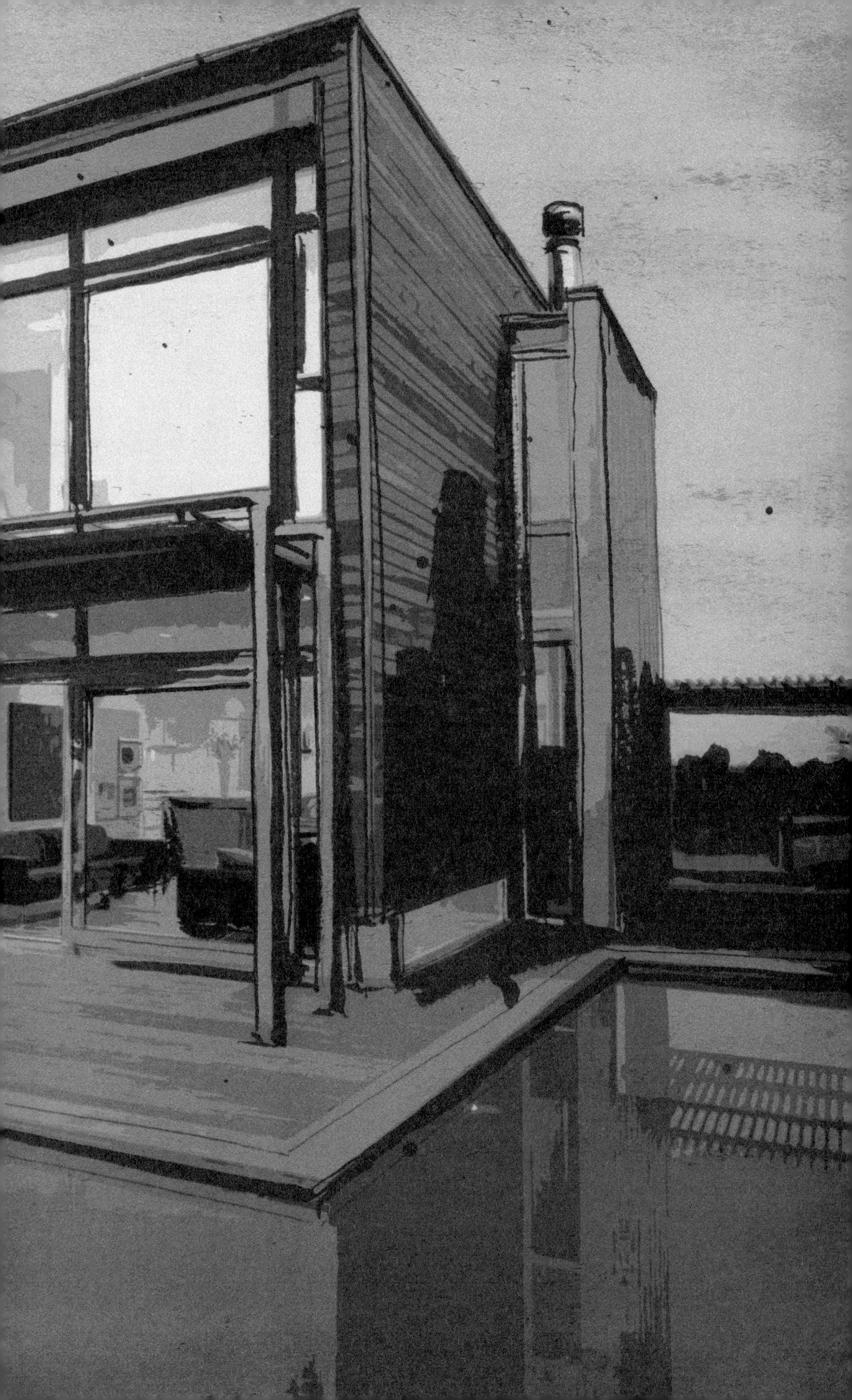

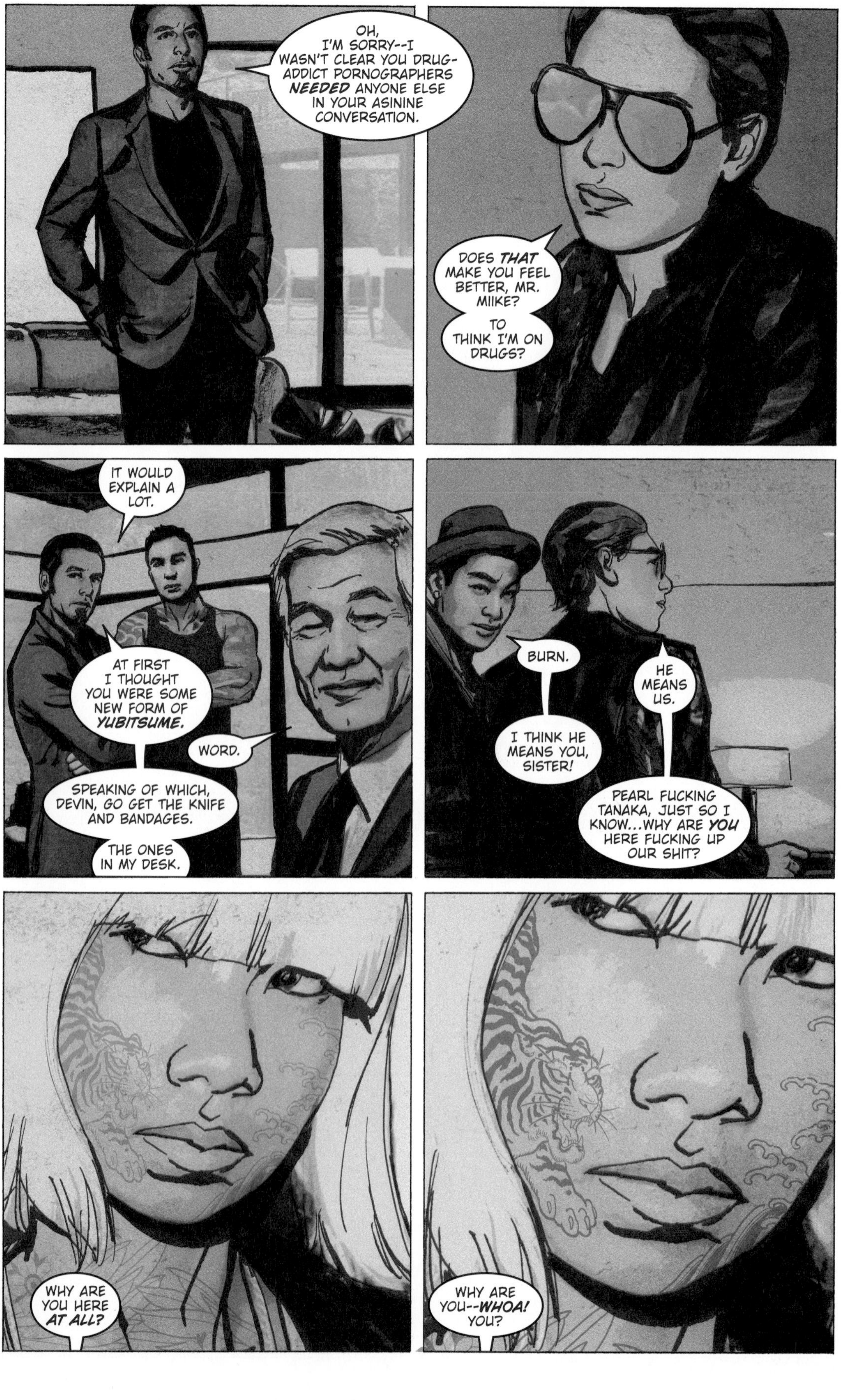
OH, I'M SORRY--I WASN'T CLEAR YOU DRUG-ADDICT PORNOGRAPHERS **NEEDED** ANYONE ELSE IN YOUR ASININE CONVERSATION.
DOES **THAT** MAKE YOU FEEL BETTER, MR. MIIKE?
TO THINK I'M ON DRUGS?
IT WOULD EXPLAIN A LOT.
AT FIRST I THOUGHT YOU WERE SOME NEW FORM OF ***YUBITSUME.***
WORD.
SPEAKING OF WHICH, DEVIN, GO GET THE KNIFE AND BANDAGES.
THE ONES IN MY DESK.
BURN.
I THINK HE MEANS YOU, SISTER!
HE MEANS US.
PEARL FUCKING TANAKA, JUST SO I KNOW...WHY ARE ***YOU*** HERE FUCKING UP OUR SHIT?
WHY ARE YOU HERE ***AT ALL?***
WHY ARE YOU--***WHOA!*** YOU?

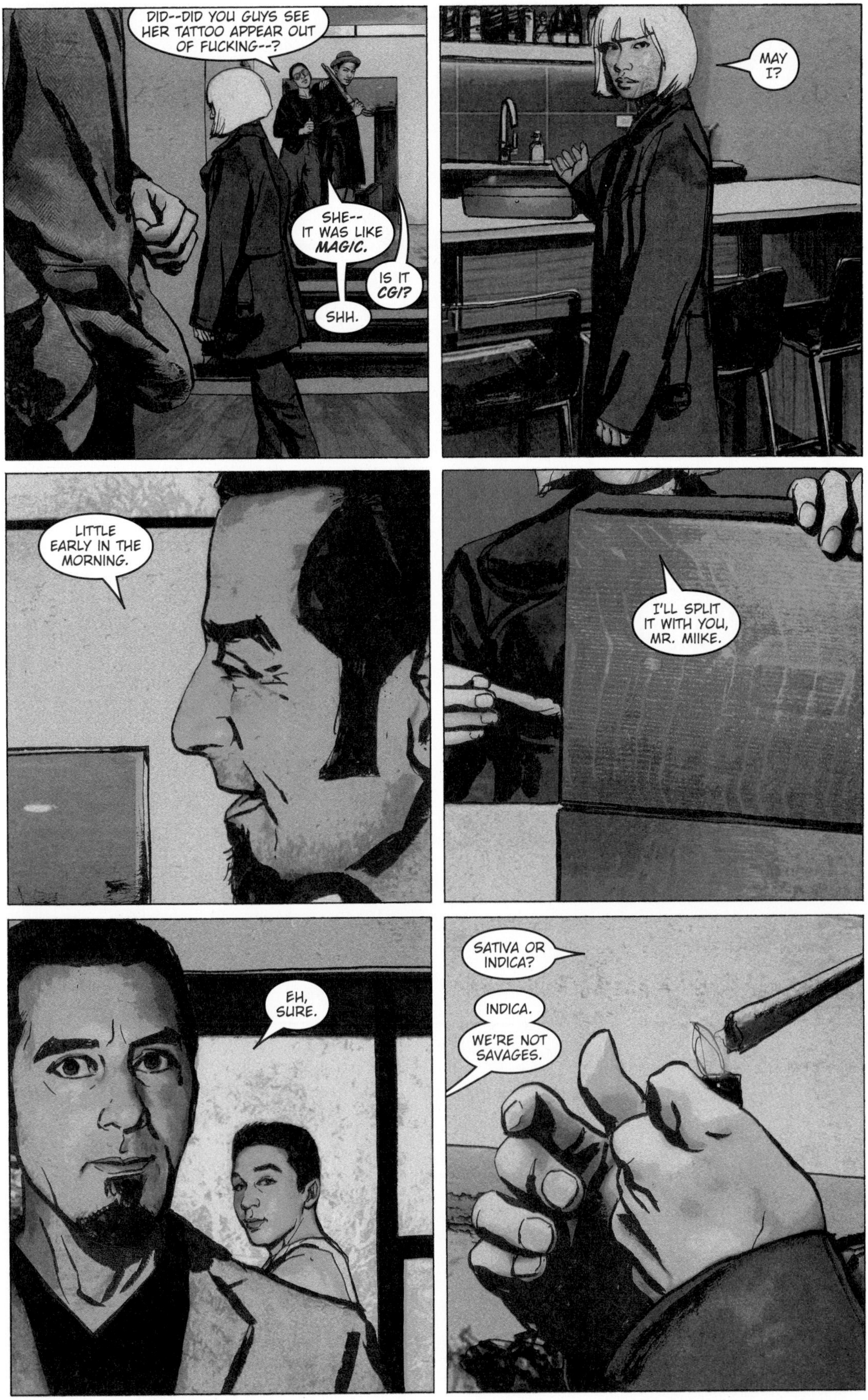
DID--DID YOU GUYS SEE HER TATTOO APPEAR OUT OF FUCKING--?
SHE-- IT WAS LIKE MAGIC.
IS IT CGI?
SHH.
MAY I?
LITTLE EARLY IN THE MORNING.
I'LL SPLIT IT WITH YOU, MR. MIIKE.
EH, SURE.
SATIVA OR INDICA?
INDICA.
WE'RE NOT SAVAGES.

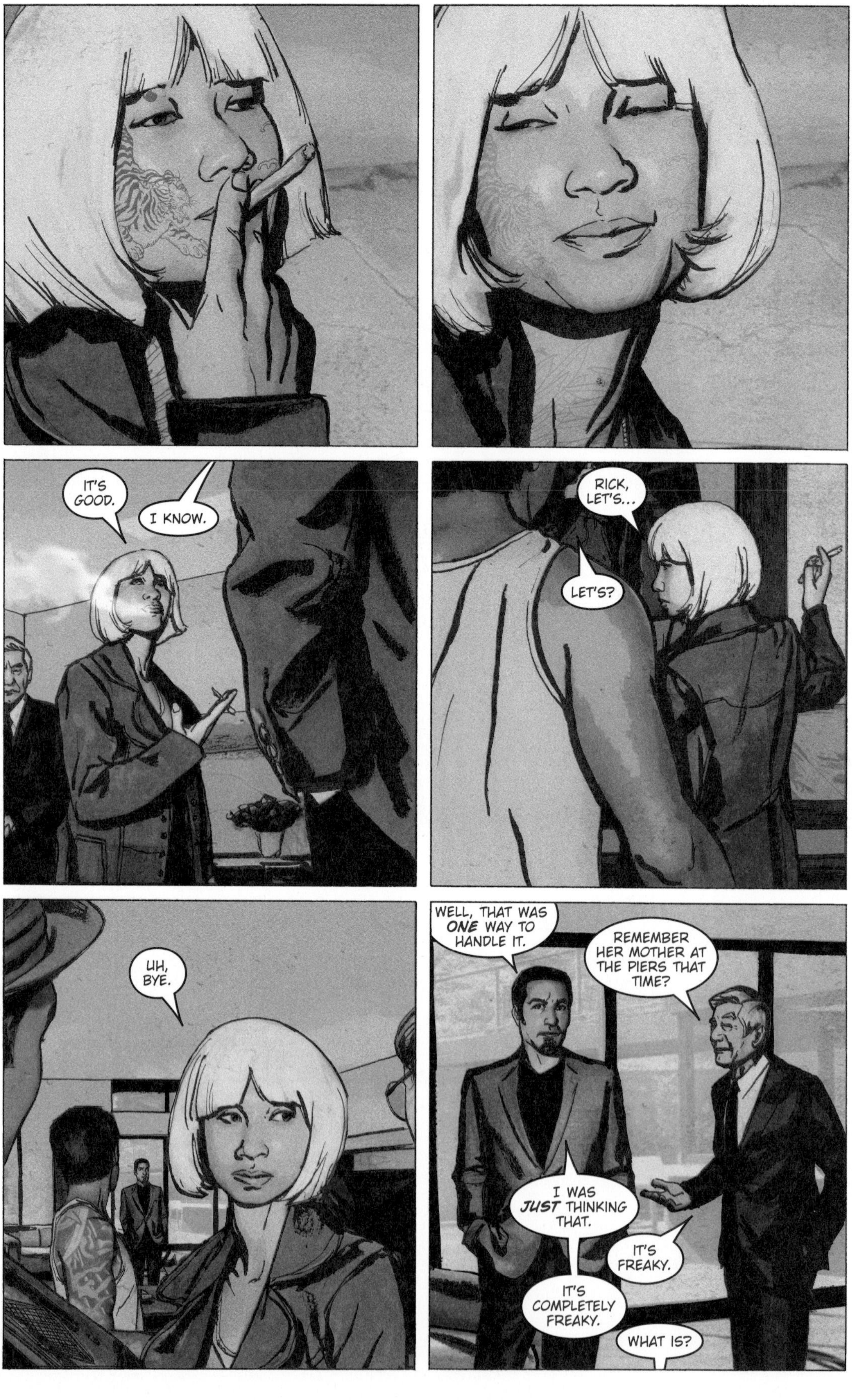
IT'S GOOD.
I KNOW.
RICK, LET'S...
LET'S?
UH, BYE.
WELL, THAT WAS ONE WAY TO HANDLE IT.
REMEMBER HER MOTHER AT THE PIERS THAT TIME?
I WAS JUST THINKING THAT.
IT'S FREAKY.
IT'S COMPLETELY FREAKY.
WHAT IS?

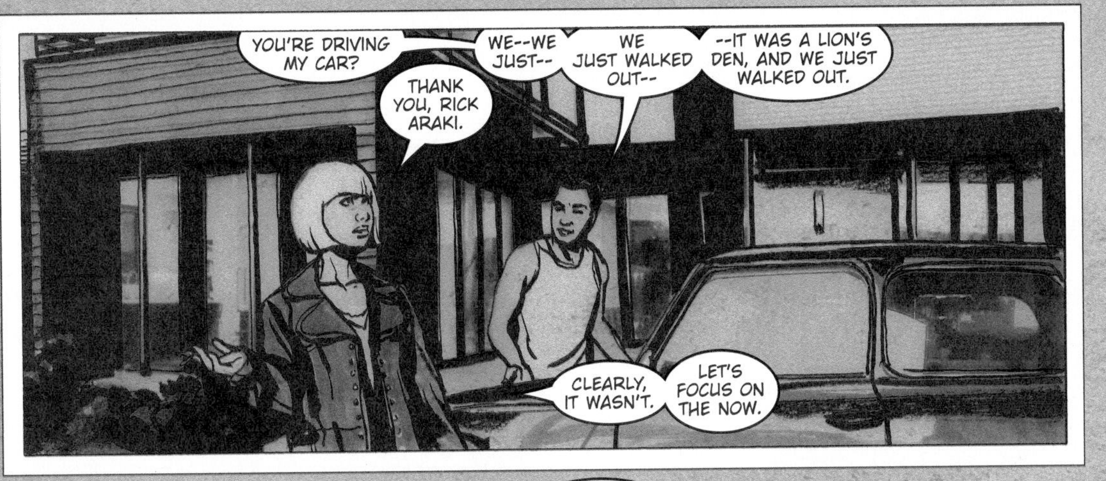
YOU'RE DRIVING MY CAR?
WE--WE JUST--
THANK YOU, RICK ARAKI.
WE JUST WALKED OUT--
--IT WAS A LION'S DEN, AND WE JUST WALKED OUT.
CLEARLY, IT WASN'T.
LET'S FOCUS ON THE NOW.

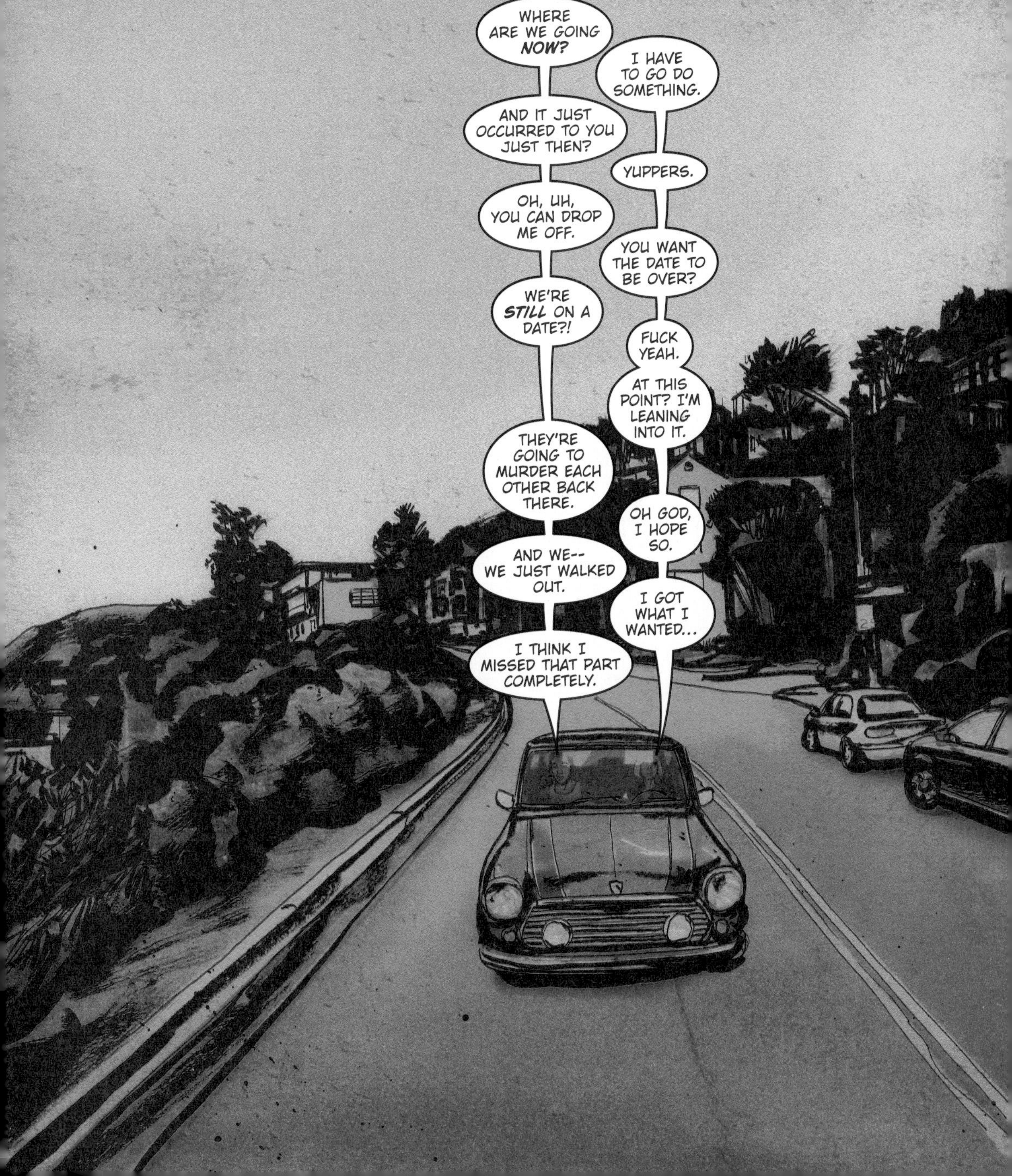
WHERE ARE WE GOING *NOW?*
I HAVE TO GO DO SOMETHING.
AND IT JUST OCCURRED TO YOU JUST THEN?
YUPPERS.
OH, UH, YOU CAN DROP ME OFF.
YOU WANT THE DATE TO BE OVER?
WE'RE *STILL* ON A DATE?!
FUCK YEAH.
AT THIS POINT? I'M LEANING INTO IT.
THEY'RE GOING TO MURDER EACH OTHER BACK THERE.
OH GOD, I HOPE SO.
AND WE-- WE JUST WALKED OUT.
I GOT WHAT I WANTED...
I THINK I MISSED THAT PART COMPLETELY.

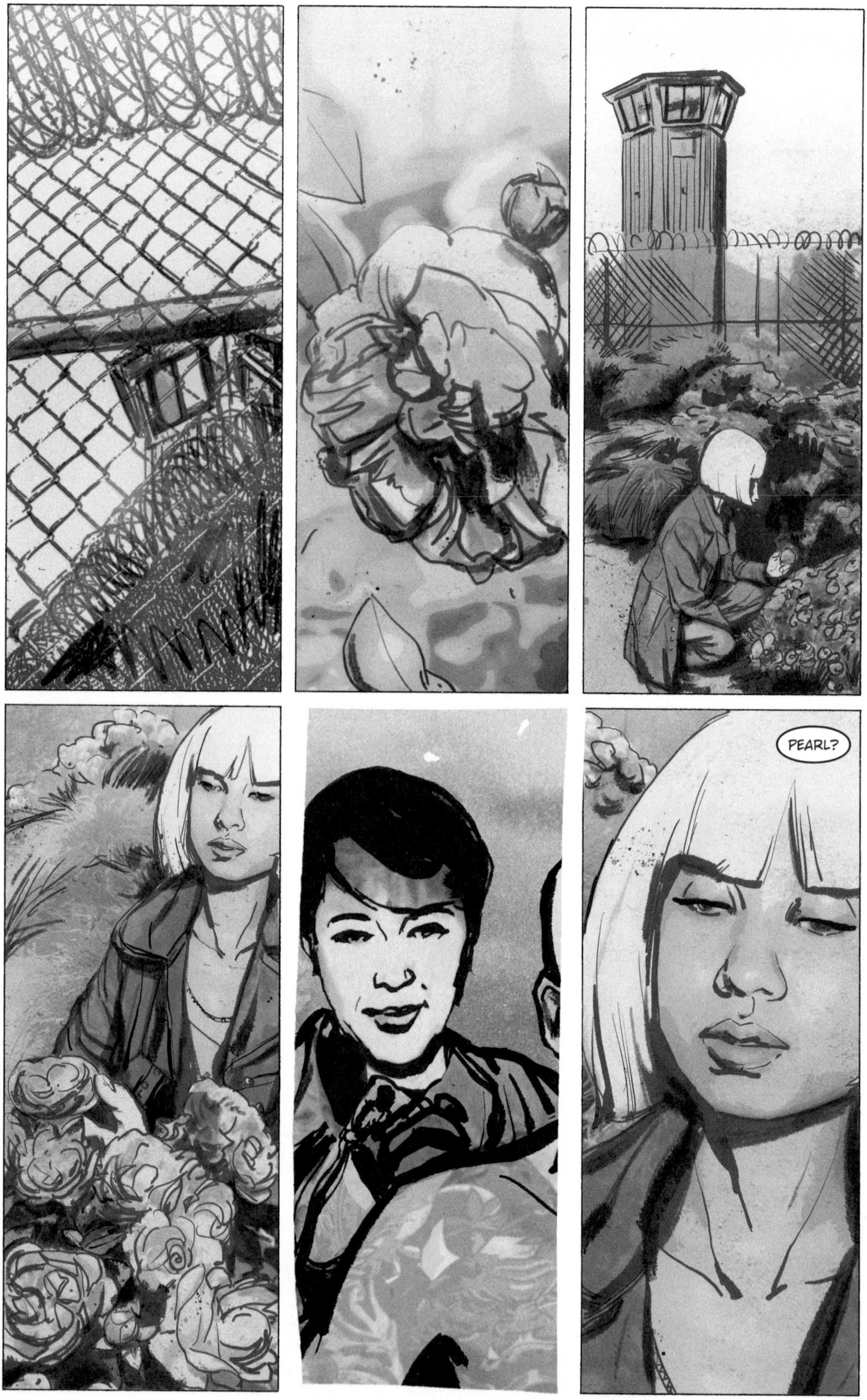
PEARL?

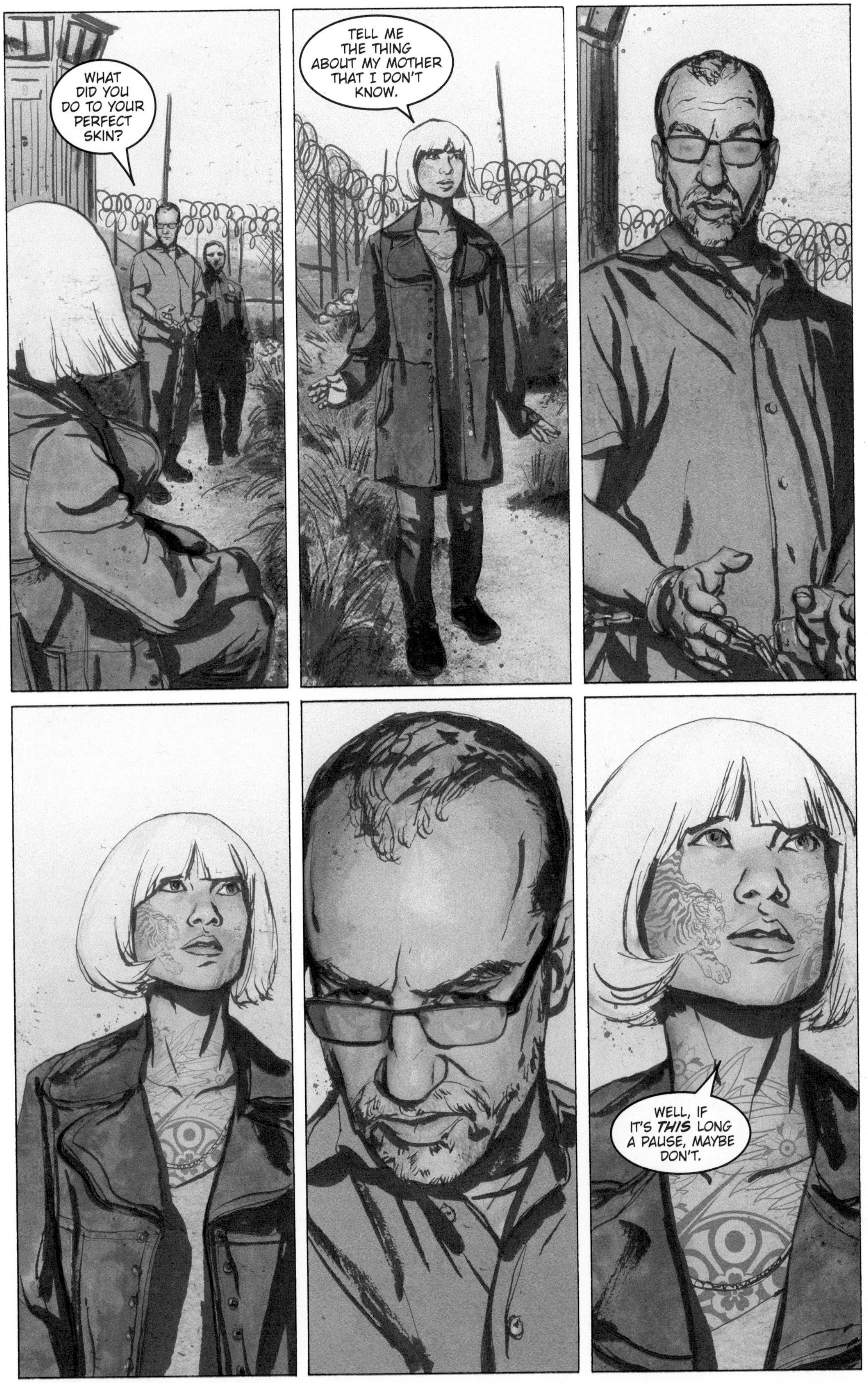
WHAT DID YOU DO TO YOUR PERFECT SKIN?
TELL ME THE THING ABOUT MY MOTHER THAT I DON'T KNOW.
WELL, IF IT'S *THIS* LONG A PAUSE, MAYBE DON'T.

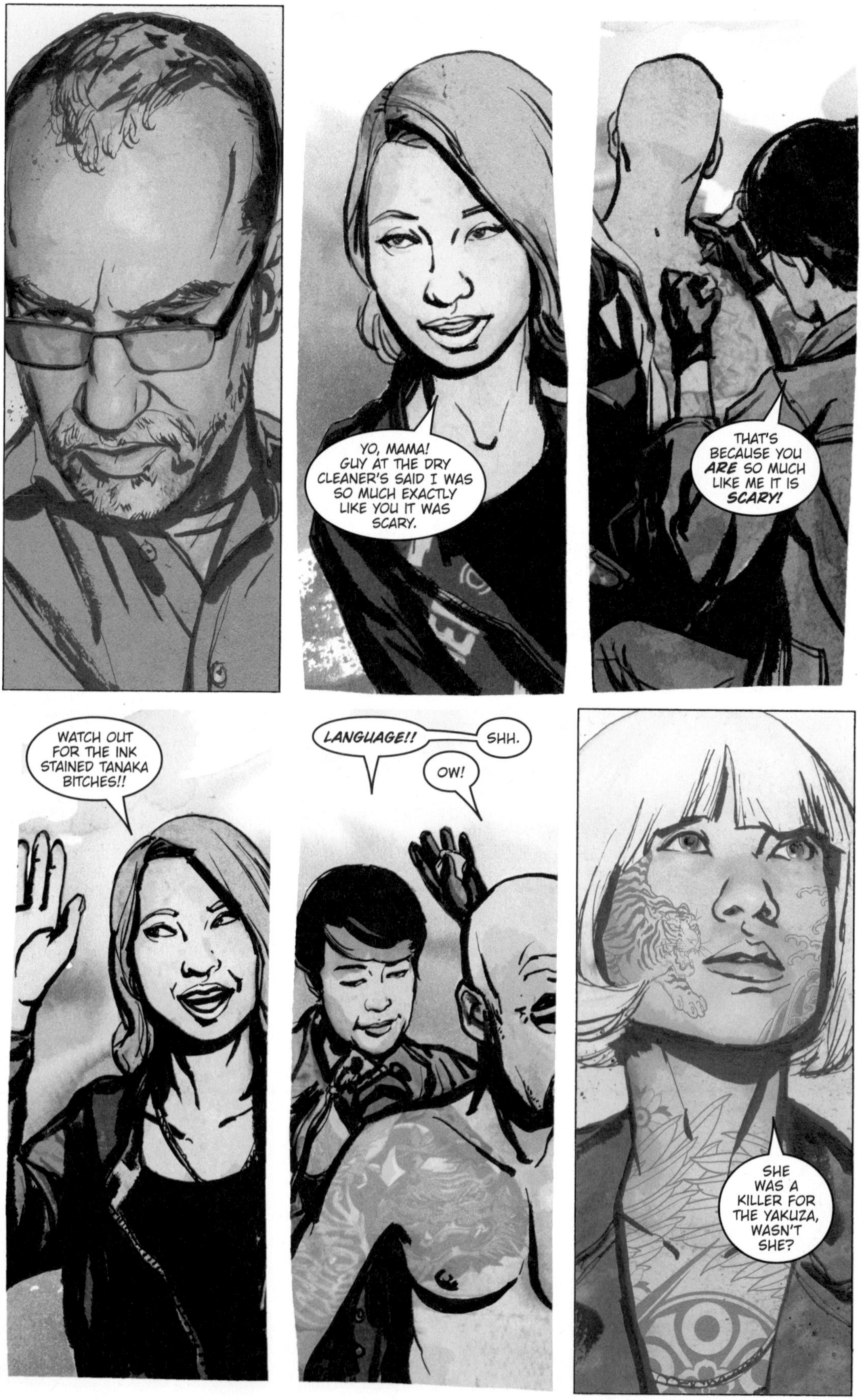
YO, MAMA! GUY AT THE DRY CLEANER'S SAID I WAS SO MUCH EXACTLY LIKE YOU IT WAS SCARY.
THAT'S BECAUSE YOU **ARE** SO MUCH LIKE ME IT IS **SCARY!**
WATCH OUT FOR THE INK STAINED TANAKA BITCHES!!
LANGUAGE!!
SHH.
OW!
SHE WAS A KILLER FOR THE YAKUZA, WASN'T SHE?

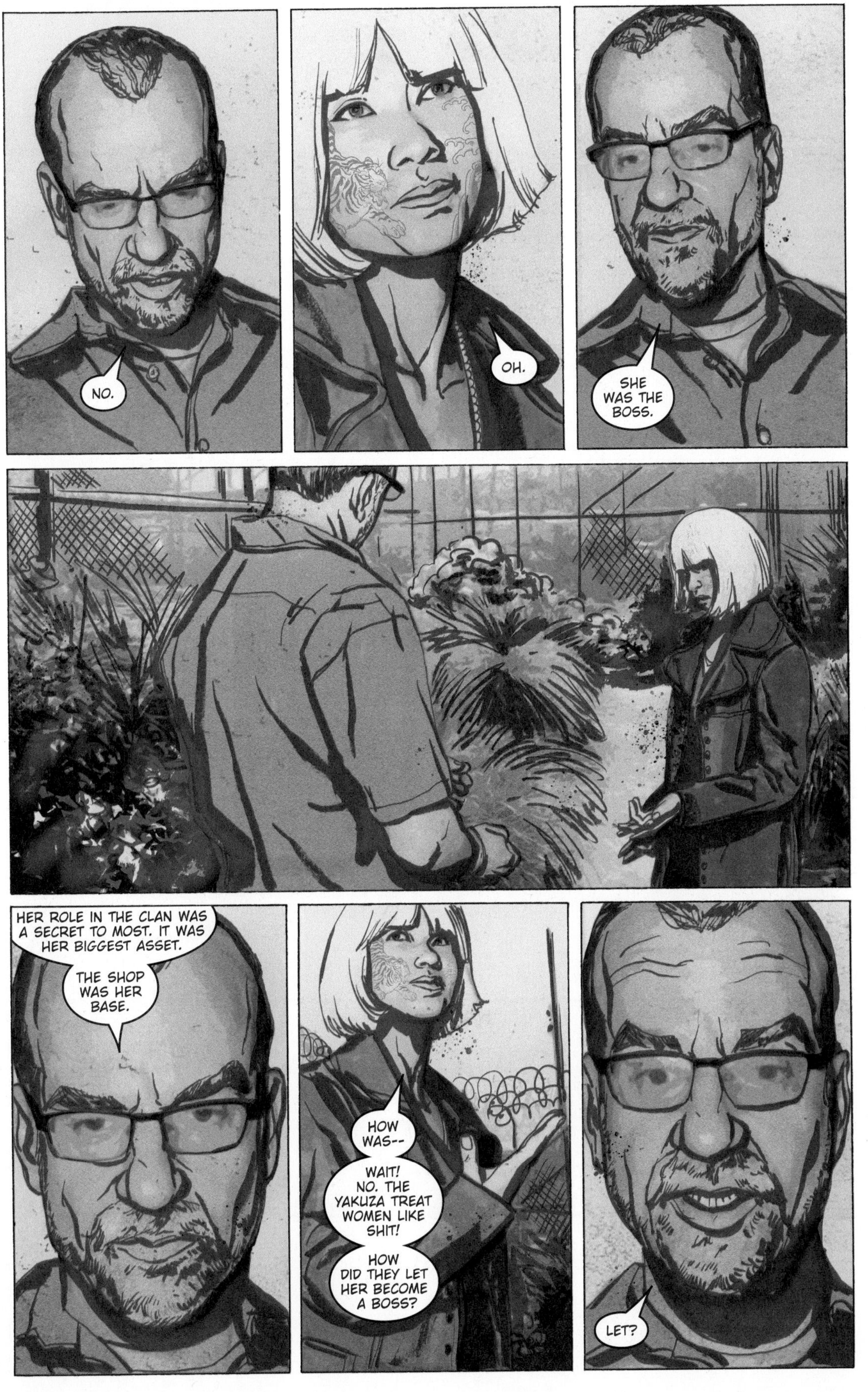
NO.
OH.
SHE WAS THE BOSS.
HER ROLE IN THE CLAN WAS A SECRET TO MOST. IT WAS HER BIGGEST ASSET.
THE SHOP WAS HER BASE.
HOW WAS--
WAIT! NO. THE YAKUZA TREAT WOMEN LIKE SHIT!
HOW DID THEY LET HER BECOME A BOSS?
LET?

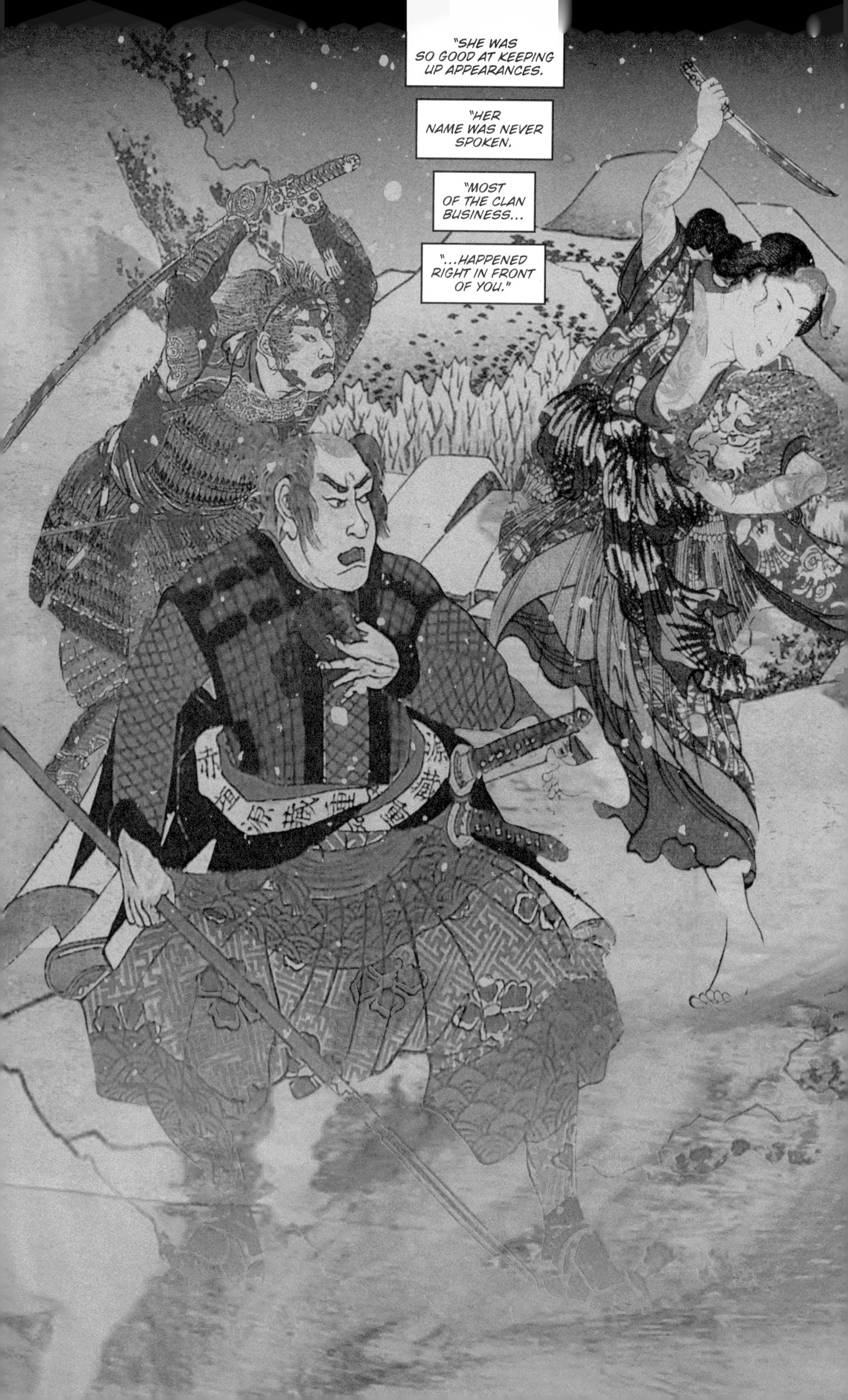
"SHE WAS SO GOOD AT KEEPING UP APPEARANCES.
"HER NAME WAS NEVER SPOKEN.
"MOST OF THE CLAN BUSINESS...
"...HAPPENED RIGHT IN FRONT OF YOU."

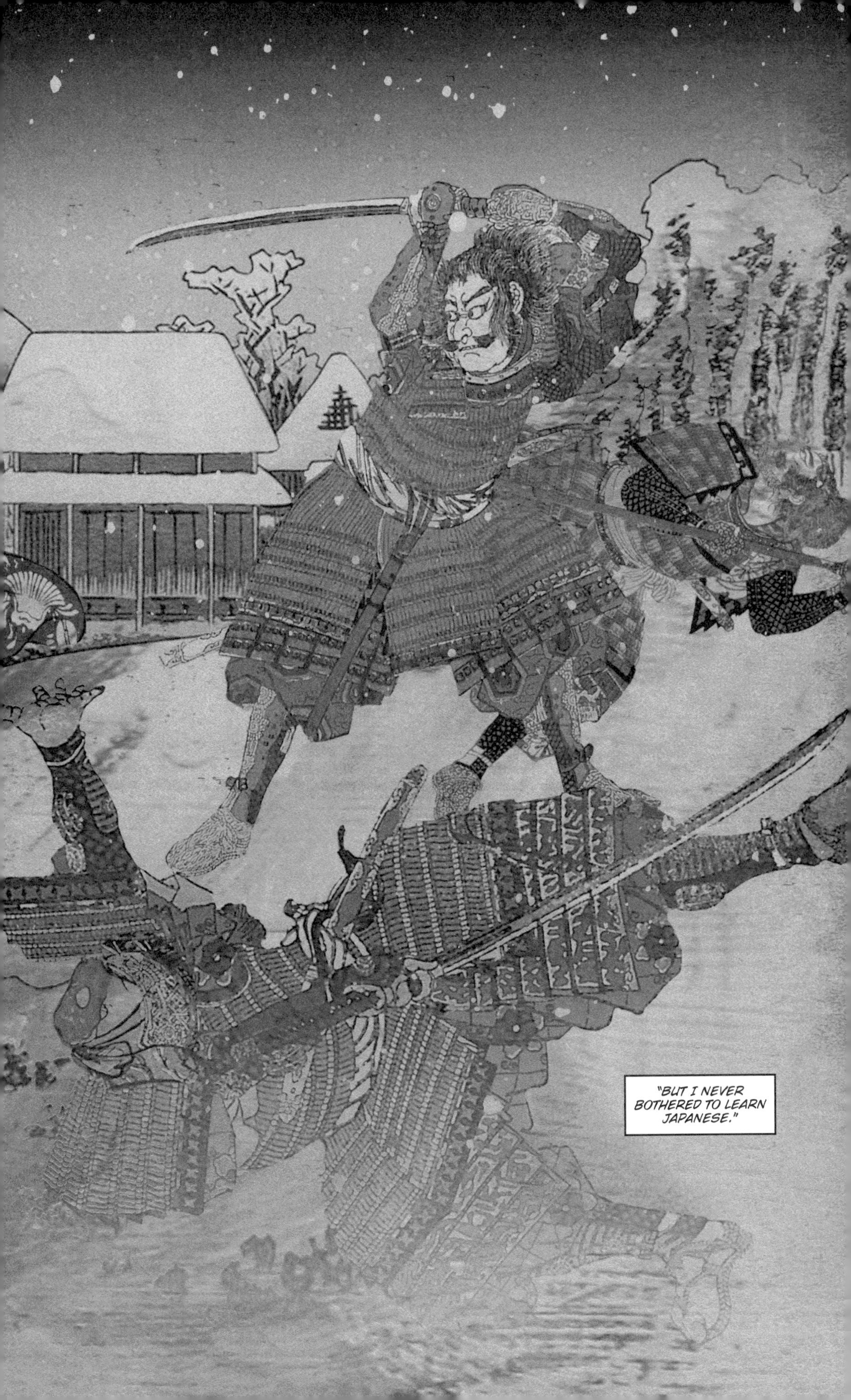
"BUT I NEVER BOTHERED TO LEARN JAPANESE."

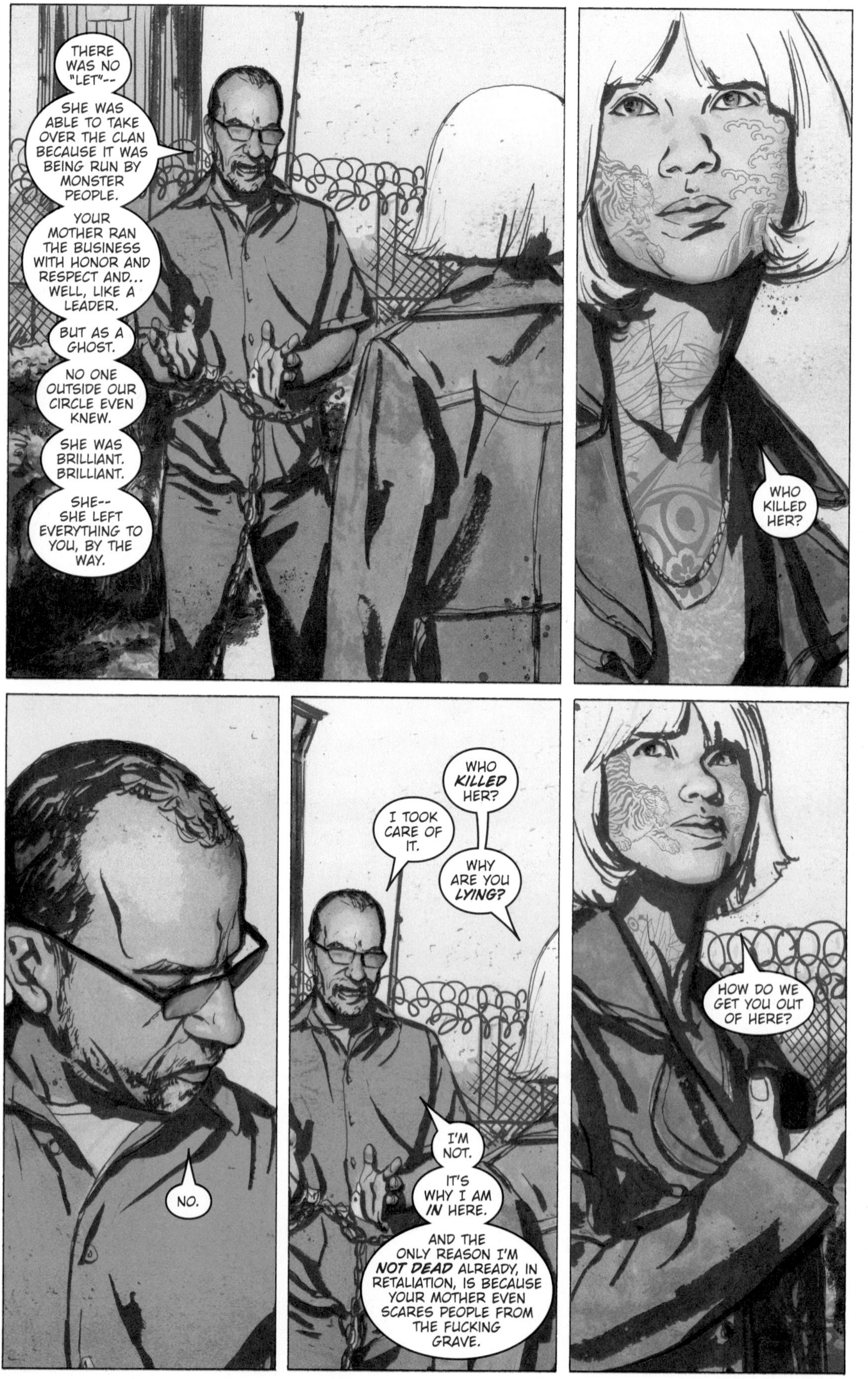
THERE WAS NO "LET"--
SHE WAS ABLE TO TAKE OVER THE CLAN BECAUSE IT WAS BEING RUN BY MONSTER PEOPLE.
YOUR MOTHER RAN THE BUSINESS WITH HONOR AND RESPECT AND... WELL, LIKE A LEADER.
BUT AS A GHOST.
NO ONE OUTSIDE OUR CIRCLE EVEN KNEW.
SHE WAS BRILLIANT. BRILLIANT.
SHE-- SHE LEFT EVERYTHING TO YOU, BY THE WAY.
WHO KILLED HER?
NO.
WHO *KILLED* HER?
I TOOK CARE OF IT.
WHY ARE YOU *LYING?*
I'M NOT.
IT'S WHY I AM *IN* HERE.
AND THE ONLY REASON I'M *NOT DEAD* ALREADY, IN RETALIATION, IS BECAUSE YOUR MOTHER EVEN SCARES PEOPLE FROM THE FUCKING GRAVE.
HOW DO WE GET YOU OUT OF HERE?

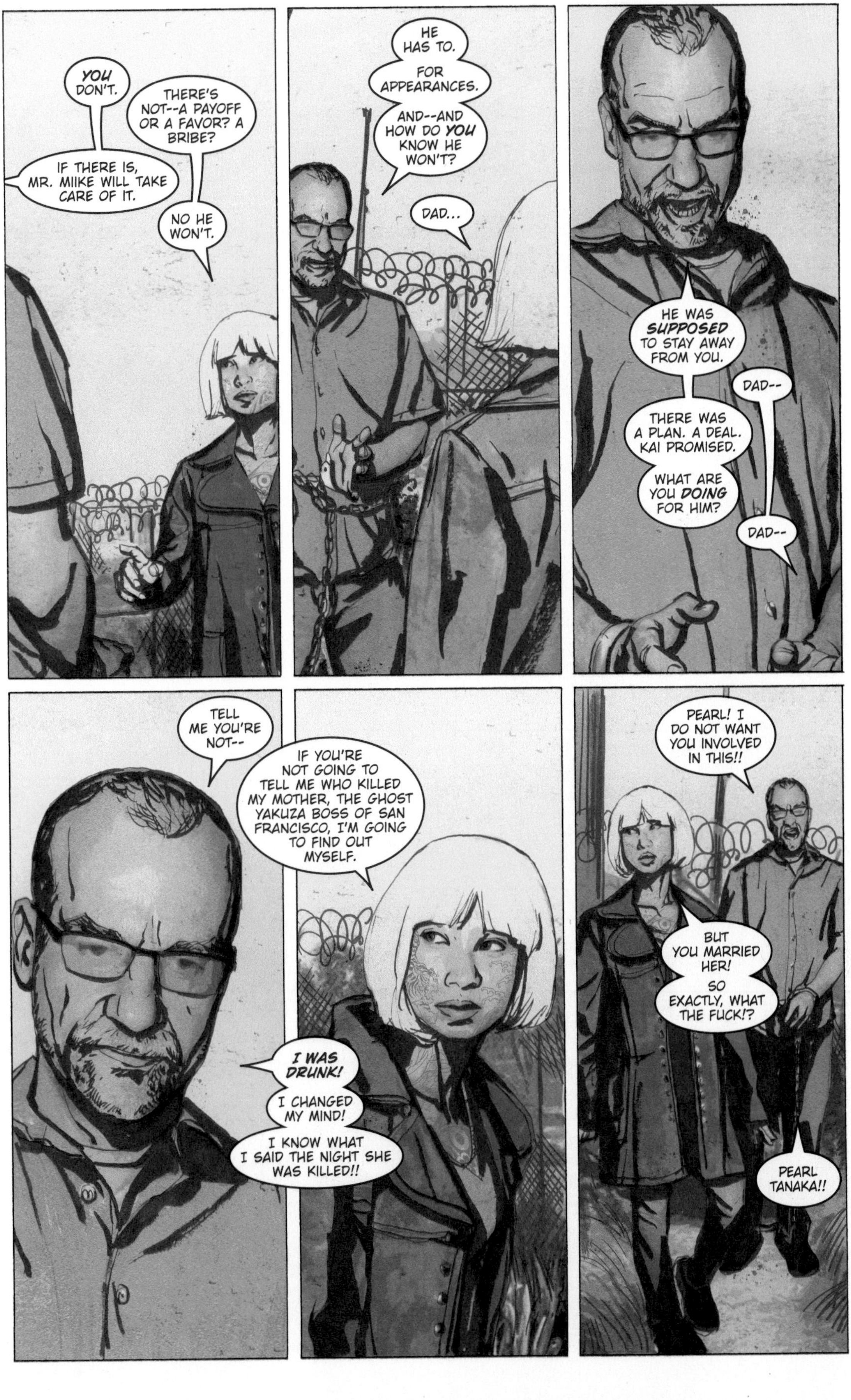

YOU DON'T.
THERE'S NOT--A PAYOFF OR A FAVOR? A BRIBE?
IF THERE IS, MR. MIIKE WILL TAKE CARE OF IT.
NO HE WON'T.
HE HAS TO.
FOR APPEARANCES.
AND--AND HOW DO YOU KNOW HE WON'T?
DAD...
HE WAS SUPPOSED TO STAY AWAY FROM YOU.
THERE WAS A PLAN. A DEAL. KAI PROMISED.
WHAT ARE YOU DOING FOR HIM?
DAD--
DAD--
TELL ME YOU'RE NOT--
IF YOU'RE NOT GOING TO TELL ME WHO KILLED MY MOTHER, THE GHOST YAKUZA BOSS OF SAN FRANCISCO, I'M GOING TO FIND OUT MYSELF.
I WAS DRUNK!
I CHANGED MY MIND!
I KNOW WHAT I SAID THE NIGHT SHE WAS KILLED!!
PEARL! I DO NOT WANT YOU INVOLVED IN THIS!!
BUT YOU MARRIED HER!
SO EXACTLY, WHAT THE FUCK!?
PEARL TANAKA!!

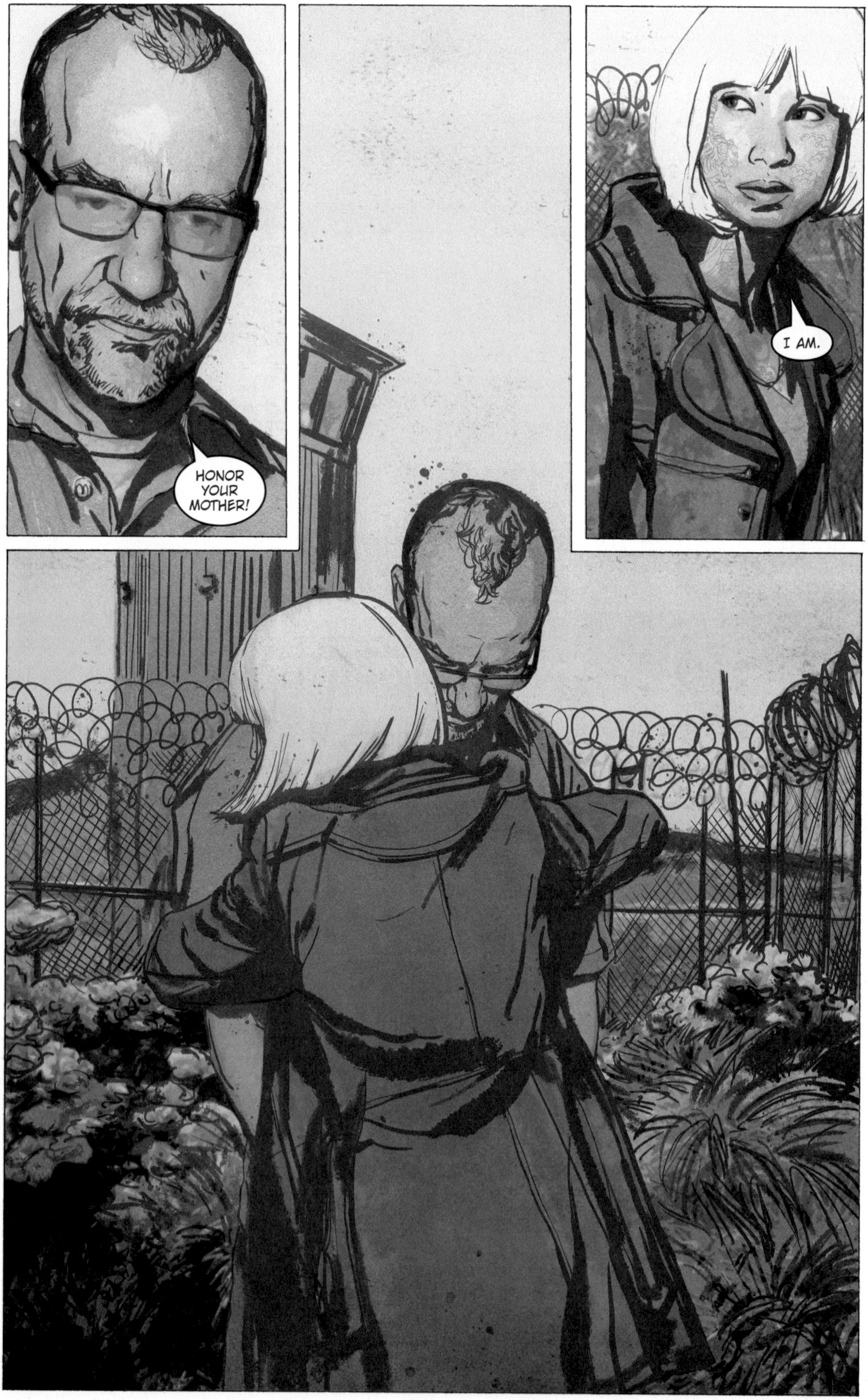
HONOR YOUR MOTHER!
I AM.

IS THE DATE OVER YET?

HOW DID YOUR IMPRISONED YAKUZA SOLDIER DAD TAKE IT WHEN YOU TOLD HIM WE MADE OUT?

WE DID NOT SPEAK OF THAT.

WE SOMEHOW HAD BIGGER FISH TO FRY THAN WHAT HE IS GOING TO DO TO YOU WHEN HE GETS OUT.

NOT TERRIBLY FUNNY AFTER THE NIGHT WE'VE JUST HAD.

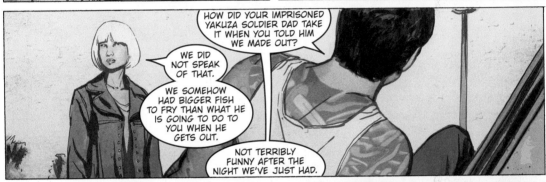

OR IT'S *HILARIOUS* AFTER THE NIGHT WE'VE HAD.

YOU OKAY?

NO.

ARE WE IN TROUBLE?

SO THAT'S...A YES.

SHIT.

NO.

I *LOVE* THIS ABOUT YOU.

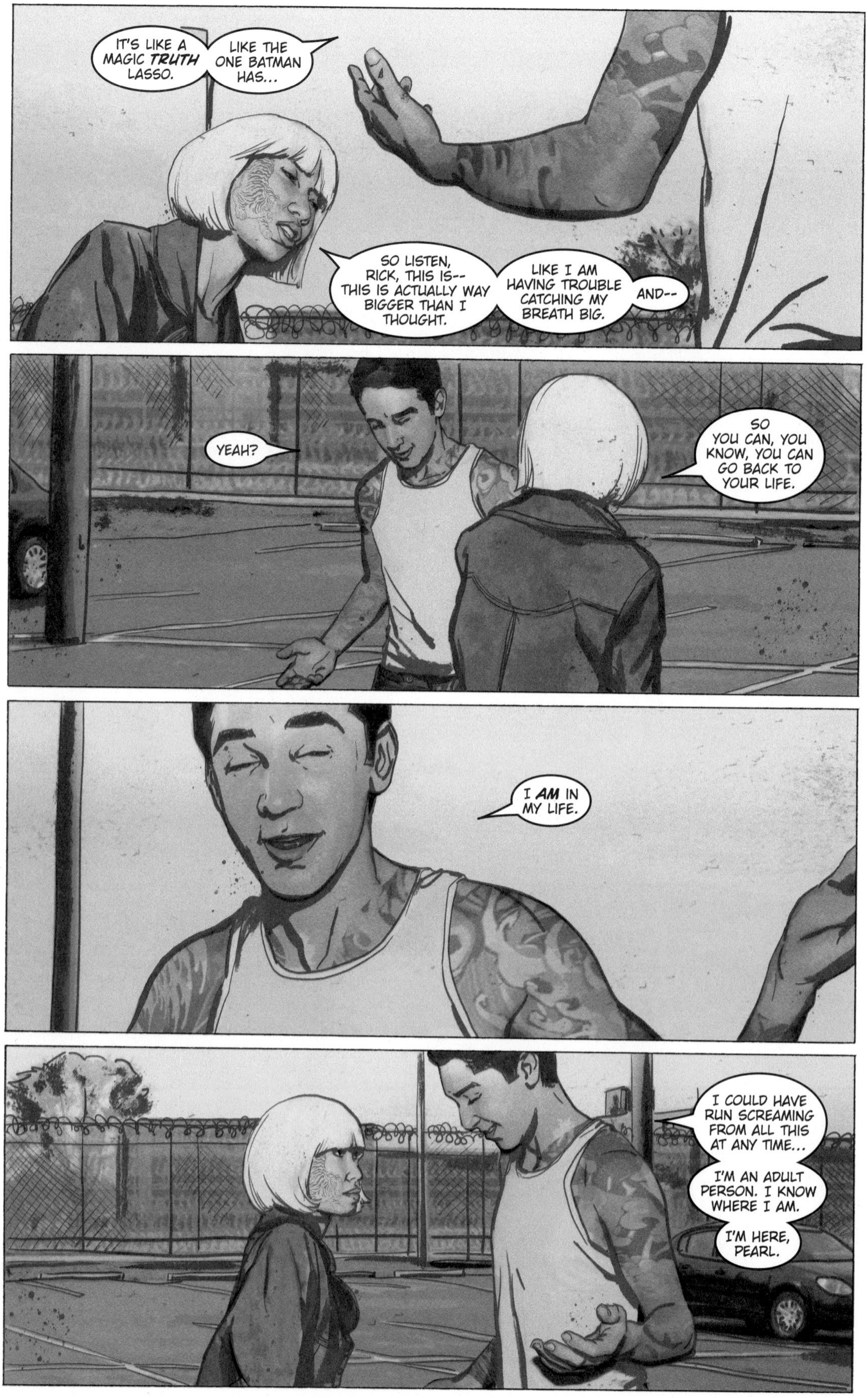
IT'S LIKE A MAGIC *TRUTH* LASSO.
LIKE THE ONE BATMAN HAS...
SO LISTEN, RICK, THIS IS-- THIS IS ACTUALLY WAY BIGGER THAN I THOUGHT.
LIKE I AM HAVING TROUBLE CATCHING MY BREATH BIG.
AND--
YEAH?
SO YOU CAN, YOU KNOW, YOU CAN GO BACK TO YOUR LIFE.
I *AM* IN MY LIFE.
I COULD HAVE RUN SCREAMING FROM ALL THIS AT ANY TIME...
I'M AN ADULT PERSON. I KNOW WHERE I AM.
I'M HERE, PEARL.

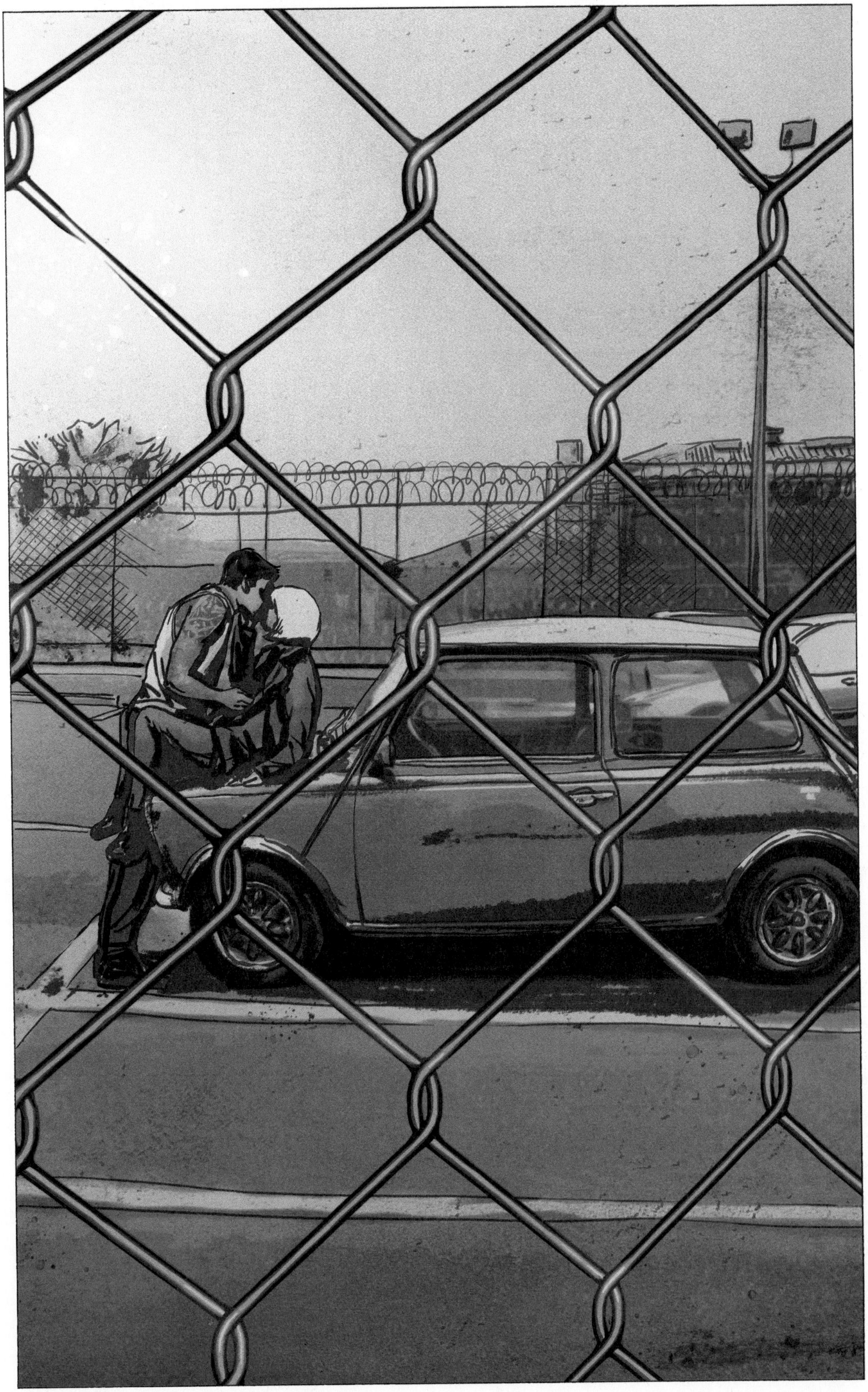

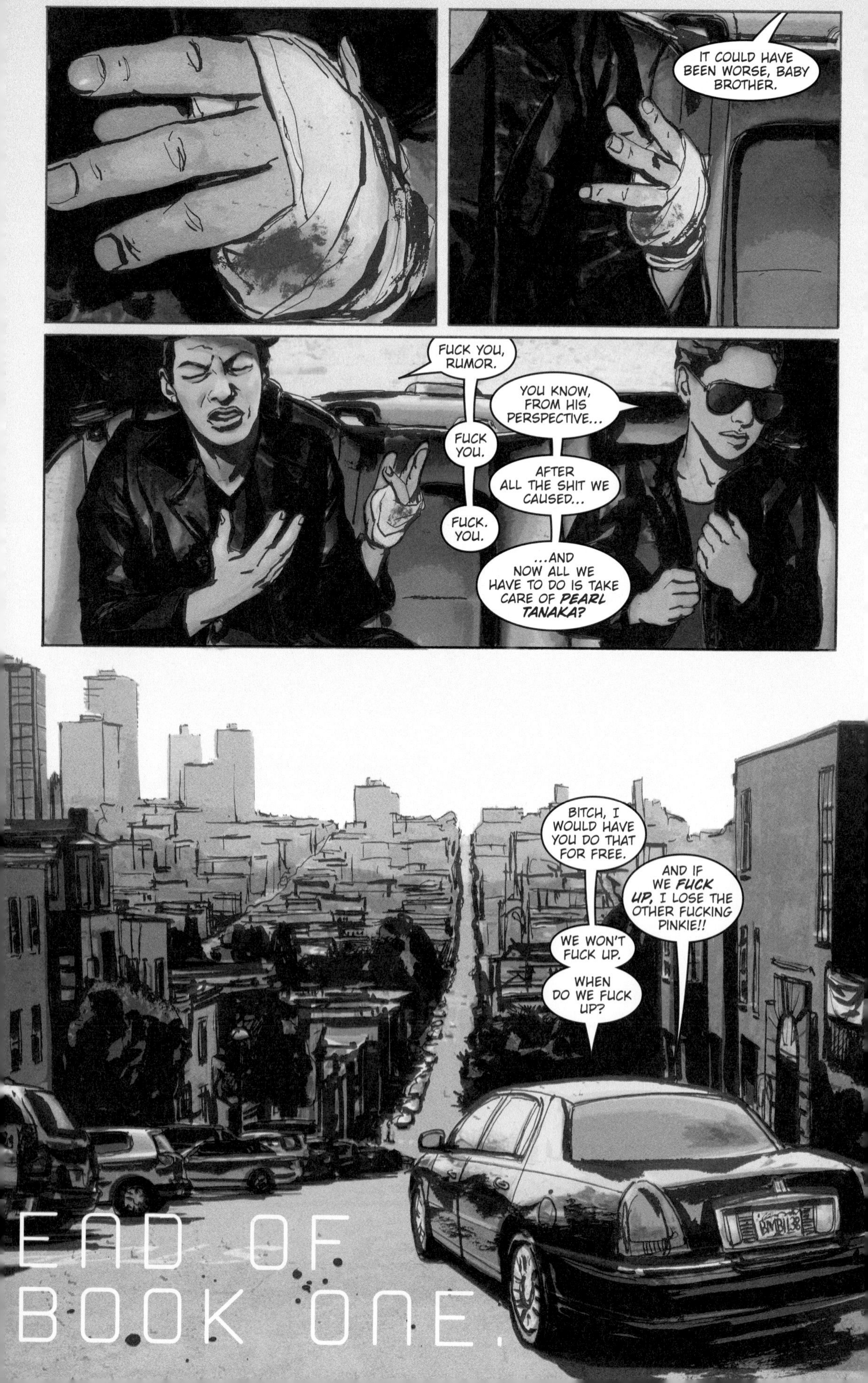
IT COULD HAVE BEEN WORSE, BABY BROTHER.
FUCK YOU, RUMOR.
FUCK YOU.
FUCK. YOU.
YOU KNOW, FROM HIS PERSPECTIVE...
AFTER ALL THE SHIT WE CAUSED...
...AND NOW ALL WE HAVE TO DO IS TAKE CARE OF PEARL TANAKA?
BITCH, I WOULD HAVE YOU DO THAT FOR FREE.
AND IF WE FUCK UP, I LOSE THE OTHER FUCKING PINKIE!!
WE WON'T FUCK UP.
WHEN DO WE FUCK UP?
END OF BOOK ONE.

INTERVIEW by Ernie Estrella for Syfy Wire

The announcement of Brian Michael Bendis' move to DC Comics came with news of writing Superman and Batman, but the most exciting aspect to the deal was that there would be new creator-owned books and extended life for his current Jinxworld catalog. The first of the new ongoing series will be PEARL and its first issue will debut this Wednesday at comic book shops and in digital format.

PEARL is set in modern-day San Francisco and centers on an incredible tattoo artist who is also an assassin for the Yakuza. Flourishing in one life, Pearl was unfortunately born into another life that she is desperately trying to free herself from, but her talents and a special ability complicate things.

Syfy Wire has exclusive preview art and an interview with co-creator Brian Michael Bendis about the new ongoing series, coming back to crime stories, Yakuza in American culture, more representation in comics and more.

AFTER JESSICA

Alias debuted in 2001, introducing the world to Jessica Jones, the foul-mouthed Avengers flunkie turned private eye. Her prominence grew over the next decade and a half, then skyrocketed with the Netflix series that stars Krysten Ritter. Bendis and artist Michael Gaydos returned to write more adventures of the hero, but with Jessica Jones so embedded in the public consciousness, PEARL represents a new space for Bendis and Gaydos to create, free from expectations and restrictions.

"Our goal was to create something that was as authentic as Jessica, but completely different in every way," Bendis tells *Syfy Wire*. "There's a history in comics, where if someone has a hit or a genre passion, they'll do a variation of that hit in a creator-owned book. I get that instinct, and I won't say if I've done that or I haven't done that (in the past). But in this particular instance, Jessica has become so out-of-our-hands iconic that we had to make sure whatever we put next in the world was unique and as inviting."

ARRESTED BY CRIME

Something that is a trademark of Bendis' creator-owned work is how steeped it is in crime fiction. While his legacy will include *Spider-Man*, SUPERMAN and *The Avengers*, street-level stories like his runs on *Sam and Twitch*, *Daredevil*, POWERS and TORSO rank among his best. Bendis told me that he attempted to steer away from the crime genre for his early Jinxworld-DC books, but in the nature of trading stories creatively, amongst creators he looked up to and his peers, especially in a comics-rich town like Portland, great crime stories would come up.

"I'm getting loaded up with great organized crime stories that I'm going to *have* to tell because I can't stop myself," he says. "Not only when I was researching PEARL did I find all of these beautiful reasons for her existence, but I was given this incredible backdrop of stories that were inspiring me to go. I was looking not to do organized crime, yet they're the best stories! It's messy people getting in trouble. Who doesn't want to read, write and analyze that?"

Bendis says that he loves the genre because it's an opportunity to tell a story about characters at their most stressed state. Crime fiction is typically about people making decisions and facing the consequences. Pearl winds up doing something in the first issue that draws her some unneeded attention.

"Now because it's crime fiction," Bendis explained, "my job is to show characters thrown against the wall and you find out what they really are. When you shake characters and put them in a crime fiction situation, it's almost a shortcut to getting to: What are they made out of? What are the choices they make in the story? I get obsessed with out-of-control characters. That's what I end up writing about."

YAKUZA IN AMERICA

PEARL features an American Yakuza story, but Bendis and Gaydos made it a point to veer from the numerous clichés regarding Yakuza. The goal was to avoid creating things like the 1989 Ridley Scott film *Black Rain*. Instead, Bendis looked to other '80s films like Jonathan Demme's *Something Wild* (1986) and *Married to the Mob* (1988) for inspiration.

"These movies remove all the clichés of the story you're used to hearing from gangster stories and came back with something completely charming, because they broke every rule," Bendis admired. "I wanted to apply that to this. I wanted to attack this story about the Yakuza by removing all the clichés, all the stuff you see all the time in films like *Black Rain* and get into something more real and maybe more fun."

It's a change from what he did in earlier books, such as *Daredevil*'s Yakuza storyline. As a Filipino-American, I was curious about Bendis' thoughts on that *Daredevil* arc while working on PEARL, and writing an Asian-American story and his choice to feature an Asian woman and as his protagonist along with her culture.

"If I could go back I'd represent those Yakuza characters differently," he admits. "There's more I could have done but I was very focused on Matt Murdock, but here I am with more years under my belt. I thought of *Daredevil* when I was doing PEARL. Then, doing research, a woman was telling me a story last year in San Francisco. She was just a person telling me a story of her life and her dealing with Yakuza-tinged organized crime and it had so much different and fascinating color that I was a bit embarrassed by the Yakuza story that I had told in *Daredevil*."

Gaydos and Bendis began talking about how the Yakuza in particular were being represented in American culture and wanting to add something different to the conversation.

"I am a Ridley Scott fan, and I looked at *Black Rain* and that film is filled with clichés. (Another) one was *Rising Sun*," he says. "I caught a bit of that recently, it's difficult for me to watch. These are good storytellers with some lousy representation in their story that begs for it. So, I said, let's try to do the opposite of that, because it's true and it makes a better story."

SKIN DEEP AND BENEATH

What separates PEARL from the average bit of crime fiction is its elements of science fiction. Tattoos emerge on Pearl's skin in response to her changing emotions.

"It's a unique skin condition and (is just) one of her unique situations. We started talking with everyone about tattoo stuff and tattoo guns and (Michael) mentioned that someone very close to him had a rare skin condition, that when the person got angry or excited, the scars fills in. Another artist had pointed out that they had tattooed themselves with an empty tattoo gun, and it fills in when they're angry. You couldn't see the ink. There's no ink there, but the scar was there, and this idea of having someone having a skin condition when they get flushed, becomes a tattoo, is a very exciting visual. After that we were off to the races!"

Pearl is also an albino, and albinism has always largely been ignored in comics, save for defining traits in the occasional villain. PEARL encompasses the complexities of being many things to many different cultures, but most importantly, the lead character.

"That was another thing I was happy to get rid of: albinos always being the creepy assassin. I read an article about how there are no lead albino heroes or characters. So as we're talking about representation in comics and media, then there seems to be a good one to fix. I was happy to course correct as much as we can. Pearl's a very unique person; no else has this."

Beyond Pearl herself, the comic draws from largely true stories. When visiting San Francisco one day, Bendis found himself in a once-segregated neighborhood that banned Asian residents.

"As a Jewish person, I can relate to someone being told they're not allowed in," he says. "I was boiling. In PEARL, the crime boss actually buys the once 'No Oriental' San Fran neighborhood. That's based on a true story. That's one example, but there are dozens more in the first issue."

BEING AUTHENTIC
IS BEING TRUE TO YOURSELF

Now to me, good stories reflect well on the storytellers, regardless of who that storyteller is. Bendis has a history of creating and writing diverse characters, including Luke Cage, Riri Williams, Miles Morales and Jessica Jones. Writing about an Asian woman will open him up for criticism again, but he takes it all in stride, letting his gut and his instinct lead the way.

"No writer is perfect and always makes the perfect choices," he says. "It's art. It's messy. Listen, I spend all day looking for truth and honest moments. I do the work. I do the research. I keep my eyes and heart open to the world around me and I try to reflect it in my work. That's the point of doing this. I listen to everything. Especially stuff I don't like or understand."

Still, criticism can persist, and it gets understandably pointed when a storyteller is visiting unfamiliar cultures and lands. Countless things swirl around amidst the neuroses of a writer, that it's only human to second-guess and wonder what Bendis thinks of when trying to broaden the scope of the stories we get to read.

"I do contemplate if I'm the right person to tell a story or not. It's not even about a cultural thing. Like, watching *Ready Player One* I was saying, was Spielberg really the right person to direct that movie? Should someone else have done that because it was really about him?" he notes. "When I was sick in the hospital, these Jinxworld books, and Superman, were what kept me focused and not screaming into the abyss. So I know, this time at least, that these are the stories I need to tell and the people I need to tell them with."

THE ART OF WAR

Fans of *Alias* and *Jessica Jones* will tell you that it was visually a very dark series, as if the scenes on the page were lit with old yellow bulbs. PEARL offers a different aesthetic, with a white fluorescence and loads of visual eye candy. Gaydos is fully painting PEARL and it's arguably his best work to date.

In constructing the world of a tattoo artist, Bendis has even contemplated getting ink himself and has the artists narrowed down a New York artist who goes by the name Yuuz, who works out of Bang Bang NYC. Who could resist?

"Someday, I'll come to New York and have the guts to have a tattoo by Yuuz," Bendis gushed before pausing. "But, I am a little Jewish boy and I have a little voice that says tattoos are *verboten!—don't do it!* I don't get into it in the book, but as a Jewish person we were told no tattoos and that was our religion and tattoos were used as a punishment in the camps. Part of this book is looking at all of this, as the art that it is."

Thank you to *Syfy Wire* for allowing the reprinting of this article and thanks so much to you, readers, for making the launch of Jinxworld one of the great joys of my already overstuffed life.

I platonically hug you from afar,
BENDIS!

MICHAEL GAYDOS sketchbook

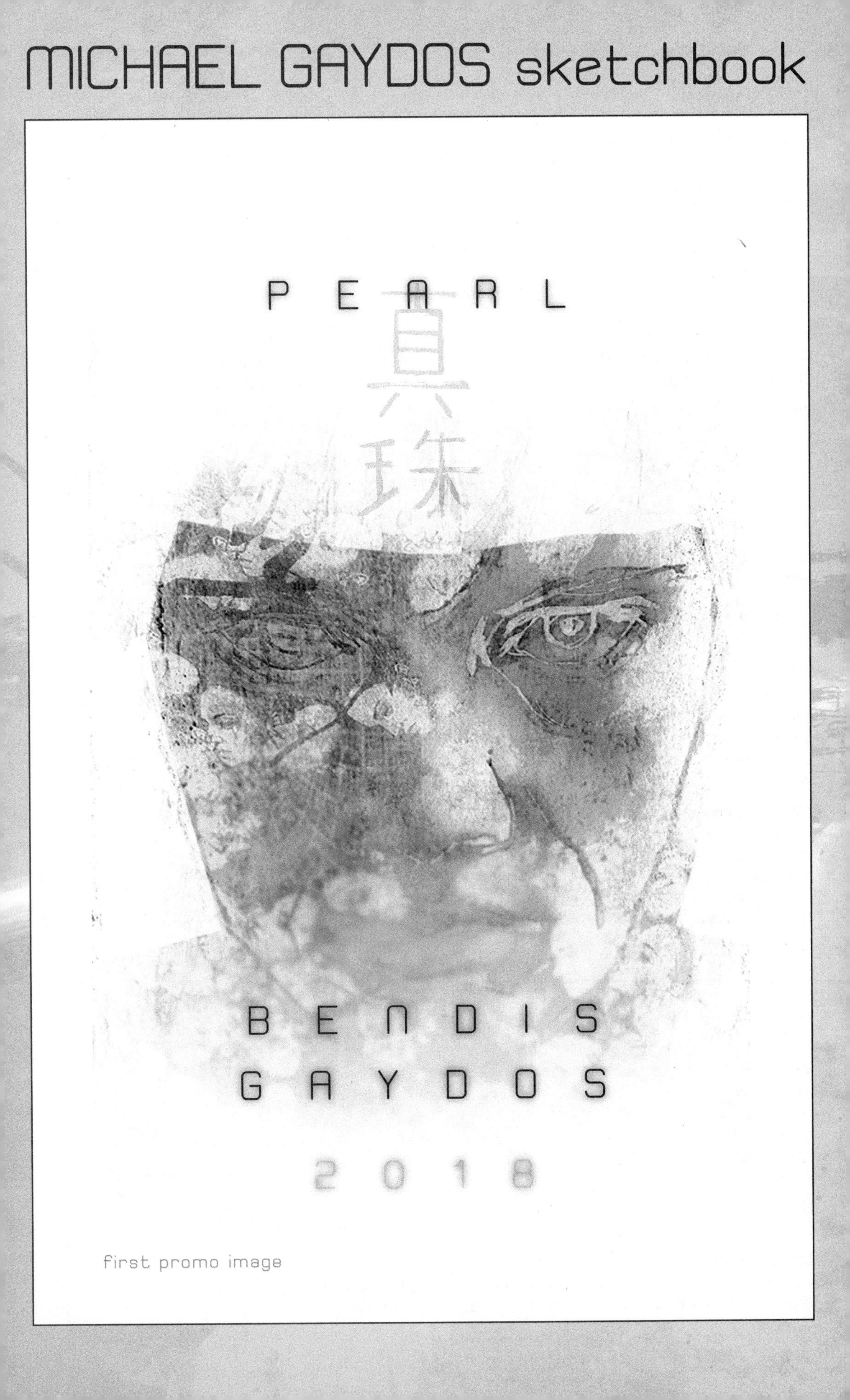
P E A R L
真珠
B E N D I S
G A Y D O S
2 0 1 8

first promo image

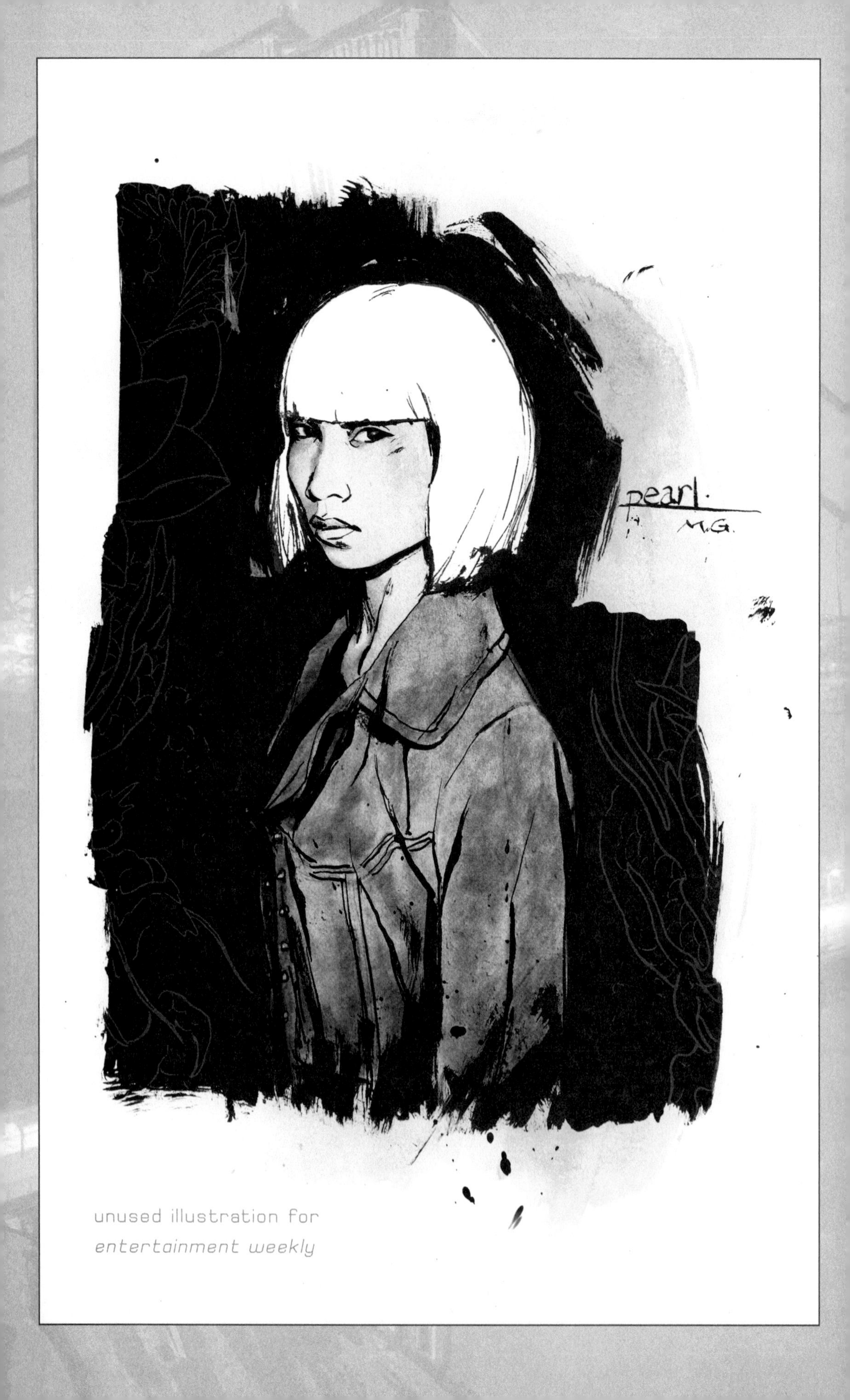
pearl.
M.G.

unused illustration for
entertainment weekly

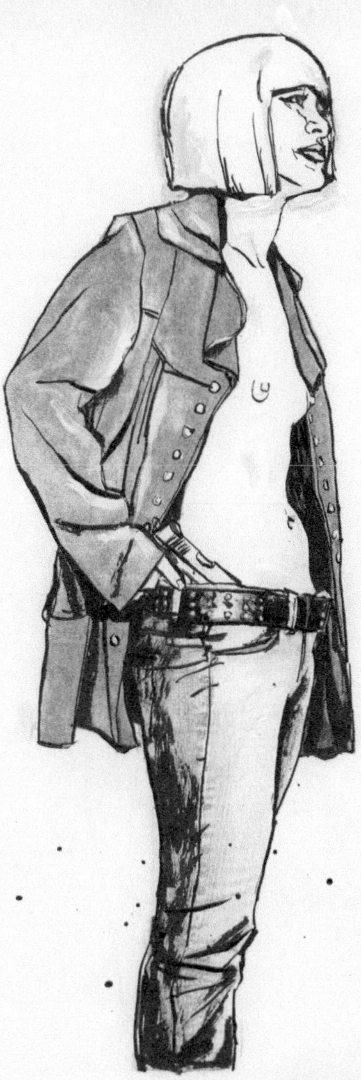

cover #2 original art

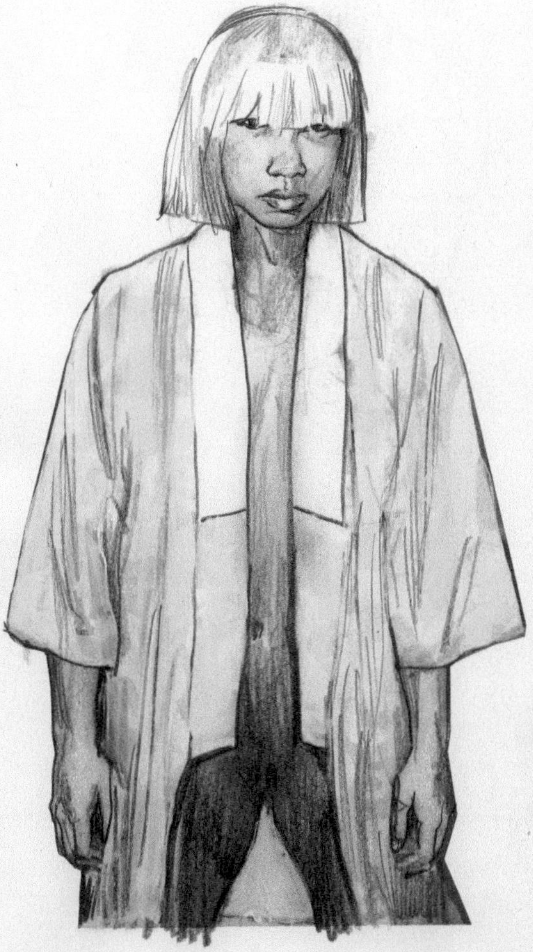

cover #6 original art

cover #3 original art

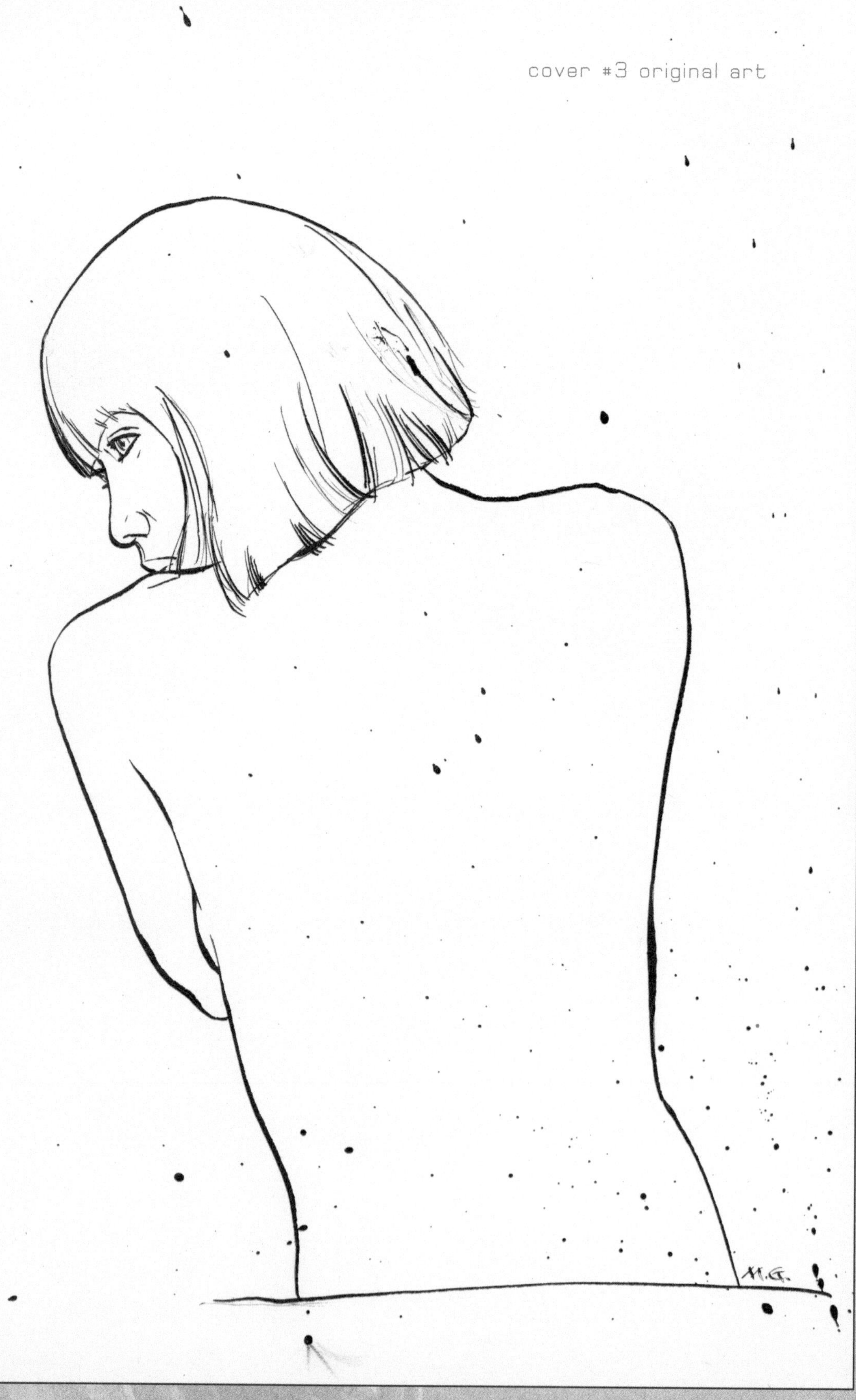
M.G.

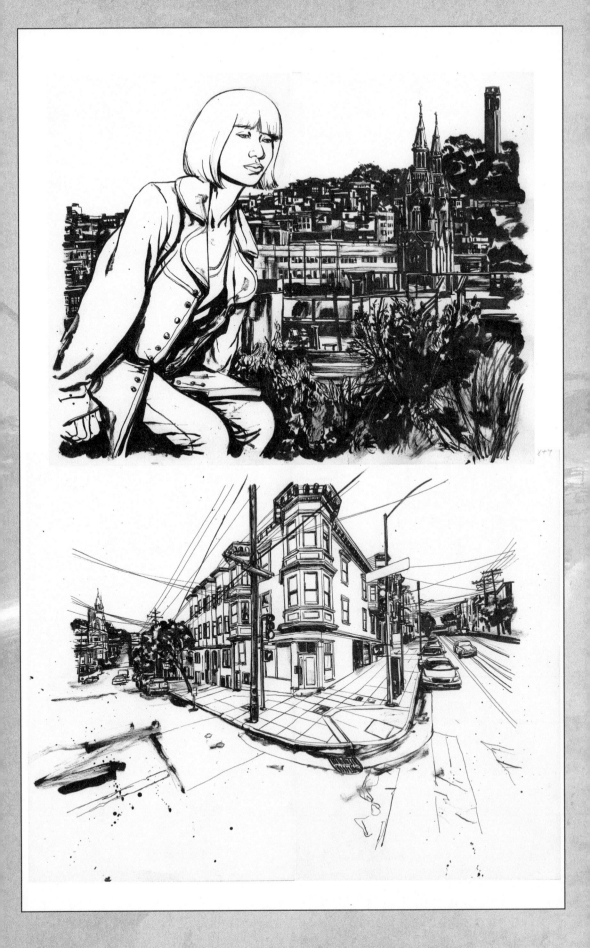

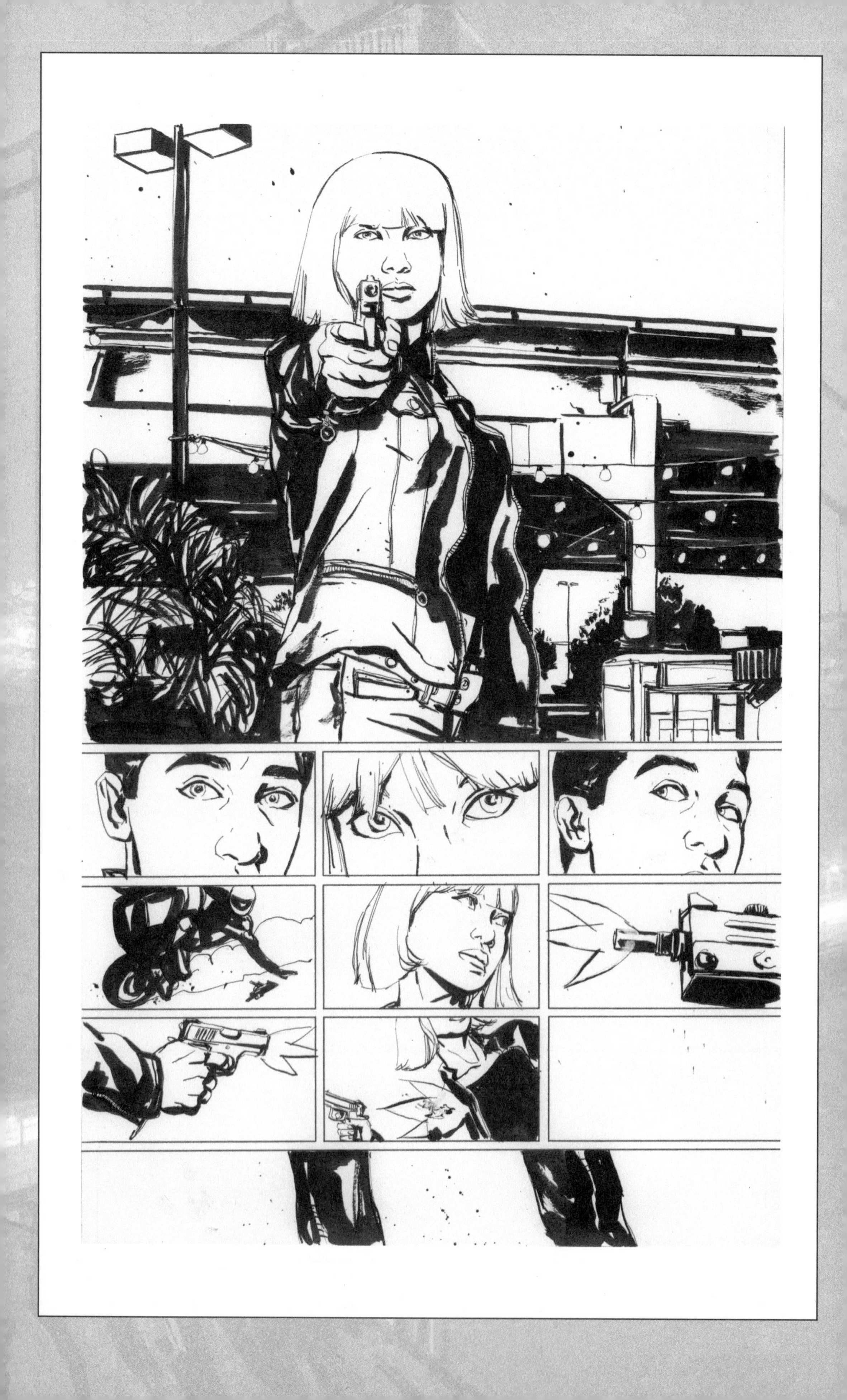

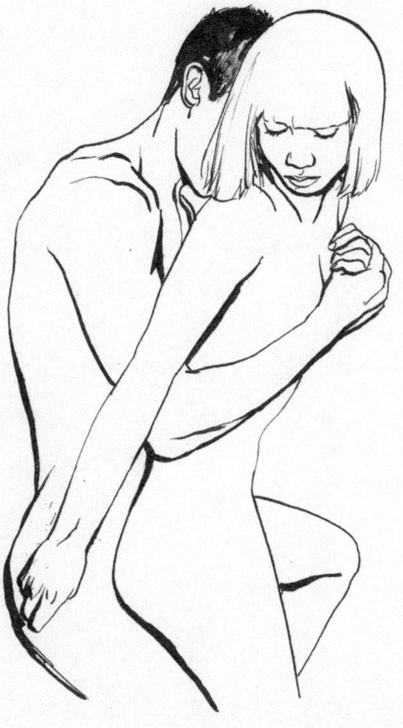

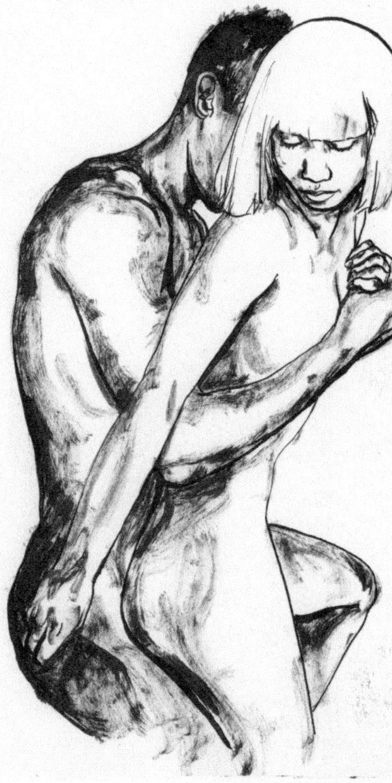

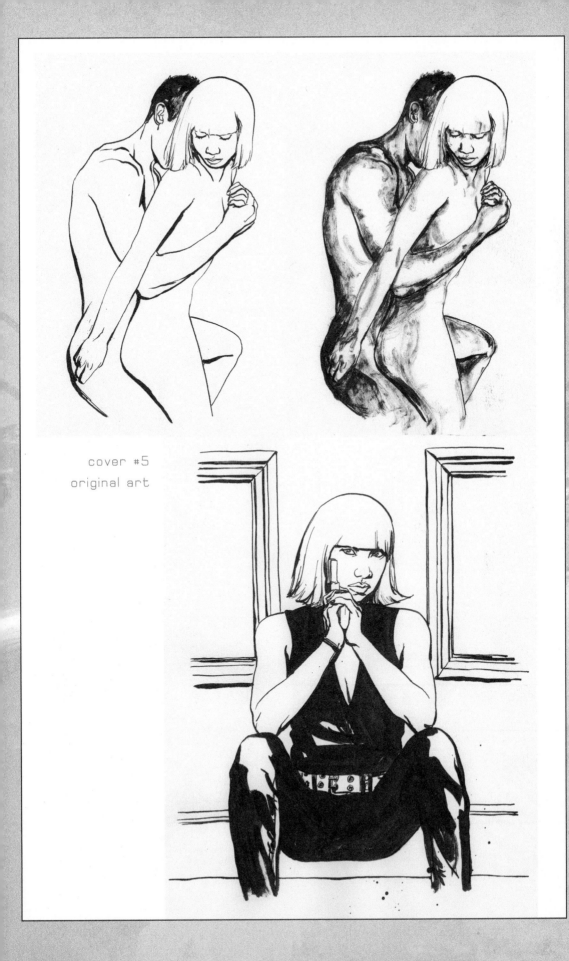

cover #5
original art

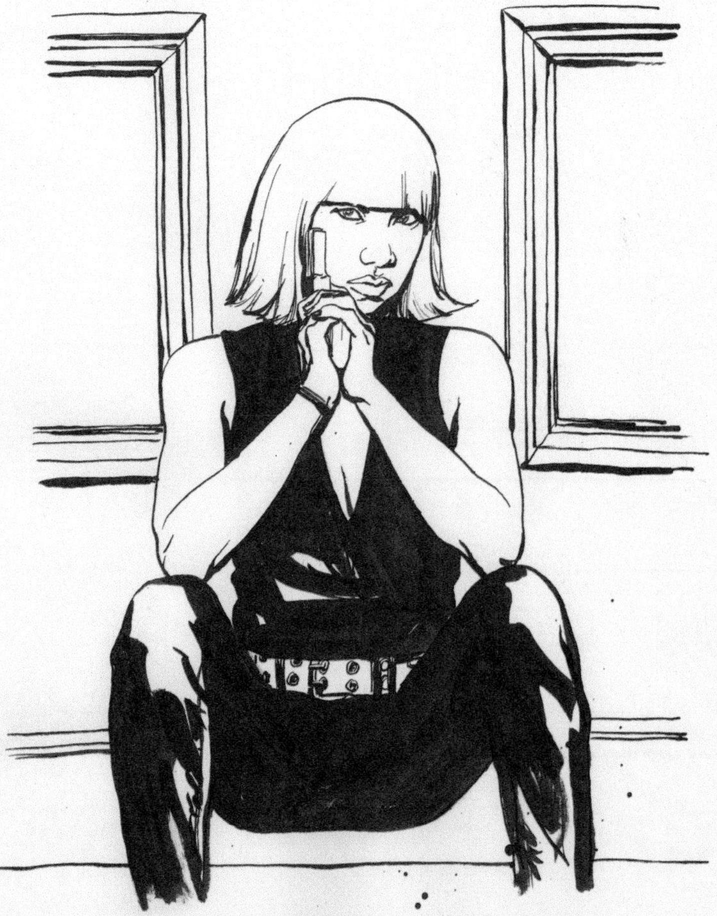

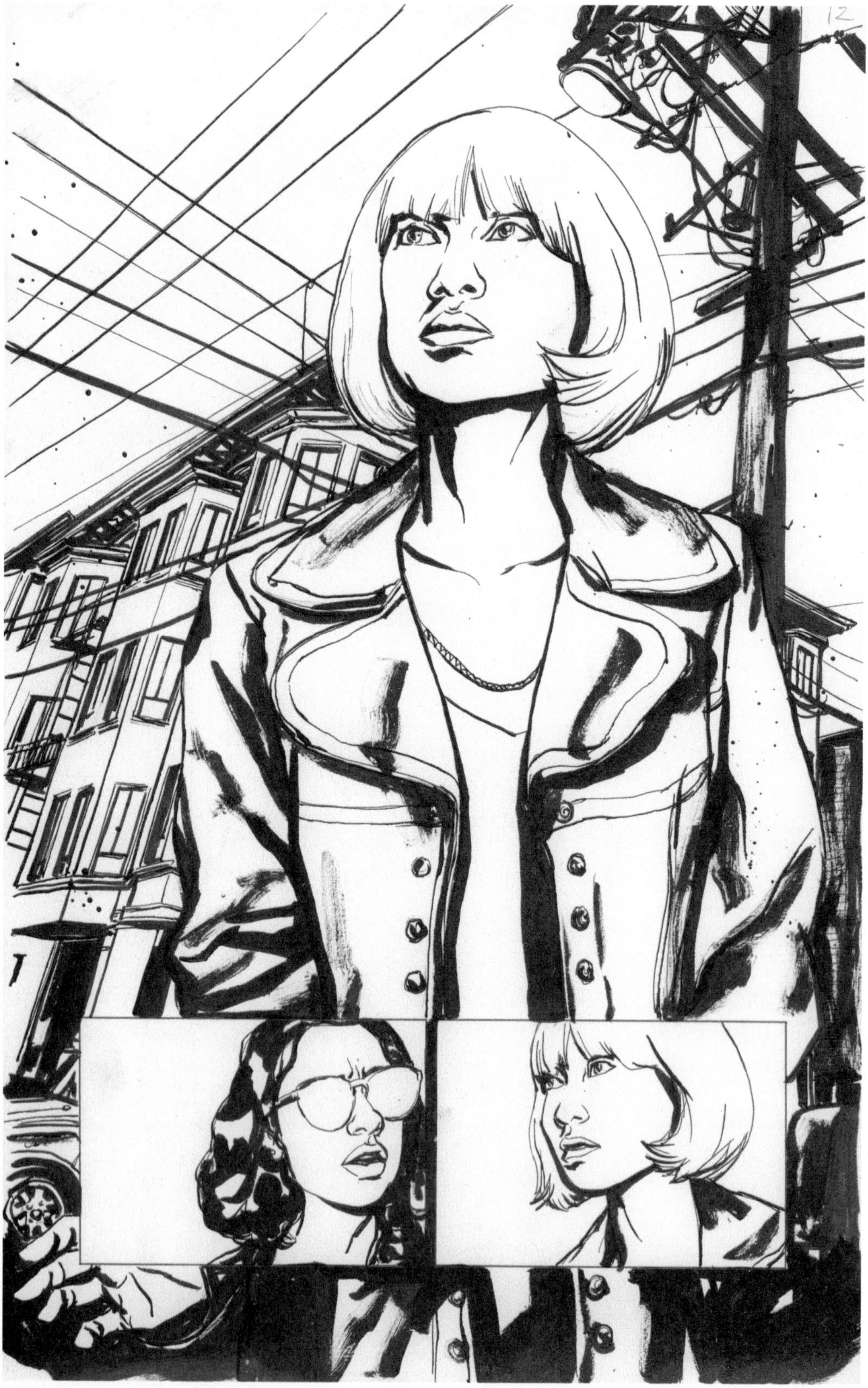
12